Ministry
of the Master
by
Donald W. Bartow

Life Enrichment Publishers
Canton • Ohio

Published by
Life Enrichment Publishers
Box 526 MM
Canton, Ohio 44701

A personal word from Pastor Bartow

The MINISTRY OF THE MASTER is a devotional guide to help you understand you are, and can continue to be, an effective channel of healing. It is not written simply to inspire, but to inform and to impart the truth that Jesus is the Great Physician.

It is my prayer it will help you develop the soil of your mind and heart to produce an abundance of faith and hope. It is important for you to have positive and powerful teaching from the Word each day.

The Apostle Paul did not say you will be transformed by renewing your heart, but he said you would be transformed by the renewing of your mind. It is very important what you feed your mind each day. The MINISTRY OF THE MASTER provides good food for you and for those you love. Feast upon it, because it leads you to the Bread of Life and the Water of Life.

I suggest the following:

1. That you faithfully use the MINISTRY OF THE MASTER each day.

2. That you encourage your loved ones to use it each day. The more they study concerning wholeness the more effective will be your ministry unto them and their ministry unto you.

3. That you encourage others in your church to make daily use of the MINISTRY OF THE MASTER. Can you imagine what it would be like in your church if several were faithfully studying the Word concerning healing? Here is a channel for achieving this end. Why not use it to the fullest.

4. That you believe God for great things. He is willing and able to heal to the uttermost.

About the Cover:

Susan Vitale, Artist

Jesus is white because of His purity and because He is described as a being of Light.

The rainbow ends in a blue sky to indicate **peace**:

> *Peace I leave with you; my own peace I now give and bequeath to you. Not as the world gives do I give to you. Do not let your heart be troubled, neither let it be afraid — stop allowing yourselves to be agitated and disturbed; and do not permit yourselves to be fearful and intimidated and cowardly and unsettled.* John 14:27

The silhouetted figures represent men, women and children of every size, shape and color who came to Jesus, each with their own need. The scars on Jesus' wrists indicate He has already died for our sins; no one coming to Him can be "good enough" to earn or deserve healing, help or salvation. The people come to Him humbly, reaching out to Him **only** as their source. The holes in them represent each need:

The heart — all emotional problems and needs including grief

The lungs — all physical needs both for the body and caring for
    the needs of the body, such as financial needs

The brain — all mental problems

The dove — baptism in the Holy Spirit

As they stand in His presence, each need is met as His Light perfectly fills and heals each hole.

> *And His brightness was like the sunlight; rays streamed from His hand; and there in the sun-like splendor was the hiding place of His power.* Habakkuk 3:4

The dove represents the Holy Spirit.

Books by Pastor Bartow

ADVENTURES OF HEALING — Perhaps the most complete book available concerning healing. A 208-page gold mine of practical, easy to understand, yet biblical guidelines to an effective healing ministry. Jim Brown, a retired Presbyterian pastor, sums this book up best: *". . . your book . . . is the most sane and sensible and Biblical . . . I've ever read. Thank you for it. If it were taken seriously, it would clear up a thousand misconceptions and help restore the healing ministry of our Lord to the total congregation and its responsibility to 'heal the sick and preach the gospel.'"*

A MINISTRY OF PRAYER (plus devotional cassette) — A guide to a thirty-day prayer pilgrimage. Groups and individuals have used this program to revolutionize their prayer life. Many churches have taken several groups through this pilgrimage. *"An excellent tool for understanding about prayer. It is a super pilgrimage. I gained so much personally from the experience. As a pastor, one of the thrilling things about this pilgrimage is that it can be led by a lay person. The format is so logical and the steps for implementation so easy to follow. I recommend it to one and all."* Jay Schmidt, Pastor, Grace United Church of Christ, Canton, Ohio.

PERSONAL PRAYER LIST — This checkbook-size booklet is ideal for listing your prayer concerns and also recording the answers to your prayers. There is space to list your daily prayer concerns as well as the answers to these requests. Your high calling as a believer who prays will be better fulfilled through the use of this book. There are several inspirational comments about prayer. These make perfect gifts for friends. Sunday School class members, prayer group members, etc. You will want to help yourself and others to become more effective in prayer.

PRESCRIPTION FOR WHOLENESS — This 5½ by 4½ inch, 20-page booklet will enhance your ministry to the hospital patient, the ill at home, those in nursing homes, and any others who need an encouraging Word from the Lord. It contains 30 daily inspirational scripture verses, prayer and suggested daily Bible readings. There is a place in the front for you to write a personal note and to write the name of the one to whom it is being sent. Each booklet has a beautiful envelope in which it can be mailed for one first class stamp.

Members of your official board, Sunday School class, or prayer group may want to sign the PRESCRIPTION FOR WHOLENESS booklet prior to it being sent. The signatures add to the joy and excitement experienced by the recipient.

For more information, contact the publisher.

Table of Contents

WHAT IS SPIRITUAL HEALING?

The goal of spiritual healing is wholeness. It is the healing of the whole person in body, mind, and spirit.

It believes healing may be received through the spiritual practice of prayer, laying on of hands with prayer, anointing with oil, the prayer of confession, the sacraments, etc. All of these become channels of power in response to our faith in God through Jesus Christ.

Although it may result in physical healings, spiritual healing is not a substitute for medicine or surgery.

It does not attempt to prescribe in the area of medicine, surgery, psychiatry, and psychology. It works closely with all involved in these allied professions dedicated to healing.

It adds another dimension to one's search for healing. All healing is of God. Individuals, in whatever profession, are instruments in His hands.

I cannot stress enough that spiritual healing is firmly based on orthodox Christian theology. It is based on the teaching and practice of our Lord Jesus Christ. It is in keeping with the teaching and practice of the early church. It is a present day obedient response to the Divine Commission given by Jesus to "go preach and heal."

It is evident that the acceptance and practice of spiritual healing inspires individuals to greater devotion and leads them to richer experiences in worship. It deepens their understanding of New Testament teachings.

Hundreds of congregations now conduct regular healing services weekly or monthly because they believe the healing power of the Lord should be proclaimed.

"I am come that you might have life and that you might have it more abundant." John 10:10

POINTS TO PONDER

1. Do you feel individuals want to be whole?
2. What does being healed through spiritual healing mean to you?
3. What is meant by the "abundant life?"

9

WHAT IS SPIRITUAL HEALING?

1. ...Why has thou smitten us, and there is no _____ for us? *Jer. 14:19*
2. ...the leaves of the tree were the _____ of the nations. *Rev. 22:2*
3. He that ministereth to you the Spirit, and worketh _____ _____ among you, ... *Gal. 3:5*
4. ...No man can do these _____ that thou doest, except God be with him. *John 3:2*
5. ...I will _____ you backslidings. *Jer. 3:22*
6. ...Is it lawful to _____ on the sabbath day? *Lu. 14:3*
7. ...He that believeth on me, the _____ that I do shall he do also. *John 14:12*
8. ...He put his _____ on them and blessed them. *Mk. 10:16*
9. A merry heart doeth good like a _____. *Pro. 17:22*
10. Then they laid their _____ on them. *Acts 8:17*
11. _____ without ceasing. *I Thess. 5:17*
12. Jesus Christ the same _____, today, and forever. *Heb. 13:8*
13. Those having not the _____ are a _____ unto themselves. *Rom. 2:14*
14. Bear one another's burdens, and so fulfill the _____ of Christ. *Gal. 6:2*

DAILY SCRIPTURE

Mon.   Acts 28:2-6
Tues.   II Kings 6:1-7
Wed.   Luke 14:1-6
Thurs. Mark 10:13-16
Fri.   Acts 8:14-22
Sat.   Heb. 13:1-17
Sun.   Gal. 5:22-26

PRAYER CONCERNS

Your Family & Relatives
Government Leaders
Missionaries
For the Unbelievers
Churches & Denominations
Your Own Church
Prayer and Praise

NOTE: You will be spiritually strengthened by completing two questions each day, reading the suggested scripture, and ministering in prayer for the concerns of the day.

THE MINISTRY OF THE MASTER—MONDAY
A Spirit Lifter

A panhandler approached a prosperous man asking for a dollar.

"Look at you," replied the prospect. "You sleep on park benches, your clothes are in tatters, and you're hungry. Why don't you go to work?"

"Go to work?" growled the loafer in disgust. "What for — to support a bum like me?"

God's Promise

"And not only so, but we glory in tribulations also; knowing that tribulation worketh patience; And patience, experience; and experience, hope." (Romans 5:3,4, KJV)

Practicing His Presence

Through what incident or person did you sense the presence of the Lord yesterday?

What Is Spiritual Healing?

What is spiritual healing? What is the wholeness the church should be seeking for individuals and groups?

Some years ago I received a letter from a pastor after conducting a healing service in his church. The healings he reported beautifully conveyed what is meant by the healing we seek.

One healing was of a man who had severe arthritis. He was in constant pain and could not carry on the normal functions of life. He was instantly delivered of the pain and his joints were made free. He went back to work on Monday and this service was held Sunday afternoon.

He mentioned a woman who had arthritis who was not delivered of this affliction. However, she told her pastor that she was healed of a terrible resentment she had carried for years.

He also told of a Lutheran pastor who had come to the meeting with a very defeated spirit. He planned to leave the pastorate because of the members in his church. When he received the laying-on-of-hands he was set free. He realized the problem was not the members, but himself. He decided to remain in the pastorate.

Three instances of healing involving a healing of the body, a healing of emotions, a healing of spirit. All three areas are important because of the power and presence of the Lord.

PRAYER: *Father, help me to believe you desire wholeness for me. Amen.*

THE MINISTRY OF THE MASTER—TUESDAY
A Spirit Lifter

When a diner complained that he couldn't eat the soup that he had been served, the waiter called the manager. "I'm very sorry, sir, I'll call the chef!" When the chef arrived, the diner still insisted that he couldn't eat the soup. "What's wrong with it?" demanded the chef. "Nothing," calmly answered the diner, "I just don't have a spoon."

God's Promise

"My brothers, what good is it to profess faith without practicing it? Such faith has no power to save one, has it?" (James 2:14, NAB)

Practicing His Presence

Through what incident or person did you sense the presence of the Lord yesterday?

What Is Spiritual Healing?

It is obvious that Spiritual Healing is not simply physical healings. Miracles are more varied and more inclusive than only what happens in the life of a terminal cancer patient.

I believe that miracles are taking place before our very eyes every day. A proper understanding of the Lord's healing power and of His constant presence will help you to behold the miracles around you each day.

One thing which disturbs me is that Christians have great power at their disposal and often they do not take advantage of this power. I call to your attention the ministry of prayer, of the laying-on-of-hands, anointing with oil, the prayers of absolution, confession, Holy Communion, baptism, private and corporate worship, and the presence of the Holy Spirit.

The Lord has ordained that His power be released through the above expressions of faith and worship. Isn't it strange the church as a whole has neglected many of these things?

Matthew 25:43 says that the Lord is ministered unto you as you minister unto the sick. Now, may I ask *"Should a Christian visit the sick with only medicine?"* Of course not, but the Christian should also minister to the ill in the way that the Master ministered unto the sick.

Your problems and condition are worthy of the total ministry of the Christian community. Do not neglect prayer, and anointing with oil, etc. any more than you should neglect to seek the best professional help available.

PRAYER: *Lord Jesus, may I behold your miracles in my life this day. Amen.*

A Spirit Lifter

Motorist: "I ran over your cat and I want to replace him."
Housewife: "Well, get busy! There's a mouse in the pantry."

God's Promise

"O give thanks to the Lord, for he is good; for his mercy endures forever." (Psalm 136:1, Lamsa)

Practicing His Presence

Through what incident or person did you sense the presence of the Lord yesterday?

What Is Spiritual Healing?

I cannot emphasize enough that the healing of which I speak does not neglect the insights and advances of modern medicine. Healing and wholeness do include the ministry of science. Neither you nor I want to delete from society the advances of technology, medicine, physicians, the allied professions or nursing, pharmacy, etc. All of these are important instruments of the Lord to bring wholeness to many people.

They become meaningful and significant instruments of wholeness through the power of the Holy Spirit as we respond by faith to the Father through the Great Physician, the Lord Jesus Christ.

The Church's healing ministry is not a substitute for medicine or for surgery. It does not speak disparagingly of the advances of modern medicine. I feel we need to realize that the Lord has revealed many things to many people which contribute to the wholeness so desperately desired.

Many in the field of medicine acknowledge that the Lord is the healer. They may treat, but God heals. Some years ago I was participating in a conference where Dr. Karl Menninger was also one of the leaders. I will never forget his comments to me concerning my emphasis upon the Church's healing ministry. He said, *"Young man, there are not near as many of us doctors opposed to what you are teaching as some would lead you to believe."*

He knew the value of blending the ministry of faith with the insights of medicine.

PRAYER: *Father, may every physician and nurse realize you use them as a channel of healing. Amen.*

THE MINISTRY OF THE MASTER—THURSDAY
A Spirit Lifter

"Teacher, I don't want to scare you, but Papa said if I don't get better grades, someone is due for a licking!"

God's Promise

"If any man will do his will, he shall know of the doctrine, whether it be of God..." (John 7:17, KJV)

Practicing His Presence

Through what incident or person did you sense the presence of the Lord yesterday?

What Is Spiritual Healing?

Have you been to see a doctor recently? Have you had someone pray specifically for you recently?

Either experience can very well be of the Lord. It is the Lord who heals regardless of how and through whom He chooses to do the healing. The Lord is the healer regardless of the individuals involved or the instrument He may choose to use for the healing. In whatever profession one may be, if he is helping in the healing process, he is but an instrument of the Lord.

I wish I could impart to you that the Lord does desire your wholeness. You and your loved ones have an open invitation from Him to come for wholeness. Jesus proclaimed wholeness. He knew that the big step toward faith in Him could be taken more easily because of a healing than because of being stricken with an illness.

Jesus would not do anything contrary to the will of His Father. He perfectly fulfilled the will of His heavenly Father. In carrying out this will he cast out demons, healed the emotions of distressed persons, and brought wholeness to the deaf, the lame, and the blind.

The acceptance of His desire for your wholeness is in keeping with the very nature of His ministry. The Lord has never told His people that He has ceased to be concerned and that He no longer wants to heal. He is the same today as always.

PRAYER: *Jesus, I acknowledge you are the Great Physician. Help me to always believe this. Amen.*

THE MINISTRY OF THE MASTER—FRIDAY
A Spirit Lifter

Golfer (in trap): "The traps on this course are quite annoying, aren't they?"
Second golfer (trying to putt): "They sure are. Would you mind closing yours?"

God's Promise

"Even though I walk in the dark valley I fear no evil; for you are at my side with your rod and your staff that give me courage." (Psalm 23:4, NAB)

Practicing His Presence

Through what incident or person did you sense the presence of the Lord yesterday?

What Is Spiritual Healing?

Have you ever seen a miracle? Take a few moments to contemplate this question.

I have asked this question in many groups and under many different circumstances. Most people reply they have not ever really seen a miracle.

However, a few will say they have seen a miracle. They then go on to give an account of some spectacular physical healing which they have experienced, seen in a friend or family member, or heard about in the life of a person they do not personally know.

It is obvious they definitely associate healing only with the physical body and only in ways which they feel are beyond the knowledge of science. It is immediately apparent they do not understand or appreciate what is meant by spiritual healing. They fail to understand how it is received and how it is maintained in the life of an individual.

There are miracles taking place within and around you every day. It is my prayer you will not miss them.

A little boy was having a serious talk with his grandfather. He asked, *"Grandpa, have you ever seen any miracles?" "Yes, many of them,"* he replied. *"How have you seen them?"* the little boy asked. He said, *"Because I look for them."*

Open your life to the things of the spirit and you will be amazed at the many miracles you will see. Yes, you will see them even today!

PRAYER: *Lord, help me this day to be open to the things of the Spirit. Amen.*

15

THE MINISTRY OF THE MASTER—SATURDAY

A Spirit Lifter

The boy scout remarked to his father at the breakfast table that it had been easy to do his good deed that morning.

"I saw Mr. Smith going for the 7:45 bus and he was afraid he'd miss it. So I let the bulldog loose and he was just in time!"

God's Promise

"If any of you lack wisdom, let him ask of God, that giveth to all men liberally, and unbraideth not; and it shall be given him." (James 1:5, KJV)

Practicing His Presence

Through what incident or person did you sense the presence of the Lord yesterday?

What Is Spiritual Healing?

Miracles are not simply of the physical body. Miracles take place in all areas of life.

The healing which is encompassed in the Christian message is the healing of body, mind, and spirit. The goal of healing is wholeness. This wholeness is to be in all areas of life. It does include the body, but includes much more.

It includes the mind, the emotions, relationships, and even in the area of the physical world. After all, the Bible records many miracles even in the realm of nature. The Red Sea incident, the floating axe, and Jesus walking on the water are just a few of them.

Mary, my wife, was in a meeting when the group was discussing miracles. One lady said she had never seen a miracle in an individual. She had never really felt she had witnessed a miraculous healing in the life of anyone. However, she said I have seen the miracle of a church being healed. She had experienced a strife torn church being made whole through the healing power of the Lord Jesus. She experienced wholeness in relationships.

The healing of relationships within her local parish was a miracle. The wages of sin were being distributed generously in her church. The enthusiasm for Christ was almost dead. The desire for a vital church was dead. The miracle of new life had come.

This miracle convinced her of the power of Christ to heal. I feel this is healing at its highest level. You and I need more of this in our lives and in the life of the church to which we belong.

PRAYER: *Father, enable me to mend all broken relationships and to live to your glory. Amen.*

THE MINISTRY OF THE MASTER—SUNDAY
A Spirit Lifter

Policeman: "Hey you, didn't you hear me say 'Pull over'?"
Driver: "Oh, I thought you said, 'Good morning, Mayor'!"
Policeman: "It is a nice morning, isn't it?"

God's Promise

"For thou hast made him a little lower than the angels, and hast crowned him with glory and honour." (Psalm 8:5, KJV)

Practicing His Presence

Through what incident or person did you sense the presence of the Lord yesterday?

What Is Spiritual Healing?

As I close this week with visiting with you as to *"What Is Spiritual Healing?"*, I want to emphasize that it is not magic, nor sleight of hand, or some hockus-pokus activity.

The foundation of wholeness is the practice and belief in the laws and ways of the Lord. Some individuals feel they can violate the laws of nature and the spirit and then in an instant receive wholeness from the Lord with one attendance at a healing service.

This is not true. Wholeness involves the living of the ways of the Lord. There are natural laws which have been discovered and harnessed which make possible the ministry of medicine. There are spiritual laws which must be pursued just as diligently as physical laws. The ways of the spirit involve faith, love, forgiveness, trust, praise, etc.

The many miracles which happen today do not break God's laws. They fulfill them. They take place within the framework of what He has established. Miracles are the result of higher laws which we cannot understand.

A few years ago the leading scientists would all agree that a heavier than air machine could not fly. This could be proven conclusively. However, there is the law of aerodynamics which was not understood.

God is not constantly inventing new laws. We are constantly discovering and understanding the old ones. Thus, He has provided a way for your wholeness.

PRAYER: *Father, may I believe you for what may appear to be the impossible. Amen.*

Theme for the Week
MEDICINE AND SPIRITUAL HEALING

Is medicine of the Lord? Should Christians receive the ministry of physicians, psychiatrists, hospitals? Should Christians depend upon pills at all?

These and other questions are frequently expressed by devout individuals. There are many more who have these questions go through their minds, but are hesitant to verbalize them. They seem to feel to do so would expose a lack of faith on their part.

One of the portions of scripture used to back up their feeling is Luke 8:43-48. The account reveals the woman had spent all of her living on physicians and had not been helped. She touched the hem of Jesus' garment and she was instantly healed.

You and I know of individuals who have exhausted all medical resources and who have not been cured. Some of them have been touched by the Lord and miraculously helped. Does this mean that everyone should abandon the medical field and *"trust only in the Lord?"*

I believe the real truth is that there should be proper use of both the laws of the spirit and the laws of science. It is not a question of either/or but one of both/and.

Jesus Christ never spoke disparagingly of physicians. He ministered in the area of wholeness, but He did not seek to curtail the efforts of others in this area. Even though it mentions the physicians were unable to help this woman, Jesus did not point out that physicians were useless.

He also went on to bring her a healing which no person can ever impart. He gave her peace of mind and forgiveness of sins. These things can never be imparted except by Jesus Christ.

Tradition maintains that Luke was a physician. We have no record of his forsaking this profession. He knew that the Lord heals through the efforts of the physician.

POINTS TO PONDER

1. Should a Christian ever go to a physician?
2. Do you feel Jesus taught people to forsake the ministry of physicians?
3. Do you feel there are people who believe pills and physicians are all they need for their wholeness?

MEDICINE AND SPIRITUAL HEALING

1. Jesus said, Somebody has _____. *Lu. 8:46*
2. And Joseph commanded the_____to embalm his father. *Gen. 50:2*
3. Asa...sought not to the Lord, but to the _____. *II Chron. 16:12*
4. Is there no balm in Gilead; is there no _____ there. *Jer. 8:22*
5. They that are whole need not a _____. *Mt. 9:12*
6. _____heal thyself. *Lu. 4:23*
7. Luke, the beloved _____, and Demas, greet you. *Col. 4:14*
8. A merry heart doeth good like a _____. *Pro. 17:22*
9. ...in vain thou shalt use many_____. *Jer. 46:11*
10. ...and the fruit thereof shall be for meat and the leaf for _____
    _____. *Ezk. 47:12*
11. They took and laid it on the boil and he _____. *II Kings 20:7*
12. And went to him, and bound up his _____. *Luke 10:34*
13. Use a little wine for thy stomach's sake and thine often _____
    _____. *I Tim. 5:23*
14. The_____of faith shall save the sick. *James 5:15*

DAILY SCRIPTURE

Mon.	Luke 8:43-48
Tues.	II Chron. 16:11-14
Wed.	Jer. 8:18-21
Thurs.	Ezk. 47:7-12
Fri.	Lu. 10:29-37
Sat.	I Tim. 5:23-24
Sun.	James 5:13-18

PRAYER CONCERNS

Your Family & Relatives
Government Leaders
Missionaries
For the Unbelievers
Churches & Denominations
Your Own Church
Prayer and Praise

NOTE: You will be spiritually strengthened by completing two questions each day, reading the suggested scripture, and ministering in prayer for the concerns of the day.

THE MINISTRY OF THE MASTER—MONDAY
A Spirit Lifter

An absent-minded professor tripped on a suitcase and fell all the way to the bottom. Picking himself up, he said, "I wonder what in the world all that noise was about."

God's Promise

"Trust in the Lord, and do good; so shalt thou dwell in the land, and verily thou shalt be fed." (Psalm 37:3)

Practicing His Presence

Through what incident or person did you sense the presence oi the Lord yesterday?

Medicine And Spiritual Healing

I feel there is much confusion on the part of some Christians concerning the relationship between medicine and healing through the power and presence of the Lord.

This fact was really brought home to me a few years ago. I was helping with a large conference and conducting the workshop on healing. A young lady seemed especially touched by what I had taught. It was with hesitation that she approached me concerning some deep concerns.

Why was she hesitant to seek further ministry from me? What made her doubt my ability to perhaps help her? It was because I wore glasses. The glasses, to her, were an outward sign of my inability to really believe the Lord. To her, if I really had faith I would have no need of glasses. My eyes would be immediately and completely healed.

She went on to say that she had eye trouble. However, several years before she had put her entire trust in the Lord and thrown her glasses away.

She had sat under teaching which stressed faith and the display of faith by not wearing glasses again. She had witnessed to her healing and did not want to reveal lack of faith by going back to the use of glasses.

To me it is tragic that she could not see the healing power of the Lord through the use of the insights of science and medicine which made glasses possible.

PRAYER: *Father, may I see your hand working through the marvels of modern medicine. Amen.*

20

THE MINISTRY OF THE MASTER—TUESDAY
A Spirit Lifter

Jamie was behaving badly all day. His mother said to him: "How do you ever expect to get into Heaven?"

Jamie replied, "Well, I'll just run in and out and keep slamming the door until St. Peter says 'For Heaven's sake, come in or stay out'!"

God's Promise

"Therefore, I say unto you, what things so ever ye desire, when ye pray, believe that ye receive them, and ye shall have them." (Mark 11:24, KJV)

Practicing His Presence

Through what incident or person did you sense the presence of the Lord yesterday?

Medicine And Spiritual Healing

Medicine and faith are not in competition nor are they at odds with each other. Both are needed and both have their place in your life and mind. The Lord has ordained certain laws and they are fulfilled in many ways. There are some things which no one can do, but there are areas which must be accomplished by individuals.

I believe the relationship between the Lord's part and the efforts of people is beautifully illustrated by this story.

A man moved into the neighborhood and began to refurbish an old home and to clean up the yard. A couple years after he had moved in, the house was in good shape and the lawn and his flower garden beautiful. One of his friends remarked, *"Isn't it amazing what the Lord can do?"* as he surveyed the beauty of his flowers and lawn.

The owner replied, *"Perhaps so, but you should have seen this place when the Lord had it."* Only God can bring and maintain growth, but there are things you and I can do to cooperate with His laws. He has chosen to reveal Himself and to reveal His power through our efforts.

This does not take away from the power and glory of the Lord, but only enhances it in our midst. Thus, the proper use of medicine is not a denial of the power of the Lord but the sensible use of the revealed truths of the Lord.

PRAYER: *Lord Jesus, grant me the strength to do my part to maintain my wholeness. Amen.*

THE MINISTRY OF THE MASTER—WEDNESDAY

A Spirit Lifter

"So Lefty, not content with stealing $5,000 in cash, you went back and took a couple of watches, 6 diamond rings, and a pearl necklace?"

"Yes, Your Honor. I remembered that money alone doesn't bring happiness."

God's Promise

"Know ye not that ye are the temple of God, and, that the Spirit of God dwelleth in you?" (I Corinthians 3:16)

Practicing His Presence

Through what incident or person did you sense the presence of the Lord yesterday?

Medicine And Spiritual Healing

It was in May 1959 that I conducted my first public service of healing. Since then I have ministered unto thousands of individuals. It has been amazing to me how many are troubled by the fact they have not received instant and what they feel to be divine healing for their illness.

I believe one of the reasons for individuals to feel they are guilty for seeking medical help, is the concept *"If I had enough faith I would never, never be ill and I would never need to see a physician."*

This is such an insidious thought because it puts all the problems and illnesses which the individual experiences upon their lack of faith. This then leaves the person living with almost constant guilt. It leads to the individual feeling even more unworthy and often can bring a state of depression and sometimes despair.

I believe this concept is far more prevalent than would first appear. There are many who feel this way, but are hesitant to express it because they don't want others to feel they lack faith or ever doubt their relationship with the Lord.

It is not a lack of faith on your part to make sensible use of all the insights the Lord has granted through science and through medicine. I believe these things are from Him and should be accepted with gratefulness and not with hesitancy or fear of being less than a Christian act.

PRAYER: *Jesus, help me to trust you for the healing you are bringing into my life. Amen.*

THE MINISTRY OF THE MASTER—THURSDAY
A Spirit Lifter

Farmer: "Hi there! What are you doing up in my cherry tree?"
Youngster: "There's a sign down there that says 'Keep off the grass'."

God's Promise

"...I am the bread of life: he that cometh to me shall never hunger; and he that believeth on me shall never thirst." (John 6:35)

Practicing His Presence

Through what incident or person did you sense the presence of the Lord yesterday?

Medicine And Spiritual Healing

Even though there are Christians who feel they are sinning when receiving any type of medical attention, there is a more serious teaching abroad in our land.

This error is that prayer is only psychological. It is the feeling that faith and prayer have no effect whatsoever on physical illness. This false concept must be rebuked by believers.

Prayer is power. Prayer is a channel through which the power of the Lord is released. When anyone proclaims that prayer is only psychological and can only help to bring some healing in the area of psychosomatic illnesses, that person misunderstands the way of the Lord and the power of prayer.

It has been through prayer that I have seen lumps disappear, legs lengthened, the crippled walk, diseased skin immediately healed, and many other almost unbelievable things.

When a person teaches that prayer is only psychological, that one misunderstands the ways and power of the Lord. Of course, prayer can help emotionally and spiritually, but it can also affect the physical.

The ministry of the Lord Jesus was one which saw the power of prayer revealed in every facet of life. Medicine and faith are blended when we do not limit the power of the Lord and at the same time when we make use of all the insights of our modern day.

PRAYER: *Father, may I see every facet of life as sacred and help me to live accordingly. Amen.*

THE MINISTRY OF THE MASTER—FRIDAY
A Spirit Lifter

First Clerk: "Yes, the boss is mean all right, but he's fair."
Second Clerk: "What do you mean, he's fair?"
First Clerk: "He's mean to everyone!"

God's Promise

"And God shall wipe away all tears from their eyes; and there shall be no more death, neither sorrow, nor crying, neither shall there be any more pain: for the former things are passed away." (Revelation 21:4)

Practicing His Presence

Through what incident or person did you sense the presence of the Lord yesterday?

Medicine And Spiritual Healing

I hope it becomes obvious throughout this week that I believe the church's healing ministry is in no way contradictory to the efforts of the medical profession. In fact, many of the ardent devotees of the healing ministry are members of the allied professions of medicine.

Also, the leaders in the healing ministry do not hesitate to seek the services of physicians.

Spiritual healing is not a matter of pills versus prayer or prayer versus pills. It is a matter of making use of all the revelations God has given to help us have health, strength, and power of body, mind, and spirit.

All the prayer in the world will not care for the problem of malnutrition resulting from lack of proper food. So we need the efforts of everyone in agriculture, research, etc. to bring all that is needed to all peoples on earth.

We do not want to become so pious we neglect the practical things the Lord has provided. At the same time we do not want to become so pragmatic that we neglect the spiritual aspects of life.

The Lord has provided many instruments of ministry to our well being. May all be used to His glory and to our good.

PRAYER: *O God, may I be willing to accept all the channels of healing available for me. Amen.*

THE MINISTRY OF THE MASTER—SATURDAY

A Spirit Lifter

"Pardon me, does this train stop at Tenth Street?"
"Yes, watch me and get off one station before I do."

God's Promise

"And we know that all things work together for good to them that love God, to them who are called according to His purpose." (Romans 8:28)

Practicing His Presence

Through what incident or person did you sense the presence of the Lord yesterday?

Medicine And Spiritual Healing

How do you blend medicine and faith? What are some practical things to keep in mind?

I would suggest that you realize you have not done everything you can for yourself and others until you have—

1. Prayed.
2. Shared your concerns and had others minister unto you with prayer.
3. Until you have sought the best professional help available.

The professional help may be a counselor, a physician, a psychiatrist, an attorney, financial consultant, etc. The point is you must avail yourself of all the help possible.

After you have done the above there is nothing left but to leave the results with the Lord. You have done everything humanly possible and now you must leave the fruit and the growth to Him.

It is somewhat like planting your garden. You prepare the soil, plant good seed, cultivate and till the crop, provide the moisture and then wait for results. There is nothing else you can do.

I see many who do not do all they can. They either seek only the professional advice and neglect prayer or they pray and neglect the other resources. All things must be blended together in proper proportion to have the best results.

PRAYER: *Father, thank you for the ones who minister unto me with prayer. Amen.*

THE MINISTRY OF THE MASTER—SUNDAY
A Spirit Lifter

Professor: "What is the principle contribution of the automobile age?"
Student: "Well, it's practically stopped horse stealing."

God's Promise

"For all the promises of God are in him, Amen, unto the glory of God by us." (II Corinthians 1:20)

Practicing His Presence

Through what incident or person did you sense the presence of the Lord yesterday?

Medicine And Spiritual Healing

I cannot close our talks together this week without expressing the fact that many today are far too dependent upon pills and the wonders of science. Millions are running from physician to physician, gobbling down pills and taking all types of medicines, who have never found an answer to their illnesses of mind, body, and spirit.

The proper balance between faith and medicine will be better maintained if the following suggestions are pursued.

1. Appreciate that the Lord is the Healer regardless of the channel.
2. Realize medicine will never have the complete answer for the illnesses and problems of the human race.
3. Permit the Living Christ to rule your life and actions.
4. Do not become dependent upon the wonders of medicine. Do not let it become a crutch. There are no magic pills which care for all ills.
5. Realize that spiritual healing is the most important goal. The wholeness of spirit is basically your greatest need. Jesus Himself said, *"Rejoice not that the spirits are subject to you, but rather rejoice, because your names are written in heaven."* (Luke 10:20)
6. Give thanks and praise unto the Lord for healing regardless of the method or channel He may be using.
7. Minister with prayer unto all who are in any way involved in a ministry of healing.

PRAYER: *Above all else, Father, I want to know my sins are forgiven and that I am yours. Amen.*

Theme for the Week
PRAYER AND SPIRITUAL HEALING

I am sure it is obvious to you that prayer is a vital part of any ministry of healing for yourself and for those to whom you minister. A healing ministry which is not undergirded with prayer is like a body without breath.

We know a person can exist only a few minutes without oxygen, and it is just as true that a healing ministry cannot exist for any length of time without prayer. A body, without oxygen for a few moments, will suffer permanent damage to the brain, and if the time elapse is for several minutes, the person will die.

There are many churches which are spiritually dead because they do not have a vital prayer life. Others are spiritually sick because of this lack of prayer and very little is happening as far as redemption of souls, ministry of healing to body, mind and spirit, and other important aspects are concerned.

William James said, *"Prayer is the very soul and essence of religion."*

He further said *"...there is no intimate converse, no interior dialogue, no interchange, no action of God and man, no return of man to God...without prayer."*

I cannot express enough that an individual has not done all he can about any problem until:

1. he has prayed
2. he has prayed with others
3. others have prayed with him and for him.

My strong emphasis upon prayer is not to be interpreted that professional help should be ignored or neglected.

The goal of every believer should be to develop the art of prayer to the point of praying without ceasing. This cannot be accomplished overnight but must be developed over a period of years.

I trust that this week will be a time of challenge for you in regard to prayer and to your relationship with the Lord.

POINTS TO PONDER

1. Is prayer the real work of the church?
2. What pattern of prayer do you faithfully follow?
3. Do you seek to regularly minister to others with prayer?

27

PRAYER AND SPIRITUAL HEALING

1. _____ for them which despitefully use you, and persecute you. *Mt. 5:44*
2. _____ and pray, that ye enter not into temptation. *Mt. 26:41*
3. ...strive together with me in your _____ to God for me. *Rom. 15:30*
4. Is anyone among you_____? Let him pray. *James 5:13*
5. _____, and it shall be given you. *Mt. 7:7*
6. ...that men ought always to pray, and not to _____. *Lu. 18:1*
7. Be _____ for nothing; but in every thing by prayer. *Phil. 4:6*
8. And it shall come to pass, that before they _____, I will answer. *Isa. 65:24*
9. All things, whatsoever ye shall ask in prayer, _____, ye shall receive. *Mk. 11:24*
10. O thou that _____ prayer, unto thee shall all flesh come. *Ps. 65:2*
11. At that day ye shall ask in my _____. *John 16:26*
12. ...by stretching forth thine hand to _____. *Acts 4:30*
13. And when ye stand praying, _____, if ye have ought against any. *Mk. 11:25*
14. Solomon stood before the altar of the Lord...and spread forth his _____ toward heaven. *I Kings 8:22*

DAILY SCRIPTURE

Mon.   Mt. 5:43-48
Tues. Rom. 15:30-33
Wed.   Mt. 7:7-12
Thurs. John 16:25-33
Fri.   Acts 4:23-31
Sat.   Mk. 11:20-26
Sun.   I Kings 8:22-26

PRAYER CONCERNS

Your Family & Relatives
Government Leaders
Missionaries
For the Unbelievers
Churches & Denominations
Your Own Church
Prayer and Praise

NOTE: You will be spiritually strengthened by completing two questions each day, reading the suggested scripture, and ministering in prayer for the concerns of the day.

THE MINISTRY OF THE MASTER—MONDAY
A Spirit Lifter

Tom: "Say, Bob, how did you get that swelling on your nose?"
Bob: "Oh, I bent down to smell a brose in my garden."
Tom: "Not brose, Bob, rose. There's no 'Be' in rose."
Bob: "There was in this one!"

God's Promise

"I love them that love me; and those that seek me early shall find me." (Proverbs 8:17)

Practicing His Presence

Through what incident or person did you sense the presence of the Lord yesterday?

Prayer And Spiritual Healing

Oswald Chambers has said,

"Prayer does not fit us for the greater works; prayer is the greater work. We think of prayer as a common sense exercise of our higher powers in order to prepare us for God's work. In the teaching of Jesus Christ, prayer is the working of the miracle of redemption in me which produces the miracle of redemption of others by the power of God."

He goes on to point out that many will not pray unless,

"...we get thrills, that is the intensest form of spiritual selfishness. We have to labor along the line of God's direction, and...there is nothing thrilling about a laboring man's work, but it is the laboring man who makes the conceptions of the genius possible; and it is the laboring Saint who makes the conceptions of his Master possible. You labor at prayer and the results happen all the time from his standpoint."

I hope you will begin this week realizing the importance of prayer. You may be ever so active in your church organization. You may be extremely busy at your work. Your family may be demanding upon your time and energy. However, regardless of your circumstance, you need to develop a life of prayer.

You must be so much in communication with the Father that you know He is with you and you with Him.

PRAYER: *Father, help me to realize prayer is the highest work to which you have called me. Amen.*

THE MINISTRY OF THE MASTER—TUESDAY
A Spirit Lifter

A neighborhood squabble brought several housewives to court, each eager to tell the judge why the problem was someone else's fault. "One at a time, ladies," said the judge. "You'll each get a chance to testify. I'll hear the evidence from the oldest among you first." The case was dismissed for lack of any evidence.

God's Promise

"For it is God which worketh in you both to will and to do his good pleasure." (Philippians 2:13)

Practicing His Presence

Through what incident or person did you sense the presence of the Lord yesterday?

Prayer And Spiritual Healing

The Holy Scriptures reveal the importance of prayer beyond a shadow of a doubt. *"You ought always to pray and not to faint."* (Lu. 18:1) *"Pray without ceasing."* (I Thess. 5:17) *"The effectual and fervent prayer of a righteous man availeth much."* (James 5:16)

There is no end to quotations from scripture and famous people concerning prayer. We are called to deep communion and precious fellowship with the Triune God. God is never far away nor difficult to commune with, if we sincerely seek Him.

I am sure one of the reasons many cannot make contact with God is because they are seeking the gifts. He has to offer rather than seeking Him, the Giver of these many gifts.

It is when we are using people that we find ourselves alienated from people. In like manner, if we are only using God, it will be impossible to really relate to Him in a deep and meaningful way.

George Matheson has said, *"It is Thee and not Thy gifts I crave."* This should be your goal and it should be my goal.

Prayer is important because it is communion with God. It is not seeking to move God to fulfill our selfish desires. It is not magic, nor a tool to be used only in a "pinch." It is not an avenue for special favors from the Lord, nor the key to getting God to change His mind.

PRAYER: *Give me a strong heart, O God, and a broken and contrite spirit. Amen.*

THE MINISTRY OF THE MASTER—WEDNESDAY
A Spirit Lifter

Jennifer asked her father if all fairy tales began with "Once upon a time." Her father answered, "No, this year they start with 'If I am elected'."

God's Promise

"Wait on the Lord: be of good courage, and he shall strengthen thine heart: wait, I say on the Lord. "
(Psalm 27:14)

Practicing His Presence

Through what incident or person did you sense the presence of the Lord yesterday?

Prayer And Spiritual Healing

There are many who will admit that prayer has psychological power. It helps to encourage a person and to give them inward strength. This they can accept and will encourage others to prayer.

However, the Christian position is that prayer is effective in all areas of life. It even makes a difference in the physical aspects of your being. I certainly do not understand all the laws of this universe and especially the laws in the area of the Spirit.

However, I have beheld the wonders as a result of prayer for individuals who are physically ill.

Dr. Alexis Carrel has stated it well when he said,

"A doctor who sees a patient give himself to prayer can indeed rejoice. The calm ingendered by prayer is a powerful aid to healing. It is by prayer that man reaches to God and that God enters into him. Prayer appears indispensible to our highest development."

Dr. Carrel knew the value of prayer in physical distress and as a channel of healing of the body as well as the mind and spirit. Many of your illnesses will be gone when you learn to properly relate to the Lord in prayer. Your relationship of all of your being to yourself and to others.

PRAYER: *Father, may I appropriate the power of prayer in my life every moment of today. Amen.*

THE MINISTRY OF THE MASTER—THURSDAY

A Spirit Lifter

New Pastor: "What did you think of Sunday's sermon, Mrs. Swanson?" Member: "It was great, preacher. We didn't know what sin was until you came here!"

God's Promise

"Surely the righteous shall give thanks to thy name; the upright shall dwell in thy presence." (Psalm 140:13, Lamsa)

Practicing His Presence

Through what incident or person did you sense the presence of the Lord yesterday?

Prayer And Spiritual Healing

Many times individuals have asked me what they can do for their illness or other problems. They have in most cases, sought help from someone and are in desperate need for further guidance. It is at this time that I usually try to point out the power and presence of prayer in their lives.

You need to hear again and again the importance of prayer to your wholeness of body, mind, and spirit. Your goal is to achieve the point where you pray without ceasing. This cannot be accomplished overnight but is an art developed over a period of years. There are some tangible steps and I will mention some of them.

First, every believer should sense the importance of spending some time each day in prayer and in meditation. Many of your ailments and many problems of this world could be solved if we all would spend some time alone with God every day. It might be for five minutes or for two hours, but it should be a very definite period of time.

I don't necessarily mean the same time each day, but a definite time of quietness before the Lord regardless of when it is done.

It is not easy to quiet the mind and to put aside all which would detract from the power of the Lord being released in and through you. That which is not easy is essential.

I appreciate being reminded that I am not called to do the easy, but to do the essential. Prayer is essential.

PRAYER: *In the rush of today, O Lord, give me the strength to quiet my whole being. Amen.*

THE MINISTRY OF THE MASTER—FRIDAY
A Spirit Lifter

After the death of her cat, a little girl was consoled by her mother, "Tabby is in Heaven now."
The girl said, "Gee, Mom, what would God want with a dead cat?"

God's Promise

"If any man will do his will, he shall know of the doctrine, whether it be of God..." (John 7:17, KJV)

Practicing His Presence

Through what incident or person did you sense the presence of the Lord yesterday?

Prayer And Spiritual Healing

Have you ever given yourself to prayer for what seems a long time and discovered it was only a few minutes? As a young man in the pastorate and seeking to develop my prayer time, I discovered I was concerned about the amount of time that I was in communion with the Lord. It was at this time that I did a very practical thing. I took an alarm clock and set it for one hour. This took the worry out of time.

This may sound too tangible for you, but it helped me a great deal. It is surprising how fast the time went by when I wasn't worrying about it. You may set your alarm for 10, 15, 30 or 60 minutes. I suggest this because I know many believers have difficulty giving themselves to much time in prayer and Bible Study.

One of the greatest scientists is reported to have said that the world would be changed in a day if everyone would take a half hour in silence each day. He knew the communion, which is deep, has to be developed. He knew this development could come only with concentrated effort. He knew that prayer is the *real* avenue of *real* help to *real* problems.

Wouldn't your day be different if you gave yourself to a period of time of looking only at your source of help, instead of at your problems? Take time to pray and you will have victory in Jesus.

PRAYER: *Lord, may I see you as my only real source of help and comfort. Amen.*

THE MINISTRY OF THE MASTER—SATURDAY

A Spirit Lifter

A guy phoned the airport to ask how long it takes to fly to Kansas City.
"Just a minute, sir," requested the clerk.
"Thanks," he said and hung up.

God's Promise

"But now abideth faith, hope, love, these three; and the greatest of these is love." (I Corinthians 13:13, RSV)

Practicing His Presence

Through what incident or person did you sense the presence of the Lord yesterday?

Prayer And Spiritual Healing

Prayer is ministry. Prayer is work. It is more than a little exercise in self discipline or self help. I believe the highest form of prayer is intercessory prayer. It is giving ourselves to being a channel of the power of the Lord to others because we are a child of the Lord.

I believe your prayer life will be expanded if you concentrate on a different area of concern each day. In my book, *"A Ministry of Prayer,"* I suggest the following areas for each day of the week.

Mondays—Your family and relatives
Tuesdays—Government leaders of the nations of the world
Wednesdays—Missionaries
Thursdays—For unbelievers and for atheistic countries
Fridays—For other churches and denominations
Saturdays—For your own church
Sundays—Prayer and praise for the many facets of ministry of your church

The suggestions do not limit you to only these concerns on any special day. However, it does help to expand your concerns and to realize all of life is in need of prayer.

The time spent each day for the above is more than moments begging God. It is a time of ministering unto others. It truly expands your prayer life.

PRAYER: *Father, enlarge my prayer vision and my prayer concerns. Amen.*

THE MINISTRY OF THE MASTER—SUNDAY
A Spirit Lifter

Finally, when he had to call the wrecker for the tenth time, he remarked to his traveling companion as the wrecker came into sight. "Well, here comes my lemon-aide!"

God's Promise

"So, do not fear, for I am with you; do not be dismayed, for I am your God. I will strengthen you and help you..." (Isaiah 41:10, NIV)

Practicing His Presence

Through what incident or person did you sense the presence of the Lord yesterday?

Prayer And Spiritual Healing

I cannot close this week of prayer and healing without saying that I believe you should participate in a prayer group. This is a must for me, and I really encourage others to participate in one.

The group may be large or small, but the important thing is that you are meeting with others. I especially like going to a prayer breakfast which is handled by lay people. There is something very refreshing and helpful in such meetings and the power and guidance received is so helpful to me. If you have a prayer group in your area I would urge you to attend. If you do not have one in your area I would urge you to begin one. *The Ministry Of The Master* could even serve as a basis of your group's study and growth in the Lord.

I further believe you will be helped a great deal if you participate in a regular healing service. Mary and I have found a weekly healing service to be a source of great power for us. It means so much to be able to take the prayer concerns of people to a service where we seek to blend our faith with others. It is a time of emphasizing the power of the Lord to heal. It is a time when our prayers can become directed and specific.

Again, you need to hear the words of I Samuel 12:23, *"But God forbid that I should sin against the Lord in ceasing to pray for you."*

PRAYER: *Deliver me, Father, from the sin of neglecting to minister in prayer unto others. Amen.*

DOES JESUS CHRIST HEAL TODAY?

"There lives a man, a singular character, whose name is Jesus Christ. He lives in Judea. The barbarians esteem Him as a prophet, but His own followers adore Him as the immediate offspring of the immortal God.

"He is endowed with such unparalleied virtue as to call the dead from their graves. And to heal every kind of disease with a word or a touch.

"This person is tall and eloquently shaped. His aspect is amiable and reverent. His hair flows into beautiful shades which no united color can match. Falling into graceful curves below His ears, agreeably couching upon His shoulders, and parting on His head like the head of a Nazarite.

"His forehead is smooth and large. His cheeks without either spot, save that of a lovely red. His nose is smooth and formed with exquisite symmetry. His beard is this and of a color suitable to the hair of his head, reaching a little below the chin and parted in the middle like a forge.

"He rebukes with majesty, commands with mildness and invites with the most tender and persuasive language. His whole address in deed or word being eloquently graceful in characteristic of so exalted a being.

No man has ever seen Him laugh. But many have seen Him weep. And so persuasive are His tears, that the multitude cannot withhold theirs when joining in sympathy with Him.

"He is very temperate, modest, and wise. And in short, whatever this phenomenon may turn out in the end, He seems a heavenly present from His excellent bearing and divine perfection, and in every way surpassing the greatest of men."

The above is a beautiful description of our Lord Jesus Christ. However, it falls far short of really depicting the reality of His presence today.

He is alive. He does desire to bring His healing to all. He is the Christ who heals today!

POINTS TO PONDER

1. Do most people really understand who Jesus Christ is?
2. What difference does Christ make in the life of an individual?
3. How can Christ make you righteous?

DOES JESUS CHRIST HEAL TODAY?

1. Christ was to be called _____.*Luke 1:35*
2. Christ the Lord is a_____.*Luke 2:11*
3. Christ is the _____ which takes away the sin of the world. *John 1:29*
4. Christ is a faithful _____.*Heb. 2:17*
5. Christ is the_____ of the New Testament or covenant. *Heb. 9:15*
6. Christ is the end of the_____for righteousness for all who believe. *Rom. 10:4*
7. Christ is the good_____. *John 10:11*
8. Christ is the _____. *John 1:1*
9. Christ is the Lord of_____. *Acts 10:36*
10. Christ is _____. *Rev. 19:16*
11. Christ is _____. *Rev. 22:13*
12. Christ is _____. *John 6:35*
13. Christ is the _____. *John 11:25*
14. Christ is the_____. *John 15:1*

DAILY SCRIPTURE

Mon.   Luke 1:26-38
Tues.   John 1:29-34
Wed.   Heb. 2:14-18
Thurs.   Acts 10:34-43
Fri.   Rev. 19:11-21
Sat.   John 11:17-27
Sun.   John 15:1-11

PRAYER CONCERNS

Your Family & Relatives
Government Leaders
Missionaries
For the Unbelievers
Churches & Denominations
Your Own Church
Prayer and Praise

NOTE: You will be spiritually strengthened by completing two questions each day, reading the suggested scripture, and ministering in prayer for the concerns of the day.

THE MINISTRY OF THE MASTER—MONDAY
A Spirit Lifter

There was a terrible earthquake and many of the inhabitants of the area fled for fear of more of the same. One couple sent their four children to stay with an aunt and uncle in another area. A week later the parents received this telegram:

"Am returning your children. Send earthquake."

God's Promise

"There is that speaketh like the piercings of a sword: but the tongue of the wise is health." (Proverbs 12:18)

Practicing His Presence

Through what incident or person did you sense the presence of the Lord yesterday?

Does Jesus Christ Heal Today?

Our belief that Jesus heals today will be determined to a large degree by understanding who He is. I believe one of the best ways to do this is to consider the many times He said *"I AM..."*

If He is all that He said then certainly He is able to heal today as when He ministered with His disciples of old.

The woman Christ met at the well refers to the Messiah. Jesus said to her, *"I am He,"* that is, I am the Messiah.

I am the bread of life—John 6:35
I am from above—John 8:23
I am the eternal One—John 8:58
I am the light of the world—John 9:5
I am the door—John 10:7
I am the resurrection and the life—John 11:35
I am the Lord and Master—John 13:13
I am the Way, the Truth, and the Life—John 14:6
I am the true vine—John 15:1
I am Alpha and Omega—Revelation 1:8
I am the first and the last—Revelation 1:17

PRAYER: *Father, help me to really believe your Son is my Great Physician. Amen.*

THE MINISTRY OF THE MASTER—TUESDAY
A Spirit Lifter

A Sunday School teacher was expounding on the first chapter of Mark verse 34 where it says, "...he healed many people of divers diseases."

The teacher tried to bring this teaching down to modern times and said that if we were putting it in our language we would say he healed people of "swimming cramps."

God's Promise

"...God had made me to laugh, so that all that hear will laugh with me..." (Genesis 21:6)

Practicing His Presence

Through what incident or person did you sense the presence of the Lord yesterday?

Does Christ Jesus Heal Today?

Jesus Christ is not only revealed by the statements of Whom He is, but also by what He says He is willing to do. A person's character is certainly revealed more by action than by words. Today I would encourage you to meditate upon the *"I will"* aspect of our Lord Jesus. They will present to you His desire for your life in a very vivid and profound manner.

To His heavenly Father, *"not as I will—*Mt. 26:39

To the leper, *"I will, be thou clean"*—Luke 5:13

To the believer, *"I will raise him unto life eternal"*—John 6:40

To the sinful world, *"I will draw all unto me"*—John 12:32

To impart hope to believers, *"I will come again"*—John 14:3

To all who have been given to Him, *"I will that they be with me"*—John 17:24

To what is expected of each person, *"If I will that he tarry"*—John 21:22

The above are strong and wonderful statements. You and I can bank our life on them. They remain our source of strength and help.

It is my prayer and hope that you and I can say unto the Lord, *"I will"* instead of *I won't."* He desires an obedient and faithful response from each of us.

PRAYER: *As Jesus performed His miracles in the past, may I believe He does so today. Amen.*

THE MINISTRY OF THE MASTER—WEDNESDAY
A Spirit Lifter

The bride wrote me several days after the wedding.

In the letter she stated, "I want to thank you, Pastor Bartow, for *maring* Jim and me."

Well, I thought then and have since, I wonder how many are maried, instead of married."

God's Promise

"Now our Lord Jesus Christ himself, and God, even our Father, which hath loved us, and hath given us everlasting consolation and good hope through grace; comfort your hearts, and establish you in every good word and work." (II Thessalonians 2:16,17)

Practicing His Presence

Through what incident or person did you sense the presence of the Lord yesterday? Are you more conscious of His presence than you were a year ago?

Does Jesus Christ Heal Today?

I can't help but get all excited when I seek to write about Jesus. He is the bright and glorious light of my life and I am sure you feel the same.

Others have so eloquently written of Him, and so I quote some comments which I feel are really great.

"There was a knight of Bethlehem
Whose wealth was tears and sorrows.
His men at arms were little lambs,
His sentinels were sparrows.

"His castle was a wooden cross,
Where on he hung so high.
His helmet was a crown of thorns,
Whose crest did touch the sky."

Jesus will be with you today. You must seek to be spiritually alert so as to be aware of His presence. There are precious truths on every hand and most of them are overlooked by most of us. The One who is the Truth is near at hand. If you are not careful you will miss Him. He is willing and able to heal today. Open your life to Him.

PRAYER: *Father, help me to be aware of the presence of Jesus in all of my activities today. Amen.*

THE MINISTRY OF THE MASTER—THURSDAY
A Spirit Lifter

In exasperation she said, "Johnny, you are an incorrigible." He raised himself to full height and proudly replied, "I am not, I am a Presbyterian."

God's Promise

"If my people, which are called by my name, shall humble themselves, and pray, and seek my face, and turn from their wicked ways; then will I hear from heaven, and will forgive their sins, and will heal their lands." (II Chronicles 7:14)

Practicing His Presence

Through what incident or person did you sense the presence of the Lord yesterday?

Does Jesus Christ Heal Today?

Someone asked the renowned Tennyson what he thought of Jesus. He replied in his own poetic fashion, *"What the sun is to that flower, so Jesus is to me."*

The flower would soon be dead without light. The reason many are dead in their heart and soul today, even though they seem alive physically, is because they have not permitted the light of the world to enter into their innermost being.

Jesus did not have a long public ministry, but His truths are for all ages and all peoples.

Socrates taught for approximately forty years. Plato was a famous teacher for fifty years. Aristotle taught for about forty years. Yet, their influence is very little compared to the impact of the teachings of Jesus Christ.

We cannot talk about whom He is without acknowledging Him as the greatest influencer that ever lived. Jesus painted no pictures, for instance. Yet He has inspired literally thousands and thousands of pictures. Can you name any picture which is the result of inspiration of the artist by Socrates, Plato, etc.? Of course not. The impact of Jesus was not simply His teaching, but the fact that He lives and heals today.

PRAYER: *May I remain rooted in my source of strength and help, ever you, Lord Jesus. Amen.*

THE MINISTRY OF THE MASTER—FRIDAY
A Spirit Lifter

Women's roles are still being challenged by various groups but this student summed up her interpretation easily.

After reading a medieval ballad on the Virgin Mary, a parochial schoolgirl wrote: "The theme of this poem is that behind every successful man there is a woman."

God's Promise

"For the righteous Lord loveth righteousness; his countenance doth behold the upright." (Psalm 11:7)

Practicing His Presence

Through what incident or person did you sense the presence of the Lord yesterday?

Does Jesus Christ Heal Today?

Someone has written concerning Jesus.

His birth was contrary to the laws of nature—He was born of the virgin Mary.

His life was lived contrary to others—He always sought to serve and desired not to have others minister unto Him.

His death was contrary to the laws of the nation—for it was a false trial.

He had no corn fields or fisheries, but yet He could feed over five thousand at one time and from a few loaves of bread and a few fish.

He walked on no beautiful carpets or velvet rugs—yet He walked on the sea of Galilee.

He ended up being killed—yet, He brought life to all.

Every effort on my part to encourage you to really permit Jesus Christ to be Lord of your life is energy well expended.

One of the earliest and most simple of the creeds of the church stated, *"Christ is Lord."*

Your believing and yielding to this truth will lead to the abundant life for you and yours. He will heal you now.

PRAYER: *Father, may I spare no energy or effort to remain faithful and loyal to your Son, Jesus. Amen.*

THE MINISTRY OF THE MASTER—SATURDAY
A Spirit Lifter

A country housewife had good intentions, but little knowledge concerning the making of doughnuts. Hers came out very heavy. She couldn't get anybody in the family to take more than one bite of them. In disgust she threw them out to the ducks. An hour later two of the neighborhood urchins tapped at her door and said, "Say lady, your ducks have sunk."

God's Promise

"God is our refuge and strength, a very present help in time of trouble." (Psalm 46:1)

Practicing His Presence

Through what incident or person did you sense the presence of the Lord yesterday?

Does Jesus Christ Heal Today?

You are opening yourself unto the One who knows you perfectly. Jesus Christ is aware of your thoughts, motives, desires, and actions. He is Lord of all.

Who is Jesus? He is the One who can put music in your life. He is the One who has inspired the great music you will hear in church worship. Jesus never wrote a word of music and yet Hayden, Handel, Beethoven, Bach, Mendelson, and many other famous composers were inspired by Him.

He is the One who must be born in your heart. He is the One to whom you must give an account of your decision for Him and for your actions.

> *"Even through Christ in Bethlehem*
> *A thousand times be born.*
> *If He is not born within your heart,*
> *Thou art most forlorn."*

PRAYER: *All that I am or ever hope to be I lift unto you at this moment, Lord Jesus. Amen.*

THE MINISTRY OF THE MASTER—SUNDAY
A Spirit Lifter

A man returned from vacation and said to his friends, "I will never figure out a woman. Last year we went on a vacation up in the mountains. She couldn't decide what to put on. This year we went to the beach and she couldn't decide what to take off."

God's Promise

"For all the promises of God in him are yea, and in him, Amen, unto the glory of God by us." (II Corinthians 1:20)

Practicing His Presence

Through what incident or person did you sense the presence of the Lord yesterday?

Does Jesus Christ Heal Today?

The Bible tells us who Jesus is with the use of fitting names. It is said that He is the beloved Son of God. At the time of His baptism the voice from heaven designated Him as such.

"And there came a voice from heaven, saying, Thou art my beloved Son, in whom I am well pleased." Mark 1:1

Jesus is often referred to as the Son of God. Many of the people of His day spoke of Him as the Son of God.

"Then they that were in the ship came and worshipped him, saying, Of a truth thou art the Son of God." Mt. 14:33

The title which seems most appropriate as I close this week of devotions is King of Kings. He is the One who is going to reign forever and ever.

"Which in his times he shall show, who is the blessed and only Potentate, the King of Kings, and Lord of Lords." I Timothy 6:15

You and I must someday face the One who is the King. It is our responsibility as well as privilege to make Him King of our life now. He desires and must sit on the throne of your heart. He wants to give you wholeness. Permit Him to do so.

PRAYER: *Thank you, Father, for the blessed hope of reigning forever with Your blessed Son. Amen.*

GOD'S CHANNEL OF HEALING

It is my firm conviction that every believer is called to be a channel of God's wholeness. The channel He uses is not confined to the professional clergy. The channel is not confined to a few who can reach out to thousands. Every humble believer is called of Him to be a source of wholeness to someone else.

A fruitful channel is not determined by sex or even age. I have known young children who have been used of the Lord to impart wholeness. Sometimes children have prayed and even laid on hands and the Lord has honored their prayer of faith.

Our grandson, Dennis, as a first grader, came forward one Wednesday night during the healing service to help me and his grandma lay on hands. The people who came while he was there seemed to really be touched by his ministry. One of them happened to be a little four-year-old boy with leukemia. This little boy was really drawn to Dennis and it meant a lot to him.

A fruitful channel is not determined by one's past life nor by one's present perfect physical condition. After all, there are no perfect individuals either in action or in health. You cannot wait until you are perfect before being willing to be used of the Lord. If you wait for this to happen you will never minister unto others.

The channel the Lord desires is one which is open to His presence and power. It is one which believes He is the healer and that He works through imperfect individuals. He does not demand.

The eleventh chapter of Hebrews mentions many heroes of the faith. There is not a one who has a perfect record, but the redeeming factor was their faith in God. They believed God and this belief translated into action which stimulated many people. They were channels of God's revelation and as such they brought His power and love into the midst of the people.

POINT TO PONDER

1. What is meant by being a channel of God's power and love?
2. What do you feel are essential qualities of a channel of God's wholeness?
3. How do you feel you can be a more effective channel?

Daily Bible Study and Daily Prayer Concerns

GOD'S CHANNEL OF HEALING

1. _____ is the substance of things hoped for.
   Heb. 11:1
2. ...and he that is chief, as he that doth _____.
   Luke 22:26
3. The elders which are among you I _____.
   I Peter 5:1
4. Is there _____ with God? *Rom. 9:14.*
5. ...I love in the _____. *II John v. 1*
6. ...thou art worthy to take the _____.
   Rev. 5:9
7. ...a great multitude, which no man could _____
   _____. *Rev. 7:9*
8. For this my son was dead, and is _____
   again... *Luke 15:24*
9. ...let them pray over him, _____ him
   with oil... *James 5:14*
10. James a _____ of God, and of the Lord
    Jesus Christ... *James 1:1*
11. ...the word spoken by angels was _____.
    Heb. 2:2
12. ...ye received of us how ye ought to walk and to please God, so ye
    would _____ more and more. *I Th. 4:1*
13. ...we were bold in our God to speak unto you the _____
    _____ of God. *I Th. 2:2.*
14. ...present your bodies a _____ sacrifice.
    Rom. 12:1

DAILY SCRIPTURE

Mon.	Heb. 11:1-5
Tues.	Luke 22:24-27
Wed.	II John 1-3
Thurs.	Rev. 5:9-12
Fri.	James 1:1-5
Sat.	Heb. 2:1-4
Sun.	I Th. 2:1-4

PRAYER CONCERNS

Your Family & Relatives
Government Leaders
Missionaries
For the Unbelievers
Churches & Denominations
Your Own Church
Prayer and Praise

NOTE: You will be spiritually strengthened by completing two questions each day, reading the suggested scripture, and ministering in prayer for the concerns of the day.

THE MINISTRY OF THE MASTER—MONDAY
A Spirit Lifter

Husband: "It was a good cake, but it defied the laws of gravity."
Bride: "How?"
Husband: "It was heavy as lead, but wouldn't go down."

God's Promise

"I lie down and sleep; I wake again, for the Lord sustains me." (Psalm 3:5, RSV)

Practicing His Presence

Through what incident or person did you sense the presence of the Lord yesterday?

God's Channel Of Healing

One of the first things about an effective channel of the Lord's wholeness is the realization that the Lord Jesus is central in the ministry of healing. It is unto Him that all things should be submitted. Everything you ever plan, perform, or even anticipate will ultimately be cast at the feet of Jesus.

Revelation 4:10 tells us that the 24 elders cast their crowns before the throne singing, *"Worthy art thou, worthy art thou."* Whether it be the crown of righteousness, the crown of victory, or the crown you receive as a spiritual leader, they will all be cast at the feet of Jesus.

A channel of God's wholeness is not a person who seeks to comply with every whim and fancy of every person. You are not called to nurse every complaint. You are called to set a pace of spiritual leadership which ultimately leads individuals to acknowledge Jesus as Lord and as the great physician.

A pastor once told me that his church's ministry of healing was based on eastern religions. It was in no way distinctly Christian. After several in their congregation had read my book, *"The Adventures of Healing,"* the ministry became Christocentric. The individuals had come to realize they were channels of God's wholeness because they had become His children through Jesus Christ. Anything less than Jesus as the focal point of the healing ministry is missing the mark.

PRAYER: *Father, I want to be an effective channel of healing. Help me, I pray. Amen.*

THE MINISTRY OF THE MASTER—TUESDAY
A Spirit Lifter

Father: "Why were you kept in at school?"
Son: "I didn't know where the Azores were."
Father: "Well, in the future, just remember where you put things."

God's Promise

"When the Spirit of truth comes, he will lead you to the complete truth, since he will not be speaking as from himself but will say only what he has learned." (John 16:13, JB)

Practicing His Presence

Through what incident or person did you sense the presence of the Lord yesterday?

God's Channel Of Healing

I often meet people who say, *"If God knows all I need before I even ask Him then why do I have to pray for healing or receive laying-on-of-hands, etc.?"* This is a good question and I can appreciate the thought.

It is impossible for me to answer all the complex aspects of the universe, but I will say this. The Lord knows you have need of food. He knows every person must eat to remain alive. However, He does not miraculously produce a harvest. Of course, growth is beyond human power. But the planting of the wheat after the soil has been prepared is done by human beings. The Lord never automatically provided a wheat field. There were things which had to be done by individuals. It is agreed the harvest came from the Lord, but only after much work had been done by people.

I see the same thing in the healing ministry. If individuals do as the Lord has instructed there is a great harvest of healings. If these things are neglected or ignored there are not as many healings. The harvest is not as bountiful.

It is important for you to realize the methods of the Master must be duplicated by His followers. When you wonder, for instance, about the validity of the ministry of the laying-on-of-hands then I urge you to consider such passages as Luke 4:40. *"...and he laid his hands on every one of them, and healed them."*

PRAYER: *Father, I make my request known unto You because You have invited me to do so. Amen.*

A Spirit Lifter

The two men hadn't met for years.

"And is your wife still as pretty as she used to be?" asked the first.

"Oh yes," replied the second, "but it takes her a little longer."

God's Promise

"Whoever would love life and see good days must keep his tongue from evil and his lips from deceitful speech." (I Peter 3:10, NIV)

Practicing His Presence

Through what incident or person did you sense the presence of the Lord yesterday?

God's Channel Of Healing

I do not want to emphasize the concept of the channel of healing to the degree that I neglect the power behind the channel. It is Jesus Christ alone who is worthy of the glory and honor for all healing. He is the One who makes us whole and who keeps us whole. He is the One who has called us unto Himself and who set the example of ministry which focuses upon need and which meets these needs.

John's vision as recorded in the book of Revelation reveals the worthiness of the Lord Jesus.

"And I saw in the right hand of him who was seated on the throne a scroll written within and on the back, sealed with seven seals; and I saw a strong angel proclaiming with a loud voice, 'Who is worthy to open the scroll and break its seals'?" Rev. 5:1

There was no one worthy. It was then that one of the elders said, *"Weep not; lo, the Lion of the tribe of Judah, the Root of David, has conquered..." Rev. 5:4*

In the healing ministry it is only Jesus who can break the seal which binds people with illnesses of body, mind, and spirit. He alone is worthy to look unto for complete healing. I may be a channel. You may be a channel. This is only to lead to Jesus and to Him alone.

PRAYER: *Though I am unworthy, O Father, I am grateful You use me as a channel of Your healing. Amen.*

THE MINISTRY OF THE MASTER—THURSDAY
A Spirit Lifter

A sign in the gift shop read: "For the man who has everything: a calendar to remind him when the payments are due."

God's Promise

"Praise the Lord! For all who fear God and trust in him are blessed beyond expression. Yes, happy is the man who delights in doing his commands." (Psalm 112:1, TLB)

Practicing His Presence

Through what incident or person did you sense the presence of the Lord yesterday?

God's Channel of Healing

I want to continue today to consider the fact that only Jesus is worthy of our devotion in the healing ministry. There is no angel good enough. There is no person worthy of the honor or glory. This truth is capsuled with these words.

"...Worthy is the Lamb that was slain to receive power, and riches, and wisdom, and strength, and honour, and glory, and blessing."
Rev. 5:12

Years ago I saw a cartoon which depicts the fact that anything less than loyalty to the highest is wrong. There was pictured a flower growing by a basement window. There was a cobweb over the window. The window was dirty and inside you could see a sixty-watt light burning.

Above was a brilliant sun. It was shining in all its glory. However, the flower was leaning toward the basement window rather than upward toward the sun. The caption for this picture was but one word, *"infidelity."* The flower had chosen the lesser light.

Any ministry of healing which is not firmly grounded upon the Lord Jesus Christ is looking to a lesser light. You cannot be a channel as you ought to be if you permit anyone or anything other than Jesus to be your point of power.

PRAYER: *Father, may I be loyal to You and to You alone. Keep me from my wayward tendencies. Amen.*

THE MINISTRY OF THE MASTER—FRIDAY

A Spirit Lifter

Grandpa: "My little man, you shouldn't say 'I ain't going.' You should say, ' I am not going,' 'He is not going,' 'They are not going,' 'We are not going,' 'You are not going.' "

Little Teddy: "Ain't nobody going?"

God's Promise

"Let us run with endurance the race that is set before us, looking to Jesus, the author and finisher of our faith." (Hebrews 12:1,2)

Practicing His Presence

Through what incident or person did you sense the presence of the Lord yesterday?

God's Channel Of Healing

Prayer is a vital part of the persons seeking to be a channel of the healing power of the Lord. This is especially significant in the light of the comments concerning the saints.

"...and four and twenty elders fell down before the Lamb, having every one of them harps, and golden vials full of odours, which are the prayers of the saints." Rev. 5:8

The vials were not filled with sweet odours of Bible study, or committee activity, or choir time, visitation, etc. They were filled with the prayers of the saints. I do not intend to say the other things are not important, but I am attempting to say prayer is the most important.

It is through prayer that we become the most effective channel. Prayer is the key to the many things you desire and to being used of the Lord in a fruitful way.

There is no way you are going to reason a person into the Kingdom. There is no way you are going to bulldoze someone to accept the healing ministry. It is the spirit of the Lord which must lead and direct.

The Lord has ordained that His channels are most effective when they pray effectively. This is the secret. If you want to be an effective channel then develop your prayer life and be a source of power.

PRAYER: *Father, the secret of power is so open to all who seek. Help me to pray always. Amen.*

THE MINISTRY OF THE MASTER—SATURDAY
A Spirit Lifter

Ted: "Since he lost his money, half his friends don't know him any more."
Fred: "And the other half?"
Ted: "They don't know yet that he has lost it."

God's Promise

"Before they call I will answer, while they are still speaking I will hear." (Jeremiah 29:12, RSV)

Practicing His Presence

Through what incident or person did you sense the presence of the Lord yesterday?

God's Channel Of Healing

I don't want to imply that there are certain mechanical things which will make you a more fruitful channel of God's healing power. It is more than the mechanics.

A fruitful channel is one who is open to the power and presence of the Lord. It is not one who folds hands a certain way or uses just certain words. This type of structure can stifle the power instead of release it.

There are people who like to raise their hands in worship while others are ill at ease doing this. I believe it doesn't make any difference to the Lord. The important point is do you believe He is the healing and are you willing to proclaim this truth.

We are told that *"...the four and twenty elders fell down and worshipped him that liveth forever and ever."* (Rev. 5:14) I have never witnessed an entire congregation falling down and worshipping at the throne of grace. I have seen an entire congregation seek to humble themselves in spirit before the Lord.

Again it is not the posture as much as the attitude and the faith. The important thing is to realize that the channel should be a worshipping channel. The failure to worship will result in a weakness of ministry.

PRAYER: *May I worship You in Spirit and in truth, dear Lord. Amen.*

THE MINISTRY OF THE MASTER—SUNDAY
A Spirit Lifter

Frank: "Alan is so conceited!"
Bob: "Yes, on his last birthday he sent a telegram of congratulations to his mother."

God's Promise

"The Lord said, I will cause all my goodness to pass in front of you, and I will proclaim my name, the Lord, in your presence." (Exodus 33:19, NIV)

Practicing His Presence

Through what incident or person did you sense the presence of the Lord yesterday?

God's Channel Of Healing

How many people does the Lord want as a channel of healing? How many will be included in His ministry of wholeness?

I believe He desires that every believer appreciate the fact that the Lord wants all of His children to be a channel of power. He desires to reach out to all and to have all reach out to others.

The final revelation certainly doesn't restrict the number of the Lord's chosen to a few people. There are countless individuals who have been redeemed by the Lord and who come into His presence.

"After this I beheld, and lo, a great multitude, which no man could number, of all nations, and kindreds, and people, and tongues, stood before the throne, and before the Lamb, ..." Rev. 7:9

Sometimes I get the feeling some Christians feel the Lord's desire is for only a few to be productive. I sincerely believe the Scripture teaches that every believer can be fruitful for Him. The important thing is to point people to the Lord Jesus.

You are, and can continue to be, a channel of God's healing. You, as a believer, are counted among those who will gather with the multitudes to glorify the Lord. May you begin to do this now by putting your trust and hope in Him.

PRAYER: *Father, help me to be a fruitful child of Yours and to believe for great things. Amen.*

GOD'S CHANNEL OF HEALING (continued)

Most people I meet are seeking to have more of the Lord's power to surge into them. They are constantly seeking to know the Word better, to be able to verbalize prayer better, to have a better feeling, and other things which keep them constantly looking inward.

Many of them feel they are unworthy to be channels of the Lord's healing and are striving to reach the point where they are really completely yielded as far as they are concerned.

All of the above are not bad, but when they become ends they are bad. The goal of your life and mine is not any of these, but it is to be used of the Lord to His glory. He cannot pour into a vessel which is already full. In most cases the vessel is full of self. The channel concept implies that some flows out as well as into a person. In fact, there cannot be more flow in until something has gone out.

You are not destined to be a dead sea into which the living water runs, but from whence there is no outlet.

You are to be a sparkling lake with water running in and out. The lake will never go dry regardless of how much runs out because the river of life flowing from the heart of our Master is inexhaustible. There is no limit to the living water available.

I feel that the ministry of healing is one where you will have ample opportunity to permit the Living Christ to flow through you. A channel of healing need never fear having no opportunity to minister.

You can pause for 20 seconds and think of several people you personally know who are in need of wholeness. You may not even get beyond yourself, because you may be in desperate need of healing. The ministry of healing is not a forced form of evangelism. It is a natural expression of concern and there are plenty of candidates for your ministry. Your prayers, visits, ministry of laying-on-of-hands, anointing with oil, etc. will be helpful to many people.

POINTS TO PONDER

1. Do you feel most people want to take in and not give out of the power of the Lord?
2. How can room be made for more Living Water in your life?
3. How many people can you list in five minute who need the message of healing?

GOD'S CHANNEL OF HEALING (Continued)

1. These are those who come out of the great _____.
   Rev. 7:14
2. And they sung as it were a _____ song.
   Rev. 14:3
3. ...Salvation, glory, honour, and power, unto the _____
   _____our God. *Rev. 19:1*
4. My flesh and my heart faileth: but God is the _____
   _____ of my heart. *Ps. 73:26*
5. Howbeit, when he, the Spirit of truth, is come he will guide you into
   all_____. *John 16:13*
6. For the Father Himself_____you. *John 16:27*
7. ...The powers that be are _____ of God.
   Rom. 13:1
8. ...It is the same God which _____ in all.
   I Cor. 12:6
9. We then, as _____ together with Him.
   II Cor. 6:1
10. _____not the Holy Spirit. *Eph. 4:30*
11. Our light affliction is but for the _____.
   II Cor. 4:17
12. If thine enemy be hungry, give him _____
    to eat. *Pro. 25:21*
13. _____ ye my people says your God.
    Isa. 40:1
14. Let thy _____ come also unto me, O Lord.
    Ps. 119:41

DAILY SCRIPTURE

Mon.	Rev. 7:13-17
Tues.	Rev. 19:1-4
Wed.	John 16:24-28
Thurs.	II Cor. 6:1-6
Fri.	II Cor. 4:14-17
Sat.	Isa. 40:1-5
Sun.	Ps. 119:41

PRAYER CONCERNS

Your Family & Relatives
Government Leaders
Missionaries
For the Unbelievers
Churches & Denominations
Your Own Church
Prayer and Praise

NOTE: You will be spiritually strengthened by completing two questions each day, reading the suggested scripture, and ministering in prayer for the concerns of the day.

THE MINISTRY OF THE MASTER—MONDAY
A Spirit Lifter

Driving Instructor: "Don't you know that you should always give half of the road to a woman driver?"

Student: "I always do when I find out which half of the road she wants."

God's Promise

"Understand, therefore, that the Lord your God is the faithful God who for a thousand generations keeps his promises and constantly loves those who love him and who obey his commands." (Deuteronomy 7:9)

Practicing His Presence

Through what incident or person did you sense the presence of the Lord yesterday?

God's Channel Of Healing (Continued)

I seek to be very practical as I present *"The Ministry Of The Master."* It is my feeling the methods of Jesus are simple and direct. He wants each of His followers to reach out to others and to be a blessing and thus be blessed.

The suggestion I have for you today is to write down the names of the people you know who are in need of healing. I want you to actually make a list of these people. You will want to ask the Holy Spirit to guide you as you open your heart to hear His still small voice speak of loved ones, friends and acquaintances who need the message of healing.

After you have done this, may I suggest you take some time to consider specific ways you can be a channel of healing for these individuals. Is it that you are to lift them into the light and love of the Lord and minister in prayer unto them? Is it that you will go personally to them and minister in prayer or laying-on-of-hands? Perhaps you will make them a matter of special prayer in your prayer group. You may seek to develop a spirit of faith as you are in their presence and seek to exhibit a spirit of faith. It may be you will want to give them a copy of *"The Ministry Of The Master."* Whatever it is, remember you are a channel of healing. May you live accordingly.

PRAYER: *Father, may I never forget that I am a channel of Your healing power. Amen.*

THE MINISTRY OF THE MASTER—TUESDAY
A Spirit Lifter

Tracey came running to her Grandmother holding a dry, pressed leaf, obviously the relic of a day long gone by. "I found it in the big Bible, Grandma," she said. "Do you s'pose it belonged to Eve?"

God's Promise

"Whether you turn to the right or to the left, your ears will hear a Voice behind you, saying, 'This is the way; walk in it.' " (Isaiah 30:21, NIV)

Practicing His Presence

Through what incident or person did you sense the presence of the Lord yesterday?

God's Channel Of Healing (Continued)

A channel of healing is most effective when you are aware of the suffering many people have to endure. You appreciate the relief which can come when you have empathy with the suffering which exists.

All the problems of life do not automatically disappear, but they are certainly made bearable when there is an understanding friend with whom they can be shared. One of the misunderstandings of the healing ministry is that if a person is not immediately healed he is not helped. This is not true. The very fact of ministry by a concerned friend is comfort and encouragement to the distressed.

The ultimate comfort comes in the world to come. However, there is much comfort on the pilgrimage if someone will sincerely minister to a person. There will come a time when,

"They shall hunger no more, neither thirst any more; neither shall the sun light on them, nor the heat." Rev. 7:16

In the meantime these are difficult days for many people. They need someone to bring to them the hope which is in Christ. They need the positive message that there is a better life and that wholeness can be theirs in a manner they have not had. You have a ministry to someone suffering today.

PRAYER: *My earthly pilgrimage is often so frustrating, Father, and I need Your comfort and guidance. Amen.*

THE MINISTRY OF THE MASTER—WEDNESDAY

A Spirit Lifter

Jane: "Is your brother a good salesman?"
Lucy: "Well, he got two orders today."
Jane: "What for?"
Lucy: "One to get out and the other to stay out."

God's Promise

"Do not take revenge on someone who wrongs you. If anyone slaps you on the right cheek, let him slap your left cheek, too. And if someone takes you to court to sue you for your shirt, let him have your coat as well." (Matthew 5:39,40, TEV)

Practicing His Presence

Through what incident or person did you sense the presence of the Lord yesterday?

God's Channel Of Healing (Continued)

I often say that people do not need hell, but they need hope. They have had enough hell and are crying to be delivered. You and I can serve as a channel to bring this deliverance. God will use willing people to fulfill His will.

He is not looking for perfect people because they do not exist. His would be a hopeless task if He waited for a perfect one before He would release His power through them.

I believe the Lord is looking for someone who will bring hope to the hopeless. If you feel hopeless today, you know how desperately you yearn to have someone, just anyone, come and bring you some hope. If this be true for you, are you not aware of the fact that there are many in the same condition? They, too, yearn for someone who cares and for a channel who will bring hope.

When I minister unto a person I do not make rash promises. At the same time I do not sell short the power of the Lord. I seek to always open the door of hope and to leave it open. It is then, that through my ministry, I seek to help people walk through that open door of hope.

PRAYER: *Thank you for the hope which You bring to me, O Lord Jesus. Amen.*

THE MINISTRY OF THE MASTER—THURSDAY
A Spirit Lifter

A reporter, interviewing a man who had reached his 99th birthday, said, "I certainly hope I can come back next year and see you reach 100."

"Can't see why not, young feller," the old timer replied, "you look healthy enough to me."

God's Promise

"God will fulfill all your needs, in christ Jesus, as lavishly as only God can." (Philippians 4:19, JB)

Practicing His Presence

Through what incident or person did you sense the presence of the Lord yesterday?

God's Channel Of Healing

When should a channel of healing reach out and permit the flow of God into the life of others? I feel we should do this without ceasing. It is a constant and consistent type of ministry. It is not to be turned on and off at will, but it is to be our lifestyle.

I am not called to reach out to only those who have small problems. It is my high calling to minister to the desperate. It is my calling to take the ministry of healing to so-called "terminal" cases as well as those who are apparently in good health. I cannot choose as to which ones need ministry. Everybody does in one way or another. This fact leaves me with a field white unto harvest and with thousands who are seeking to hear a message of hope.

It is relatively easy to be a contented believer and to let the hurts of this world go by. It is a different ball game when you are willing to be a channel of wholeness to those in desperate need. A channel of healing cannot dry up but must keep the flood gates open to permit the abundance of God's love to flow out to others. Each channel becomes more effective with use, and becomes clogged and ineffective with lack of use.

PRAYER: *The desperate needs in my life and in those around me make me dependent on You, Father. Amen.*

THE MINISTRY OF THE MASTER—FRIDAY
A Spirit Lifter

A patient was informed by his psychiatrist that he could consider himself cured of his delusion that he was Napoleon.
"Oh wonderful!" cried the happy man. "Where's the phone? I must call Josephine and tell her the great news."

God's Promise

"I will forgive their wickedness and will remember their sins no more." (Jeremiah 31:34, NIV)

Practicing His Presence

Through what incident or person did you sense the presence of the Lord yesterday?

God's Channel Of Healing (Continued)

It is a source of great encouragement to people to let them know that Jesus Christ has achieved the victory. He is the victor. He is not the victim. He is the One who has conquered. He has not been defeated.

I know one of the reasons Christ must be held high is because He is the Physician. An individual cannot heal. They can be a channel of healing, but are not the One who heals.

The note of victory in Jesus needs to be heard by the ill and the depressed and defeated. This positive proclamation is a necessity. It is essential if hope is to be instilled in the hopeless.

The Bible emphatically speaks of the victory of Jesus.

"We give thanks, O Lord God Almighty, which are, and wast, and art to come; because thou hast taken to thee thy great power, and hast reigned." Rev. 11:17

The day will come when this power will be displayed perfectly and the reign of sin will be over. Until this day we still see the power of the Lord revealed as He takes control over sickness and other adverse situations. He reveals His power often and dramatically.

It is not a perfect world, but it is a place where the power of the Lord is released with the degree of frequency to convince us of His presence and love. You can with confidence say that Jesus hears and will answer. Look to Him!

PRAYER: *Thank you for the victory I have in You, O Lord Jesus. Amen.*

60

THE MINISTRY OF THE MASTER—SATURDAY
A Spirit Lifter

"Yes, stamp collecting is educational," said the fond mother to the visitor. "For instance, where is Hungary, Dennis?"

Without looking up from his stamp book, the young philatelist answered promptly, "Two pages in front of Italy."

God's Promise

"This is how we know that love is: Jesus Christ laid down his life for us." (I John 3:16)

Practicing His Presence

Through what incident or person did you sense the presence of the Lord yesterday?

God's Channel Of Healing

It is music to my ears to hear discouraged people singing a new song. The song of victorty is a classic of joy even if expressed poorly. The delivery is not near as important as sincerity and realizing Jesus is the healer.

A gentleman attended our healing service for the first time with the problem of being unable to sleep. He had gone over six years without an entire night of sleep. He had received much medical treatment but all to no avail.

The following Wednesday night he was present and I asked during the service what had happened since last Wednesday. He replied that he had slept better than for all the years since his illness and the night before had slept all night. He spoke with a note of joy in his heart and life. He knew the Lord had touched him. The community of believers had served as a channel of healing for him. The Lord honored the channel and extended healing in a wonderful way.

I believe one reason he could accept the channel was because of the note of victory he could sense in the meeting and in the lives of people who were present. It was a new song for him and he loved it. Now he joined with others in this song of victory.

PRAYER: *Thank you for the new song You have put in my heart, Jesus. May it ever be sung. Amen.*

THE MINISTRY OF THE MASTER—SUNDAY
A Spirit Lifter

Joe: "I'm starting on my second million."

Bill: "Your second million? You haven't got the first million yet."

Joe; "Yeah—they always say making your second million is the easiest."

God's Promise

"The Kingdom we are given is unshakable; let us therefore give thanks to God, and so worship, with reverence and awe, for our God is a devouring fire." (Hebrews 12:28,29, NEB)

Practicing His Presence

Through what incident or person did you sense the presence of the Lord yesterday?

God's Channel Of Healing (Continued)

Rudyard Kipling wrote a poem, "When Earth's Last Picture Is Painted." One day I was stirred to write of heaven instead of earth. I want to include my poem as it depicts the ultimate healing which will be yours.

When heaven's first glimpse is seen and earth's pull restricts me no more.
When Christ in His splendor does beam and I cross my Jordan to heaven's shore,
There shall be rest I have longed for and the absence of all pain so severe,
Sorrows are vanquished by the Comforter and I'll shout as they disappear.

All who are faithful will be there. They shall surround the throne with glad cries.
They shall busy themselves with praises, and I'll be welcomed as one who never dies.

I shall see the great saints of the past, prophets, priests, loved ones great and small.
I shall fellowship with them through the ages, until I come to know them all.

The smile of the Master is present, the welcome of His Father and mine
No one is better than another, no place, no spirit so sublime.

Each from the depth of the soul, expresses great thanks and great praise
And as the perpetual ages roll, the glad shout of redemption I'll raise.

PRAYER: *Thank you, Father, for the promise of wholeness throughout all eternity. Amen.*

Theme for the Week
ACCORDING TO THY WILL

Often I am asked how a person should pray in the face of illness or other difficulty. Many leave the impression that they should be resigned to whatever lot or illness has befallen them.

I have a problem with the approach of praying for an illness or problem with the main emphasis being the words, *"if it be thy will."*

It is impossible for me to believe illness is God's will. It is self-evident that He uses illness to reach people and to redirect their lives. But to say it is His will to use distress to bring devotion is contrary to scripture and to selfhood. He would much prefer that we trust Him by simple faith instead of having to be put in a corner before trusting Him.

The approach of *"if it be thy will,"* I feel, leads to the logical conclusion that when we pray for wholeness or seek to alleviate illness it may be thwarting His will. I can't believe this is true.

It is *"according to the will"* of God that we can minister unto all with the aim of wholeness being imparted. So the *"if"* can be eliminated. Scripture, common sense, and all the efforts of the field of medicine tell us that wholeness is a worthy and proper goal.

Just stop and think for a moment about the teaching, *"if it be thy will."* It is hinting at least that sometimes God does not want a person whole. If this is not His will, then you are expending a lot of money and time through hospitalization insurance, doctors, medicines, prayers, and other things and all of them may be to thwart His will if you are to be sick.

Now you might respond by saying, *"I'm doing all of this because I'm not sure whether my illness is His will or whether it isn't. But time will reveal the answer, because if I dont' get well, then I know it was God's will that I be ill."*

Now this appears to me as a backdoor way of saying that you really do not believe that God desires the very best for you.

POINTS TO PONDER

1. Is God in the business of making people ill?
2. Do you feel some people believe their illness is a sign of their being close to God?
3. Do you really believe God wants you whole? Why?

Daily Bible Study and Daily Prayer Concerns
ACCORDING TO THY WILL

1. ...Thy will be done in _____, as it is in heaven. *Mt. 6:10*
2. If ye then, being evil, know how to give good gifts unto your children, how much more shall your Father in heaven give_____ things to them that ask him? *Mt. 7:7-12*
3. ...Jesus said, I_____be thou clean. *Mt. 8:3*
4. Come unto me...and I will give you _____. *Mt. 11:28*
5. ...I will build my church and the gates of _____ shall not prevail against it. *Mt. 16:18*
6. ...it is not the will of your Father...that one of these little ones should _____. *Mt. 18:14*
7. ...his father saw him, and had _____, and ran, and fell on his neck and kissed him. *Lu. 15:20*
8. ...I will pour out of my Spirit upon _____. *Acts. 2:17*
9. Who will render to every man according to his _____. *Rom. 2:6*
10. Paul an apostle of Jesus Christ by the _____ of God. *II Cor. 1:1*
11. Who will have all men to be _____. *I Tim. 2:4*
12. ...their iniquities will I remember no _____ Heb. 8:12
13. ...I will never _____ thee nor forsake thee. *Heb. 13:5*
14. ...I will be his _____, and he shall be my son. *Rev. 21:7*

DAILY SCRIPTURE

Mon.   Mt. 6:7-15
Tues.   Mt. 7:7-12
Wed.   Mt. 11:25-30
Thurs. Mt. 12:40-45
Fri.   Acts 2:14-21
Sat.   Heb. 13:1-6
Sun.   Rev. 21:1-7

PRAYER CONCERNS

Your Family & Relatives
Government Leaders
Missionaries
For the Unbelievers
Churches & Denominations
Your Own Church
Prayer and Praise

NOTE: You will be spiritually strengthened by completing two questions each day, reading the suggested scripture, and ministering in prayer for the concerns of the day.

THE MINISTRY OF THE MASTER—MONDAY
A Spirit Lifter

During the holiday season an enthusiastic youth group caroler was going door to door with the collection box. She went to the door of a good old lady and asked if she would like to help the carolers.

"I'd love to dearie," replied the old lady croakily, "but I've got the bronchitis and I couldn't sing a note."

God's Promise

"He has removed our sins as far away from us as the east is from the west." (Psalms 103:12, TLB)

Practicing His Presence

Through what incident or person did you sense the presence of the Lord yesterday?

According To Thy Will

Mark 1:40-42 records the encounter by Jesus with the leper. Jesus responded that He willed wholeness for this man. If a leper can be the object of wholeness for the Lord, then certainly you and I are individuals whom the Lord wants to be whole.

I pray that at the very beginning of this week you would remove the old tape from your mind and heart which plays the tune *"Maybe God wants me sick. Perhaps God wants me defeated. Maybe he wants me to be cast down."* Replace that tape with the message of hope which Jesus brought to the leper. Replace it with the tape that God wants you whole and that He loves you and cares for you.

Do you realize that if illness is God's will for any person, then hospitals must be termed dens of iniquity and doctors called the grossest of sinners because they are seeking to thwart the will of God for sick people? I do not agree with this. I believe hospitals are places of mercy and doctors are instruments of God's healing.

I do not want to imply that all are healed because of the efforts of concerned people; but simply because you or someone you know is not healed, is no sign God does not desire the healing. Many other factors are involved.

PRAYER: *Father, may my mind be renewed to believe You want wholeness for me. Amen.*

THE MINISTRY OF THE MASTER—TUESDAY
A Spirit Lifter

Andrew told his teacher: "I'm going to be an astronaut when I grow up." Teacher: "Do you really want to fly in space?" "No," admitted Andrew. "I just want to go eight days without a bath."

God's Promise

"The world passeth away and the lust thereof, but he that doeth the will of God abideth forever." (I John 2:17)

Practicing His Presence

Through what incident or person did you sense the presence of the Lord yesterday?

According To Thy Will

A very logical question is, *"Why is there so much suffering and so much illness?"* This is a very difficult and complex question and practically impossible to answer. However, I will give a few possible reasons.

First, we know there is sickness, suffering, and imperfections in the world not because it is God's ultimate will, but because of sin being in the world. There was no illness previous to the time man yielded to sin. God did not desire the fall of man. He fell by his choice. Sin in all of its power brings many problems of illness as well as many other difficulties.

In the second place, illness may be the result of man's ignorance. Today, if someone has appendicitis, he goes to the hospital, has an operation, and is soon well. Years ago, many such patients would have died. No one would have known the technique to adequately care for the problem.

In the third place, failure to believe and practice the spiritual laws results in much illness. I deal constantly with individuals who have resentment, fear, and guilt. They harbor evil thoughts which result in evil actions. They are not willing to leave the tomorrows in God's hands so that their todays will be meaningful and relatively free of tension.

PRAYER: *Lord, the fears, resentments, and guilt feelings I give to You. Amen.*

THE MINISTRY OF THE MASTER—WEDNESDAY
A Spirit Lifter

The recruit was puffing as he fell over the last hurdle during his first day of rugged training on the obstacle course.

"My leg, sergeant," groaned the man. "I think I broke it."

"Well then, don't waste time just lying there—do push ups until the medics get here!"

God's Promise

"And the Lord will continually guide you, and satisfy your desire in scorched places, and give strength to your bones; and you will be like a watered garden, and like a spring of water whose waters do not fail." (Isaiah 58:11, NASV)

Practicing His Presence

Through what incident or person did you sense the presence of the Lord yesterday?

According To Thy Will

I believe as fervently that the Lord desires your wholeness in all areas as I do that He desires you receive the gift of eternal life. Consider the words,

"The Lord is not slack concerning his promise, as some men count slackness; but is longsuffering to us-ward; not willing that any should perish, but that all should come to repentance." II Peter 3:9

Now, from the truth presented in this verse, can anyone say that the Lord does not want all to come to know Him? Of course not! However, do they all come? No! Can we blame God? Not at all! The opportunity is there. The decision is left to each person. It is a great decision. It is a decision many feel impossible to make in a positive manner.

Thus, with the message of wholeness. The Lord does desire that you be whole. He is not in the business of making you miserable or making you ill. I feel the complexities of life and the many things over which you have no control plus other factors bring suffering and illness. Simply to blame God and say that illness is His will is an expression of gross misunderstanding of the very nature of God.

PRAYER: *May I never forget Your faithfulness, Father. Help me to live with this truth. Amen.*

THE MINISTRY OF THE MASTER—THURSDAY
A Spirit Lifter

Girl: "A man down the street just insulted me."
Beau: "I'll knock his block off. What did he look like?"
Girl: "A great big brute with a scar on his cheek."
Beau: "Oh well, —forget it—he was probably joking."

God's Promise

"Jesus said unto him, If thou canst believe, all things are possible to him that believeth." (Mark 9:23, KJV)

Practicing His Presence

Through what incident or person did you sense the presence of the Lord yesterday?

According To Thy Will

I would like to present some very definite reasons why I feel we can pray *"according to thy will"* and do not have to pray *"if it be thy will."* My task is to try and remove all blocks to your healing. I want you to trust the Lord to meet your every need. I pray you will believe He desires your wholeness and that you have a right to put forth concerted effort to have that wholeness.

This approach sets you free from the bind that maybe it is His will that you be ill. Now with a clear conscience you can receive the ministry of the church and the discoveries of science for healing. You should realize that efforts toward wholeness are not efforts to thwart God's will, but are in keeping with His desires for you.

You can accept this premise for several reasons. One of them is because the very nature of the triune God is to heal. God is more concerned for your well-being than you are yourself. The Lord Jesus summed it well with,

"If ye then, being evil, know how to give good gifts unto your children, how much more shall your Father which is in heaven give good things to them that ask him?" Mt. 7:11

Sometimes you will be guilty of failing to believe He is seeking to help and to heal. However, forget these weak moments and move on to a faith which appropriates His healing power to your situation.

PRAYER: *Father, may I really believe you want me to be whole. Thank you for helping me. Amen.*

THE MINISTRY OF THE MASTER—FRIDAY
A Spirit Lifter

A farmer's friend says he's used to hard times. "I got nothing from my old man. Once on my birthday, he gave me a bat. The first day I played with it, it flew away."

God's Promise

"Where two or three gather together because they are mine, I will be there among them." (Matthew 18:20, TLB)

Practicing His Presence

Through what incident or person did you sense the presence of the Lord yesterday?

According To Thy Will

You can with confidence pray *"according to thy will"* because of the ministry of our Lord Jesus Christ. His ministry was to the needs of individuals. He did not stop with spiritual homilies. He launched His public ministry with a miracle and He maintained this pace.

He forgave sins, but just as effectively and specifically He healed the body. He did not make a distinction between illness and sin. He treated them both as evil. He said in word and demonstrated in power that both are to be defeated.

The four friends dropped the sick man through the roof and to the feet of Jesus. He was not insulted nor was He frustrated by this apparent intrusion. He simply said, *"...thy sins are forgiven."* (Luke 5:20)

The prevalent thought of His day was that illness was always a consequence of sin. Jesus took care of the root problem. He healed the sin.

It was then that He cared for the problem of physical illness. In response to the religious leaders who said no one can forgive sins but God, Jesus acted in keeping with the nature of His being and ministry.

He said,

"Which is easier to say, Thy sins be forgiven thee; or to say, Rise up and walk?" Luke 5:23

PRAYER: *Above all else, Lord Jesus, help me to accept Your forgiveness of my sins. Amen.*

THE MINISTRY OF THE MASTER—SATURDAY
A Spirit Lifter

"Those new people across the street seem very devoted. Every time he goes out he kisses her and he goes on throwing kisses all the way down the street. Alan, why don't you do that?"

"Me? I don't even know her!"

God's Promise

"Therefore, my beloved brethren, be ye steadfast, unmoveable, always abounding in the work of the Lord, forasmuch as ye know that your labour is not in vain in the Lord." (I Corinthians 15:58, KJV)

Practicing His Presence

Through what incident or person did you sense the presence of the Lord yesterday?

According To Thy Will

Today I want to drive the point deeper that the Lord is not the giver of illness and that He desires to heal. It is the very nature of a loving God and the chief characteristic of the public ministry of His blessed Son.

You and I know that the Bible teaches the Lord Jesus faithfully and completely fulfilled the will of His heavenly Father. He never did anything which was against His Father's will. He maintained a deep and abiding communion with the Father. His was not an on and off again relationship of devotion. Your life and mine may appear as a yo-yo with ups and downs in regard to our devotional status. Not so with Jesus, but He was always devoted and faithful.

The church through the centuries has accepted the concept of His complete devotion to the Lord. Most people in the church believe this today. Therefore, I feel you can truly believe it is the Lord's desire to heal and to help. This is not to make the claim that all situations will immediately become rosy nor that all illnesses will be physically healed. There are many stumbling blocks to wholeness.

I find it much more in keeping with the total message of scripture to acknowledge hindrances to healing than to say that sometimes God doesn't want a person well.

PRAYER: *Loving Father, forgive me for my failures and help me to believe in Your faithfulness. Amen.*

70

THE MINISTRY OF THE MASTER—SUNDAY
A Spirit Lifter

"Sir, my stenographer, being a lady, cannot type what I think of you. I, being a gentleman, cannot think it. You, being neither, will understand just what I mean."

God's Promise

"Trust the Lord completely; don't ever trust yourself. In everything you do, put God first, and he will direct you and crown your efforts with success." (Proverbs 3:5,6, TLB)

Practicing His Presence

Through what incident or person did you sense the presence of the Lord yesterday?

According To Thy Will

This week I have appreciated being able to visit with you each day concerning the Lord's desire for your wholeness. I hope your mind and heart have been helped to see that you can pray *"according to thy will."*

Peter gives a wonderful summary of the ministry of our Lord. He says,

"How God anointed Jesus of Nazareth with the Holy Ghost and with power; who went about doing good, and healing all that were oppressed of the devil; for God was with him." Acts 10:38

Peter, through the inspiration of the Holy Spirit, teaches it is the devil who oppresses. He also conveyed the wholeness Jesus brought to individuals. The good deeds of Jesus were more than kind words or drawing water for a sick person or taking an offering for the needy. He healed the sick.

All of this was done because God was with Him. It was not done contrary to God's will nor in spite of God. It was done in accordance to the will of God and because of the Father. He was pleased with the ministry of His Son.

Many of the people at Nazareth, his home town, did not receive a healing. However, we are told it was because of their unbelief. It was not because the Lord did not desire to heal them. The failures resulted from their indifference and unbelief.

PRAYER: *Father, You do you want to heal. Help me to prepare the soil of my mind and heart for healing. Amen.*

ACCORDING TO THY WILL (Continued)

I feel the insight that you can pray *"according to thy will"* is so important that I want to devote another week to this theme. It is impossible to have an effective healing ministry if limits are placed on the Lord. He has called you to a ministry of obedience. He has not called you to a ministry of trying to out guess Him.

There are those who will say, *"Well, does this mean everyone will be automatically healed?"* No, it does not mean this at all. Certainly it does not mean that everyone will be physically healed at all times. There comes a point when the body is overcome with the stress of sin and disease and must succumb to this onslaught.

You and I are not called to be percentage prayers. We are not called to only pray for the people it seems obvious will soon recover. We are called to minister to the difficult and the not so difficult. In each case we can minister in confidence that the Lord desires wholeness.

I do not want to waste time and energy seeking knowledge from the Lord if a person should receive the ministries of the healing ministry. I settled this long ago. The Lord taught me He desires wholeness. Therefore, all of my energies are expended to achieve this goal. It is not always achieved, but this failure is not because of lack of desire on the part of the Lord. There are many factors which prevent and prohibit healing of body, mind, and spirit.

The individual who believes the Lord is willing and able to heal will have a fruitful ministry. The congregation which moves in the direction of believing the Lord desires wholeness will be blessed abundantly.

The healing ministry must be seen not as a program within a local parish, but rather as a lifestyle of Christian living. The Lord is our healer and all activities of the parish should be conducted from this viewpoint.

POINTS TO PONDER

1. When will individuals probably not be healed physically?
2. What do you feel is meant by the statement that the healing ministry is a lifestyle?
3. Can healing be put into a compartment of church life?

ACCORDING TO THY WILL (Continued)

1. ...the spirit is willing, but the_____is weak.
   Mt. 26:41
2. ...with perfect_____they offered willingly
   unto the Lord. *I Chr. 29:9*
3. I will pray with the spirit and I will _____
   with the understanding. *I Cor. 14:15*
4. ...I will be their God, and they shall be my _____
   _____. *II Cor. 6:16*
5. ...that ye might be filled with the knowledge of his _____
   _____. *Col. 1:9*
6. If there be first a _____ mind. *II Cor. 8:12*
7. Ye ought to say, If the Lord _____, we shall
   live, and do this, or that. *James 4:15*
8. For so is the will of God, that with well doing ye may put to silence
   the_____ of foolish men. *I Pet. 2:15*
9. For he that will love life, and see good days, let him refrain his
   _____from evil. *I Pet. 3:10*
10. It is better, if the will of God be so, that _____
    for well doing, than for evil doing. *I Peter 3:17*
11. For the prophecy came not in old time by the _____
    of man. *II Pet. 1:21*
12. ...he that doeth the _____ of God abides forever.
    I John 2:17
13. The Lord is not _____that any should perish.
    II Pet. 3:9
14. Believe not every spirit, but try the spirits whether they are of_____
    _____. *I John 4:1*

DAILY SCRIPTURE

Mon.	Mt. 26:36-46
Tues.	I Chron. 29:6-9
Wed.	I Cor. 14:13-19
Thurs.	I Pet. 3:13-22
Fri.	I John 2:15-17
Sat.	I John 4:1-6
Sun.	James 4:13-17

PRAYER CONCERNS

Your Family & Relatives
Government Leaders
Missionaries
For the Unbelievers
Churches & Denominations
Your Own Church
Prayer and Praise

NOTE: You will be spiritually strengthened by completing two questions each day, reading the suggested scripture, and ministering in prayer for the concerns of the day.

THE MINISTRY OF THE MASTER—MONDAY
A Spirit Lifter

"My small son has swallowed my fountain pen," Mr. Casey telephoned the Doctor. "Please come at once."

The physician inquired, "But what are you doing in the meantime?"

Mr. Casey answered, "Using a pencil."

God's Promise

"Hope deferred makes the heart sick, but desire fulfilled is a tree of life." (Proverbs 13:12, NASV)

Practicing His Presence

Through what incident or person did you sense the presence of the Lord yesterday?

According To Thy Will (Continued)

Your approach concerning healing is more than mere words. It is not a matter of just saying *"if it be thy will"* or *"according to thy will."* I feel your entire approach to life is revealed by your feelings toward these two statements.

If I accept the fact the Lord desires wholeness, it is easier for me to accept all the ministries of healing available in our world today. The physicians, nurses, hospitals, churches, pastors, lay believers, etc. are all viewed as instruments of the Lord. I don't have to challenge their validity nor struggle with their goals. Although many may not acknowledge His lordship, they are still instruments used by Him for healing.

One of the most difficult things for me is to convey to our parish and to others the fact that the healing ministry is not an extra program. It is not a program to be adopted or refused. It is a lifestyle. It is an approach to all life. The ministry of the Lord Jesus was not one of worship, social activities, work and play. His ministry was one of wholeness. All that He did was done in the light of His goal of bringing individuals to a state of greater wholeness.

I realize for convenience sake, I speak of the spiritual healing ministry. It is my prayer that the Lord will grant to me the insights and the words to convey to myself and others that wholeness is an integral part of all life.

PRAYER: *Father, may my church sense the reality of the message of healing. Amen.*

THE MINISTRY OF THE MASTER—TUESDAY
A Spirit Lifter

Father: "I'm worried about your being at the bottom of the class."
Son: "Don't worry, Dad, they teach the same stuff at both ends."

God's Promise

"How wonderful it is, how pleasant, when brothers live in harmony." (Psalms 133:1, TLB)

Practicing His Presence

Through what incident or person did you sense the presence of the Lord yesterday?

According To Thy Will (Continued)

"Why are you so interested in healing?" This is a question which I have been asked many times. It appears strange to me that any Christian would not be interested in healing. The very nature and desire of the universe is for wholeness. Paul says the entire creation *"groaneth and travaileth in pain together until now."* (Rom. 8:22)

Wholeness is not a part of all of life. However, it is the goal of all of life. It is that goal for which I seek and the one I would encourage you to seek.

I feel the Lord's will is wholeness because the body He gave to you is designed for wholeness. It is constructed for wholeness. All the resources at the command of the body rush to its defense when it is attacked by any disease.

It is reported that someone remarked to a famous Harvard medical school doctor:

"When you see how many diseases there are, you wonder how anyone is ever well."

His answer was,

"Oh, no! When you know something about the human body and its tremendous resources for health, you wonder why anyone is ever sick. The human body is so constructed as to go on functioning almost indefinitely without becoming sick. Once sick, the human body and the human mind have tremendous power to heal themselves."

PRAYER: *Thank you, Father, for the wonders of my body. Keep me whole and wholesome. Amen.*

THE MINISTRY OF THE MASTER—WEDNESDAY
A Spirit Lifter

Mrs. Wolf: "She told me that you told her the secret I told you not to tell her."
Mrs. Jones: "That mean thing! I told her not to tell you I told her."
Mrs. Wolf: "Well, don't tell her that I told you she told me."

God's Promise

"When someone becomes a Christian, he becomes a brand new person inside. He is not the same any more. A new life has begun." (II Corinthians 5:17, TLB)

Practicing His Presence

Through what incident or person did you sense the presence of the Lord yesterday?

According To Thy Will (Continued)

Some people seem to delight in their illnesses. I am aware of this. Some even try to leave the impression God has chosen to chastise them through illness and therefore they may be superior to others as far as their spiritual life is concerned.

This is a sad condition, because the Lord has called us to fight illness and not to revel in it. When the physical, mental, and spiritual healings are an integral part of the church there is power and strength with the believers.

I believe it was a healing church which *"turned the world upside down."* There is no doubt but what the apostolic church believed it was the Lord's will to heal. They did not seem to struggle with the decision of His will and then minister after this had been determined. They knew He desired wholeness. Their lifestyle was in the light of this conviction.

The ministry of the early church was one of help and healing. It was not one of helplessness and hopelessness in the face of illness. This does not mean that the entire world accepted the fullness of God's providential power. They did not. There were pockets of believers in the midst of many unbelievers.

It is no different today. My experience has been that only a few grasp the joy of believing the Lord really wants the best for them. Many verbalize this, but only a few really appropriate it to their life.

PRAYER: *Thank you, Lord, that I can have a ministry of help and hope unto others. Amen.*

THE MINISTRY OF THE MASTER—THURSDAY
A Spirit Lifter

Customer: "You served me twice as much yesterday."
Waiter: "Where were you sitting?"
Customer: "Over there by the window."
Waiter: "Oh, that was for advertising."

God's Promise

"For the power of the life-giving spirit — and this power is mine through Christ Jesus — has freed me from the vicious circle of sin and death." (Romans 8:2, TLB)

Practicing His Presence

Through what incident or person did you sense the presence of the Lord yesterday?

According To Thy Will (Continued)

A reason that convinces me you can pray *"according to thy will"* is the plain teaching of scripture. This undergirds the other four reasons:

1. The very nature of the triune God.
2. The nature and ministry of the Lord Jesus.
3. The nature of your body which is designed for wholeness.
4. The practice of the apostolic church.

Jesus said, *"I have come that you might have life and that you might have it more abundant."* (John 10:10) This is not a statement which would support a life of defeat through illness.

The epistles abound with references to the abundant power of the Lord to save and to heal. He worked wonders wherever the messengers took the message. Paul says he fully preached the gospel. How did he do it?

"...by word and deed, through mighty signs and wonders, by the power of the Spirit of God..." Rom. 15:19

How could Paul have preached the gospel fully if he would have taught that the Lord wanted some of the people to be ill and bedfast. The signs and wonders were the proof of the presence of the Lord. These signs and wonders were not his eloquent preaching or correct theological insights. They were the healing miracles received through his ministries.

PRAYER: *Father, I give thanks for the evidence of Your presence each and every day. Amen.*

THE MINISTRY OF THE MASTER—FRIDAY
A Spirit Lifter

The bus driver for the Christian School was urging his young passengers to move to the rear but was having little success.

Finally in desperation he shouted, "Fill up the back — just like you do in church!"

God's Promise

"Everyone who hates his brother is a murderer; and you know that no murderer has eternal life abiding in Him." (I John 3:15, NASV)

Practicing His Presence

Through what incident or person did you sense the presence of the Lord yesterday?

According To Thy Will (Continued)

I want to continue to present the spiritual basis for believing we can pray *"according to thy will."* You and I do not violate the plan of God nor His will when we pray this way.

The apostles were faithful servants. They never stopped with just teaching about a great God or a loving Son of God. They trusted Him for miracles. The evidence of an apostle in the midst of believers was not his eloquence but his effectiveness.

"Truly the signs of an apostle were wrought among you in all patience, in signs, and wonders, and mighty deeds." (II Cor. 12:12) This statement attaches guidelines to an apostle. He must be one who does the signs of an apostle. What did he do? He released the power of the Lord by faith and healings resulted.

The apostles did not go from church to church setting up a healing ministry. They went with the Lord's ministry which is a healing ministry. Today I talk about the healing ministry because it has been abandoned by most churches. It is tragic that we cannot see that all that the local church does should be aimed at making people whole.

Paul didn't pull up the tent of faith and say there is no hope, but he pitched the tent of faith and proclaimed *"according to His will"* you can be whole.

PRAYER: *Lord, may I pitch the tent of faith in the very center of my problems and frustrations. Amen.*

THE MINISTRY OF THE MASTER—SATURDAY
A Spirit Lifter

Tourist Guide: "Just think, some of those ruins are 5,000 years old."
Tourist: "Say, I'm not that dumb!"
Tourist Guide: "Don't you believe they are 5,000 years old?"
Tourist: "How could they be — it's only 1984."

God's Promise

"Blessed are the pure in heart, for they shall see God." (Matthew 5:8, NASV)

Practicing His Presence

Through what incident or person did you sense the presence of the Lord yesterday?

According To Thy Will (Continued)

It is fitting that together we consider more scripture in regard to our belief in healing being a lifestyle and not a separate ministry. The writer of the book of Hebrews does not say the church had a ministry of healing in addition to classes for children, youth, and adults. The church had a total ministry and that ministry was for wholeness.

The Lord bore witness to faith and faithfulness through healings. The lifestyle of the teachers and how they taught was one of great expectation and wholeness.

"God also bearing them witness, both with signs and wonders, and with divers miracles, and gifts of the Holy Ghost, according to his own will." (Heb. 2:4) His will was that the miracles take place. He asked for the fulfillment of the spiritual laws and said the results would be miraculous.

There is no record that He said to the apostles to limit their message of wholeness. The challenge is to greater things and not to lesser. The challenge is to believe for wholeness and not wallow in illness.

"According to the will of God" the faithful believer can bank on His faithfulness.

PRAYER: *Thank you, Father, for the evidence of Your presence through signs and wonders.*

THE MINISTRY OF THE MASTER—SUNDAY
A Spirit Lifter

Susan: "There's a black cat in the dining room."
Helen: "Black cats are unlucky."
Susan: "This one isn't. It just ate your dinner!"

God's Promise

"When the poor and needy seek water, and there is none, and their tongue faileth for thirst, I the Lord will hear them, I the God of Israel will not forsake them." (Isaiah 41:17, KJV)

Practicing His Presence

Through what incident or person did you sense the presence of the Lord yesterday?

According To Thy Will (Continued)

There are many portions of scripture which lend support to the concept of healing being a lifestyle. It was not a separate ministry of the early church, but a way of life for the believers. When the apostle Paul speaks of the gifts of the Spirit he does not break them into separate ministries within the local church. They are different functions of the total ministry.

I Cor. 12:28-30 speaks of the gift of miracles as well as the gift of healing. These two are not relegated to a compartmentalized ministry within the local church. They are expressions of a complete ministry.

This scripture leaves no doubt concerning the Lord's desire for wholeness. It accents this desire. It says beyond a shadow of a doubt that the church moved with the concept of *"according to thy will."*

I realize some have carried this verse to extremes but it is still part of the Bible *"...by whose stripes ye were healed."* (I Pet. 2:24) The entire church can accept the fact that the death of Jesus brought redemption, but far fewer can grasp that this includes the total person, even the physical body. The Lord did not separate His ministry to a segment of life. He ministered to it all.

Jesus never said *"I will teach you how to love the Lord by having you continue in your affliction and in your suffering."* He rather said, *"I will, be thou made whole."*

PRAYER: *Thank you, Jesus, for making me whole. Thank you for redeeming my soul. Amen.*

Theme for the Week
THE IMPORTANCE OF PRAYER

The poet Tennyson has written,
"More things are wrought by prayer
Than this world dreams of.
Wherefore, let thy voice rise like a fountain for me night and day
For what are men better than sheep or goats
That nourish a blind life within the brain,
If, knowing God, they lift not hands of prayer
Both for themselves and those who call them friend."
I believe he was inspired by the Lord to impart to us the importance of prayer.

What is prayer and how important is it? These are important questions which I hope to consider with you in the weeks ahead.

I believe that prayer is a relationship with God. It is a lifestyle of commitment and fellowship with our heavenly Father through the Lord Jesus Christ and the power of the Holy Spirit. I believe it is a corporate experience. You are not alone. The Holy Spirit is your prayer partner. In addition, other believers have and are experiencing prayer in their lives to a greater or lesser degree.

F.J. Huegel has written, *"Prayer is work of such a sublime order that it lies beyond the imagination of men."* Charles Spurgeon was right on when he said, *"Prayer itself is an art which only the Holy Ghost can teach us. He is the giver of all prayer. Pray for prayer. Pray till you can pray."* Thus, prayer is not the right use of the right words, but the life in tune with God.

POINTS TO PONDER

1. What do you feel is a good definition of prayer?
2. How important is prayer in the life of an individual?
3. Is prayer worth high priority in your life? Why?

THE IMPORTANCE OF PRAYER

1. Men began to_____upon the name of the Lord.
   Gen. 4:26
2. Abraham_____upon the name of the Lord.
   Gen. 12:8
3. The King answered and said _____ for me.
   I Kings 13:6
4. The Lord turned the captivity of Job when he prayed, for his_____
   _____. *Job 42:10*
5. Evening, and morning, and at noon, will I _____.
   Ps. 55:17
6. Whatsoever ye shall_____in my name.
   John 14:13
7. Ask, and it shall be_____you. *Mt. 7:7*
8. Your Father in heaven will give_____things
   to them that ask him. *Mt 7:11*
9. If we ask according to His_____He hears us.
   I John 5:14
10. Thou shalt find the Lord if you seek him with all thy _____
    _____and soul. *Deut. 4:29*
11. The Lord is not_____from everyone of us.
    Acts. 17:27
12. Ye shall find me when ye _____ for me with all
    your heart. *Jer. 29:13*
13. Jesus said, I am the _____, the truth, and
    the life. *John 14:6*
14. Men ought always to _____. *Luke 18:1*

DAILY SCRIPTURE

Mon.	Gen. 12:1-9
Tues.	Job 42:1-10
Wed.	John 14:12-14
Thurs.	Mt. 7:7-12
Fri.	I John 5:13-21
Sat.	Acts 17:22-31
Sun.	Luke 18:1-5

PRAYER CONCERNS

Your Family & Relatives
Government Leaders
Missionaries
For the Unbelievers
Churches & Denominations
Your Own Church
Prayer and Praise

NOTE: You will be spiritually strengthened by completing two questions each day, reading the suggested scripture, and ministering in prayer for the concerns of the day.

THE MINISTRY OF THE MASTER—MONDAY
A Spirit Lifter

"Hello, that you, Jake?" "Yep, this is Jake." "It does not sound like Jake." "Well, this is Jake all right. What can I do for you?" The caller went on with, "Are you sure this is Jake?" "Yes, I am sure!" "Well, Jake, this is your friend, Henry. Would you lend me fifty dollars?" The voice at the other end nervously replied, "What's your number, Henry? I'll have Jake return your call when he comes in."

God's Promise

"Now that you have faith in Christ Jesus you are all sons of God." (Galatians 3:26, Phillips)

Practicing His Presence

Today consciously practice His presence. May you seek to quiet your body, mind, and spirit. He is with you.

The Importance Of Prayer

I firmly believe that prayer is the work of the church. It is not an exercise which you learn to do to help you with the work of the church. It is the work of the church. It is not to undergird you to do the work of the church. It is the work of the church.

Now, I realize this runs counter to the thinking of many However, it certainly does not run counter to the teaching of the Bible. The disciples never asked Jesus to help them develop skills for preaching, calling, organizing, or public relations. The did ask Jesus to teach them to pray.

"Lord, teach us to pray, as John taught his disciples to pray." Luke 11:1

Every follower of Jesus should be making the same request.

Serving on committees and feverishly working for the church is not the work of the church. I do not want to speak disparagingly of these activities, but they must be put in their proper perspective. Prayer cannot be put at the bottom of our list and the church remain a channel of God's power and purpose. It is my prayer that each of us will come to appreciate that prayer is the work of His Church.

PRAYER: *Father, help me to put prayer high on my priorities and to be faithful in my prayer life. Amen.*

THE MINISTRY OF THE MASTER—TUESDAY
A Spirit Lifter

The chairperson of a club made the following comment about one of the committees which had worked long and hard all year:

"In most kindred associations half the committee does all the work, while the other half does nothing. I am pleased to place on record that, for this committee over which I have had the honor to preside this year, it is just the reverse."

God's Promise

"He guides the humble in what is right and teaches them His way." (Psalm 25:9)

Practicing His Presence

It takes conscious effort to be aware of the Lord in the small things in life. How did this consciousness affect your day yesterday?

The Importance Of Prayer

Some years ago a high school student came to see me concerning some very frustrating problems. She was disturbed about a number of things, but especially disturbed about the advisor of their literary society. This girl was a senior and had been a member of the literary society for over three years.

The new advisor was upsetting all the members. Would you believe that this advisor was suggesting, and even insisting, that the members read books, report on them, and then discuss them? The members were disturbed because they were neglecting the social times formerly enjoyed by the society. They did not want to read books and to spend time discussing them.

As we talked I asked the purpose of the society. The girl replied that it was organized to help high school students to become familiar with great literature. It was obvious to her that the society had drifted completely from its purposes.

It is not difficult to relate this incident to the life of most Christians and most churches. Many have drifted entirely from the true purpose. Pious activity has replaced powerful prayer and meaningful worship.

PRAYER: *Lord, help me to keep my life focused on true purpose and yielded to you. Amen.*

THE MINISTRY OF THE MASTER—WEDNESDAY
A Spirit Lifter

"Yep, my family can trace its ancestry back to William the Conqueror." His friend sneered and retorted, "I suppose you'll be telling me that your ancestors were on the Ark with Noah?"

"Certainly not," said the other. "My people had a boat of their own."

God's Promise

"Where you have envy and selfish ambition, there you find disorder and every evil practice. But the wisdom that comes from heaven is first of all pure, then peace-loving, considerate, submissive, full of mercy and good fruit, impartial and sincere." (James 3:16,17, NIV)

Practicing His Presence

Can you recall a spiritual feast you had yesterday as you sensed the Lord's presence? Isn't it neat to be aware of the Lord in daily work and play?

The Importance Of Prayer

Has all your busyness brought peace to you? Have your accomplishments at work, in your community, in your home, brought joy to you? Have you found a purpose in life which overshadows everything and brings a pervading purpose?

Practically everything you have will be dumped by you before your life is over. When it comes down to the final wire, all you have left is your relationship to the Lord. Possessions, fame, and fortune will mean little to you in the long run. Why not decide now to put forth what will ultimately be first anyhow?

Your relationship with God will be your final support. Strengthen that relationship now through prayer. Have you heard of the man who connived and labored to get gold. He mined some and robbed for more. While he was being pursued by the law, he came upon a river.

There was no recourse but to attempt to cross it. He forced his horse into the stream. Soon the horse was exhausted. The man was on his own to swim across the river. However, the gold was so heavy he could not swim. He had to let the money belt sink. He was willing to lose all to save his life. At the end even gold was not worth his life. I suggest that you and I drop off the unneeded and put the proper emphasis on a life of prayer.

PRAYER: *Lord Jesus, enable me to take a long look at life and to put first things first. Amen.*

THE MINISTRY OF THE MASTER—THURSDAY
A Spirit Lifter

"John, I understand that the Chinese have an invariable rule to settle all their debts on New Year's Day, isn't that a wonderful custom?"

Shirley, his wife, replied, "It sure is, but remember, the Chinese don't have a Christmas the week before."

God's Promise

Praise Jesus! There is light at the end of the tunnel.

"If God is for us, who can be against us?" (Romans 8:31, NIV)

Practicing His Presence

Through what incident or person did you sense the Lord's presence yesterday? How did this make you feel?

The Importance Of Prayer

Isn't it interesting to hear the fans instruct the football team and its coaches? I have attended several Ohio State football games. I have been present when they have had a season in which they won each game; but let a bad play develop, and some fans screamed bloody murder. I have heard them curse Woody and a few minutes later with execution of a good play they would bless him. It is easy to second guess and to be a coach from the bleachers.

I believe many are like this in their relationship with the Lord. Let everything be going as they feel it should and they are on top for the Lord. If any obstacle appears or a problem arises, they are at odds with God. Prayer for them is seen as a means to trigger God to action in their lives. It is not a relationship which is deep, personal and constant.

It is prayer which will enable you to keep from second guessing God. It will help you to see that the Lord is working out His plan in your life regardless of the outward circumstances and the puzzling events. Prayer will be the stabilizing force to keep you on course for Him. You will not want to be the head coach, but will leave that position up to the Lord.

PRAYER: *Father, enable me to desire to keep in close relationship with you regardless of outward circumstances. Amen.*

THE MINISTRY OF THE MASTER—FRIDAY
A Spirit Lifter

A very religious lady noticed that each morning as she went to work there was a rather down-and-out looking gentleman waiting for the bus. She shoved a dollar bill into his hand and whispered, "Never despair."

Some days later she was startled when he stopped her and with a glowing countenance handed her nine dollars. "What does this mean?" she asked.

"It means, ma'am," came his proud response, "that 'Never Despair' won at 8 to 1."

God's Promise

"Thus says the Lord, your Redeemer, the Holy One of Israel: 'I am the Lord your God, who teaches you to profit, who leads you in the way you should go.'" (Isaiah 48:17, NASB)

Practicing His Presence

I believe as you exercise your spiritual powers you will become more aware of the spiritual side of life. How did you sense the presence of His Spirit yesterday?

The Importance Of Prayer

Jesus never made prayer an option to His followers. He says, *"when you pray..."* Mt. 6:5 is not *"if you pray."* There is a world of difference between *"when"* and *"if."*

Therefore, if we are to pray, then should not each of us seek to develop the art of prayer? I believe courses should be given to help individuals to pray. Several years ago we offered such a course in our church. After it had concluded all who participated were thrilled with what they had learned.

One participant had a penetrating insight. She said to me, *"Pastor, I have been active in church work for over forty years. I have served several years as a missionary of our denomination. I have been constantly admonished to pray. However, this is the first time I have ever been presented with an opportunity to be taught how to pray. This is the first course I have ever had presented to me in the area of prayer."*

I thought of the tragedy of this comment. If prayer is important, should you not take advantage of opportunities to learn to pray? And should not the church be presenting these opportunities for you?

PRAYER: *Lord, teach me to pray and help me to teach others the art of communing with you. Amen.*

THE MINISTRY OF THE MASTER—SATURDAY
A Spirit Lifter

"Did the patent medicine you purchased cure your aunt?"
"My goodness, no! She read the label on the bottle as to what it would cure and ended up with two other diseases."

God's Promise

"If the Son sets you free, you will be free indeed." (John 8:36, NIV)

Practicing His Presence

May you seek to quiet yourself this day and hear "the still small voice" speak to you. How were you aware of His presence yesterday?

The Importance Of Prayer

As many saints through the years have discovered, *"God has no problems. He has only great plans."* This thought is tremendous. The Lord does have great plans for you. He has great plans for me. He has great plans for His world.

It is prayer which will enable you to believe and accept this fact. Prayer will keep you in tune with the reality of a plan. It will enable you to accept the fact the Lord is with you even when it seems He is not. It will strengthen you even when you feel you are going to faint. It will buoy you up when it appears that you are going to sink and drown in the difficulties of life.

It is impossible for you or me to straighten everyone out and to make them believe and behave as we think they should. Life is not that way and never will be. The world is not going to roll over and play dead until we catch our breath and get things figured out in our own lives.

It is a mad and complex world. Yet, in the midst of it all looms God's plans for you. As you deepen your prayer life, you will discover the plan overshadowing the frustrations. Your purpose in life will be accepted as God's purpose for you. Herein is the peace that passeth understanding.

PRAYER: *Thank you, Father, for the plan you have for my life. Enable me to believe that your plan is best for me. Amen.*

THE MINISTRY OF THE MASTER—SUNDAY
A Spirit Lifter

"Did you give the Governor any message?"

The not-too-bright delivery boy said, "Yes, sire, but there ain't no use sendin' that man any notes. He's blind as a bat."

"Blind, well that's news to me," replied the polished politician.

"Course he's blind. Twice he asked me where my hat was, and there it was in plain sight on my head all the time. Yes, sire, I'd say he's blind as a bat!"

God's Promise

"The nearer you go to God, the nearer He will come to you." (James 4:8, JB)

Practicing His Presence

It is sometimes difficult to remember a specific incident in which you really felt His presence, isn't it?

The Importance Of Prayer

What problem are you facing today which seems too much for you? How are you ever going to face it? More importantly, how are you going to overcome it?

May I suggest prayer? When you are given the inner strength to face the outer onslaughts, you will know prayer is real. You will know that your relationship with the Father is essential and also very stabilizing for your life.

When you consciously come into the presence of God, something happens. It always does. Something happens to you. The story is told of a young man who went to see Phillips Brooks and concerning a problem. He needed and desired guidance and help.

After the visit a friend asked whether the problem had been solved through discussing it with Dr. Brooks. The young man replied, *"You know, I forgot to mention it. It just didn't seem important after I started talking with him."* Then, as he walked away, his friend heard him say, *"It doesn't seem insurmountable now."*

You see, he had come into the presence of power. It was not the details which brought the answer. It was the presence. This is the way it is with prayer and with your relationship with God.

PRAYER: *Father, help me not to get caught up in the details of life but dedicate myself to You. Amen.*

Theme for the Week
THE PRAYER LIFE OF JESUS

The public ministry of our Lord Jesus is considered to be three years. This amounts to 1095 days. He had much to accomplish and little time in which to do it. Therefore, He had to be busy working all the time. He certainly did not have time to waste on worship, prayer meetings, retreats, etc. These spiritual disciplines are all right for people who have much time on their hands. They are practically impossible for busy people and those with big goals.

Wait one minute. Take a good look at the life of our Lord Jesus. Yes, He had a short time. Yes, He had much to accomplish. But what did He really do? He gave Himself to a life of prayer and developed a deep devotional lifestyle.

May I break down His years of public ministry in this fashion? He started with forty days of prayer and fasting in the wilderness. We are told that He went to the synagogue on the Sabbath as was His custom. This would be 156 days out of 1095.

He went to the religious feast observances faithfully. This would total at least 60 days over the three-year period.

We read where He withdrew for a time of prayer. Let's presume He did this 15 times in the three-year period. A conservative total days devoted to prayer during public ministry of Jesus would be 271.

This means that approximately one day out of every five the Lord gave to devotional time. He gave a double tithe of His time to prayer and devotional commitment.

Jesus knew He could not accomplish anything lasting on His own. If the Father did not bless the efforts it would all be in vain. He realized He was a worker *with the Father. Prayer was important to Jesus because He knew the source and benefits of this power.*

POINTS TO PONDER

1. Why do you feel Jesus spent so much time in prayer?
2. Do you feel you could accomplish more if you prayed more?
3. How can a person today withdraw from the hustle and bustle of modern life?

THE PRAYER LIFE OF JESUS

1. Many for a_____make long prayers.
   Mk. 12:40
2. Jesus continued all_____in prayer.
   Lu. 6:12
3. Jesus was praying _____. *Lu. 9:18*
4. Jesus prayed in a_____place. *Lu. 11:1*
5. My house shall be a house of _____. *Lu. 19:46*
6. My house shall be called a house of _____
   for all people. *Isa. 56:7*
7. Jesus _____ up from prayer. *Lu. 22:45*
8. Jesus fell on his_____and prayed.
   Mt. 26:39
9. Jesus went into a _____ place to pray.
   Mk. 1:35
10. Jesus withdrew into the _____ and prayed.
    Lu. 5:16
11. Jesus knew that the Father heard him _____.
    John 11:42
12. Jesus went up into the_____to pray.
    Mt. 14:23
13. Jesus prays unto the_____. *John 14:16*
14. Jesus prayed that believers be kept from the _____.
    John 17:15

DAILY SCRIPTURE   PRAYER CONCERNS

Mon.	Mk. 12:38-40	Your Family & Relatives
Tues.	Lu. 6:12-16	Government Leaders
Wed.	Lu. 19:45-48	Missionaries
Thurs.	Lu. 22:39-46	For the Unbelievers
Fri.	Mk. 1:35-39	Churches & Denominations
Sat.	John 14:15-24	Your Own Church
Sun.	John 17:6-19	Prayer and Praise

NOTE: You will be spiritually strengthened by completing two questions each day, reading the suggested scripture, and ministering in prayer for the concerns of the day.

THE MINISTRY OF THE MASTER—MONDAY
A Spirit Lifter

Sherlock Holmes — "Ah, dear Watson, I see you have on your winter long johns."

Watson — "Marvelous, Holmes, marvelous! And how did you ever deduce that?"

Sherlock — "Well, for one thing, you've forgotten to put on your trousers."

God's Promise

"He will never let me stumble, slip, or fall. For He is always watching, never sleeping. Jehovah himself is caring for you! He is your defender. He protects you day and night." (Psalm 121:3-5, TLB)

Practicing His Presence

Can you recall a specific incident or person which helped your awareness of the Lord's presence yesterday?

The Prayer Life Of Jesus

Centuries ago a famous rabbi said, *"Great is prayer. It is greater than all good works."*

I believe Jesus believed in the power and importance of prayer. His entire life displayed the fact that prayer was a vital part of His life. It was prayer which enabled Him to ignore the negative criticism and to triumph in obedience to the Father. When He faced the ultimate choices of life, He did it on His knees in prayer in the Garden of Gethsemane.

The devout of the past have said, *"He who prays in his house surrounds it with a wall that is stronger than iron."* There is nothing which will protect you and yours more than prayer.

All the defenses available through the advances of science cannot protect you from inward destruction. It is prayer which is able to accomplish this feat.

If prayer was a part of the life of the Master, then I want it to be a vital and important part of my life. I cannot improve upon the methods of the Master. I am not called to improve upon them. I am called to emulate them. This I seek to do constantly. May I encourage you to do likewise.

PRAYER: *Father, help me to surround myself and those I love with fervent prayer. Amen.*

THE MINISTRY OF THE MASTER—TUESDAY
A Spirit Lifter

The relatives telephoned the florist and gave instructions. The ribbon was to be extra wide with "Rest in Peace" on both sides; and if there was room, the words "We Shall Meet in Heaven" were also to be on the ribbon. The ribbon was extra wide as requested, but the message was a bit unusual as follows: "Rest in peace on both sides; and, if there is room, we shall meet in heaven."

God's Promise

"I have the strength for anything through Him who gives me power." (Philippians 4:13, NEB)

Practicing His Presence

I have sought to remind you each day to be aware of the presence of our Lord. How do you find this taking place and what is it doing for you?

The Prayer Life Of Jesus

The Jewish people have produced more religious leaders who have influenced the world than any other group of people. They have produced more religious literature which is used worldwide by millions than any other group of people.

Why is this? What made the difference? Granted it is stated they are God's chosen people. Some may feel it is because of this. However, may I offer another facet of this interesting fact?

The point I want to make is that many of the Jewish leaders were individuals of deep devotional life. Also, their entire social and family life was permeated by a spirit of prayer. The result was men and women who became great leaders in the area of faith.

You do not gather oranges within the Arctic circle. In like manner, you do not have icebergs in Miami, Florida. The climate determines what is present.

In like manner, the religious climate is important if deeply devout people are forthcoming. Jesus grew up in the midst of people who believed and stressed the importance of prayer. Prayer was a part of His life because He had been taught. It made a difference.

PRAYER: *Father, help me to understand that as I prepare my heart through prayer that you reveal more to me. Amen.*

THE MINISTRY OF THE MASTER—WEDNESDAY
A Spirit Lifter

A man in Gary, Indiana was grumbling about the intense heat and about the fact that there was no breeze at all. His friend had just returned from a trip down south and assured him that he hadn't ever experienced a really hot day. His comment was:

"Hot! Friend, you don't know what hot is! One day last week when I was in Mississippi I saw a dog chasing a cat, and would you believe it was so hot they were both walking?"

God's Promise

"He personally bore our sins in His own body on the cross, so that we might be dead to sin and be alive to all that is good. It was the suffering that He bore which has healed you." (I Peter 2:24, Philips)

Practicing His Presence

I hope these have been exciting days for you. Being aware of the Lord's presence is sure to add some enthusiasm. Continue to make your days exciting. Praise Jesus!

The Prayer Life Of Jesus

Did you hear about the little girl who had been taught the importance of prayer? She also had been instructed how to pray each night prior to jumping into bed. Often she would be sleepy and it was difficult for her to think of something to say. So she wrote out a prayer which she would read each night.

After a few nights she discovered herself so sleepy she could hardly read through the prayer. Finally she hit upon a wonderful idea. She taped the written prayer to the wall by her bed and then each night she would say,

"There it is, God. I'm sleepy so please read it yourself!"

Many of us are more like this little girl than we are willing to admit. Not so with Jesus. He knew and understood the power and value of prayer. He did not sleep, but admonished the disciples who had fallen asleep. He knew what it was to spend all night in agonizing prayer.

The prayer life of Jesus did not start because He was in water over His head. It started because of his being instructed to pray. It continued because He knew He could not completely fulfill the Father's will unless He kept tuned into the things of the Spirit.

PRAYER: *Give me a desire, O Lord, to give my best to prayer. Amen.*

THE MINISTRY OF THE MASTER—THURSDAY
A Spirit Lifter

"How could you be so deceitful, as to tell Miss Woodly she was pretty?"

"What do you mean, deceitful? I told her the absolute truth!"

"But you don't really think she is pretty, do you?"

"Of course not, but didn't you notice that I phrased it, 'You are as pretty as you can be'?"

God's Promise

Do you ever wonder how God views you? Take in this neat promise! *"Worship the Lord with the beauty of holy lives."* (Psalm 96:9, TLB)

Practicing His Presence

Through what incident or person did you sense the presence of the Lord yesterday? Was the reality of this presence a conscious effort on your part?

The Prayer Life Of Jesus

Jesus faced the realities of the cross. He had to make a monumental decision. He was being tempted by Satan and feeling the natural repulsion to death which is a part of every person's being.

This moment called for action. Isn't it interesting that the action Jesus chose was prayer? He went to His favorite prayer spot. He took disciples with Him, but He wrestled alone when it came to the final decision.

The prayer life of Jesus certainly involved the great decisions of His life. I believe that the victory on Calvary was achieved in the garden. The final act took place on the hill, but the victory took place on His knees. He gave Himself to prayer that He might give Himself to all of us.

The victory you desire will be won on the inside if you keep in the right relationship with the Father. Jesus could say, *"Thy will be done,"* not because He bargained with the Father, but because He related to the Father.

He did not go to the Garden to dicker, but to dedicate Himself afresh. This displayed the place and power of prayer in His life in a very real way.

PRAYER: *May I not run away from my problems, Father, but face them with prayer. Amen.*

THE MINISTRY OF THE MASTER—FRIDAY
A Spirit Lifter

"What are you doing pacing back and forth in front of this house at this hour?"

"Officer, no problem. It is simply that I forgot my key, and I'm waiting for my kids to get home so they can let me in."

God's Promise

"Do not be anxious about your life, what you shall eat, nor about your body, what you shall put on. For life is more than food and the body more than clothing." (Luke 12:22,23)

Practicing His Presence

I pray that being aware of His presence each day is a meaningful experience for you. How did you sense His presence yesterday?

The Prayer Life of Jesus

There are individuals who feel the power of prayer lies in the length of the prayer. Jesus instructed that the one who thinks he will be heard because of his long prayer is sadly mistaken. It is the intent of the heart which is important.

Consider the worship services in many of the churches of Scotland in the sixteenth century. There would be an hour's teaching concerning a selected portion of scripture. After this the sermon of almost always an hour in length would be presented.

Intermingled between the hour of teaching and the sermon would be prayers. Some of them would be very long. Many pious individuals would be offended by a short prayer.

As there was not much else to do on Sunday, the people were willing to be subjected to this religious form of righteousness even though many denied the power of prayer.

Jesus endeavored to impart the reality of the presence rather than the power of performance. It was a matter of the heart and not of the form which made prayer purposeful and powerful.

PRAYER: *Father, may I not get encumbered with words, but remain yielded in spirit to all you have for us. Amen.*

THE MINISTRY OF THE MASTER—SATURDAY
A Spirit Lifter

The point under discussion was the new church graveyard. The one deacon had become so exasperated that he exclaimed, "I'll never be buried in that place as long as I live."

"How obstinate and stubborn can you be!" shouted another member of the board.

"If my life is spared, I will!"

God's Promise

"When the Holy Spirit controls our lives He will produce this kind of fruit in us: love, joy, peace, patience, kindness, goodness, faithfulness, gentleness and self-control." (Galatians 5:22, TLB)

Practicing His Presence

You may have had a busy day yesterday. I pray that, amidst your activity, you were able to pull apart and sense the Lord's presence.

The Prayer Life Of Jesus

May I mention a further word about formality and informality? It is very difficult to remain free and open unto the Lord. We will drift into a form before we know it, and often when it appears we are free.

I recall as a young man that the rural church members I served took pride in their informality. In fact, several of them were outspoken against the formal city churches. They were especially negatively critical of the worship service bulletin used by other churches. They didn't want to be tied to this formality. Yet, you knew what was going to happen at every Sunday morning worship service at that church. Their apparent freedom was as rigid as the form of worship they were attacking.

The prayer life of Jesus was vital and alive. He prayed in the wilderness. He prayed all night. He prayed at the grave site of His friend Lazarus. He prayed and expected others to pray at the temple. He stressed prayer at the temple so much that He chased out the money changers and proclaimed to all that the temple *"...should be a house of prayer."*

I believe the smallest and the largest events of life are worthy of prayer. I believe we should be in a spirit of prayer constantly. I believe this because Jesus lived this way and taught by word and example that we should do the same.

PRAYER: *Wherever I am and whatever I am doing may I remain in a spirit of prayer, Father. Amen.*

97

THE MINISTRY OF THE MASTER—SUNDAY

A Spirit Lifter

"I dreamed last night that I had invented a new type of breakfast food. I was just at the point of consuming a large sampling of it when..."

"Yes, yes, go on! Was it really good?"

"Well, when I woke up I discovered a corner of the mattress was gone."

God's Promise

"I shall put my spirit in you, and make you keep my laws and sincerely respect my observances." (Ezekiel 36:27)

Practicing His Presence

I believe you will have a great day if you are aware of the Lord's presence. How did you do this yesterday?

The Prayer Life Of Jesus

I am always amazed that the gospel accounts of our Lord always depict Him as apparently having things under control. He doesn't appear to be ruffled by problems nor overcome by burdens. He could even take His time getting to His friend's home when told that Lazarus was sick unto death. He pursued a measured pace which is astounding.

I believe one of the biggest reasons for this was His close walk with the Father. He knew that He couldn't be the Saviour by activity. He had to be the Saviour by accepting the reality of the Father's presence and power.

The way that Jesus stayed in tune with His mission was through prayer. His prayer life not only brought stability to Him, but His prayer life helped maintain that stability.

You have read or heard of Jesus being a good man. A good man He was. However, a more accurate and stirring description would be that Jesus was a praying man. He gave Himself to a life of prayer that He might give Himself.

If you practice His presence each moment of the day, you too will be coming closer to the prayer life of Jesus. Prayer will become a lifestyle and not merely verbalization.

PRAYER: *Help me, dear God, to be like your Son. May I give myself to prayer. Amen.*

PATTERN OF PRAYER—QUIET

"Be still and know that I am God." Psalms 46:10 is a statement you and I need to ponder at depth. Most of the time we live as if the way to know that He is God is to be very active, to study a lot, or to be in constant fellowship with others.

Isn't is interesting that the psalmist says that quietness is a key to really knowing God? How do you become quiet? How do you develop this art? How essential is it to a deep and meaningful devotional life?

The first step in my pattern of prayer is to seek to be quiet before the Lord. It is a big step toward the realization of the power of the Lord in your life.

You can be quiet in spirit and soul without withdrawing completely from life. I believe I can be in the midst of many activities and around many people and still have quiet in my soul. The quietness the Psalmist is suggesting is not the life of a recluse. Rather, it is the life of a person who rests in the quiet assurance of the presence and power of the Lord in all areas of life and at all times.

Dr. Albert E. Day has said, *"Right prayer demands a quieting of the whole being. The truest prayer begins when we pass beyond words into deep silence. When lips are hushed, when racing thoughts are stilled, when emotions are placid as the dawning over the waveless ocean."*

I believe that frequently the most sacred and close moments of life are periods of silence. It is a time of holy hushness. It is not a time of constant babbling or great activity.

POINTS TO PONDER

1. How important do you feel it is to seek to find quiet time each day?
2. How difficult do you find it to be quiet in your heart and soul?
3. How do you commune in spirit with the living God?

Daily Bible Study and Daily Prayer Concerns
PATTERN OF PRAYER—QUIET

1. Be_____and know that I am God.
   Ps. 46:10
2. And that ye study to be _____. *I Thess. 4:11*
3. The pagans _____ aloud and cut themselves
   after their•manner. *I Kings 18:28*
4. _____ me, O Lord, that this people may
   know you are the Lord God. *I Kings 18:37*
5. After the fire a _____ small voice.
   I Kings 19:12
6. Stand still and_____what the Lord will
   command. *Num. 9:8*
7. Stand thou still a while, that I may _____
   thee the word of God. *I Sam. 9:27*
8. Stand still, that I may _____ with you before
   the Lord. *I Sam. 12:7*
9. Stand still and consider the wondrous _____
   of God. *Job. 37:14*
10. Commune with your own_____and be still.
    Ps. 4:4
11. He that _____ his lips is wise. *Pro. 10:19*
12. He was oppressed, and he was afflicted, yet he opened not his _____
    _____. *Isa. 53:7*
13. But Jesus held His _____.*Mt. 26:63*
14. He answered him _____. *Lu. 23:9*

DAILY SCRIPTURE

Mon.	Ps. 46:1-11
Tues.	I Thess. 4:9-12
Wed.	Num. 9:1-8
Thurs.	I Sam. 12:6-18
Fri.	Job. 37:14-24
Sat.	Mt. 26:57-68
Sun.	Lu. 23:6-12

PRAYER CONCERNS

Your Family & Relatives
Government Leaders
Missionaries
For the Unbelievers
Churches & Denominations
Your Own Church
Prayer and Praise

NOTE: You will be spiritually strengthened by completing two questions each day, reading the suggested scripture, and ministering in prayer for the concerns of the day.

THE MINISTRY OF THE MASTER—MONDAY
A Spirit Lifter

A rather haughty and sophisticated lady had purchased a stamp. The postman had given the stamp to her and ignored the fact that she had laid the envelope in front of him. She retorted, "Must I stick it on myself?"

His calm and cutting remark was, "Do as you choose, Ma'am, but it will accomplish a great deal more if you stick it on the envelope."

God's Promise

"The young lions do lack and suffer hunger; but they who seek the Lord shall not be in want of any good thing." (Psalm 34:10, NASB)

Practicing His Presence

It may be that you had a difficult day yesterday. I do hope, however, that you were able to take the time to be aware of His presence.

A Pattern Of Prayer—Quiet

I spend very little time praying for individuals. During past years I did a great deal of this, but have in recent years been led to a different approach. Now I give myself to a ministry of prayer unto individuals.

I have become convinced that prayer is a ministry. It is work. It is an art. It is not petitioning the Lord to bend His will to my pet project or particular deep concern.

Prayer is opening myself and others up to the presence, power, and purpose of the Lord. It is permitting myself to be a channel of His power to myself and to others. It is not constantly begging the Lord for favors.

I was visiting a patient in the hospital who was very disturbed and uptight. As we talked you could see the individual becoming more relaxed and free. Presently he remarked about the change which had come over him and asked me what had happened.

My response was that even while we were talking I had been endeavoring to be a channel of the power of the Lord and to have the Spirit of the Lord permeate his very being. I believe this happened. I had lifted him into the light and love of the Lord and the result was the Lord's power made a difference.

PRAYER: *Father, help me to open myself unto you as a flower opens to the rain and sunshine. Amen.*

THE MINISTRY OF THE MASTER—TUESDAY
A Spirit Lifter

They had just arrived in an area where figs were raised by the acres. The woman was intrigued by a certain tree and asked the guide what it was. He nonchalantly replied, "That, my dear lady, is a fig tree." She stood several moments with a puzzled expression upon her face, and then she said, "But that can't be a fig tree!" "But is it, madam, it is!"

After a long pause fellow passengers heard her mumble, "But I thought the leaves were larger than that!"

God's Promise

"The Lord can rescue you and me from the temptations that surround us." (II Peter 2:9, TLB)

Practicing His Presence

Do you find that an awareness of His presence is determined to some degree by how you feel?

A Pattern Of Prayer—Quiet

I believe that the power of the Lord is often released in the moment of quietness. Certainly it is released from and through the quiet soul. The soul reposed in the assurance of the Lord's love and goodness and power.

The prophet of old grasped essential truth when he wrote,

"...Not by might, nor by power, but by my spirit, saith the Lord of hosts." Zech. 4:6

If anything lasting is to be accomplished, it must be of the Lord. I cannot really change anyone or accomplish feats. Thus, it is necessary that I remain open to the power which is available to me.

Today I would encourage you to try to maintain a quiet spirit and to let the presence of the Lord be felt in you and flow through you. Perhaps you could seek to move from begging God to being open to Him. You may seek to be like the flower which is open to the sunshine and the rain, but does not beg for it.

Prayer is the work of the church. Prayer is your vital ministry, but it does not have to be a certain mode of verbalization. It is relating to the Father as one.

PRAYER: *May I quiet all of my being in your presence, O Lord. Amen.*

THE MINISTRY OF THE MASTER—WEDNESDAY
A Spirit Lifter

A widow was trying to get him to guess her age. He was hesitant, and she said, "You must have some idea, surely."

His sage response was, "I have several ideas. The only trouble is I hesitate whether to make you ten years younger on account of your looks, or ten years older on account of your intelligence."

God's Promise

"When you lie down, you will not be afraid; when you lie down, your sleep will be sweet." (Proverbs 3:24, NIV)

Practicing His Presence

Are you finding being aware of His presence exciting? Did you have an exciting day yesterday?

A Pattern Of Prayer—Quiet

May I minister unto you with prayer today? I am going to talk with each of you as I would to one who came into my office for prayer.

I am going to suggest that you seek to quiet your entire being. You are perhaps tense, frustrated, and worried. How do you get rid of this spirit? How can you achieve any relief?

May you for at least the next few minutes try to quiet your mind. Put aside all your worried thoughts and think only of the presence of the Lord. Seek to picture His light and love engulfing you. Then may you seek to quiet your emotions. Your heart may be fearful, but at least for a short time put aside the fear and relax the heart before the Lord.

Now I am going to ask that you even quiet your body. Begin with the top of your head and just let yourself relax down through every member of your body unto the tips of your toes.

At least for a few moments you will be freer than you have been for a long time. Even a rubber band cannot be kept tight all the time without the elasticity being lost. A rubber band which is stretched for a while and then released from strain for a while will last indefinitely. In like manner, your life needs moments of release.

PRAYER: *It isn't easy, Father, to quiet my whole being, but please help me to do so. Amen.*

THE MINISTRY OF THE MASTER—THURSDAY

A Spirit Lifter

There were two old sailors sitting in their favorite barroom. The place had been completely modernized and refurbished. It was clean and very sanitary now. The one said to the other:

"I suppose it's all right, Bill, these new-fashioned trappings, but I miss the old spittoon."

"Yep, you always did, Jim."

God's Promise

"Jesus said, 'If you hold to my teaching, you are really my disciples. Then you will know the truth, and the truth will set you free.' " (John 8:31,32, NIV)

Practicing His Presence

It's amazing to me how often the Lord has felt so near while I am involved in the ordinary experiences of life. Is this true of your life?

A Pattern Of Prayer—Quiet

I read of an experiment which illustrates the necessity of quieting yourself before the Lord. An individual had a two-ounce weight attached to her index finger. She was then asked to raise and lower the weight as many times as she could. Several hundred times later her finger was absolutely exhausted. She could not lift it one more time.

Another person had the same weight attached to her index finger. She was asked to raise and lower the weight three times and then rest the finger for three seconds. She was to repeat this procedure for as long as possible. In this case the experiment was called off after several hours, because there was no way the finger could be exhausted. If anything, it got stronger.

The difference is obvious. The one was a continual stress situation. The other provided moments of quietness and rest. I believe your spiritual life is the same. You need times of becoming quiet in the Lord. These moments of rest enable you to recuperate from the moments of stress.

A ministry of prayer unto you by another person can be a source of great strength. Prayer is a ministry you should receive and a ministry you should render.

PRAYER: *The stress and strain of life is sometimes too much for me, Father. Please help me to give my burdens to you. Amen.*

THE MINISTRY OF THE MASTER—FRIDAY
A Spirit Lifter

The American history teacher had spent some weeks concerning the history of our early years as a nation. She asked, "Why did the Puritans come to this country?"

There were several responses, but the classic was from one of the boys, "To worship in their own way and make other people do the same."

God's Promise

"The righteous will flourish like a palm tree, they will grow like a cedar of Lebanon; they will still bear fruit in old age, they will stay fresh and green."
(Psalm 92:12,14, NIV)

Practicing His Presence

Was there at least a little time during your busy schedule when you sensed His presence yesterday? How did this make you feel?

A Pattern Of Prayer—Quiet

Has a quiet spirit been an experience of yours this week? It is reported that Dr. Albert Einstein once said,

"The best formula for success in life is that $A = X + Y + Z$. Now X is work, and Y is play." Someone then asked him, *"If X is work, and Y is play, then what is Z?"* Dr. Einstein replied, *"Z stands for keeping your mouth shut."*

He knew the value of the quiet spirit. I am not too enthusiastic about the theory that I should storm the gates of heaven. Or that I should beat upon those doors with my prayers until the Lord hears me. I do not believe the Lord is deaf nor is He unattentive. I need not shout to be heard, but I need to be open to be blessed.

I read of no account in the gospels of Jesus' screaming unto the Lord in prayer. On the contrary, He spent time in private prayer, but when He ministered in public it was only a word, a touch, a brief comment used to release healing power. He had been in touch with the Father and thus could move in confidence and pray with power.

PRAYER: *The confidence I need to face life must come from you, Father. Help me to believe this. Amen.*

105

A Spirit Lifter

The group had been making a tour of the piano factory. The guide was proudly pointing to the beautiful ivory keys of their prize instruments. "Why, it takes 5,000 elephants a year to make our piano keys."

A voice in the back of the group responded, "Isn't it remarkable what those intelligent beasts can be trained to do! What will they think of next for them to do!"

God's Promise

"Where, O death, is your victory? Where, O death, is your sting? Thanks be to God! He gives us the victory through our Lord Jesus Christ." (I Cor. 15:55,57, NIV)

Practicing His Presence

May you continually remain sensitive to the Spirit. How were you aware of His presence yesterday, and how did this make you feel?

A Pattern Of Prayer—Quiet

You have heard the statements *"quiet as a mouse,"* or *"quiet as a monastery."* There is truth to them, but the truth we need is to become as "quiet as a believer." I am speaking of the quietness of your innermost being.

The great forces of the universe are exerted in quietness. The tornado makes a terrible noise. I have heard one pass within a few hundred yards of my home. It was as a roaring train. The hurricane blows with great noise and obvious destructive force. The volcano erupts with a deafening roar.

However, as powerful as these acts of nature are, they are not the greatest force in the world. There is more water evaporating every day than is contained in the world. There is more water evaporating every day than is contained in the worst flood. Yet, you do not hear this.

Gravity has more power than any earthquake or tornado, and yet it exerts its great power in quietness.

The growth of a tiny seed can ultimately split a huge rock as the tree grows, but there is no sound which issues forth. You need but stop and think to realize that there is a marvel to the silence of the powers of the universe. In like manner, there is great power to the quiet soul.

The quietness of the believer is the heart fully confident that the Lord loves, hears, and answers His children.

PRAYER: *May your still small voice speak volumes to my soul this day, Father. Amen.*

THE MINISTRY OF THE MASTER—SUNDAY
A Spirit Lifter

"I can't think why the board at the opera company makes such a fuss over Miss Smith's voice. I feel that Miss Bartly has a much richer voice."

"They do, too, but Miss Smith has a much richer father."

God's Promise

"He who guards his mouth and his tongue guards his soul from troubles." (Proverbs 21:23, NASB)

Practicing His Presence

Are you anticipating being aware of His presence throughout this day? If so, I am sure this will be a wonderful day for you.

A Pattern Of Prayer—Quiet

I will close this week of considering the quiet spirit by mentioning my search through the Scriptures for loud and long prayer. I could find no reference to any in the New Testament. I then turned to the Old Testament. It was there I found reference to loud prayers.

However, it was interesting to me that the loud prayers were offered by individuals who did not worship the true and living God. They were the prophets of Baal. This incident is recorded in I Kings, chapter 18.

Elijah had challenged the prophets of Baal. The sacrifice was prepared. They had opportunity to call upon their god. It says they went to the extreme and,

"They cried aloud, and cut themselves after their manner with knives and lancets, till the blood gushed out upon them." I Kings 18:28

Nothing happened. All the noise they could make did not accomplish their goal. It is then that Elijah offered a prayer which takes about twenty-five seconds to pray (I Kings 18:36,37). The fire descended and consumed the sacrifice. The true believer did not have to shout to a deaf God. He merely had to open himself to the Living God.

PRAYER: *Father, I am grateful that I do not have to shout to be heard by you, but that even a whispered prayer opens the portals of heaven. Amen.*

A PATTERN OF PRAYER—LIFT

The second step in my Pattern of Prayer is lift. I use this word because I feel so keenly that all of our concerns and burdens can and must be borne by the Lord. You and I cannot bear them alone.

In addition, we have the admonition of the Lord to bring our burdens to Him. He is not only willing that we bring them, but He is always able to care for them. He does not say, *"Just call me when you need me,"* and then not respond when the call is made. He said, *"Come,"* and is always there when you call.

Last week I dealt with the quiet spirit. May I suggest as you quiet yourself before the Lord that you picture all of your being and cares being lifted unto Him.

How do you imagine lifting all things unto Him? I will tell you how I do it. I picture the Lord as light and love.

Love I cannot perceive in any material way, but light I can. I can behold in my mind and heart a light which permeates every facet of my being. I can then imagine that love is a part of all that light.

I find this approach to be helpful because it gets my mind and heart off of myself and problems unto the Lord. I can never solve my own problems nor the problems of anyone else. Only the Lord can really do that.

Therefore, in my prayer experiences I must get my eyes on the Problem Solver and off the problems I am endeavoring to solve.

The more you dwell upon a problem, the more engrained it becomes in your life. The more you look to the One who can care for your problem, the more you are spiritually enriched.

POINTS TO PONDER

1. What are some properties of light which help us understand spiritual truths?
2. Why do you find it so difficult to get your eyes off of your problems?
3. What is love and in whom do you feel love existing?

A PATTERN OF PRAYER—LIFT

1. Come unto me and I will give you_____.
   Mt. 11:28
2. He_____for you. *I Pet. 5:7*
3. I am come a _____ into the world.
   John 12:46
4. The _____ was the light of men.
   John 1:4
5. The _____ is the light thereof.
   Rev. 21:23
6. _____ is love. *I John 4:8*
7. He that followeth me shall not walk in_____.
   John 8:12
8. God said let there be _____. *Gen. 1:3*
9. I have loved you with an _____ love.
   Jer. 31:3
10. But God commendeth his _____ toward us.
    Rom. 5:8
11. Behold, what manner of _____ the
    Father hath bestowed upon us. *I John 3:1*
12. The Lord direct your _____ into the
    Love of God. *II Thess. 3:5*
13. We have known and_____the love that
    God hath to us. *I John 4:16*
14. And to know the love of Christ, which passeth _____
    _____. *Eph. 3:19*

DAILY SCRIPTURE

Mon.   Mt. 11:25-28
Tues.   I Pet. 5:6-11
Wed.   John 12:44-50
Thurs.   I John 4:7-21
Fri.   II Thess. 3:1-5
Sat.   Eph. 3:14-19
Sun.   *Rev. 21:22-27*

PRAYER CONCERNS

Your Family & Relatives
Government Leaders
Missionaries
For the Unbelievers
Churches & Denominations
Your Own Church
Prayer and Praise

NOTE: You will be spiritually strengthened by completing two questions each day, reading the suggested scripture, and ministering in prayer for the concerns of the day.

THE MINISTRY OF THE MASTER—MONDAY
A Spirit Lifter

"He always plays in the spirit of Christian charity."

"Christian charity!" exclaimed his puzzled friend. "How can you play with Christian charity?"

"With him it is easy. His right hand does not know what his left hand is doing."

God's Promise

"You will show me the path that leads to life; your presence fills me with joy and brings me pleasure forever." (Psalm 16:11, TEV)

Practicing His Presence

Through what incident or person did you sense the presence of the Lord yesterday? How did this make you feel?

A Pattern Of Prayer—Lift

Approximately twenty years ago I went through a period of illness which left me in constant pain. This pain was with me night and day. I could not walk without pain. I could not sit without pain. In fact, I had to hook my leg over the edge of the bed to get up in the morning. I tried everything I knew to alleviate the pain.

I purchased a new chair for my study. I tried using other chairs which would perhaps provide more comfort. I spent times praying the Lord would bring me some relief from pain.

It was during this time that I learned a valuable lesson. The best way for me to receive some relief was to lift myself into the light and love of the Lord.

When I prayed directly for the pain, it was as if this intensified it. However, when I quieted my spirit and lifted myself into the light and love of the Lord, my mind was off the pain and on the Lord Jesus. This made a great difference.

Today I would encourage you to lift your physical, emotional, and spiritual being into the light and love of the Lord and permit Him to permeate every aspect of your being.

PRAYER: *May I lift all of my concerns into your light and love this day, O Lord. Amen.*

THE MINISTRY OF THE MASTER—TUESDAY
A Spirit Lifter

"I'm convinced that the publishers have a conspiracy against me," was the comment of Fred Brown.

"But why would you say this?" said his friend. "You haven't even had a book published yet!"

"But can't you see? That's where the conspiracy is. Ten of them have now refused the same book."

God's Promise

"For it is God who is at work within you, giving you the will and the power to achieve His purpose." (Philippians 2:13, Phillips)

Practicing His Presence

I pray you were very much aware of the Lord's presence in your life yesterday. Can you recall some specific incident or person which helped this awareness?

A Pattern Of Prayer—Lift

Why do I use the concept of light in my pattern of prayer? I do so because this is a description which our Lord used of Himself.

"I am the light of the world..." John 12:35

"...Yet a little while is the light with you..." John 12:35

Elsewhere Scripture speaks of the fact that Christ brings light.

"For God, who commanded the light to shine out of darkness, hath shined in our hearts..." II Cor. 4:6

"...and Christ shall give the light." Eph. 5:14

"And the city had no need of the sun, neither of the moon, to shine in it; for the glory of God did lighten it, and the Lamb is the light thereof." Rev. 21:23

The Scriptures also speak of God as light.

"The Lord is my light and my salvation..." Ps. 27:1

"...the Lord shall be a light unto me." Micah 7:8

"...God is light, and in Him is no darkness at all." I John 1:5

If there are so many references to the Lord as light, then I feel this is a good concept for me to develop. It helps me to appreciate that He is able to know all about me and to become completely identified with my needs and answers.

PRAYER: *I want to follow the light, O Father, which leads me to you and to your will. Amen.*

111

THE MINISTRY OF THE MASTER—WEDNESDAY
A Spirit Lifter

Two persons were hotly discussing the merits of a book. Finally, one of them, himself an author, said to the other:

"No, John, you can't appreciate it. You never wrote a book yourself and you have no idea of a book's quality."

"Perhaps, Harry, but remember I have never laid an egg, but I'm a far better judge of an omelet than any hen."

God's Promise

"You will call upon me and come and pray to me, and I will hear you." Jeremiah 29:12, RSV)

Practicing His Presence

If you are like me, you sometimes experience things which seem to cloud the reality of His presence. What do you do when this happens to you?

A Pattern Of Prayer—Lift

The properties of light are interesting and can readily be applied to the spiritual life. The first thing I stress is that light travels faster than anything known to man. In like manner, the Spirit of the Lord reaches us faster than anything known in the universe.

Light is essential for growth. Light dispels darkness. Light reveals flaws and weaknesses. Light guides. Light transmits heat. Light can even transmit voices. Light is a source of energy. Light is all of these and more.

You can readily seen how the above characteristics can be applied in a spiritual sense.

Scientists tell us that light is not solid. It is a constant flowing stream of pulsating particles. Isn't this a beautiful analogy of the love of God as light pulsating out to you and me every moment of every day and in every situation?

The light of the Lord can permeate the trillions of cells of your body and sweep through the millions of thoughts of your mind. It is a tangible way of depicting the intangibles of the spirit.

PRAYER: *Your light and love can permeate every aspect of my being, Father. Help me to believe this. Amen.*

THE MINISTRY OF THE MASTER—THURSDAY
A Spirit Lifter

A group was being addressed by a famous author. His lecture was finished and the question and answer period had progressed very well.

Near the close of this session he was asked: "Which of your works of fiction do you consider to be your best, Dr. Martin?" Without hesitation he replied, "My last income tax return."

God's Promise

"The God who made both earth and heaven, the seas and everything in them. He is the God who keeps every promise." (Psalm 146:6, TLB)

Practicing His Presence

I do hope that you were able to pull apart yesterday, and be aware of the Lord's presence in the small things of life. What did this do for you?

A Pattern Of Prayer—Lift

The victorious life is one which is lived in the pathway of the light and love of the Lord Jesus. It is not a life which is aware of the light, but the one which walks in that light.

I was reared on a farm where it was obvious that lack of light stunted growth. If a plant in the house was becoming pale, it would be placed where there was more available light.

If a bean happened to be covered by a small rock, it could not come through to the light and remained yellow and unhealthy in appearance. Expose this plant to the light and it soon came to full development.

I urge you to seek to walk in the light of the Lord. Keep your life lifted into His light. Lift into His light those unto whom you minister in prayer.

There are many who feel the victorious Christian life is through a knowledge of the Bible. Now I am not discouraging Bible study, but it is not the secret of the Christian life. The secret is walking in the light of obedience before the Lord.

PRAYER: *Father, I want to walk in the light of complete obedience to you. Thank you for the joy this brings. Amen.*

THE MINISTRY OF THE MASTER—FRIDAY
A Spirit Lifter

A man and wife were in deep argument over the controversy concerning the author of the plays attributed to Shakespeare. The woman insisted that Bacon really wrote them, and the husband was as adamant that Shakespeare wrote them. Finally the husband said, "Well, when I get to Heaven, I am going to ask Shakespeare whether he really wrote the plays."

"But suppose he isn't there?"

"Then you ask him, my dear," was the curt response.

God's Promise

"I will instruct you, and teach you the way to go; I will watch over you and be your advisor." (Psalm 32:8, JB)

Practicing His Presence

Continually remain sensitive to the Spirit. Can you recall a specific incident yesterday in which His presence was very evident?

A Pattern Of Prayer—Lift

I feel that light and love go together beautifully. All the light which you may perceive with the eye of the imagination is filled with the love of God. He is receiving you and yours because of this love.

Love is something which can never be exhausted. I come from a family of eleven children. The love of my parents was not diminished by another child. The amount of time they would have to devote to each would be diminished, but their love was the same for each of us.

Thus, the Lord's love for each person is not diminished as the population of the world increases. He is able to love each as if there were but one person in the whole world. He is able to love the whole world as if it were but one person.

The Lord created all things. He pronounced His creation good each day. However, after the creation of man we find the statement: *"And God saw everything He made, and, behold, it was very good." Genesis 1:13*

The rainbow sign to Noah still speaks to us today. It reminds us of the lasting love of God while showing us the beauty of light when its facets are separated.

PRAYER: *I pray for a rainbow of hope today, Father. Help me to see it even through my tears and trials. Amen.*

THE MINISTRY OF THE MASTER—SATURDAY
A Spirit Lifter

Dear Editor,
Your classified ad department is fantastic. Thursday I lost a gold watch which I valued very highly. Friday I inserted an ad in your lost-and-found column. It didn't come out in the paper until Saturday morning. Yet, would you believe, Saturday afternoon I went home and found the watch in the pocket of another suit? God bless your paper and keep up the good work.

God's Promise

"I will honor those who honor me." (I Samuel 2:30, TEV)

Practicing His Presence

May you seek to quiet yourself this day. How were you aware of His presence yesterday?

A Pattern Of Prayer—Lift

I once read of an eminent pediatrician who had a standard treatment for frail babies. He would write out this prescription for every mother with such a baby.

"This baby is to be loved every three hours."

Now he realized the parents loved the child all the time. However, the baby needed to be assured of this love in a tangible way. Love which is expressed is love which is precious and helpful.

Tests have shown that even rabbits respond to love. A scientific experiment revealed that rabbits shown much attention and love ended up with a lower cholesterol count than those which were ignored.

You render a most helpful ministry to others when you deliberately seek to lift them into the light and love of the Lord. It is a better treatment than probably anything else you could do for them at the moment.

I was touched by the story of a little boy sitting on the porch. The old collie dog was also sleeping nearby. A neighbor came by and remarked, *"Are you watching him?"* The beautiful answer was, *"No, I'm loving him."* God is loving you all the time, and He is watching those unto whom you minister in prayer.

PRAYER: *Your love surrounds me, dwells within me, and sustains me. I thank you, O God. Amen.*

THE MINISTRY OF THE MASTER—SUNDAY
A Spirit Lifter

"I'm sorry," said the diner, who hoped to get away with it, "but I haven't any money to pay for that meal."

"That's all right," said the cashier. "We'll write your name on the wall and you can pay the next time you come in."

"Oh, don't do that. Everybody who comes in will see it."

"Oh, no, they won't. Your overcoat will be hanging over it."

God's Promise

"The Lord is faithful. He will strengthen you and keep you safe from the Evil One." (II Thess. 3:3, TEV)

Practicing His Presence

May you continually remain sensitive to the Spirit. How did this sensitivity affect your day yesterday?

A Pattern Of Prayer—Lift

There is the legend of a rabbi who had a very special dream.

His dream revealed a set of scales on which was piled all the precious values of the world, precious gems and other items of great worth.

The weight of the precious things lowered the one side of the huge scales and the other side disappeared into the heavens. It was then that the rabbi saw a pulsating heart of a living person. The heart was placed on the other side of the scales.

Slowly, but surely, the scales began to tip the other way. Over a period of a few minutes all the precious gems and riches of the world had disappeared into the heavens. The one heart had outweighed them all.

Jesus said that He loved you more than the whole world. You are worth more than the whole world. Those unto whom you minister in prayer are worth more than the whole world.

The only thing which really endures is love. Therefore, may you develop the art of prayer to the point that you lift others into the light and love of the Lord as well as lifting yourself there.

PRAYER: *I want others to be in my prayers, Father. I come in behalf of those for whom I am concerned. Amen.*

A PATTERN OF PRAYER—VISUALIZE

I would like to emphasize, that to visualize is to develop the ability to see already fulfilled, that for which you are praying. This is not easy to do, but is a rewarding step in your pilgrimage of prayer.

Who can deny the effect the mind has upon the life? This is often witnessed from a negative viewpoint. I am suggesting you turn this power to a positive force in your life.

Have you ever known anyone who was made almost ill through remarks of other people? If you have not witnessed this, you have at least heard of it.

A person is told he doesn't look too well. A few minutes later someone else calls attention to how pale he is. Then another asks if he is all right. By this time, the person is headed for a mirror to observe for himself. Sure enough, he doesn't look too good.

Another comment by an acquaintance and he is sick enough to go home and may be to the point that he feels he has some dreaded disease. It is almost as if by mid-afternoon he is dying of dreaded cancer.

All of this has been imparted in the mind. He began to visualize problems and sure enough they appeared.

It is my position that in your prayer life you should visualize the positive power of God in your life. You will want to develop the ability to visualize the fulfillment of that for which you are praying.

This, in a sense, is saying that wholeness is in the mind. It is easy for most to say that illness is in the mind. We need to be disciplined to realize that wholeness can be in the mind also.

I am now seeking to visualize each one reading this book for this week being open to the positive power of the Lord. May you visualize this as well, and be blessed abundantly in so doing.

POINTS TO PONDER

1. Are you able to visualize your problems being helped or solved?
2. Are you plagued with visualizing problems, failure, illness, etc.?
3. What do you feel is the value of visualizing the positive power of the Lord in every facet of your life?

A PATTERN OF PRAYER—VISUALIZE

1. As a person_____so is he. *Pro. 23:7*
2. Not by power, nor by might, but by my _____
   saith the Lord of hosts. *Zec. 4:6*
3. Let this_____be in you which was also
   in Christ Jesus. *Phil 2:5*
4. The peace of God shall keep your hearts and _____
   through Christ Jesus. *Phil 4:7*
5. Be ye transformed by the renewing of your_____.
   Rom. 12:2
6. Where the Spirit of the Lord is there is _____.
   II Cor. 3:17
7. If anyone be in Christ they are a_____
   creature. *II Cor. 5:17*
8. Thou wilt keep him in perfect peace, whose _____
   is stayed on thee. *Isa. 26:3*
9. Thou shalt love the Lord with all thy heart, and with all thy soul, and
   with all thy _____. *Mt. 22:37*
10. They received the word with all readiness of _____.
    Acts 17:11
11. Be renewed in the spirit of your_____.
    Eph. 4:23
12. The believer should put on humbleness of_____
    Col. 3:12
13. God hath not given you the spirit of fear, but of power, love, and of
    a sound _____. *II Tim. 1:7*
14. Feed the flock of God with a ready_____.
    I Pet. 5:2

DAILY SCRIPTURE

Mon.	Phil. 2:1-11
Tues.	Rom. 8:1-8
Wed.	II Cor. 5:16-21
Thurs.	Isa. 26:1-9
Fri.	Eph. 4:17-24
Sat.	Col. 3:12-17
Sun.	II Tim.1:3-7

PRAYER CONCERNS

Your Family & Relatives
Government Leaders
Missionaries
For the Unbelievers
Churches & Denominations
Your Own Church
Prayer and Praise

NOTE: You will be spiritually strengthened by completing two questions each day, reading the suggested scripture, and ministering in prayer for the concerns of the day.

THE MINISTRY OF THE MASTER—MONDAY
A Spirit Lifter

The old lady entered the drugstore and approached the young man who was in charge of the soda fountain.

"Are you a doctor?" she asked, peering over her horn-rimmed glasses.

The young man, not wanting to miss this opportunity to elevate himself, replied, "Yes, you might say so, Madam. But then I'm actually a fizzician."

God's Promise

"You are no longer foreigners and aliens, but fellow citizens with God's people and members of God's household." (Eph. 2:19, NIV)

Practicing His Presence

Begin today to consciously practice His presence.May you seek to quiet your body, mind, and spirit. "Our God reigns!"

A Pattern Of Prayer—Visualize

What you see yourself to be is to a large extent what you will be. Shakespeare said it this way.

"Some men never seem to grow old — always active in thought, always ready to adopt new ideas, they are never foggy and cast down. They are never satisfied and yet satisfied, settled and yet unsettled. They always enjoy the best of what is and are the first to find the best of what will be."

It is obvious that these individuals have an outlook that is positive. They have developed the art of visualizing the good and positive and powerful. I feel that as Christians we should draw upon the power of visualizing. This is not an evil gift, but rather is a gracious gift from the Lord. He wants you and me to use it properly and continually.

You need not dwell upon all the dread fears which could possess you. It is my prayer you will seek that the Lord is with you. Seek to visualize His presence and wholeness in your life right now.

PRAYER: *Father, I am going to try to visualize your presence with me every moment of this day. This is my promise. Amen.*

THE MINISTRY OF THE MASTER—TUESDAY
A Spirit Lifter

"Private Morris, is there any medical reason why you should not continue in the Army?" asked the doctor as he examined the new recruit who was requesting discharge.

"Believe me, Doctor, there is. Why, half my insides are missing!"

"What? Which parts are missing?" asked the startled physician.

"I have no guts," was the quick retort.

God's Promise

"Just as you trusted Christ to save you, trust him, too, for each day's problems; live in vital union with him." (Col. 2:6, TLB)

Practicing His Presence

It takes an added effort to be aware of the Lord in the small things in life. Were you able to pull apart yesterday and reflect upon the small things?

A Pattern Of Praise—Visualize

What are some practical aspects of being able to visualize the power and presence of the Lord in a situation? Let me explain it by relaying how I minister to individuals who come to me for counseling.

If someone comes to me for marriage counseling I seek to listen in the Spirit and to help them. This includes prayer. When I minister unto them with the laying-on-of-hands with prayer I seek to visualize a home that is a contented home. I seek to picture a home where peace is present. I try to see a home where there is compatibility and openness.

This approach does not guarantee a perfect answer to all the complexities of life, but it certainly does help release the positive power of the Lord. I do not have the answer and no one else has the answer. The power of the Holy Spirit must be released into the situation.

I feel I am a channel to help release His power. You can be a channel, too, as you lift your prayer concerns unto Him and visualize the answer already received.

PRAYER: *Thank you, Father, for helping me to see by faith the answer before it becomes a fact. Amen.*

THE MINISTRY OF THE MASTER—WEDNESDAY
A Spirit Lifter

A group of Boy Scouts was visiting the local FBI office. They viewed the pictures of the ten most wanted men in the U.S.A. One little boy pointed to a picture and asked if that was the photograph of the wanted person. When he was informed that it was, he asked the $64,000 question.

"If that is him, why didn't you keep him when you took his picture?"

God's Promise

"He has made known to us in all wisdom and insight the mystery of his will, according to his purpose which he set forth in Christ." (Ephesians 1:9, RSV)

Practicing His Presence

Were you able to practice His presence yesterday? If so, how did this awareness make you feel?

A Pattern Of Prayer—Visualize

It is not always easy to visualize in prayer what you would like to see in fact. However, the power of visualization is tremendous and I seek to develop this art and I encourage you to do the same.

A few years ago I visited a man in the hospital who was in the last stages of cirrhosis of the liver. He was so thin and emaciated and his stomach was swollen many times its regular size. I ministered unto him with the laying-on-of-hands with prayer and explained to him how I was seeking to visualize the stomach restored to normalcy.

The next day he told me that about 20 minutes after I had departed someone took hold of his upper left arm. He was sitting on the edge of the bed. There was no one in the room. Yet the grasp was firm, real, and definitely the touch of a person.

Immediately the swelling began to recede and in a day or so, his stomach was flat. He dynamically experienced the presence of the Lord and was instrumental in leading several to Christ before his death.

What we had sought to visualize together had come to pass and he was used of the Lord in a great way. He believed he had been touched by God.

PRAYER: *May I feel the touch of your presence, Father. I do not ask for physical touch, but the touch of the inward spirit of your love for me. Amen.*

THE MINISTRY OF THE MASTER—THURSDAY
A Spirit Lifter

Four-year-old Betty had crawled in bed without saying her prayers. Her mother noticed and called this neglect to her attention. The little girl had a perfect answer as she responded, "There are some nights when I don't want anything."

God's Promise

"Only test me! Open your mouth wide and see if I won't fill it. You will receive every blessing you can use!" (Psalm 81:10)

Practicing His Presence

I believe as you exercise your spiritual powers you will become more aware of the spiritual side of life. How did you sense the presence of His Spirit yesterday?

A Pattern Of Prayer—Visualize

I read one time about a man who was very disturbed by his wife. The thing which so irritated him was her apparent lack of concern about important matters. In fact, he got to the place where he worried about the fact that she did not worry.

Finally, after an upsetting experience in their family, he could take it no longer and blurted out, *"What is wrong with you? We have almost had a catastrophe and you act like you don't ever care!"*

The wife's reply is a classic because she had the ability to visualize the power and presence of the Lord. She could picture Him at work and could rest in the assurance of His love.

"Well, years ago I made up my mind that when anything went wrong, I would ask myself honestly and earnestly — can I do any good by thinking and worrying about it? Am I to blame in any way? If so, do not spare me, nor let me spare myself. Can I do anything to put a better face on it? Now, if after looking at it honestly from all angles, I found I could do no good, I made up my mind that I would give up thinking about it and worrying about it."

PRAYER: *The assurance that you are working in my behalf at all times is a comfort for which I give thanks, Father. Amen.*

THE MINISTRY OF THE MASTER—FRIDAY
A Spirit Lifter

The nine-month-old baby brother had been crying loudly for some time. His five-year-old brother was getting bothered. In exasperation he said to his mother, "Didn't you tell me that Freddy came from heaven?"

"Yes, dear, I did." replied the mother.

"Well, no wonder they threw him out."

God's Promise

"Commit everything you do to the Lord. Trust him to help you do it and he will." (Psalm 37:5, TLB)

Practicing His Presence

Stop, look, and listen! If you do, I am certain this will be an exciting day for you.

A Pattern Of Prayer—Visualize

Are you able to picture yourself surrounded, yea engulfed, by the love and light of the Lord? I would encourage you to try to visualize this fact at this moment. The Lord is with you. He is over you, under you, behind you, in front of you, and even in you.

I frequently minister unto individuals with prayer, the concept that the light and love of the Lord is permeating their every thought, emotion, and cell and fiber.

There is power in visualizing the power and presence of the Lord. A doctor in Texas instructs his patients to visualize the cancer cells as raw hamburger or raw liver. Then the patient is to visualize healthy cells devouring the hamburger. He reports that the individuals who can really develop a strong power of visualization have a much higher rate of recovery than those who cannot, or will not, visualize the consumption of the diseased cells.

There is more to what he prescribes than simply the power of positive thinking. There is the opening of one's self to the power of the ever present Lord.

PRAYER: *Father, right now I want to open every aspect of my being unto all your power and purity. Amen.*

THE MINISTRY OF THE MASTER—SATURDAY
A Spirit Lifter

A woman enrolled in night school and told her instructor that she wanted to learn French as fast as possible.

"What's the big rush?" exclaimed the teacher. "Learning French will take some time."

"Well, we have just adopted a six-month-old French baby, and we want to be able to understand him when he begins to talk."

God's Promise

"The Lord your God is with you ...He will take great delight in you, he will quiet you with his love, he will rejoice over you with singing." (Zephaniah 3:17)

Practicing His Presence

Can you recall some specific incident or person which helped your awareness of the Lord's presence yesterday?

A Pattern Of Prayer—Visualize

Isn't it amazing that every local body of believers tells people they should pray. However, very few of them really teach individuals how to pray. What would be the end result if every congregation really appropriated the power of prayer into their experiences?

You begin to exercise faith when you begin to visualize and accomplish what you are bringing to the Lord in prayer. Negative barriers are knocked down when you place in your mind a concept of the answer you expect.

The Bible teaches that believers should seek to "renew" their minds. This means that you replace the defeated and negative aspects and let the positive power of the Lord reign supreme.

Hazlett has said, *"Great thoughts reduced to practice become great acts."* Lord Byron observed, *"The power of thought is the magic of the mind."* Jesus taught that our actions originate in the mind and heart. What you visualize is what you will be doing and expecting.

I would encourage you today to seek to have your prayer time become more vital through visualizing the presence of the Lord in your problem and in the answer He gives.

PRAYER: *Help me, Father, to get my eyes off my problems and to focus them upon you, my Problem Solver. Amen.*

THE MINISTRY OF THE MASTER—SUNDAY
A Spirit Lifter

A gentleman told of the 21-day tour he was offered by a company. He said that it included the company flying him to London and then flying him home from Tokyo.

He asked, "But how do I get from London to Tokyo?"

The agent replied, "That's why we give you twenty-one days."

God's Promise

"The name of the Lord is a strong tower; the righteous run to it and are safe." (Prov. 18:10)

Practicing His Presence

It is sometimes difficult to remember a specific incident in which you felt the Lord's presence, isn't it?

A Pattern Of Prayer—Visualize

You and I are called to look unto the Lord. It is as we look unto Him and believe that we will be consistently blessed and strengthened.

It is true that there is some overflow of blessings even when we neglect to trust Him. However, the consistent victorious life is the product of constantly looking unto Him.

I read about a person who was always disgruntled and walked looking down all the time. One day he found a five dollar bill. It so impressed him that for the next forty years he walked looking down.

At the end of the 40 years he had accumulated 29,516 buttons, 54,172 straight and safety pins, 78 pennies, 4 quarters, and other junk. In addition, he had a bent back and a miserable disposition.

He received what he had visualized and that for which he was looking. You are not called to live this way. You are called to look and live.

Emerson wrote, *"Thoughts rule the world. All thoughts that mold the age, begin deep down within the primitive soul."* Your thoughts are your visualization experiences. Make them positive ones!

PRAYER: *Father, may I keep my heart and mind from the little things of life and look unto you for real meaning and purpose. Amen.*

A PATTERN OF PRAYER—BELIEVE

The Lord Jesus said, *"...all things are possible to him that believeth."* (Mark 9:23) It is evident that believing was very important to Him. He felt it was very important to His followers.

The dictionary defines believe,

"To accept as true on testimony or authority: be convinced of, as the result of study or reasoning. To credit a person with veracity; accept the word of it. To be sure of the existence or truth of anything. To have confidence in the truth or integrity of a person, the strength of a thing..."

It is important that you understand the importance the Bible attaches to our being able to really believe the Lord.

"...for he that cometh to God must believe that He is, and that He is a rewarder of them that diligently seek Him." (Hebrews 11:6)

When I minister unto someone with prayer I seek to lead them to the place of really believing that the Lord is present and that He loves them. This is not always easy to do. Most of us come to the Lord out of deep distress. We do not come because of our deep devotion and great belief.

The situation which has brought most of us to the point that we want to believe God exists, and that He cares for us, usually is of a nature which retards belief rather than strengthens it. Thus, even though believing is necessary we often find it almost impossible to believe. It is in the throes of this dilemma that I feel my pattern of prayer is helpful.

There is power released when you really believe the Lord. There is great gain for you when you can even say, *"Lord, I believe! Help my belief."* (Mark 9:24) It is wonderful that our belief does not have to be 100% pure, but even a grain of belief accomplishes great things. The Lord wants our confidence to be in Him and He will honor our belief.

POINTS TO PONDER

1. What do you feel it means to really believe God?
2. How do you know what to believe?
3. How do you know who to believe?

A PATTERN OF PRAYER—BELIEVE

1. The apostles asked Jesus to increase their _____.
   Lu. 17:5
2. He that comes to God must _____
   that He is. *Heb. 11:6*
3. Jesus said that whoever _____ on Him
   shall not abide in darkness. *John 12:46*
4. It is through believing that we have _____
   through the name of Jesus. *John 20:31*
5. We are not to be afraid, but only _____.
   Mark 5:36

6. A person _____ with his heart. *Rom. 10:10*
7. The _____ shall live by faith. *Hab. 2:4*
8. Daughter, thy faith has made you _____.
   Mark 5:34
9. Thy faith has _____ thee. *Luke 7:50*
10. If ye had faith as a_____of
    mustard seed. *Luke 17:6*
11. He had faith to be _____.*Acts 14:9*
12. The_____of faith shall save the sick.
    James 5:15
13. Being _____ by faith we have peace.
    Rom. 5:1
14. Now abideth _____, hope and charity.
    I Cor. 13:13

DAILY SCRIPTURE

Mon.	Lu. 17:5,6
Tues.	Heb. 11:1-7
Wed.	John 20:26-31
Thurs.	Mk. 5:35-43
Fri.	Acts 14:8-18
Sat.	Rom. 5:1-18
Sun.	James 5:13-18

PRAYER CONCERNS

Your Family & Relatives
Government Leaders
Missionaries
For the Unbelievers
Churches & Denominations
Your Own Church
Prayer and Praise

NOTE: You will be spiritually strengthened by completing two questions each day, reading the suggested scripture, and ministering in prayer for the concerns of the day.

THE MINISTRY OF THE MASTER—MONDAY
A Spirit Lifter

The pastor was calmly performing the wedding ceremony. The groom was not nearly so calm and was sweating profusely.

The pastor asked this nervous groom, "Wilt thou take this woman as thy lawful wedded wife?" The groom stammered, "I wilt."

God's Promise

"The Lord saves righteous men and protects them in times of trouble. He helps them and rescues them." (Psalm 37:39,40)

Practicing His Presence

Through what incident or person did you sense the presence of Christ yesterday? How did it make you feel?

A Pattern Of Prayer—Believe

Belief is action. This is not a passive word. It is not a willingness to conform to a set of statements, nor is it simply an acceptance of a creed.

Many people are what I term *"fat-goose"* Christians. They are without vibrancy or vitality. They desire more Bible Study. They want to be fed more. They want to be taught all the details of the Bible. They are even willing to be taught about prayer.

All of this feeding leaves them fat and flabby. They do not really believe. They want to study about believing instead of maintaining a lifestyle of believing.

The goose is put in a small pen. It is then fed constantly. The idea is to fatten the goose for market. The goose will exert no positive influence in life, but will live a dull overfed life until its death.

It is my prayer that you will seek to live out the teaching of the Word. The life of believing is what the Lord desires. Exercise your faith for great things today, and don't remain flabby spiritually. You do not need a dull, overfed spiritual life. You deserve to be alive in the Spirit.

PRAYER: *Father, may I be a channel through which will flow the water of life to myself and others. Amen.*

THE MINISTRY OF THE MASTER—TUESDAY
A Spirit Lifter

A lady was excitedly discussing her recent trip to China. She described how she was transported on her sightseeing experiences. "We went riding in one of those rickshaws, and believe it or not, they have horses in China that look just like men."

God's Promise

"You will increase my honor and comfort me once again." (Psalm 71:21, NIV)

Practicing His Presence

As you exercise your spiritual powers, you will become more aware of the spiritual side of life.

A Pattern Of Prayer—Believe

Probably everyone at one time or another has wondered about the existence of God. You have no doubt had those moments when you have thought that you needed tangible proof of the existence of God.

Although these thoughts may cross the mind, the truth is, we must believe the Lord exists and that He is a rewarder of those who seek Him. He is the Creator and Sustainer of all life.

Hudson Taylor was once asked, *"What proof do you have that there is a God?"* I feel his answer is worthy of our consideration. *"Only little things can be proved. Great things do not need it. They prove themselves."*

The Bible does not have a passage seeking to prove the existence of God. It assumes this and is written from this viewpoint. Your life and mine should not be lived trying to prove the existence of God. It should be lived believing God.

The Lord is not Someone who merely exists. He is Someone who is constantly at work in our midst. You can believe this moment that He is with you. He is and will continue to be.

PRAYER: *Thank you, Father, that you are the everlasting God and also that you are concerned about me and my problems. Amen.*

A Spirit Lifter

A chronic eavesdropper overheard this gem aboard the bus after working hours.

"You know, I wouldn't say anything about Dolly unless I could say something good. And, oh brother, is this ever good!"

God's Promise

"...We, too, are weak in our bodies, as He was, but now we live and are strong, as He is, and have all of God's power." (II Cor. 13:4, TLB)

Practicing His Presence

May you seek to quiet your mind, heart, and body to hear "the still small voice" speak to you today. He is certainly with you.

A Pattern Of Prayer—Believe

It is important that you believe God is very much interested in you and in every aspect of your life.

You do not need a fantastic miracle three times a week to keep believing in the Lord. You are to walk by faith. He is your friend and He is not going to forsake you.

You do not have your dear friend call you three times a day and say, *"I'm your friend. Don't you forget it!"* You just know that your friend is there and will be with you through thick and thin.

Thus, it is with God. He is with you. He doesn't have to come every day and say, *"Remember, I still exist. I am God. I am real."* No! It boils down to you believing He is with you always. The joy of His presence is assured through believing Him. I like the words of the prophet who displayed great faith.

"Though the fig tree does not blossom, nor fruit be on the vines, the produce of the olive fail and the fields yield no food, the flock be cut off from the fold and there be no herd in the stall, yet I will... joy in the God of my salvation."
(Habakkuk 3:17-18)

PRAYER: *Thank you, Father, that I can have your joy regardless of outward circumstances or inward feelings. Amen.*

THE MINISTRY OF THE MASTER—THURSDAY
A Spirit Lifter

The traffic officer stopped the motorist and said, "I'm going to give you a ticket for driving without a taillight."

The motorist got out to investigate and gave out a wail of dismay. He was practically distraught with anguish. "Come now," said the officer, "it's not as serious as all that. Just a little taillight."

"It's not the taillight I'm worried about. What's become of my trailer?"

God's Promise

"Is anyone among you suffering? Let him pray." (James 5:13)

Practicing His Presence

Are you consciously making the effort to be aware of the Lord in the small aspects of life?

A Pattern Of Prayer—Believe

If I were to come to your house and find you at the foot of the stairs with a broken leg, broken back, and other injuries, would it not be cruel to say, *"You better get up and call the doctor."* You'd reply, *"But I can't. I'm crippled."* How cruel if I would reply, *"But if you really wanted to, you could."*

It is obvious that a person injured to this degree has to depend upon someone else to summon help. Do you realize this same thing is true spiritually? There are individuals who cannot help themselves in the area of believing. They need the faith and belief of another person to undergird them at the moment.

This is one of the reasons I frequently encourage seriously ill individuals to take some of my faith. I share my belief in the Lord's healing power with them. They are too sick to pray or to muster much belief. They need me and their friends at that moment.

Today if you find it almost impossible to really believe the Lord cares, then may I suggest you stop and think about the fact that I am praying for you. I am believing that the Lord will undergird and bless you. He is with you. This I know and this I believe. May your realization of my sharing my faith with you help you to believe.

PRAYER: *Father, I pray that today my faith may blend with someone who needs help and that they will be undergirded with hope. Amen.*

THE MINISTRY OF THE MASTER—FRIDAY
A Spirit Lifter

The following is reported to have appeared in the newspaper years ago. "The world's largest shipment of hot dogs arrived from France last Monday because they owe us three million francs."

God's Promise

"He has made everything beautiful in its time." (Eccl.3:11, RSV)

Practicing His Presence

Through what incident or person did you sense His presence yesterday?

A Pattern Of Prayer—Believe

You and I are called to develop a climate of belief in which the fruitful aspects of the spirit can be manifest. If this climate exists many aspects of life will naturally care for themselves.

When we moved to Canton, the lot next to us was vacant and had been used as a dumping ground for years. The weeds were several feet high and the amount of rubbish on it was amazing. I began to clean up this lot. During the winter when the weeds were dead, I put the rubbish in piles. During the spring I would pull the weeds as they began to grow.

We ended up owning the lot. It was then that I had a bulldozer in to clear it. The man clearing the lot took away twenty-ton loads of rubbish from it.

Now the interesting thing to me is that today it is a beautiful lot. I never planted one ounce of grass seed on it. Yet I have a beautiful stand of grass. All I did was to clean up the mess and I had beauty. All the believing in the world would not have made the lot beautiful. I had to clean it up first.

Your faith will be stronger and your life more victorious if you would rid yourself of all that hinders your believing. Clean out the weeds in your life and let the fruit grow to God's glory. Believe that He will help you do this.

PRAYER: *Remove all trash from my life, Father. May I be willing to have you do this today. Amen.*

THE MINISTRY OF THE MASTER—SATURDAY
A Spirit Lifter

The telephone operator had placed a person-to-person call for Mr. Jones. When a child answered, the operator had a difficult time trying to convey to him that she had a person-to-person call for Mr. Alonso Jones. Finally, in desperation, she asked whether there was any other person at home.

The little boy said his brother was there. The operator asked whether she might talk to him. About three minutes later the little boy came back and said, "I can't lift him out of his play pen."

God's Promise

"You will keep in perfect peace him whose mind is steadfast, because he trusts in you." (Isaiah 26:3, NIV)

Practicing His Presence

I pray that being aware of His presence each day has been a meaningful experience for you.

A Pattern Of Prayer—Believe

It is reported that the famed astronomer, Russell Norris, was presenting a lecture concerning the Milky Way. He dramatically conveyed the tremendous size of the Milky Way. During the question and answer period a lady asked, *"If our world is so little, and the universe is so big, can we believe God pays attention to an individual?"*

Dr. Norris replied, *"My dear lady, this all depends upon how big a God you believe in."* How true this is. The belief Jesus desires is the one which believes God is big enough to care for every detail of your life.

Today is the day to begin to believe as never before that the Lord is interested in every facet of your being. There is no area of your life so insignificant that He is not concerned. He is not only concerned, but He is desirous of being a part of every area of your life.

May you believe that He is with you. I pray that you may believe in a big God today. A big God is One who is interested in little things. Nothing in your life is too small for Him."

PRAYER: *Father, may I never forget that you are a big God. A really big God. Amen.*

THE MINISTRY OF THE MASTER—SUNDAY

A Spirit Lifter

A lady tells of driving by a used car lot. There was a large shade tree on the lot and a nice picnic table under it. This was not unique, but the sign on the table was, because it read,

"Shady deals made here!"

God's Promise

"Be patient, brother, until the Lord's coming. Think of a farmer: how patiently he waits for the precious fruit of the ground. You, too, have to be patient; do not lose heart." (James 5:7,8, JB)

Practicing His Presence

I pray that amidst your busy day yesterday you were able to pull apart and sense the Lord's presence. How did this make you feel?

A Pattern Of Prayer—Believe

The apostle Paul gives to us a standard of belief which is shockingly simple. Yet, it is profound in its power.

"...Still I am not ashamed, for I know — I perceive, have knowledge of and am acquainted with Him — Whom I have believed (adhered to and trusted in and relied on), and I am (positively) persuaded that He is able to guard and keep that which has been entrusted to me and which I have committed (to Him), until that day." II Timothy 1:12 (amplified)

When Michael Faraday was at the point of death a friend asked, *"What are your speculations?"* Faraday's response was, *"Speculations! I have none. I am resting on certainty for I know in Whom I have believed."*

This is the victorious life we all are seeking. I feel that as we believe the Lord is with us, our prayer life becomes what it ought to be. It moves from believing only when we have had a specific answer to a prayer to believing in the face of all things.

The Lord is with you. Prayer becomes the fellowship with our Father and moves from a method of manipulating our Father.

PRAYER: *Thank you, Lord Jesus, for the certainty of your presence. I love you. Amen.*

A PATTERN OF PRAYER—PRAISE

Did you know that the word praise appears 151 times in the Psalms and twice in the heading of the Psalms? It appears 57 times from Psalms through the book of Revelation. Even Jeremiah, the weeping prophet, speaks of praise eleven times in his book. There is no doubt but what praise is part and parcel of the experience of worship in biblical days.

The word praise is an exciting word. I can't even say it without becoming more enthused. It brings a zest to my spirits, and gives to me a spiritual lift. Why don't you experiment with what it will do for you? Say three times *"Praise the Lord, praise the Lord, praise the Lord!"* Now try it again and this time say it outloud. Now didn't it do something for you?

Consider the meaning of praise and you will understand why you are lifted in spirit by praising the Lord.

The dictionary says —

"Commendation expressed, as of a person for his virtues, or concerning meritorious actions, applause. Thanksgiving for blessings conferred; laudation to God. The object, ground, reason, or subject of praise. ...Praise is the hearty approval of an individual, or of a number or multitude considered individually, and is expressed by spoken or written words; applause, the spontaneous outburst of many at one time. Applause is expressed in any way, by stamping of feet, clapping of hands, waving of handkerchiefs, etc., as well as by voice..."

The definition itself sounds exciting, doesn't it? When praise is part of your pattern of prayer it will bring new excitement to your prayer time. It will be part of the pattern which you can practice all day long.

Praise is not confined to a few moments during your devotional period. It is an attitude. It is a living expression of the living presence of the living Lord.

POINTS TO PONDER

1. How does a person praise the Lord?
2. Do we help or hinder others if we constantly praise the Lord?
3. Is it really possible to praise the Lord in any and all situations?

A PATTERN OF PRAYER—PRAISE

1. Let all the people _____ the Lord.
   Ps.67:3
2. The_____which should be offered to
   God continually is praise. *Heb. 13:15*
3. Those called out of darkness should show forth the _____
   of God. *I Pet. 2:9*
4. The_____led the whole multitude of
   disciples to rejoice and praise God. *Lu. 19:37*
5. A voice came out of the throne saying _____
   our God. *Rev. 19:5*
6. _____ praises to the Lord. *Ps. 9:11*
7. Paul and Silas _____ praises unto God
   at midnight. *Acts. 16:25*
8. The Levites praised the Lord with _____
   II Chron. 29:30
9. Four thousand praised the Lord with _____.
   I Chron. 23:5
10. His praise shall continually be in my_____.
    Ps. 34:1
11. _____ ye the Lord. *Ps. 148:1*
12. Let_____that has breath praise the Lord.
    Ps. 150:6
13. Bless the _____, O my soul. *Ps. 103:1*
14. _____ be the God and Father of our
    Lord Jesus Christ. *I Pet. 1:3*

DAILY SCRIPTURE

Mon.	Heb. 13:7-16
Tues.	I Pet. 2:4-10
Wed.	Lu. 19:28-40
Thurs.	Rev. 19:1-10
Fri.	Acts 16:25-34
Sat.	Ps. 150:1-6
Sun.	I Pet. 1:3-9

PRAYER CONCERNS

Your Family & Relatives
Government Leaders
Missionaries
For the Unbelievers
Churches & Denominations
Your Own Church
Prayer and Praise

NOTE: You will be spiritually strengthened by completing two questions each day, reading the suggested scripture, and ministering in prayer for the concerns of the day.

THE MINISTRY OF THE MASTER—MONDAY
A Spirit Lifter

The deeply religious missionary had just been put into the big pot by the cannibals. As he was being prepared for the upcoming feast, he whispered to a friend,

"Well, at least they will get a taste of religion. '

God's Promise

"I lie down and sleep; I wake again, for the Lord sustains me." (Psalm 3:5, RSV)

Practicing His Presence

I believe this will be a tremendous day for you if you take time to be aware of the Lord's presence.

A Pattern Of Prayer—Praise

I really am intrigued with the number of times the word praise and its many tenses appear in the Bible. Consider—

Praise—236 times
Praised—26 times
Praiseth—1 time
Praising—10 times
Praises—27 times

It is evident that believers are to praise the Lord and to rejoice in their relationship with Him. Your prayer life will be greatly enhanced if there is time devoted to conscious praise.

When I minister unto an individual with prayer it includes a time of praise. I praise the Lord that He is working in the life and that His wholeness is being extended. I praise the Lord for prayer and for the opportunity to release His power into the situation.

It is these moments of praise which helps me to deal with the difficulties so often faced. I do not know how the Lord will answer them or when, but I do know that I can always praise Him. This is a high point of my prayer time.

PRAYER: *Teach me to praise you, O Lord, and to lift high your Holy Name. Amen.*

137

THE MINISTRY OF THE MASTER—TUESDAY
A Spirit Lifter

The definition of a fisherman is a sportsman who catches fish sometimes by patience, sometimes by luck, but more often by the tale.

God's Promise

"When the spirit of truth comes he will lead you to the complete truth, since he will not be speaking as from himself but will say only what he has learned." (John 16:13, JB)

Practicing His Presence

You may have had a difficult day yesterday. I do hope, however, that you were able to pull apart and be aware of His presence. How did this make you feel?

A Pattern Of Prayer—Praise

What sacrifice should a believer make today? What should be brought unto the Lord as a sacrifice? The New Testament gives a clear cut answer to these questions.

"Through Him (Christ) therefore let us constantly and at all times offer up to God a sacrifice of praise, which is the fruit of lips that thankfully acknowledge and confess and glorify His name." Hebrews 13:15 (amplified)

Many feel that the true sacrifice is to give up some beloved habit or object. Others feel it is doing a super abundance of work. Others feel it is to submit to a form of self deprivation. All of these may have some value, but the sacrifice the Lord seeks is that of praise.

Praise can and should be lifted unto Him. Your time of prayer is really not complete if you have not praised the Lord. When praise is present we can rejoice regardless of what is happening. The victory is in Him. It is not in the answers. We are to be persons of praise.

PRAYER: *Teach me afresh that the sacrifices you love are the ones of praise, O Lord. Amen.*

THE MINISTRY OF THE MASTER—WEDNESDAY
A Spirit Lifter

The patient phoned his dentist for an immediate appointment. The tooth was aching to the point of being almost unbearable.

"I'd love to take you now," said the dentist, "but I'm very busy. In fact, this afternoon I have eighteen cavities to fill."

Whereupon, he hung up the phone, picked up his golf bag, and departed.

God's Promise

"Whoever would love life and see good days must keep his tongue from evil and his lips from deceitful speech." (I Peter 3:10, NIV)

Practicing His Presence

Was there any time yesterday when you knew the spiritual life was the most important aspect of your being?

A Pattern Of Prayer—Praise

Thomas Carlisle was a great writer and deep thinker. However, it is said that he was so attached to his mother that he made life miserable for everyone around him. Seldom, if ever, did he have a good word of praise for anyone. He especially ignored his wife.

After the death of his wife the following entry was found in her diary.

"Carlisle never praises me. If he says nothing, I have to be content that things are allright."

The absence of any praise was to be taken as tacit approval.

What a terrible way to die. She hungered for a little praise and received none. She longed for some recognition and appreciation and it was not forthcoming.

One of the ways you can praise the Lord today is to express some sincere praise to someone you know. Express appreciation to a member of your family or to a close friend. Even if you must force yourself to do it, I would suggest that you verbalize appreciation to someone today.

I am sure you would appreciate a word of praise from your boss, husband, wife, sister, brother, etc. There are many who would gladly work for less money if they received more praise. Just as we minister unto Jesus as we help the *"least of these,"* we also praise the Lord when we praise others.

PRAYER: *Set me free, Father, from any attachment to persons or things which would keep me from being loving. Amen.*

THE MINISTRY OF THE MASTER—THURSDAY
A Spirit Lifter

"Good heavens, Mother," cried Whistler when he saw the aged woman scrubbing the floor.

"Have you gone off your rocker?"

God's Promise

"Praise the Lord! For all who fear God and trust in him are blessed beyond expression. Yes, happy is the man who delights in doing his commands." (Psalm 112:1, TLB)

Practicing His Presence

Are you finding that being aware of His presence is exciting? I certainly am! Did you have an exciting day yesterday?

A Pattern Of Prayer—Praise

Again today, I want to emphasize the importance of praising God through sincerely praising others. The expression of praise toward another is uplifting to you and to the one you praise.

The importance of praise has been conveyed well by this unknown author.

"If with pleasure you are viewing
Any work a man is doing,
If you like him or you love him tell him now.
Don't withhold your approbation till
The preacher makes oration
And he lies with snowy lilies on his grave.
For no matter how you shout it,
He won't know how many tear drops you have shed,
If you think some praise is due him,
Now's the time to slip it to him,
For he cannot read his tombstone when he's dead."

PRAYER: *It is my prayer that I will tell you today that I love you, O Lord.*

THE MINISTRY OF THE MASTER—FRIDAY
A Spirit Lifter

The young bridegroom was patiently awaiting his cold drink. Finally, he could bear it no longer and went into the kitchen to check on his bride.

"And what is my snookums doing in here so long?" he asked.

The worried bride explained, "I rinsed the ice cubes in this warm water and now I can't find them."

God's Promise

"Let us run with endurance the race that is set before us, looking to Jesus, the author and finisher of our faith." (Heb. 12:1,2)

Practicing His Presence

The more I practice His presence, the more I behold Him in all things. Is this true of your life?

A Pattern Of Prayer—Praise

I read the following account of a divorce. The judge asked the couple if they really wanted the divorce.

The man replied, *"I think so."* The wife said, *"I really do."*

The judge said to the wife, *"Why are you so certain you want a divorce?"*

"All these 16 years I have kept this house, got his meals, mended his clothes, and cared for him in many other ways."

The judge said, *"Well, did he find any fault with you because of this loyalty?"*

She emotionally responded, *"No, that's not the problem. The problem is in all that time, after all that I have done for him, there was not one time when he said I had done a good job. I can't take it any longer."*

This husband would have indeed praised the Lord through praising his wife.

Sometimes we think praising God is some mystical verbalization. This is not true. We serve the Lord as we serve others. In like manner, we praise the Lord as we praise others.

PRAYER: *Father, help me to see that I bring praise to you through praising others in proper spirit and ways. Amen.*

141

THE MINISTRY OF THE MASTER—SATURDAY
A Spirit Lifter

The pastor had assured his congregation in this way, "Every blade of grass is a sermon."

A couple of days later the good Reverend was mowing his lawn. One of his beloved members passed by and gave evidence of having heard the last sermon and desiring a change in future ones. He said, "That's the stuff, Reverend! Cut your sermons short!"

God's Promise

"Before they call I will answer, while they are still speaking I will hear." (Jeremiah 29:12, RSV)

Practicing His Presence

Was there at least a little time during your busy schedule when you sensed His presence yesterday?

A Pattern Of Prayer—Praise

Kathryn II of Russia said, *"I praise loudly! I blame softly."* Wouldn't this make your day different? Why not try it today?

A Greek teacher is reported to have observed, *"Many men know how to flatter, but few men know how to praise."* A wise person observed, *"The sweetest of all sounds is praise."*

Prayer is not a detachment from life. Prayer is confrontation with all the realities of life. My concept of the pattern of prayer includes praise, but I do not detach praise from the common experiences of life. I believe praise should be forthcoming often and should be directed toward important people in your life. This is praising the Lord. This is a tangible expression of a meaningful experience.

I often speak of the fact that prayer is an art. Art is something which must be developed. Practice is an essential element. The practice of praise will help open your life to the power and presence of the Lord.

I praise the Lord for you and your willingness to read this devotional book and to develop your prayer life. Praise Jesus for you and yours.

PRAYER: *Help me today, Father, to speak a word of praise to someone who is very close to me. Amen.*

THE MINISTRY OF THE MASTER—SUNDAY
A Spirit Lifter

"Dear Mom,
Please send me something to eat. All we ever get to eat around here is breakfast, dinner and supper."

God's Promise

"The Lord said, I will cause all my goodness to pass in front of you, and I will proclaim my name, the Lord, in your presence." (Exodus 33:19, NIV)

Practicing His Presence

May you continually remain sensitive to the Spirit. How were you aware of His presence yesterday, and how did this make you feel?

A Pattern Of Prayer—Praise

I don't want to stress praising others so much that I neglect to emphasize praising the Lord directly. I believe there are times when privately and times when publicly you should praise the Lord.

1. In your prayer time say, *"Praise You, Jesus,"* or *"Praise You, Father,"* or *"Praise You, Holy Spirit."* You may want to repeat one or all of these statements. Try it today. It will really help lift your spirit.

2. Remember that when you praise the Lord you acknowledge He is in control. This is a great feeling. God does know what He is doing. In the midst of all your troubles and trials, you can praise Him. He is at work in and through you and praise is appropriate. Your self-pity party will be of little value to you and of no value to your friends. Your praising the Lord will be of great value to you and immense value to your friends.

My friend, Arthur J. Rait, wrote in 1963 — *"...through all eternity to thee a joyful song I'll raise; but all eternity is too short to utter all thy praise. Amen."*

PRAYER: *Father, even though I can never praise you enough may I not neglect to praise you often. Amen.*

Theme for the Week
A PATTERN OF PRAYER— TRUST

Trust is defined as *"a confident reliance on the integrity, veracity, or justice of another; confidence, faith. Something committed to one's care for use or safekeeping; a charge, responsibility. The state or position of one who has received an important charge."*

It is obvious from the above that trust is an essential aspect of a meaningful pattern of prayer. There must be the willingness to believe the Lord has your best interest in mind at all times. He does care for you and His ultimate will for your life is for your good and His glory.

It is interesting to note the number of times trust and kindred words appear in the Bible.

Trust—132 times. It occurs 17 times prior to the Psalms, 49 times in Psalms, 39 times in the Old Testament after Psalms and 27 times in the New Testament.

Trusted—28 times

Trustedest—3 times
Trusteth—23 times
Trusting—1 time
Trustee—1 time

You are called to a complete trust in the Lord even though you cannot, with the senses, prove the existence and love of God. He is too big to be proved and too loving to neglect anyone. We can trust Him completely.

The trust you need must begin on the inside. The Kingdom of God is within and it is in His Kingdom that trust may reign supreme. There is no other place where your trust can be placed with complete confidence.

Everyone and everything will at one time or another let you down. However, the Creator and Sustainer of the universe will never forsake you nor let you down. He is always there and is always interested in your wholeness. He has no ulterior motives, but reaches out to you in untarnished love. He, you can trust!

POINTS TO PONDER

1. Are you acquainted with anyone you feel you can completely trust?
2. What does it mean to really trust the Lord?
3. What is perfect peace and is it possible to attain it?

Daily Bibly Study and Daily Prayer Concerns
A PATTERN OF PRAYER—TRUST

1. It is better to_____in the Lord than to put confidence in men. *Ps. 118:8*
2. Trust in the Lord with all your _____. *Pro. 3:5*
3. _____ shall be with the one who trusts in the Lord. *Ps. 32:10*
4. The one who really trusts in the Lord shall be kept in perfect _____ _____. *Isa. 26:3*
5. I will look unto the _____. *Micah 7:7*
6. The Lord_____them that trust in Him. *Nahum 1:7*
7. We trust in the_____God. *I Tim. 4:10*
8. _____ is the one who trusts in the Lord. *Ps. 34:8*
9. He that trusts in_____shall fall. *Pro. 11:28*
10. _____ is the one who trusts in the Lord. *Pro. 16:20*
11. He that trusts in his own heart is a _____. *Pro. 28:26*
12. _____is the man who trusts in man. *Jer. 17:5*
13. Blessed is the man that trusts in the _____. *Jer. 17:7*
14. Let all the earth keep_____ before the Lord. *Hab. 2:20*

DAILY SCRIPTURE

Mon. Hab. 2:18-20
Tues. Ps. 32:8-11
Wed. Isa. 26:1-9
Thurs. I Tim. 4:6-10
Fri. Ps. 118:5-9
Sat. Pro. 16:12-24
Sun. Jer. 17:5-10

PRAYER CONCERNS

Your Family & Relatives
Government Leaders
Missionaries
For the Unbelievers
Churches & Denominations
Your Own Church
Prayer and Praise

NOTE: You will be spiritually strengthened by completing two questions each day, reading the suggested scripture, and ministering in prayer for the concerns of the day.

145

THE MINISTRY OF THE MASTER—MONDAY
A Spirit Lifter

The Sunday School teacher had been imparting truth concerning sharing.
"Brett, if you had a large, good apple and a small, wormy one and were told to share it with your brother, which would you give him?"

There was no hesitancy on the part of Brett as he answered, "Do you mean my big brother or my little brother?"

God's Promise

"Understand, therefore, that the Lord your God is the faithful God who for a thousand generations keeps his promises and constantly loves those who love him and who obey his commands." (Deuteronomy 7:9)

Practicing His Presence

Are you anticipating being aware of His presence throughout this day? If so, I am certain this will be a wonderful day for you.

A Pattern Of Prayer—Trust

Trust in the Lord is a wonderful admonition and a most worthy goal. However, there has never been anyone who at all times and in all places completely trusted the Lord.

The great saints of the past had their moments of doubt. The devout souls of today experience their moments of doubt. Simply because there are times when doubts appear, it does not mean you do not trust the Lord. The important thing is to have a basic trust in His goodness and mercy. *"The Dark Night of the Soul"* is the descriptive statement of the pilgrimage of some of the outstanding Christians of bygone days. They really trusted in the Lord, but at times they would experience a period when it seemed to them God did not care nor did He act in their lives.

May I encourage you, as you begin this week, to consider the word trust. May you appraise your degree of trust in the light of God's word and not according to your personal feelings.

Feelings will vary from moment to moment. The word is steadfast and eternal. You are not called to perfection. You are called to believe and in moments of weakness to ask the Lord to help your unbelief.

PRAYER: *It is you, O Lord, that I trust. Help that I will never stray from this position. Amen.*

THE MINISTRY OF THE MASTER—TUESDAY
A Spirit Lifter

Two tramps approached an Indiana farmer for food. "Fill that shed with kindling wood and you'll get the best meal you have had in weeks."

Several minutes later the farmer came by to see how they were doing. The one tramp was leaning on the ax handle and the other was jumping around with great dexterity. "Goodness," said the farmer. "I didn't know your friend was an acrobat."

The reply, "Neither did I till I cracked him on the shin with this ax."

God's Promise

"Whether you turn to the right or to the left, your ears will hear a Voice behind you, saying 'This is the way; walk in it.' " (Isaiah 30:21, NIV)

Practicing His Presence

In order to develop spiritual awareness be aware of the Lord's presence. How did you do this yesterday and how did it make you feel?

A Pattern Of Prayer—Trust

Martin Luther is considered one of the greatest Christians. He has influenced millions to trust the Lord and to believe in Him. Yet, Luther had moments of great despair.

He wrote one time that for more than a week—

"I was close to the gates of death and the gates of hell. I trembled in all my members. Christ was wholly lost. I was shaken by desperation and blasphemy of God."

If this could happen to a person of his stature, what about you and me? But God did not cast him aside. The Holy Spirit came to strengthen and to help him through this period.

I challenge you to really trust the Lord today. I also challenge you to accept the fact that, though it is hard for you to trust the Lord, He will honor even a grain of trust. He knows the inner thoughts of your heart and even when outwardly you are disturbed, He knows you have placed your confidence in Him.

You have prayed for yourself and others. Now complete the pattern of prayer by letting the results of your ministry of prayer in the hands of the Lord.

PRAYER: *All that I have or ever will accomplish is in your hands, Father. Help me to trust you for the fruit. Amen.*

THE MINISTRY OF THE MASTER—WEDNESDAY
A Spirit Lifter

An American and a Russian were debating the merits of their respective countries.

"In the United States," said the American, "we have freedom of speech."

"We have freedom of speech in the USSR, too," retorted the Russian.

"In this country," said the American, "I can walk up to Nixon and call him a jerk."

"That's nothing," replied the Russian, "in my country I, too, can walk up to Kosygin and say, 'Nixon is a jerk!' "

God's Promise

"Do not take revenge on someone who wrongs you. If anyone slaps you on the right cheek, let him slap your left cheek, too. And if someone takes you to court to sue you for your shirt, let him have your coat as well." (Matthew 5:39,40, TEV)

Practicing His Presence

I pray that you were very much aware of the Lord's presence in your life yesterday. Can you recall some specific incident or person which helped this awareness?

A Pattern Of Prayer—Trust

Some years ago Mary and I and the children were in Las Vegas for a day. I was astounded at the immense crowds and the intenseness with which they gambled. The ladies amazed me because of the amount of time and money they spent playing the slot machines. There were men playing them, but some of the women were really caught up in this game of chance.

There existed the hope that the right figures would appear on the machine and that they would hit the jack pot. They would put in the coin and hope for the best. This reminded me of the way many pray. It is as if they drop petitions in God's prayer answering machine and by begging trigger the mechanism into action. If they are lucky there will be a good return, and if not the lemons will appear.

The throne of Grace is not a spiritual slot machine. Rather, it is a place of mercy where the Lord continually pours out His blessings. You can trust Him with your life. He will care for it tenderly. He will bless you abundantly. The confidence you place in Him will not be rewarded necessarily materially, but there will be the deep assurance of His presence, power, and love. The pattern of prayer is perfected in and through trust. Without trust it is incomplete.

PRAYER: *Thank you, Father, for the moment by moment grace which you daily give to me. Amen.*

THE MINISTRY OF THE MASTER—THURSDAY
A Spirit Lifter

The man was bragging about his new hearing aid. "I can hear a leaf drop a block away. A drop of water is like an explosion. I can hear tears in the apartment next door. This hearing aid is the greatest in the world."

"What kind is it?" asked his friend.

"It's a quarter to nine," he answered.

God's Promise

"God will fulfill all your needs, in Christ Jesus, as lavishly as only God can." (Philippians 4:19, JB)

Practicing His Presence

Your awareness of the Lord's presence sometimes gets clouded by circumstances. What do you do when this happens?

A Pattern Of Prayer—Trust

Brother Lawrence vividly describes his pilgrimage of trust. He writes concerning his entrance into religion.

> *"I took a resolution to give myself up to God as the best return I can make for His love and for the love of Him to renounce all besides. Such was my beginning and yet I must tell you that for the first ten years I suffered much. The apprehension that I was not devoted to God as I wished to be, my past sins always present to my mind and the great unmerited favors which God did me were matter and source of my sufferings. During this time I fell often and rose presently — during this time I thought of nothing but to end my days and these troubles which did not at all diminish the trust I had in God and which served only to increase my faith. I found myself changed all at once and my soul which to this time was in trouble felt a profound inward peace as if she were in a center and place of rest."*

It is evident that his pilgrimage to vital trust took many years. You and I must put our confidence in the Lord regardless of how we feel or the circumstances surrounding us.

PRAYER: *Father, you know my pilgrimage of trust is not always consistent, but thank you that you understand. Amen.*

THE MINISTRY OF THE MASTER—FRIDAY
A Spirit Lifter

The hypochondriac was complaining to the doctor. He said he had a fatal liver disease. "That's silly," the doctor said, "how would you know? With that disease there is no discomfort of any kind."

"Those are my symptoms exactly," replied the hypochondriac.

God's Promise

"I will forgive their wickedness and will remember their sins no more." (Jeremiah 31:24, NIV)

Practicing His Presence

I do hope being aware of His presence has been exciting for you. May you continually remain sensitive to the Spirit.

A Pattern Of Prayer—Trust

I cannot emphasize enough that your trust in the Lord is not dependent upon your expected specific answers to your prayers. If you have a pre-determined answer for your prayer, you have already distorted the pattern of prayer. Your prayers are to be lifted unto the Lord. Your answers are to be left in the hands and wisdom of the Lord.

Somerset Maugham tells of hearing the thought that if you prayed anything could happen. All you had to do was believe. He prayed one night for his stuttering to be taken away. He visualized it all gone. He now knew the kids wouldn't make fun of him anymore. The next morning he dashed downstairs to greet his parents. He was so excited because he had asked God to take away his stuttering, and he just knew it was gone. Almost breathlessly he said to his parents, *"Goo-goo-goo-good morning."* It was not gone. He was embarrassed again. He says he dashed to his room faster than he came downstairs and vowed never to pray again. He had put his trust in an answer and not in the One who is the Answer.

If you are going to validate prayer by your receiving the specific answer you demanded, your prayer life is at least tarnished if not finished. The Bible teaches that you are to trust the Lord. You cannot trust either your requests or your answers.

PRAYER: *Dear Lord, help me to keep my eyes off specific desires and to keep my heart open to continual communion with you. Amen.*

THE MINISTRY OF THE MASTER—SATURDAY
A Spirit Lifter

A lawyer tore excitedly into court and asked that a new trial be granted a client found guilty the day previous. "I've uncovered new evidence," declared the lawyer.

"Of what nature?" asked the judge.

"My client," the lawyer told him, "has an extra six thousand dollars. I only found out about it this morning."

God's Promise

"This is how we know that love is: Jesus Christ laid down his life for us." (I John 3:16)

Practicing His Presence

I do hope that you were able to pull apart yesterday and be aware of the Lord's presence in the small things of life.

A Pattern Of Prayer—Trust

The desire, ability, and reality of trust is not determined by your outward circumstances. This depends upon your inward spiritual depth. The storms of life may buffet, but the ship of trust cannot sink. It will remain afloat by the grace of God.

Two artists were commissioned to paint a picture of trust and confidence in the Lord. The one painted a beautiful pastoral scene. The meadow was green and aflame with blooming flowers. The sky was exotic blue and dotted with playful clouds. Cows grazed in the distance and a happy family sat on their back porch serenely surveying the tranquility of the moment.

The second picture depicted one of the most devastating storms imaginable. The sky was ominous, the lighting sharp and terrifying. The heavy rain was lashing against the rocks and added force to the raging waterfall. The trees nearly touched the ground as they bent before the onslaught of the wind.

A close inspection revealed a small bird in the cleft of a rock unruffled by the storm. Underneath the picture was the one word — PEACE. This one was chosen because it depicted the peace of God in the midst of the turmoil of the world. You can trust Him at all times and in all ways.

PRAYER: *Thank you, Father, for your peace which passeth understanding even in the midst of all our problems. Amen.*

THE MINISTRY OF THE MASTER—SUNDAY
A Spirit Lifter

The surgeon's friend was congratulating him concerning a successful operation. He pointed out that he had operated just in time. "Why, you got that patient in just in the nick of time. By tomorrow he would have been well."

God's Promise

"The Kingdom we are given is unshakable; let us therefore give thanks to God, and so worship, with reverence and awe, for our God is a devouring fire." (Hebrews 12:28,29, NEB)

Practicing His Presence

May you continually seek to quiet yourself and be aware of the Lord's presence in the small things in life. How did you do this yesterday?

The Pattern Of Prayer—Trust

There are some practical steps which will help strengthen your trust in the Lord.

1. Don't get up tight when you minister in prayer to others or to yourself. You do not have to fuss with God nor do you need to shout at Him. I would encourage you to relax in the confidence He hears your prayers. You are not the deliverer, God is. You are not the healer, God is. You are not the Answer, God is. Realizing these truths, you can trust Him.

2. Leave the results of your prayers in His hands. The Lord's reputation is not at stake. No one is going to make Him less than God, nor can your pious prayers make Him more than He is. Do not worry about your reputation if prayers are not answered as some may desire. You are not called to maintain a reputation as a great prayer warrior. You are called to be obedient unto the Lord.

3. Maintain your confidence in the Lord. The place of quiet peace and rest is not a specific spot, but rather it is an attitude. It is the spirit of confidence in God's desire for the best for you. He wants you to be whole of body, mind, and spirit. May you trust Him for all things.

PRAYER: *In quiet confidence I rest my life in you, O Lord. Thank you for caring for me now and throughout eternity. Amen.*

Theme for the Week
GOD'S HEALTH CARE PLAN—LOVE

The great emphasis upon healing today is good, but often one side of wholeness is neglected. It is the emphasis upon a life-style assuring health instead of upon the restoration to health after illness.

I believe the Lord would have us follow His health care plan and thus save us many illnesses. He has beautifully presented His plan in His holy Word. We have the privilege and responsibility to discover His plan and to follow it.

Some individuals advocate a health care plan for everyone in our nation. Some would have socialized medicine with the concept that the best in medical ministry would be available to all regardless of race, income, or creed. As commendable as these goals may be, it is still self-evident that we need God's health care plan above all others.

One of the essential ingredients of His plan is love. Love is illusive in definition, but essential to a purposeful and worthwhile life.

The biggest problem in presenting the Lord to others is convincing them that they are loved by the Lord. Most people can conceive that Christ died for the world, but it is difficult for them to understand that He died for them as individuals. The death of Christ remains generalized instead of applied specifically to them.

To ask whether God loves you is as ridiculous as to ask, *"Do birds fly? Do fish swim? Do thirsty plants require water?"* It is obvious these questions must be answered in the affirmative. Thus, with the Lord, it is obvious that He loves us, but sometimes we miss even the obvious.

"God is love" (I John 4:8,16) is not a definition of love, but is a matter-of-fact statement concerning God.

Love is experienced more than it is defined. Your life can come to a new wholeness if you permit the love of the Lord to permeate every aspect of your life.

Try this part of His health care plan now. A new wholeness will be yours in so doing.

POINTS TO PONDER

1. What is a definition of love?
2. How did God reveal His love to the whole world?
3. When do you feel you first experienced the love of another person?

GOD'S HEALTH CARE PLAN—LOVE

1. God is _____. *I John 4:8*
2. Thou shalt_____ the Lord thy God with all thine heart. *Deut. 6:5*
3. He that_____ father or mother more than me is not worthy of me. *Mt. 10:37*
4. The Lord_____all them that love him. *Ps. 145:20*
5. It has not entered into the heart the things God hath prepared for them that _____ him. *I Cor. 2:9*
6. Perfect love casts out _____. *I John 4:18*
7. A new_____I give unto you, that ye love one another. *John 13:34*
8. Ye yourselves are taught of God to_____ one another. *I Thess. 4:9*
9. This is the message that ye heard from the _____, that we should love one another. *I John 3:11*
10. Thou shalt love thy_____as thy self. *Mt. 19:19*
11. Therefore love is the _____ of the law. *Rom. 13:10*
12. God so_____the world that He gave His only begotten Son. *John 3:16*
13. The greatest of all is _____. *I Cor. 13:13*
14. He said to him the third time, Peter do you_____ _____ me. *John 21:17*

DAILY SCRIPTURE

Mon.	I John 4:7-12
Tues.	Deut. 6:1-9
Wed.	John 13:31-34
Thurs.	Rom. 13:7-14
Fri.	John 3:16-21
Sat.	John 21:15-22
Sun.	I Cor. 13:1-13

PRAYER CONCERNS

Your Family & Relatives
Government Leaders
Missionaries
For the Unbelievers
Churches & Denominations
Your Own Church
Prayer and Praise

NOTE: You will be spiritually strengthened by completing two questions each day, reading the suggested scripture, and ministering in prayer for the concerns of the day.

THE MINISTRY OF THE MASTER—MONDAY
A Spirit Lifter

Voice over the phone: "Tommie Jones will not be in Sunday School today because he is sick."

Pastor: "Oh, I am so sorry to hear that. We were going to have the test on the Ten Commandments this morning. To whom am I speaking?

Voice: "This is my father speaking."

God's Promise

Do you ever have a problem with anger? The Bible is quite blunt concerning this.

"A short-tempered man is a fool." (Proverbs 14:17, TLB)

Practicing His Presence

Seek to quiet your body, mind, and spirit. Now reflect upon your day yesterday. Was there any time you were able to draw apart and be aware of His nearness? How did this make you feel?

God's Health Care Plan—Love

Your life will be enriched as you give and as you are willing to receive love. Your release of love toward others will affect their health for the better.

An experiment involved giving a dozen rabbits tender, loving care. Their food was taken to them; they were petted and talked to almost as if they were human.

Another dozen was provided the necessities of life, but in a cold and indifferent manner. Their food was dispensed to them without any person coming close to the pen. They were ignored as completely as possible over a period of many weeks.

The examination following this test period revealed that the rabbits which had received TLC were healthier than those which had been neglected.

It is not always easy for you and me to realize how important it is that we manifest love through our words and actions. I think we would perhaps be more loving if we realized how influential the spirit of love is in the lives of those around us. God's health care plan is such that hate brings disease, and love releases the forces of healing.

"Love is what makes the world go round" is more than a song. It is an essential facet of God's health care plan. Why not enroll in His health care plan today by subscribing to acts of love on your part?

PRAYER: *Father, help me to be willing to receive the love you pour out upon me. Amen.*

THE MINISTRY OF THE MASTER—TUESDAY
A Spirit Lifter

"Dear God, take care of Mommy, and Daddy, and my little sister, and Grandma, and Grandpa, and everybody. And please God, take care of yourself, 'cause if anything happens to you, we're all sunk." This was the prayer of the little five year old.

God's Promise

The Lord provides unlimited blessings, doesn't He?

"Jesus said unto him, If thou canst believe, all things are possible to him that believeth." (Mark 9:23, KJV)

Practicing His Presence

Even in the small things in life we can sense the presence of the Lord. Did you sense His presence yesterday in some small aspect of your own life?

God's Health Care Plan—Love

God's health care plan involves love which goes two ways. It is love which flows from you to Him and from Him to you. I cannot emphasize enough the importance of love being perceived as flowing both ways. Love which is emitted, but not received, is love stifled. Love which is bestowed, but not returned, is love paralyzed.

Let me illustrate this point. Since becoming a pastor in 1948, I have counseled with many people. The most miserable, negative, and defeated persons are those who feel they love, but their love is not returned. The husband feels he desperately loves his wife, but she no longer loves him. Who is most miserable? The husband is, of course. On the other hand, the wife may desperately desire to save the marriage, but the husband says he no longer loves her because he has found a new love. Who is the most miserable? The wife is, of course. She is extending love which is not being returned.

My experience has shown that the biggest spiritual problem is not to get individuals to love God. The problem is to get them to appreciate the fact that God loves them. Most feel they give love which is not returned. Therefore, their lives remain confused, defeated, and miserable.

Some catch a glimpse of the eternal truth that God loves them. These are the individuals who are most nearly whole. They are the ones who have the spring in their steps and joy in their hearts.

PRAYER: *Lord, may I be willing to receive the love of others as well as to try to bestow love upon and toward others. Amen.*

THE MINISTRY OF THE MASTER—WEDNESDAY
A Spirit Lifter

The seven-year-old was told by his mother that he could not attend the church picnic because of his poor behavior. The next day she had changed her mind. He took the news quietly and almost indifferently although previously he had desperately wanted to attend. Bewildered, she asked, "What's the matter, don't you want to go to the picnic?"

He sighed, "Yeah, but it is too late, Mom. I've already prayed for rain."

God's Promise

I really like this promise from the Lord Jesus Himself.

"Where two or three gather together because they are mine, I will be there among them." (Matthew 18:20, TLB)

Practicing His Presence

As you exercise your spiritual powers, you will become more aware of the spiritual side of life. How did you sense the presence of His Spirit yesterday?

God's Health Care Plan—Love

Love cannot and should not remain vague or pointless. There is not great merit in saying, *"I love everybody."* There is no great power in saying, *"God loves the world."*

The impact comes when we make the decision to love someone and when we come to realize that God loves us. This makes love definite and dynamic. Sometimes we are inclined to become so general in our love that we are grasping at nothingness. This leaves a vagueness to life and a vacuum in our heart.

You may have heard of the girl who told her friend that she had received a love letter from her boyfriend which left her depressed. Her friend could not comprehend why initial enthusiasm had waned so rapidly. Then the girl said that it was a very touching and beautifully written letter; however, it was mimeographed.

How many other girls had received the same letter? The generalness of the message took away the significance of the message. You cannot love in generalities. I pray that today you will know the wholeness of giving yourself in love to your spouse, to your children, and to your God. You are not being selfish to make a decision to love someone. You are being untrue to yourself and others not to make such a decision.

PRAYER: *I thank you, Father, that your love is so specific. I thank you that Jesus loved me so much He died for me. Amen.*

THE MINISTRY OF THE MASTER—THURSDAY
A Spirit Lifter

An eager hand went up as the teacher asked the class who could repeat last week's memory verse. A little girl gave the verse and then enthusiastically said, "I even remember the zip code. It is Luke 19:10."

God's Promise

As you exercise your spiritual powers, you will become more aware of the spiritual side of life. How did you sense the presence of His Spirit yesterday?

Practicing His Presence

How did being consciously aware of His presence make you feel yesterday? Make this another wonderful day for yourself by practicing His presence.

God's Health Care Plan—Love

Do you feel fragmented and frustrated? If so, is there a possibility you are searching for scattered love instead of specific love?

I meet many people who have never really given themselves to anyone or to anything in particular. Love to them remains vague. There is no person to whom they have declared, *"I have decided to love you."* By this statement, it is meant that they have made a commitment to care and to share regardless of circumstances or actions. They desire to discipline themselves to love and care.

Discipline is important in life. It is important especially in the area of love in your life. I read that the Olympic gold medal winner, Bruce Jenner, devoted as many as ten hours a day in practice to win the decathalon. He loved to win, and he disciplined himself to this end.

May you love to love and discipline yourself to this end. The commitment in love to your spouse, your children, your church, your city, and your job will not make you a more narrow person. It will expand you as an individual.

Specific love commitments make you a better person and not a more self-centered person. Love is manifest through our actions and our devotion to specifics. It permeates all we do because it is definitely a part of what we do.

PRAYER: *Dear Jesus, I want the disciplined life. I want to have your power to be a disciplined lover of all. Amen.*

THE MINISTRY OF THE MASTER—FRIDAY
A Spirit Lifter

"Tell me, my little man," said the pastor to Jimmy, "do you say your prayers every night?"

"Oh no, sir," came the ready response. "Not every night. Some nights I don't want anything."

God's Promise

"Trust the Lord completely; don't ever trust yourself. In everything you do, put God first, and he will direct you and crown your efforts with success." (Proverbs 3:5,6 TLB)

Practicing His Presence

Amidst the activities of your busy day, pull apart a moment and think about how the Lord's presence affected your day yesterday.

God's Health Care Plan—Love

How much do you love? How much would you be willing to do for another member of your family, neighborhood, or church?

I was impressed with the heartwarming account of the capture of the Prince of Cappadocia. He, his wife, and his children were captured and taken to Rome. Augustus ordered that the Prince and the eldest son were to be killed, but his wife and youngest son were to be spared. The guards sought to follow through on this order but were stymied because each boy claimed to be the oldest son. Each wanted to die for the other.

Finally, the guards made the mother point out the oldest. She determined that the youngest should die because she felt the eldest would be most capable of caring for her. The youngest did not object and gave his life for his brother.

The emperor, Augustus, received the report of what happened and was so impressed that one would die for his brother that he brought the oldest son and the mother into his court and cared for them until their dying day.

This kind of love, that of one son for his brother, is the kind which nourishes a wholeness otherwise missing. Your life will take on new dimensions when you come really to understand that Christ has died for you. He died, not generally for the world, but specifically for you and for all others.

PRAYER: *Father, help me to love though action and not simply through words. Amen.*

159

THE MINISTRY OF THE MASTER—SATURDAY

A Spirit Lifter

He had a close call while traveling with his parents. The car door had flown open, and he was almost thrown upon the pavement. However, as he frantically held on to the arm rest, the car was brought to a halt by a worried father. After a few minutes when everyone's nerves had settled a bit, the mother said: "Why don't you thank God for saving your life today?" His comeback was typical four-year-old truthfulness. "What for? I was the one that held on!"

God's Promise

"Hope deferred makes the heart sick, but desire fulfilled is a tree of life." (Proverbs 13:12, NASV)

Practicing His Presence

Can you recall some specific incident or person which helped your awareness of the Lord's presence yesterday? Take a moment and reflect upon this.

God's Health Care Plan—Love

When and how does God love? Does He love only when you have been good and only when He has a spare moment? Does he love sparingly or is His love bestowed in abundance?

Many distressed souls feel that God loves them only when they are good or lucky. They cannot conceive that He bathes them in love constantly and that His love is more consistent than the rays of the sun.

I liken some individuals' concept of God's love to the medicine dropper approach. They picture God in heaven with His love dropper in hand. Occasionally, he squeezes the rubber top and dispenses a drop of His love upon them. He does this whenever they have done a good deed, said a nice prayer, gone to church, or just had a lucky day and happened to walk under a drop of His love. It is impossible for them to accept the fact that He loves them always.

We, who have crisscrossed several continents by plane, know that the sun shines all day long. It may be cloudy at takeoff, but in a few minutes the sun is shining beautifully as you fly above the clouds. The clouds have not destroyed the sun. They have only lessened its brightness. Our actions may lead us to feel God's love is withdrawn, but this feeling of not being loved is more wrong than thinking the sun has ceased to shine.

PRAYER: *It is your love which completely and always surrounds me which sustains me. Thank you, Father. Amen.*

THE MINISTRY OF THE MASTER—SUNDAY
A Spirit Lifter

"Daddy, why does it rain?" "Why son, God makes it rain so that the flowers will grow, the grass will be nice and green, and the leaves of the trees make a lot of shade." Pondering that answer for a few seconds, his next question was, "So, why does it rain on the sidewalk?"

God's Promise

Isn't friendship a blessing in your life?

"How wonderful it is, how pleasant, when brothers live in harmony." (Psalms 133:1, TLB)

Practicing His Presence

The presence of the Lord is our hope and comfort. What a tremendous day you will have as you are aware of His presence throughout it!

God's Health Care Plan—Love

If actions are the bricks of life, then love is the mortar which holds them in proper place. It is love which endures above all else. It is love which brings the desired harmony and wholeness to life. Someone has written,

"Rock is strong, but iron breaks it in two. Fire melts iron, but water extinguishes fire. Clouds come and take away the water. The winds drive the clouds away. Man may withstand the wind, but fear unmans man. Wine can dispel fear, but sleep overcomes wine. Death sweeps away even sleep. What then endures? Only love. Love that is deep and love that is genuine — that alone remains."

Believing the above with all our hearts would make a vast difference in the world.

Love is identifying yourself as much as possible with the one you love. Jesus completely identifies with you. He knows your joys; He knows your pain; He knows your victories; He knows where you are hurting.

One person told another of his love for him. The person said, *"Do you know what pains me?"* He replied, *"No! How can I know what pains you?"* The response was, *"Unless you know what pains me, how can you really love me?"*

You must identify to love. God's love is real and complete because His identification with your situation is real and complete.

PRAYER: *Lord Jesus, I want to be completely identified with you. I want to be one with you in spirit and truth. Amen.*

Theme for the Week
GOD'S HEALTH CARE PLAN—JOY

Frequently we read of ways to be healthier, happier, and more content. One time I made a list of suggestions and discovered that, if I did them all, there would not be time for life itself.

For instance, you should brush your hair at least one hundred strokes a day. You should lift weights for about ten minutes every day. You should take five minutes warming exercises before lifting weights. You should walk at least forty-five minutes per day. You should have someone rub your feet at least three times a week for ten minutes at a time. During the day everyone should take catnaps of from three to fifteen minutes in length. Well, the list goes on and on. It is obvious that, if we were to do all that some suggest, there would be no time left to do the essentials of life.

God has some wonderful things to say about your health and wholeness. He is interested in your total person. He is especially interested in the spiritual aspect of your being. His health care plan involves the fruit of the Spirit. Consider,

> *"But the fruit of the Spirit is love, joy, peace, longsuffering, gentleness, goodness, faith, meekness, temperance: against such there is no law."*
> *Galatians 5:22,23*

This week I want to consider joy as a part of God's health care plan. The joyful person will be a healthier person. Joy affects your entire being. The wisdom of the past is pertinent for the present. *"A merry heart doeth good like a medicine, but a broken spirit drieth the bones."*

The definition of joy is gladness, rejoicing, or a lively emotion of happiness.

Can you imagine what a difference it would make in your life this week if you possessed and imparted real joy? I suggest that right now you seek to rejoice and to lift your spirits. It is true that how you feel on the inside determines how you are on the outside.

POINTS TO PONDER

1. What is real joy?
2. Is it possible to be joyful in all situations?
3. What is meant by the statement that Christ is your joy?

GOD'S HEALTH CARE PLAN—JOY

1. The_____of the Lord is your strength.
   Neh. 8:10
2. In thy _____ is fullness of joy. *Ps. 16:11*
3. The ransomed of the Lord shall return, and come to Zion with songs and everlasting_____upon their heads.
   Isa. 35:10
4. The kingdom of God is not meat and drink, but righteousness, and peace, and_____in the Holy Ghost. *Rom. 14:17*
5. Having received the word in much affliction, with joy in the _____ _____. *I Thess. 1:6*
6. The joy of the hypocrite is but for a_____.
   Job. 20:5
7. They that sow in tears shall _____ in joy.
   Ps. 126:5
8. As sorrowful, yet always _____. *II Cor. 6:10*
9. Count it all joy when you fall into divers_____.
   James 1:2
10. Joy shall be in heaven over one sinner that _____ _____. *Luke 15:7*
11. Singing and making_____in your hearts unto the Lord. *Eph. 5:19*
12. These things I have spoken unto you, that my joy might _____ _____in you. *John 15:11*
13. Rejoice that your names are written in _____.
    Luke 10:20
14. Your sorrow shall be turned into _____.
    John 16:20

DAILY SCRIPTURE

Mon.	Neh. 8:9-12
Tues.	Isa. 35:1-10
Wed.	I Thess. 1:2-10
Thurs.	James 1:1-8
Fri.	Luke 15:1-7
Sat.	Luke 10:17-22
Sun.	John 16:19-24

PRAYER CONCERNS

Your Family & Relatives
Government Leaders
Missionaries
For the Unbelievers
Churches & Denominations
Your Own Church
Prayer and Praise

NOTE: You will be spiritually strengthened by completing two questions each day, reading the suggested scripture, and ministering in prayer for the concerns of the day.

THE MINISTRY OF THE MASTER—MONDAY
A Spirit Lifter

The parents and their children each had a prayer before going to bed. Things were as usual for all but the little four-year-old who, you might say signed off instead of closed her prayer. She ended with "...And God bless Mommy and Daddy and everybody. Amen, and FM."

God's Promise

"When the poor and needy seek water, and there is none, and their tongue faileth for thirst, I the Lord will hear them, I the God of Israel will not forsake them." (Isaiah 41:17, KJV)

Practicing His Presence

The feeling of His presence may not always be yours, but its reality is always yours. How did this affect your life yesterday?

God's Health Care Plan—Joy

Is there any relationship between joy and health? There certainly is. Pause for a moment and imagine deep joy within your total being. Now doesn't that make you feel better? Even if you are on a bed of affliction, embroiled in troubles way over your head, or plagued by contemptuous friends, a spirit of joy will give you a different approach to your problem, regardless of what it may be.

Have you heard about the gentleman who says he laughed himself to health and wholeness? The physicians said his illness was terminal. His life on this planet was limited to but a few months. He discovered a cure which may not work for all, but certainly worked for him.

He disciplined himself to remain in a room where he could put emphasis upon joy. He obtained as many cassettes and movies as he could which emphasized joy, fun, and laughter. He listened to and watched these stories and movies constantly. If visitors came, he would not permit them to say anything discouraging. In fact, he preferred that his friends tell him jokes instead of commiserating with him on his hopeless condition.

There was more to this than the laughter. It was more than constantly having a life of funny jokes. His was a life lived in joy. This spirit of joy affected his entire being. His was not a laughter of scorn, but a laughter of the deep contentment which is yours and mine when we are sincerely joyful.

PRAYER: *Thank you, Lord, for the joy you have brought to my life. It is deep and abiding and I am grateful. Amen.*

THE MINISTRY OF THE MASTER—TUESDAY
A Spirit Lifter

The instructor was teaching the wonders of the universe. Among her fascinating facts was the one that our light comes from the sun at the rate of 186,000 miles per second. Almost in awe she said, "Isn't that amazing? Why it is almost unbelievable!"

One little boy who certainly had the disposition of a pessimist, retorted, "Aw, I dunno, after all, it's downhill all the way."

God's Promise

The Lord promises us freedom in our walk with Him.

"For the power of the life-giving spirit — and this power is mine through Christ Jesus — has freed me from the vicious circle of sin and death." (Romans 8:2, TLB)

Practicing His Presence

I am amazed at how often the Lord has felt near while I am involved in the ordinary experiences of life. The more I practice His presence, the more I behold Him in all things. Is this true of your life?

God's Health Care Plan—Joy

A joyful heart can make us realize accomplishments which otherwise would evade us. Many years ago I officiated at the marriage of an older couple. Each person had lost his spouse and had found a new love in life. He had won her through his jolly spirit and joyfulness. He loved to sing songs to her which he composed and sang from the depth of his soul.

He would gaze into her eyes while singing his ballads, and she would sit enthralled with the beauty and joy of it all. They had truly discovered a wholeness which had been lacking for years.

A few months after their wedding she left him. She could not adjust to the new situation. I spent time counseling both of them. It looked hopeless to me. Yet, he was not to be denied the woman he loved. Even though she had gone to live with a son, he would visit her and keep singing the songs of joy. Even when she would not permit him to come in and talk to her, he would sing his ballads of joy and love.

In the end he got her back. Joy had won the day. She could not resist the man who maintained the song on his lips and in his heart. They continued to live together and had many wonderful years rejoicing in the presence of each other and of the Lord.

Your problems today will be lighter tomorrow if joy is permitted to permeate your soul. God says that this is part of His health care plan.

PRAYER: *Father, I want your joy to permeate the very marrow of my bones. Amen.*

THE MINISTRY OF THE MASTER—WEDNESDAY
A Spirit Lifter

A little child was in church for the first time and was fascinated by the many facets of the service. He seemed to be especially impressed by people putting money in the offering plate. He just knew each one was paying an admission charge. When the plate got to his pew, all heard this little voice exclaim, "Don't pay for me, Daddy. I'm under five."

God's Promise

"And the Lord will continually guide you, and satisfy your desire in scorched places, and give strength to your bones; and you will be like a watered garden, and like a spring of water whose waters do not fail."
(Isaiah 58:11, NASV)

Practicing His Presence

May you continually remain sensitive to the Spirit. How were you aware of His presence yesterday, and how did this make you feel?

God's Health Care Plan—Joy

Ardis Whitman has written of joy and its mystery in this way.

"Suddenly we are aware of every living thing. Every leaf, every flower, every cloud, the mayfly hovering above the pond, the crow cawing in the treetop."

She is saying that the little things of life take on a new glow when joy is present. Life is more wholesome and healthy when joy is part of your steady diet.

One of Satan's favorite tricks is to give to you a disgruntled and discouraged spirit. He delights in keeping you from rejoicing. He even makes some Christians feel pious by making them look pitiful. Your very appearance is affected by the attitude of your inner being.

"A merry heart makes a cheerful countenance, but by sorrow of the heart the spirit is broken." Proverbs 15:13

I believe that Moses' face shone after his talks with God because of his deep inner joy. He knew he was doing the Lord's will. He knew the source of his power and strength.

PRAYER: *May the joy within, Father, shine forth in my countenance, voice, and actions. Amen.*

THE MINISTRY OF THE MASTER—THURSDAY
A Spirit Lifter

"What do you mean you aren't going to school tomorrow?" demanded his mother. "Well, it's no use, and it's no fun," said the youngster. "Well, why not?" asked his mother.

"Well, I can't read. And I can't write. And the teacher won't let me talk, so what's the use?"

God's Promise

"He who goes about as a slanderer reveals secrets; therefore, do not associate with a gossip." (Proverbs 20:19, NASV)

Practicing His Presence

If you are as I am, your awareness of the Lord's presence sometimes gets clouded by certain events. What do you do when this happens to you?

God's Health Care Plan—Joy

Many touching stories have arisen concerning the life of Martin Luther. This great man of God was a real human being. He sometimes had trouble dealing with the vicissitudes of life just as you do.

It is reported that one morning his wife, Katie, asked him, *"Is God dead?"* Luther snapped back, *"He certainly isn't!"* Her retort was, *"Then why don't you stop looking and acting as if He were?"*

Too much of the time many of us look and act as if God were dead. The joy of the Lord has departed from the heart, and the glory of His presence has faded from our countenance.

Can you tell by appearance when someone is angry at you? Have you ever caught a dagger-like look thrown your way? Some friend, your spouse, or family member has sent you a message of anger and disapproval through his countenance. The emotion could not be hidden.

In like manner we can impart the message of joy. How much better it is when the emotion of joy is conveyed to others! Life then remains a joy instead of a burden.

"He that is of a merry heart hath a continual feast" Proverbs 15:15 is a verse which should be memorized by every believer. There is no need to be feasting on that which destroys. Your heart and mind need to be kept whole through the joy which is part of God's health care plan.

PRAYER: *What a joy to realize afresh each day that You are alive, Jesus. Thank you for your life. Amen.*

THE MINISTRY OF THE MASTER—FRIDAY
A Spririt Lifter

Johnny was reporting to his parents concerning his week at camp. They asked whether he had become homesick, and he told them he had not. Then they asked whether any of the other children had become homesick at all.

"Some of the kids did. The ones that have a dog."

God's Promise

"When someone becomes a Christian, he becomes a brand new person inside. He is not the same anymore. A new life has begun." (II Corinthians 5:17, TLB)

Practicing His Presence

Practice may not make perfect your relationship to His presence, but it certainly makes it more real and powerful. Were you able to practice His presence yesterday?

God's Health Care Plan—Joy

Jesus was about to leave His disciples. He desired to give them a gift. He could have chosen anything in this universe. He had the privilege of giving whatever He desired to give. He gave a gift without price.

Did He give them money? Did He give them organizational ability? Did He give them the ability to preach? Did He give them valuable keepsakes from His ministry? No, He gave them nothing of this nature. He gave them Joy. Prayerfully consider His words:

"These things have I spoken unto you, that my joy might remain in you, and that your joy might be full." John 15:11

He knew that in the long run the experiences on the inside would mean the most to them. The persecution they would face could not erase the joy they had experienced.

"And ye now therefore have sorrow: but I will see you again, and your heart shall rejoice, and your joy no man taketh from you." John 16:22

God's health care plan is not dependent upon what others may do or say. He has given you His wholeness, and no one can take it from you. It is this assurance which sustains and strengthens at all times.

PRAYER: *I am so grateful for your gift of joy to me, Lord Jesus. Thank you. Thank you. Amen.*

THE MINISTRY OF THE MASTER—SATURDAY
A Spirit Lifter

The Sunday School teacher was quizzing the class whether any of them said a prayer before eating. Most of them did, but one little boy gave a reason why he did not. He said, "I don't have to. My mom's a good cook."

God's Promise

"Everyone who hates his brother is a murderer; and you know that no murderer has eternal life abiding in Him." (I John 3:15, NASV)

Practicing His Presence

Through what incident or person did you sense His presence in your life yesterday? How did this make you feel?

God's Health Care Plan—Joy

The greatest joy comes from the commitment to the high calling of the Lord Jesus for your life. It is in the center of God's will that the joy, which is more than surface laughter, is experienced.

I often look upon my heart as concentric circles. The outside circles are often thrown out of shape. They almost pulsate with fear, distress, and sadness at times. The incidents of life affect them.

But the circles which nestle in the core of the heart are not disturbed. They remain perfectly round and constant. Even in the midst of very troublesome circumstances the inner circles remain calm and joyful. Nothing can take away my deep inner joy which issues forth from His presence and from the knowledge that I am seeking to fulfill His will in my life as He has revealed it to me.

You may have lost a loved one. You may have been forsaken by friends. You may be facing insurmountable problems. Yet, deep inside there can be His peace. God's health care plan involves this deep inner joy. It helps keep your emotions and body sound even when barraged by the difficulties of life.

"Thou wilt show me the path of life; in thy presence is fullness of joy; at thy right hand there are pleasures forevermore." Psalm 16:11

PRAYER: *I want joy in your presence regardless of my circumstances, Father. Thank you for giving me the desire and strength to do so. Amen.*

THE MINISTRY OF THE MASTER—SUNDAY
A Spirit Lifter

The Sunday School teacher sought to impart good moral teaching to her class. One day she said, "Now children, you must never do anything in private that you wouldn't do in public."

One of the pupils really liked that concept. He jumped up and yelled, "Hurray! No more baths!"

God's Promise

God wants your heart to be pure. *"Blessed are the pure in heart, for they shall see God."* (Matthew 5:8, NASV)

Practicing His Presence

Quiet yourself and be aware of the Lord's presence in the small aspects of your life. I know this will be an exciting day for you. Praise Jesus!

God's Health Care Plan—Joy

The joy of the Lord leads us to praise Him. When we praise Him, we experience joy. I feel the following from the "Manual for Discipline" discovered among the Dead Sea Scrolls is a good way to close this week of considering joy as part of God's health care plan.

"As long as I live it shall be a rule engraved on my tongue to bring praise like fruit for an offering and my lips as a sacrificial gift. I will make skillful music with lyre and harp to serve God's glory; and the flute of my lips will I raise in praise of His rule of righteousness.

"Therefore I will bless His name in all I do, before I move hand or foot, whenever I go out or come in, when I sit down and when I rise, even when lying on my couch, I will chant his praise.

"My lips shall praise Him as I sit at the table which is set for all, and before I lift my hand to partake of any nourishment from the delicious fruits of the earth.

"When fear and terror come, and there is only anguish and distress, I will still bless and thank Him for His wonderous deeds, and meditate upon His power, and lean upon His mercies all day long. For I know that in His hand is justice for all that live, and all His works are true. So when trouble comes, or salvation, I praise Him just the same."

These words speak of wholeness at its highest. Joy is the Lord and the Lord is joy.

PRAYER: *My problems are overwhelming, but your joy cannot be erased from my heart, Father. Praise your name. Amen.*

GOD'S HEALTH CARE PLAN—PEACE

Peace is such a desirable product that practically everyone in the world is pursuing it. Individuals seek it as well as nations. The state of peace is so great that it is no wonder it is coveted. Consider:

"Peace is a state of quiet or tranquility, freedom from disturbance or agitation, calm repose, freedom from mental agitation or anxiety, spiritual contentment."

These characteristics of the state of peace appeal to me and to almost all other people. Yet, it seems too few ever really achieve this state of living.

It is obvious that many seek peace in the wrong direction and through the wrong means. There are those who feel peace can be secured by running away from God instead of turning to Him. Some feel that peace is achieved through shortcuts such as drugs, the occult, or sex. They miss the mark in that peace is a Person and not a possession.

I feel that the whole world needs to hear the message that Christ is our peace. He alone can satisfy the heart completely and bring the deep and abiding inner peace which is so earnestly desired and so diligently sought.

Matthew Henry, the great Christian writer of the past, said,

"Peace is such a precious jewel that I would give anything for it, but truth."

The biggest obstacle to your inner peace is your inner being. The real stumbling blocks to your inner peace are not outward circumstances. They are your inward feelings. You may feel that peace would be yours if you had different neighbors, or different fellow employees, or if only the world thought as you do.

The Apostle Paul often began a letter with *"grace"*, *"mercy"*, and *"peace"*. He knew there could be no real peace without first having the grace and mercy of God.

POINTS TO PONDER

1. What do you feel it means to be at peace with God, yourself, and others?
2. Is is possible to have real peace in this world?
3. Will there ever be peace among groups and among nations?

GOD'S HEALTH CARE PLAN—PEACE

1. Seek_____and pursue it. *Ps. 34:14*
2. Blessed are the _____: for they shall be called the children of God. *Mt. 5:9*
3. If it be possible, live _____ with all. *Rom. 12:18*
4. God has called us to _____. *I Cor. 7:15*
5. My peace I give unto you: not as the_____ giveth. *John 14:27*
6. We have peace with God through our _____ _____. *Rom. 5:1*
7. The peace of God passeth all _____. *Phil 4:7*
8. Let the peace of God _____ in your hearts. *Col. 3:15*
9. There is no peace, saith the Lord, unto the _____ _____. *Isa. 48:22*
10. Glory to God in the highest, and on _____ peace. *Luke 2:14*
11. _____be to the brethren, and love with faith. *Eph. 6:23*
12. To be spiritually minded is_____and peace. *Rom. 8:6*
13. Follow after the things which make for _____ _____. *Rom. 14:19*
14. Follow righteousness, faith, charity, peace with them that call on the Lord out of a_____heart. *II Tim. 2:22*

DAILY SCRIPTURE

Mon.	Ps. 34:12-22
Tues.	Mt. 5:1-12
Wed.	I Cor. 7:12-16
Thurs.	Phil. 4:6-8
Fri.	Isa. 48:17-22
Sat.	II Tim. 2:22-26
Sun.	John 14:27-31

PRAYER CONCERNS

Your Family & Relatives
Government Leaders
Missionaries
For the Unbelievers
Churches & Denominations
Your Own Church
Prayer and Praise

NOTE: You will be spiritually strengthened by completing two questions each day, reading the suggested scripture, and ministering in prayer for the concerns of the day.

THE MINISTRY OF THE MASTER—MONDAY
A Spirit Lifter

The city youngster was viewing the wonders of a farm for the first time. The cows, the chickens, the pigs, and the horses fascinated him. He ran up to his parents excited about his most recent discovery. "Daddy! Daddy! I just saw a man make a horse. He had one nearly finished when I saw him, because he was just nailing on its back feet."

God's Promise

I believe you will find comfort in the following promise today.
"The eternal God is your refuge." (Deuteronomy 33:27, TLB)

Practicing His Presence

It is sometimes difficult to remember a specific incident in which you felt the Lord's presence, isn't it? I do believe, however, that it is helpful to be reminded of the spiritual awareness which each of us should develop.

God's Health Care Plan—Peace

Peace! Do you realize this is the last thing Jesus gave to His disciples? He could have given them whatever He chose. His decision was to give them peace.

"Peace I leave with you, my peace I give unto you; not as the world giveth, give I unto you. Let not your heart be troubled, neither let it be afraid."

Jesus knew peace would be the greatest legacy he could leave His disciples. He did not leave them riches nor fame, but He left them peace and spiritual power. He had no earthly possessions to divide among them, but He had an inner peace which could be given to each one in abundant portions.

There are pleasures available to quiet your troubled soul, but these delights are not found in the hurry and rush of modern or ancient life. They are derived from the One who is our peace.

I look upon the things which trouble and steal peace as I look upon a shadow. If I walk away from the light, I see my shadow. It looms before me and there is no way I can catch it or eliminate it. However, if I walk toward the light my shadow is behind me. I am not distracted by it because I cannot even see it. I have put it behind me. Thus, when I walk toward my light, Jesus Christ, the shadow of the cares of this world are behind me. He give me inner peace as I gaze upon Him. It departs only when I stray from steadfastly seeking Him and walking in the light of His fellowship.

PRAYER: *Thank you, Jesus, that you are my peace. The world cannot give me your presence nor take you from me. Amen.*

THE MINISTRY OF THE MASTER—TUESDAY
A Spirit Lifter

The Indian petitioned a judge to grant him a shorter name. The judge asked, "What is your name now?" He replied, "Chief Screeching Train Whistle." "All right then, what new name would you prefer?" He responded, "Toots."

God's Promise

May the following speak to your heart today.

"For whatever was written in earlier times was written for our instruction, that through perserverance and the encouragement of the Scriptures we might have hope." (Romans 15:14, NASV)

Practicing His Presence

At times friends can be near, yet far from us. Other times, they may be far away yet there is a bond. It is the reality of the presence which is important rather than the proximity. How were you aware of the Lord's presence in your life yesterday?

God's Health Care Plan—Peace

The peace of our Lord is evident in the events of His life as well as in His teachings. Consider John 20:26

"And after eight days again his disciples were within, and Thomas with them: then came Jesus, the doors being shut, and stood in the midst and said, Peace, be unto you."

I love this verse for the way it shows me that the Lord Jesus can come into any realm of my life at any time. I feel it is especially helpful to remember this truth in the midst of your many trials and tribulations.

You should keep in mind that, regardless of the sorrow, grief, despair, and heartaches that you may now be experiencing, the Lord Jesus can bring His peace to you.

He can go behind the closed doors of your heart, the doors that cannot be opened by others through gracious words or kind actions, as well as the doors which remain closed in spite of all your own effort.

I am thinking of the doors of such as loneliness, grief, resentment, regrets, and disillusionments. This is the real reason I often refer to this incident at a funeral service.

PRAYER: *Thank you, Father, that no amount of loneliness or grief can steal your inner peace from me. Amen.*

THE MINISTRY OF THE MASTER—WEDNESDAY
A Spirit Lifter

Two white mice were chatting through the bars of their laboratory cages. "Tell me, how are you getting along with Dr. Smith," asked the first mouse. With evident sense of accomplishment the second replied, "Oh, it took awhile, but I've finally got him trained. Now whenever I ring the bell, he brings me some food."

God's Promise

"For the oppression of the poor, for the sighing of the needy, now I will arise, saith the Lord; I will set him in safety from him that puffeth at him." (Psalm 12:5, KJV)

Practicing His Presence

I hope being aware of His presence is exciting for you. May you continually remain sensitive to the Spirit. How did this sensitivity affect your day yesterday?

God's Health Care Plan—Peace

God has designed His health care plan with the thought of keeping you healthy. Of course, there is divine healing from the hand of the Lord. However, even more important is divine health from the hand of the Lord. The greatest healing you can have is to have constantly good health.

There is no merit in your being healed of some dreadful disease. The real satisfaction in life comes from being able to appreciate life and to serve the Lord because of your good health.

One of the contributing factors to continued good health is peace of mind and heart. The peaceful spirit, heart, and body are essential to optimum health.

Have you ever known anyone who is usually tense and upset with other people? Have you ever known anyone who is disturbed by nearly everything that takes place? The chances are that these individuals have physical problems as well as emotional problems. Frequently they experience heart problems, arthritic conditions, stomach disorders, and overall nervousness.

They have no peace, and with this essential ingredient missing, the fullness of life cannot be theirs. You and I are called to remain calm in the midst of all and to possess His peace that passes understanding.

PRAYER: *Help me, O Lord, to remain calm and peaceful in the midst of all my trials and tribulations. Amen.*

THE MINISTRY OF THE MASTER—THURSDAY
A Spirit Lifter

"Miss Jones, kindly tell me what happens when a body is immersed in water?" The pretty co-ed did not hesitate a moment with her reply. "Well, professor, usually the first thing that happens is the phone rings."

God's Promise

"And he said unto me, my grace is sufficient for thee: for my strength is made perfect in weakness. Most gladly therefore will I rather glory in my infirmities, that the power of Christ may rest upon me." (II Corinthians 12:9, KJV)

Practicing His Presence

What a wonderful day you will have as you are consciously aware of His presence throughout it!

Think Christ! It will make a difference. May you choose to keep Him at the center of your thoughts.

God's Health Care Plan—Peace

The peace of the Lord cannot be yours if you walk away from Him in a lifestyle of living which is contrary to His divine laws. Wickedness never produces peace although it may bring temporary satisfaction. The prophet Isaiah stated this succinctly,

"There is no peace, saith the Lord, unto the wicked," Isaiah 48:22)

I deal with many people who want to pursue a life of wickedness and still have the peace of the Lord. The two are diametrically opposed to each other.

Some years ago I had a woman come to me for counseling. She was deeply disturbed because she could not face life as desired. She had left her husband. Friends had taken her into their homes because she had no place to live. She had been unfaithful to her husband and lived a wicked life. Now, she had become sexually involved with the husband in the home that had granted her a refuge.

I tried to point out that the peace and power of the Lord cannot be present in such a sordid situation. She wanted her cake even as she ate it.

The way of holiness is the way of peace. The forsaking of the plan of Go for you is the surest way to life without the peace you desire. The lasting peace you seek comes from loving the Lord's ways and faithfully fulfilling them.

PRAYER: *Your plan for my life is your plan for peace for me. Help me to realize this, O Lord. Amen.*

THE MINISTRY OF THE MASTER—FRIDAY
A Spirit Lifter

The dude was determined to be properly equipped for his stay at the ranch. The seasoned cowboy asked, "What kind of saddle do you want, one with a horn or without a horn?"

Revealing how thoroughly he considered matters, he pondered for a while and replied, "I guess I'll take one without a horn. There doesn't seem to be much traffic on these prairies."

God's Promise

God is a forgiving God.

"He has removed our sins as far away from us as the east is from the west." (Psalms 103:12, TLB)

Practicing His Presence

I pray that amidst your busy day yesterday you were able to pull apart and sense the Lord's presence. How did this make you feel?

God's Health Care Plan—Peace

The peace you desire is a goal you must pursue. The Psalmist said,

"Depart from evil, and do good; see peace, and pursue it."

Some actions result in peace; other actions destroy the peace of heart and soul.

The Apostle Paul tried desperately to convey to the saints of his day that the peace of God is a worthy goal. He says,

"And let the peace of God rule in your hearts..." Colossians 3:15)

The conscious effort of which he speaks is more than positive thinking. It is pure living.

The obstacles to peace are not outward circumstances. Peace is an inward problem. Many years ago a wise person wrote,

"There are five great enemies to peace. They inhabit each of us. They are wickedness, ambition, envy, anger, and pride."

You will observe he never mentioned one outward circumstance or condition. The five enemies to be banished if peace is to reign are all within you.

PRAYER: *Help me to realize, Father, that your presence is the only way of peace. Amen.*

THE MINISTRY OF THE MASTER—SATURDAY
A Spirit Lifter

How diplomatic can one become? The emotionally exhausted choir director was trying to tell the lady gracefully that she did not have a solo quality voice. Finally, she thought of the perfect answer in response to the question, "Well, how do you like my voice?"

"My dear lady, I have been playing the white keys and I have been playing the black keys. However, you are the first one I have ever heard who could sing in the cracks."

God's Promise

Do you enjoy this brief time of reflection upon God's promises?

"Trust in the Lord, and do good; so shalt thou dwell in the land, and verily thou shalt be fed." (Psalm 37:3, KJV)

Practicing His Presence

Have a good day as you are consciously aware of the Lord's presence. Recall some specific incident or person which helped your awareness yesterday.

God's Health Care Plan—Peace

What brings peace? Who gives peace? Where can you find peace? These are the questions being asked by people of our day. Peace is not only a worthy goal, but also a desirable goal. Thank God it is an attainable goal!

However, the path most people pursue will not bring the peace they desire. My heart has been broken on several occasions as I have sought to help young people and their families in the midst of a drug problem. The young people rely upon drugs for their peace. It is a dead-end street of confusion and discontentment. You never conquer a drug. It always conquers you. It does not matter whether the drug be alcohol or heroin.

I am amazed at the number of highly educated adults who are seeking peace through the occult. The occult emphasis is more prevalent and widespread than probably at any time in our history as a nation. The extreme degree of the pursuit of the occult is worship of Satan and believing Judas to be a saint.

Peace is a gift from the Living Lord. There are no peace pills available n can peace be gained from a bottle. The One who is your peace is not only your destination, but He is your traveling companion. He not only says, *"Come to me and receive my peace,"* but He also says, *"I will be with you always."* He is the answer to your questions concerning peace. Thus, the answer is not an explanation, but a Person, Jesus Christ.

PRAYER: *O what peace it is to me, Lord Jesus, to know you will always be with me. In life and in death you are mine. Amen.*

THE MINISTRY OF THE MASTER—SUNDAY
A Spirit Lifter

"The people upstairs are sure a noisy lot," complained the tenant. "Last night they stomped and banged on the floor until after midnight."

"Goodness," replied the sympathetic landlord, "did they disturb you that much?" His reply, "Well, not as much as you would think. Luckily I was practicing my tuba."

God's Promise

Perhaps you are struggling with some fear today.

"Don't be afraid, for the Lord will go before you and will be with you; he will not fail nor forsake you." (Deuteronomy 31:8, TLB)

Practicing His Presence

May you seek to quiet your mind, heart, and body to hear "the still small voice" speak to you today. He is certainly with you. How did you sense His presence yesterday?

God's Health Care Plan—Peace

May I share with you today a practical way to experience the peace of the Lord? My life is extremely busy and complex. Yours is no doubt the same. In the midst of all of this activity, what steps can be taken to appropriate the peace of the Lord to life?

One thing which I do is to try to quiet my mind, heart, and body. As I do this, I seek to visualize the most peaceful place I can imagine. I put myself in the most restful spot I have known throughout life. For me this is a place on the farm where I was reared.

In the pasture field was a rolling bank down by a spring which never went dry. There was always cool water and a pleasant sound from the trickling stream flowing from the rock. In the spring there would be mushrooms, violets, sweet williams, and other flowers in the area. I loved to lie there, and merely think, or at times not even think.

Now that I am older, I idealize the spot. I am sure there is some romanticizing about the spot now. It never was so lovely as I depict it in my mind, but to me the very thought of it brings tranquility. It helps me to understand and to appreciate the peace of the Lord.

You have your spot. May you travel there in your mind. Then remember that the peace you feel this moment can be yours the next moment as well. It is not something you have to wait until you die to receive. It is yours now!

PRAYER: *Lead me to a quiet spot, O Lord, and speak your peace to my anxious heart. Thank you. Amen.*

GOD'S HEALTH CARE PLAN—PATIENCE

"God, give me patience, and right now!" At times this is the prayer of almost every person. Patience is a virtue which is not easily acquired nor diligenty kept by most people.

We live in an age which is witnessing the mushrooming of attempts to bring better health to all people. Health care plans have been advanced by insurance companies. Our Congress is struggling with a health care plan for the entire nation. The medical professions are striving to better the health of individuals. By uniting these efforts, great strides are being made enabling more individuals to live longer.

I feel that all of our efforts in science, research, medicine, etc. would be enhanced if we would also adopt God's health care plan. He wants each of His children to bear the fruit of the Spirit and thus have a healthier life. One aspect of this is patience.

How would you define patience? One wag responded, *"Patience is what my wife doesn't have."* This negative definition may describe a personality, but the following defines the word.

"Patience is the exercise of sustained endurance and perseverance; the forbearance toward the faults or infirmities of others; tranquil waiting or expectation; the ability to await events without provocation; keeping kindness of heart on a vexatious conduct; long suffering in continued patience; an active force denoting uncomplaining steadiness in doing."

Your blood pressure, your nerves, and your mental attitude would all be affected in a positive way if patience could become a greater part of your life.

The Lord is patient with you and me. A part of our high calling is to be patient with each other and to wait patiently upon His will to be unfolded.

POINTS TO PONDER

1. Do you feel everyone has areas where impatience reigns supreme?
2. What difference would a greater degree of patience make in your life?
3. How do you handle impatient individuals?

THE LAYING ON OF HANDS WITH PRAYER

1. The patience in spirit is better than the _____ _____ _____ in spirit. *Eccl. 7:8*
2. In your_____possess ye your souls. *Lu. 21:19*
3. Strengthened with all might, according to his glorious _____ _____, unto all patience and longsuffering with joyfulness. *Col 1:11*
4. Be _____ toward all. *I Thess. 5:14*
5. After he had patiently endured, he obtained the _____ _____. *Heb. 6:15*
6. Ye have need of _____. *Heb. 10:36*
7. The trying of your _____ worketh patience. *James 1:3*
8. Be ye also patient; establish your hearts: for the _____ _____of the Lord draweth nigh. *James 5:8*
9. Ye have heard of the patience of _____. *James 5:11*
10. My son, despise not the _____ of the Lord. *Pro. 3:11*
11. Let patience have her _____ work. *James 1:4*
12. Be patient in_____. *Rom. 12:12*
13. _____ in the Lord, wait patiently for him. *Ps. 37:7*
14. I waited patiently for the _____, and he inclined unto me. *Ps. 40:1*

DAILY SCRIPTURE

Mon.	Luke 21:12-19
Tues.	I Thess. 5:12-24
Wed.	Heb. 6:13-20
Thurs.	Heb. 10:32-39
Fri.	Rom. 12:9-15
Sat.	Ps. 37:1-11
Sun.	Ps. 40:1-8

PRAYER CONCERNS

Your Family & Relatives
Government Leaders
Missionaries
For the Unbelievers
Churches & Denominations
Your Own Church
Prayer and Praise

NOTE: You will be spiritually strengthened by completing two questions each day, reading the suggested scripture, and ministering in prayer for the concerns of the day.

THE MINISTRY OF THE MASTER—MONDAY
A Spirit Lifter

Overheard on the party line was the comment, "I won't go into all the details, my dear. In fact, I've already told you more about it than I heard myself."

God's Promise

"Behold, I give unto you power to tread on serpents and scorpions, and over all the power of the enemy; and nothing shall by any means hurt you." (Luke 10:19, KJV)

Practicing His Presence

Through what incident or person did you sense the presence of Christ yesterday? How did this make you feel?

God's Health Care Plan—Patience

Sometimes we are led to believe that the saints of the past had an abundance of patience. It is as if they were almost superhuman. However, a look at some of them reveals that the greatest often lacked patience.

The children of Israel certainly became impatient after their flight from Egypt. At the same time there were moments when the impatience of Moses showed itself. Numbers 20:5 reveals the impatience of the people, but in verse 10 we read where Moses in a moment of frustration calls them rebels.

II Kings 5:11 shows that Naaman had a short fuse. He was angry at Elisha and let everyone know it.

The disciples quickly lost their patience when the woman of Canaan beseeched the Lord to heal her daughter. They wanted the woman sent away from him immediately. (Matthew 15:23)

James and John were hotheads when people acted differently from what the two disciples felt they should. When the Samaritans shunned Jesus, the two disciples were ready to call down fire from heaven to destroy them. (Luke 9:51-56)

Both Sarah and Abraham had difficulty waiting patiently for the Lord's word to be fulfilled. This spirit of impatience resulted in the birth of Ishmael to the handmaiden, Hagar. (Genesis 16:1-6)

The above examples should bring some comfort to you. Your impatience is not unique to you. This has been a trait of individuals through the ages. However, at the same time it does not excuse either you or me from seeking to develop and to live a life of patience.

PRAYER: *Father, calm my anxious spirit when I am impatient. Help me to trust you. Amen.*

THE MINISTRY OF THE MASTER—TUESDAY
A Spirit Lifter

The private had just been told that he would have to pay for the rifle he had lost. "Sir," he gulped. "suppose I lost a tank? Surely, I wouldn't have to pay for it?" "Yes, you would, even if it took the rest of your life," snapped the sergeant. "Oh," said the private, "now I know why a captain always goes down with his ship."

God's Promise

My prayer is that you have at least one true friend in this human life. *"A true friend is always loyal, in time of need."* (Proverbs 17:17, TLB)

Practicing His Presence

The Lord comes to us through others. May you place in your mind a person who is close to you in spirit and picture the love of God coming through them.

God's Health Care Plan—Patience

I like what Isaac Newton said,

"If I have ever made any valuable discoveries it has been owing more to patient attention than to any other talent. It takes patience to learn the great truths of the universe."

If this great scientist needed patience, how much more do you and I need it? The enduring truths of a purposeful life are not garnered in a day. They come as we patiently trod on our pilgrimage. The secret is to be patient enough to permit time to reveal truths.

Most church members grow weary in well-doing and in righteous living. They are sincere when they join church. They honestly want to know more about the Lord and His ways. However, most of them want this revealed during the initial weeks of the enthusiasm of their new life in Christ.

What they fail to realize is that the great truths are not gleaned from study so much as they are gathered from experience. The deep Christian life develops as one patiently seeks to serve the Lord.

Your calling is to be faithful, not to be successful. Success is relative. Faithfulness is God's standard. If you stop or lag behind in your devotion to the Lord because of lack of patience, the end result is disaster. Patiently serve the Lord and the end result is His abiding presence.

PRAYER: *Give me the patience, Father, to let your truths unfold and develop in me. Amen.*

THE MINISTRY OF THE MASTER—WEDNESDAY
A Spirit Lifter

The editor, weary of the abuse following his editorials, ran the 10 Commandments in his column.

A few days later came a letter, "Cancel my subscription, You're getting too personal."

God's Promise

"And he said unto me, my grace is sufficient for thee: for my strength is made perfect in weakness. Most gladly therefore will I rather glory in my infirmities, that the power of Christ rest upon me." (II Corinthians 12:9, KJV)

Practicing His Presence

We hear a lot about energy today. Have you thought about the fact that the greatest source of energy is the presence of the Lord in your life?

God's Health Care Plan—Patience

Milton was right when he said,

"They also serve who only stand and wait."

This is patience at its highest. Service for the Lord is not frantically rushing trying to work for Him. True service involves quietly waiting upon Him and calmly working with Him. We are not called to be dashing servants, but devoted partners with the Lord.

The tendency on my part, and I am sure your tendency as well, is to feel that I have to make things happen. I cannot wait until the grain is sprouted, matured, and come to the time of harvest.

As a lad we would plant corn with what was called a jogger. With it we were able simultaneously to deposit a few kernels of corn and some fertilizer into the ground. The spring, summer, and fall were needed for the corn to come to full development. There was no way to hurry the process.

The same thing is true of your actions. You cannot expect instant results. You may have a TV which comes on instantly, a phone which gives you the dial tone instantly, instant coffee, and instant hot rolls; but you cannot have instant insights into all the truths of life. Your patient understanding and waiting must be a part of this achievement.

PRAYER: *Help me to wait upon your guidance and help, Father. Forgive when I impatiently go my own way. Amen.*

THE MINISTRY OF THE MASTER—THURSDAY
A Spirit Lifter

The man had been looking for a good church to attend and to join. One day he entered a worship service as the pastor and congregation were reading, "We have left undone those things which we ought to have done, and we have done those things which we ought not to have done." The man dropped to his knees and sighed with relief as he said to himself, "Thank goodness! I've found my crowd at last."

God's Promise

"But he giveth more grace. Wherefore he saith, God resisteth the proud, but giveth grace unto the humble." (James 4:6, KJV)

Practicing His Presence

I would suggest that you quiet your mind, your heart, and your body. This will help your awareness of the presence of the Lord throughout your day.

God's Health Care Plan—Patience

Impatience spawns many problems. For this reason God's health care plan stresses patience or long-suffering. He knows we will be constantly upset if we do not possess a patient spirit.

Impatience produces flared tempers, unproductive shortcuts to solve problems, and ruined relationships with others. I saw a friend throw a jack handle through the windshield of his car. His impatience cost him dearly. I saw another jump up and down on the trunk of his parents' new car, damaging paint and leaving dents, all because they would not permit him to use it at that moment.

The price tag on impatience is very high. It costs in hurt feelings, ruined relationships, as well as much illness. Patience is a virtue we cannot afford to neglect.

Just as I have witnessed the above results of impatience, I have witnessed the fruit of a patient spirit. I have seen parents go through hell with children, but patiently wait for the years to bring maturity.

I have seen elderly people planting fruit trees which would never bear fruit in their lifetimes.

I have seen pastors, politicians, scientists, educators, and other leaders patiently sow seed which would take years to develop fully. Their example of patience served as a quieting spirit and positive influence in the lives of many people.

PRAYER: *Deliver me from the problems I have created through my impatience. Amen.*

THE MINISTRY OF THE MASTER—FRIDAY
A Spirit Lifter

The two pastors were of different faiths, but close friends. They often differed on theological matters and would often end in arguments. One day in the midst of a heated argument, the one said, "That's all right. We'll agree to disagree. The thing that counts is that we are friends and both doing the Lord's work, you in your way and me in HIS."

God's Promise

There is no need to worry when you know the Lord your God.

"Be still (without care) and know that I am God." (Psalms 46:10, KJV)

Practicing His Presence

The Lord often feels very near when I am involved in the ordinary routines of everyday life. What a tremendous experience! I hope this is also true in your life.

God's Health Care Plan—Patience

The story is told of Dr. Phillip Brooks' pacing the floor like a caged animal. One of his parishioners stopped by and found him in this state of frustration. He said, feeling that some great calamity had fallen upon Dr. Brooks, *"My dear man, what is the trouble?"*

Dr. Brooks replied, *"Nothing, my friend, except that I am in a hurry, and God isn't."*

Does this sound familiar? I often want a quick and easy answer. Most believers want to lift their requests unto the Lord by noon and to have His answer back by sundown.

The patient spirit is willing to accept God's timetable. There is no way you are going to hurry the Lord, and the sooner you learn this the better it will be for you and for your health.

Isn't it strange that so often we feel God should patiently wait on us? This is contrary to life and to the teachings of Scripture. The Psalmist says:

"Wait on the Lord: be of good courage, and he shall strengthen thine heart; wait, I say, on the Lord."

It is God who sets the pace of life. Our calling is to fall into step with Him. He is not our errand boy. We are His chosen children. Your prayer should be that He grant you the serenity to wait patiently for the unfolding of His perfect will.

PRAYER: *I pray for willingness to have my peace in life to be your peace in me, Father. Amen.*

THE MINISTRY OF THE MASTER—SATURDAY
A Spirit Lifter

She was dignified and had an air of superiority. Shaking hands with the pastor after the service, she said, "Wonderful sermon, Reverend. Everything you said applies to somebody or other that I know!"

God's Promise

"Let your mind dwell on whatever is true, noble, right, pure, lovely, admirable, excellent, praiseworthy." (Philippians 4:8, TLB)

Practicing His Presence

The feeling of His presence may not always be yours, but its reality is always yours. How did this reality affect your life yesterday?

God's Health Care Plan—Patience

F.W. Robertson has remarked,

"There are times when God asks nothing of His children except silence, patience, and tears."

These three things speak volumes and accomplish many worthy achievements.

The old Dutch proverb is, *"A handful of patience is worth more than a bushel of brains."* A person may be brilliant, but mar all this with an impatient spirit.

Many concerns can wait and still not affect the depth of the meaning of life. A few years ago Mary and I journeyed through Europe. We enjoyed all the countries visited. Each had its own characteristics. Holland was noted for its slowness. True or not, one person is reported to have said,

"When the world comes to an end, I'm going to Holland, because there they are always fifty years behind everybody else."

Yet, in the midst of all this I felt they were a happy people. Life went on even if the expressway wasn't completed on time and even if other things were not completed in a hurry.

The greatest accomplishment for you is the patient and understanding spirit. The flaws of administration will always be with us. The joys of ministry and of the assurance of working patiently with our Lord are our goals.

PRAYER: *Father, give to me a kind spirit today. Help me to permit this spirit to reach out to others. Amen.*

THE MINISTRY OF THE MASTER—SUNDAY
A Spirit Lifter

The sexton was laying new carpet and was not too cautious about the tacks left on the floor. The pastor saw this happening even in the pulpit area and said, "See here, James, what do you suppose would happen if I stepped on one of those tacks right in the middle of my sermon?"

"Well, preacher," he retorted, "I reckon there'd be one point you wouldn't linger on!"

God's Promise

What a wonderful promise to consider.

"Open my eyes to see wonderful things in your Word." (Psalms 119:18, TLB)

Practicing His Presence

His presence is like gravity. It holds life together and enables us to drop those things which we should.

God's Health Care Plan—Patience

"How can I really serve God?" was a question addressed to Clara Barton. Her reply is worth our serious consideration.

"Keep yourself quiet and in restraint. Reserve your energies doing those little things that lie in your way. Do each one as well as you can. Save your strength so that when God does call you to do something good and great, you will not have wasted your force and strength with useless strivings but will be ready to do the work quietly and well."

She is telling us to wait patiently on the Lord. A patient person can turn the irritants of life into stepping stones of maturity and service.

A grain of sand lodges in the oyster shell. It is so irritating that the oyster reacts. Finally, unable to rid itself of the irritant, it does the next best thing and goes on in spite of it. In fact, it begins to use the irritant as a base for the development of a pearl.

That which was irritating becomes riches instead of ruination for the oyster.

"But they that wait upon the Lord shall renew their strength; they shall mount up with wings as eagles; they shall run, and not be weary; and they shall walk, and not faint." Isaiah 41:31.

PRAYER: *Father, help me to put the proper priority on the activities of life. Amen.*

GOD'S HEALTH CARE PLAN—KINDNESS

A careful study of the good Book reveals a wonderful health care plan for each of us. He has ordained a plan which makes it possible for you to live in a healthy and victorious manner.

God's health care plan involves the fruit of the Spirit. One aspect of this fruit is gentleness. It is not easy to define gentleness. It is what we might term kindness. I like this meaning of kindness.

"Kindness is the gentle, tender, good deed which reaches out to others while at the same time reaching deep within yourself."

We all need much kindness. It is a part of life which helps bring forth wholeness. Kindness which you receive helps both you and the one bestowing it. Kindness which you render helps the one unto whom you show it and in addition, helps you deep within your inner being.

If you do not experience kindness today, it is probably because you are not looking for it. May I encourage you to look for kind acts coming your way.

Kindness is more than verbalization. It is an act in the best interest of the one for whom it is done. It blesses the one being blessed as well as the one doing the blessing in word and deed. Kindness exudes from the person who is relating to you. An ounce of kindness is worth a ton of admonition.

The spirit of kindness is not your calling for only one season. It is your calling for life. The Bible does not tell you that you should continue to be kind until someone is unkind to you and that after that you too can be unkind.

We are admonished to love the unlovable, to pray for our enemies, and to be kind to those unkind.

Kindness is a tangible step to overcome the human tendency of selfishness. A selfish, unkind life is a sick life. The selfish soul is a stiffled soul. The kind soul is the awakened soul.

POINTS TO PONDER

1. What does the word kindness mean to you?
2. Whom do you think of when you think of a kind person and why?
3. Is the spirit of kindness an attitude which can be cultivated and developed?

GOD'S HEALTH CARE PLAN—KINDNESS

1. Be _____ affectioned one to another with brotherly love. *Rom. 12:10*
2. Love suffers long and is _____; love envieth not. *I Cor. 13:4*
3. By pureness, by knowledge, by longsuffering, by_____ _____, by the Holy Spirit, by love. *II Cor. 6:6*
4. And be ye kind to another, tender-hearted, _____ _____ one another, even as God has forgiven you. *Eph. 4:32*
5. Put on therefore, as the elect of God holy and beloved, bowels of mercies, _____, humbleness of mind. *Col. 3:12*
6. And to godliness brotherly _____; and to brotherly_____ charity. *II P?t. 1:7*
7. The virtuous woman has the tongue of _____ _____. *Pro. 31:26*
8. The desire of a man is his _____. *Pro. 19:22*
9. He comforted them and spoke_____ unto them. *Gen. 50:21*
10. But the servant of the Lord must not strive, but be _____ _____unto all. *II Tim. 2:24*
11. But the fruit of the spirit is love, joy, peace, longsuffering, _____ _____. *Gal. 5:22*
12. Thy_____hath made me great. *Ps. 18:35*
13. He shall gather the lambs with his arm, and carry them in his bosom, and shall_____lead those that are with young. *Isa. 40:11*
14. I Paul myself beseech you by the meekness and _____ _____ of Christ. *II Cor. 10:1*

DAILY SCRIPTURE

Mon.	Rom. 12:9-21
Tues.	I Cor. 13:4-13
Wed.	Eph. 4:25-32
Thurs.	Col. 3:5-11
Fri.	Gen. 50:15-21
Sat.	Isa. 40:9-11
Sun.	II Pet. 1:3-11

PRAYER CONCERNS

Your Family & Relatives
Government Leaders
Missionaries
For the Unbelievers
Churches & Denominations
Your Own Church
Prayer and Praise

NOTE: You will be spiritually strengthened by completing two questions each day, reading the suggested scripture, and ministering in prayer for the concerns of the day.

THE MINISTRY OF THE MASTER—MONDAY
A Spirit Lifter

The youngster had been especially bad. Mother decided to do something about it and took him to the pastor. The pastor started out with some questions and the third one was, "Now son, where is God?" The boy replied he did not know. Again there was the questions and the firm denial.

The third time the pastor raised his voice somewhat as he asked the youngster, "Where is God?" With this the little boy ran out of the office, grabbed his mother's hand, and said, "Mom, let's get out of here quick. They've lost God around here and are trying to put the rap on me."

God's Promise

"God is our refuge and strength, a very present help in trouble. Therefore will I not fear." (Ps. 46:1,2)

Practicing His Presence

It takes conscious effort to keep in tune with the Lord. The discipline of being aware of His presence is worth all the effort.

God's Health Care Plan—Kindness

Gentleness or kindness is something practically everybody wants. I like the comment of the little boy who had just got out of bed. When his mother asked what he wanted for breakfast, his sleepy reply was,

"I would like some cereal, an egg, and a word of kindness."

Isn't that a beautiful way to start the day? It is such a worthy request. Your day and mine would be much different if we started with a word of kindness. Surely, there is someone close to you who would appreciate such a word. In fact, many people would forego the eggs and bacon if a word of kindness were on the menu.

The apostle Paul had the right idea when he said,

"Be kindly affectioned one to another with brotherly love..." Romans 12:10, KJV)

It did not matter whether you were beginning or ending the day. The attitude was to be one of kindness or gentleness. You and I are in the unique position of being able to influence the day for others. This week I pray that you will put forth special effort to influence the day for others in such a way as they will behold how kind you are. This should especially be the attitude you have toward those of your own household. Regardless of your circumstance or state of health, it is not too much to ask that you be kind.

PRAYER: *I need renewed, Father. I quiet my spirit and wait upon you to guide and direct. Amen.*

THE MINISTRY OF THE MASTER—TUESDAY
A Spirit Lifter

The rather long service having ended, one lady said to the pastor, "Reverend, I really must apologize for dozing just a little during the fine sermon." Then realizing what she had said, she attempted to convey the fact that she still got the message. She went on to say, "But I want you to know, I didn't miss a thing."

God's Promise

The Lord certainly provides many blessings, doesn't He?

"Jesus said unto him, If thou canst believe, all things are possible to him that believeth." (Mark 9:23, KJV)

Practicing His Presence

It takes conscious effort to be aware of the Lord in the small aspects in life. How did this consciousness affect your day yesterday?

God's Health Care Plan—Kindness

Henry Thoreau is reported to have said,

"The quality of life is most important and quality can be achieved through kindness. It is something to be able to paint a particular picture, make a few objects beautiful, but it is far more glorious to affect a quality of the day. This is the highest of arts."

Somewhere through your experiences today you will discover someone endeavoring to be kind. Often many do not detect kindness because they are looking only for thorns, instead of roses among the acts of life.

The kindness you receive cannot in most instances be immediately repaid to the person who did it. My wife's Grandma Bell always said,

"Kindness travels in a straight line."

It is to be received and passed on and does not have to return to the one who gave it. You and I do not live a boomerang life so far as kindness is concerned.

You should not expect a direct return from your kindness from the one to whom you are kind. Many may forget or ignore a kindness extended, but you are called to continue to be kind regardless of this fact.

PRAYER: *Although I cannot repay all who have been kind to me, help me, Father, to pass this spirit of kindness on to others. Amen.*

THE MINISTRY OF THE MASTER—WEDNESDAY
A Spirit Lifter

"Now, how many of you would like to go to heaven?" asked the Sunday School teacher. All the eager five-year-olds raised their hands except Nathan. He so sincerely said, "I'm sorry, I can't. My mother told me to come right home after Sunday School."

God's Promise

"Therefore, I say unto you, What things soever ye desire, when ye pray, believe that ye receive them, and ye shall have them." (Mark 11:24, KJV)

Practicing His Presence

Can you recall a spiritual feast you had yesterday as you sensed the Lord's presence? Be aware of the Lord in your every moment.

God's Health Care Plan—Kindness

Have you been taking kindness for granted in your life? My guess is that you have been receiving far more than you are really grateful for at this moment.

As I become older, there are past events which speak to my heart about kindness. I am more appreciative now than at the time. When I was a college student, a pastor and his wife kindly let me stay in their home. They provided me with a room and board for many months. They were my encouragement to assume a pastorate and to go on for the Lord. Since I have not seen them for many years, I keep thinking I must write them a letter. Yet, I continue to put this off. We have gone our separate busy ways, and it is a shame that I have not taken the time to thank them again for their kindnesses.

My guess is that if you look closely enough, you too will recall times when kindness was extended which you did not fully appreciate. Perhaps you will never be able to express your thanks to the ones who were kind to you. You can pass on this attitude of kindness to others.

A father asked his teenage son whether he would like to do something for which he would be paid during the rest of his life. His reply was that this would be great. Dad said,

> *"I'll tell you what and how to do it. Go two doors down and shovel the walks for the widow, Mrs. Jones. Never tell her who did it and never ask for pay."*

This young man became a famous writer and years later wrote that this was one of the greatest things that ever happened to him.

PRAYER: *Father, help me to appreciate the little kind acts and how much they will mean to me through the years. Amen.*

THE MINISTRY OF THE MASTER—THURSDAY
A Spirit Lifter

In the throes of his energetic sermon he asked whether anyone had ever known a perfect person. Imagine his astonishment when a hand went up. "You do!" The timid little man replied, "Yes, sir; my wife's first husband."

God's Promise

"And Jesus said unto them, I am the bread of life: he that cometh to me shall never hunger; and he that believeth on me shall never thirst." (John 6:35, KJV)

Practicing His Presence

I believe as you exercise your spiritual powers you will become more aware of the spiritual side of life. How did you sense the presence of His Spirit yesterday?

God's Health Care Plan—Kindness

The story is told of Dr. Dan Poling having a great struggle with what he termed the hypocrites in his church. One of his friends said to him,

"Dan, I know how you feel, but if you want to help these people and save yourself, you will have to learn to love them, my boy. You are going to have to learn to love them."

A harsh spirit could not possibly minister positively to the members of Dr. Poling's church. A kind and understanding spirit must prevail.

God's health care plan requires that we maintain a life of kindness toward others as well as a devotion unto the Lord.

In my 30-day pilgrimage, *"A Ministry of Prayer,"* I suggest, as an optional act, doing a kind deed each day. Every group which has used this book reports that the most difficult aspect is deciding upon a specific kind deed for the day and doing it.

Dr. Wiliam Barclay writes,

"...both man and woman belie their nature when they are not kind."

In other words, it is kindness which lifts you to your higher nature. It is kindness which helps release the Holy Spirit through you to others.

I urge you to realize that to cultivate kindness is a valuable part of the business of life.

PRAYER: *Lord, deliver me from just having a general spirit of kindness and not specifically being kind to someone each day. Amen.*

THE MINISTRY OF THE MASTER—FRIDAY
A Spirit Lifter

When it comes to protection, you should cover all bases. Nothing can be taken for granted.

I like this comment which is credited to Noah's wife. "Just the same, I'd feel safer if those termites were locked up in a metal box."

God's Promise

"Trust in the Lord, and do good; so shalt thou dwell in the land, and verily thou shalt be fed." (Psalm 37:3, KJV)

Practicing His Presence

I am certain this will be an exciting day for you if you seek to quiet yourself and practice His presence. Have a good day!

God's Health Care Plan—Kindness

Someone has said,

"Kindness is the golden chain by which society is bound together."

It is true that without acts of kindness we really cannot have a civilization. We certainly cannot have a Christian Church without the spirit of kindness.

There are many who credit William Penn with this beautiful thought.

"I shall pass through this world but once. Any good therefore that I can do or any kindness that I can show to any human being, let me do it now. Let me not defer or neglect it for I shall not pass this way again."

There are no reruns in life. There are no instant replays to enable you to erase actions and edit the life tape you have made. Effort must be expended to be kind now and to rejoice in the satisfaction that springs forth from these acts of kindness.

There are many people who are chained by the sins and unkind acts of their past life. These chains which bind can be replaced by chains which build. The chains of selfishness, bitterness, unkindness can and must be replaced by the golden chain of kindness. This chain will lift you higher. It will not bind you. It will free you.

PRAYER: *Lord Jesus, help me to be wrapped in the garment of kindness and love. Amen.*

THE MINISTRY OF THE MASTER—SATURDAY
A Spirit Lifter

A minister met one of the church members who had, for a long time, been inactive but recently had been in worship every Sunday. "It's so nice to see you in worship with your wife these past few Sundays," commented the pastor.

The response was "It's a matter of choice. I'd rather hear your sermon than hers."

God's Promise

"Beloved think it not strange concerning the fiery trial which is to try you, as though some strange things happened unto you: But rejoice, inasmuch as ye are partakers of Christ's sufferings..." (I Peter 4:12,13, KJV)

Practicing His Presence

May you seek to quiet yourself today and hear "the still small voice" speak to you! How were you aware of His presence yesterday?

God's Health Care Plan—Kindness

"Have you had a kindness shown
Pass it on.
It was not given for thee alone
Pass it on.
Let it travel down the years
Let it wipe another's tears.
Till in heaven the deed appears
Pass it on. Pass it on."

One kind act on your part will give birth to another. I have met some mighty fine people who have been kind to me. Through the years I have had the reputation of running out of gas. While this is not good, there has been a blessed side to it.

I recall one time when I ran out of gas on the turnpike. A man stopped and took me to the nearby exit. I secured a can of gas and returned to the exit to thumb a ride back to my car. The official at the entrance said it was illegal to thumb a ride on the turnpike. Then he said, *"Come in here with me."* When the next driver who was alone stopped to pay, the official asked him to take me to my car. He was kind indeed.

One day I ran out of gas on a lonely country road. It was over five miles to a gas station. I went to a farm home to seek help. The lady said, *"I have no gas. However, I have a can, and you may use my car to go get some."* She gave me the keys to what I discovered was a new Ford car. She was indeed kind. The day of kindness is not over.

PRAYER: *Father, remove the harsh spirit from my life and open me to the kindness of spirit I need and desire. Amen.*

THE MINISTRY OF THE MASTER—SUNDAY
A Spirit Lifter

The farmer was late returning from his weekly trip to town with his team of mules and wagon. The wife asked, "What took you so long?" "Well, I'll tell you," he replied. "On the way home I picked up the preacher, and from then on those darn mules didn't understand a thing I said."

God's Promise

You can be assured of divine protection in the Family of God.

"For the oppression of the poor, for the sighing of the needy, now will I arise, saith the Lord; I will set him in safety from him that puffeth at him." (Psalm 12:5, KJV)

Practicing His Presence

It is sometimes difficult to remember a specific incident in which you really felt His presence, isn't it? Yet, I do believe it is helpful to be reminded of the spiritual awarenss which each of us should develop.

God's Health Care Plan—Kindness

I cannot close this week's comments concerning the gentle spirit and acts of kindness without dealing with the way to receive a kindness. It is at times difficult for me to handle a kind act or a kind word.

It is sometimes embarrassing to me to have a person show kindness. I feel so unworthy and think, *"If they only know how I really was, they would not think I was so good or gracious."* I guess we all have trouble handling kindness.

One thing which has helped me is to realize that the Lord has made all things possible. Therefore, I am simply to respond with a thank you or expression of gratefulness. I must work at it to cultivate the art of receiving a kindness and receiving it in the proper spirit.

Really, none of us is worthy in ourselves to receive any of the marvelous blessings of life. We receive from the Lord and to Him be the glory and honor. The kindness of the Lord is from everlasting to everlasting. This I must not forget and must continue to realize. His kindness is released and revealed to me through others.

Your life will be more healthful, fulfilling, and productive if you develop the art of being gentle and kind. The warmth of gentleness can produce what harshness can never bring forth. It will benefit you and others.

PRAYER: *Thank you, Father, that your kindness never ends. May I ever be grateful for this. Amen.*

GOD'S HEALTH CARE PLAN—GOODNESS

Included among the aspects of the fruit of the spirit is goodness. The Apostle Paul says,

"The fruit of the spirit is love, joy, peace, long suffering, gentleness, goodness, faith, meekness, temperance: against such there is no law." Galatians 5:22,23, KJV

The definition of goodness is exciting.

"Goodness is having or characterized by admirable, moral, or spiritual qualitites, especially governed by dutiful regard for the moral and divine law. Conformed to the law of righteousness, virtuous, religious; opposed to bad, opposed to evil, viciousness, and wickedness."

All of this and more is needed to define goodness. I was amazed to discover in my dictionary over seventy-five synonyms for goodness. There were more synonyms for goodness than for any other word I have ever looked up in the dictionary.

After it had listed the 75, it summarized by saying that good may at some time be a synonym of almost any adjective in the language implying advantage, benefit, utility, and worth.

Thus, even the dictionary gave up trying to define goodness. It covers the whole gamut of life. It includes all that would lift up and benefit individuals.

Dr. William Barclay points out that the Greek word for goodness can be translated *"virtue equipped at every point."* It is a quality of life which can rebuke, correct, and discipline.

Thus within the word itself lies the inherent quality of rebuking and chastising. To do good unto another does not imply that you will never challenge or discipline them.

Jesus sought to do good, but he still upset the tables of the money changers. Goodness includes fairness, but it does not include permitting individuals to go unchallenged or unchanged throughout life.

POINTS TO PONDER

1. What does it mean to be good?
2. What are some tangible ways you can express goodness?
3. What did Jesus mean when He said, *"There is none good but one, that is, God."*? (Matthew 19:17, KJV)

GOD'S HEALTH CARE PLAN—GOODNESS

1. Depart from evil, and do _____. *Ps. 34:14*
2. Trust in the Lord and do_____. *Ps. 37:3*
3. But to do_____ and to communicate forget not. *Heb. 13:16*
4. Therefore to him that knoweth to do good, and doeth it not, to him it is _____. *James 4:17*
5. Let your light shine before men, that they may see your good_____ _____. *Mt. 5:16*
6. Let us consider one another to provoke unto love and to good _____ _____. *Heb. 10:24*
7. Do good to them that _____ you. *Mt. 5:44*
8. Follow what is_____, both among yourselves, and to all. *I Th. 5:15*
9. _____ and upright is the Lord. *Ps. 25:8*
10. O taste and see that the Lord is_____. *Ps. 34:8*
11. There is none good but one, that is, _____. *Mt. 19:17*
12. The_____is full of the goodness of the Lord. *Ps. 33:5*
13. If the salt has lost its savour it is good for _____ *Mt. 5:13*
14. Jesus anointed with the Holy Ghost went about doing _____. *Acts 10:38*

DAILY SCRIPTURE

Mon.	Ps. 34:11-22
Tues.	Ps. 37:1-11
Wed.	Heb. 13:7-16
Thurs.	Mt. 5:13-16
Fri.	Mt. 19:16-22
Sat.	Ps. 34:1-10
Sun.	Acts 10:34-43

PRAYER CONCERNS

Your Family & Relatives
Government Leaders
Missionaries
For the Unbelievers
Churches & Denominations
Your Own Church
Prayer and Praise

NOTE: You will be spiritually strengthened by completing two questions each day, reading the suggested scripture, and ministering in prayer for the concerns of the day.

THE MINISTRY OF THE MASTER—MONDAY
A Spirit Lifter

"You know, when I was a boy, I used to think Sodom and Gomorrah were man and wife." Rather sheepishly the friend replied, "Don't let that bother you. When I was younger, I used to think the Epistles were the wives of the Apostles."

God's Promise

"Do not let your hearts be troubled. Have faith in God and faith in me. In my Father's house there are many dwelling places; otherwise, how could I have told you that I was going to prepare a place for you?" (John 14:1-2, NAB)

Practicing His Presence

Can you recall a specific incident or person which helped your awareness of the Lord's presence yesterday? Take a moment and reflect upon this.

God's Health Care Plan—Goodness

The value of goodness is beautifully illustrated through the fable of the king who sent three subjects throughout the kingdom to discover and bring to him what he would most desire.

The first returned with all the curiosities he could find. He felt the king would really be pleased to have things which were unusual. Many of them were one of a kind items.

The second went throughout the kingdom proclaiming the glories of the king. He felt the king would be delighted when he learned that he had lifted the king's praises in every city, village, and hamlet.

The third man reported that throughout the kingdom he had, to the best of his ability, practiced goodness. He reported that goodness had been accomplished.

The curiosities were soon lost among the archives of the kingdom. The praises meant little as the loyalty of the subjects varied with what the king had done for them at the moment. The king chose goodness because he said it would go on forever. The ripples issuing from it would last for eternity.

He turned to the man who had majored in goodness and said,

"It is to this third man I give the coveted prize of being second in command to me in the kingdom."

Goodness is a goal worthy of your most devoted pursuit now and always.

PRAYER: *Dear Father, help me to pursue goodness with the fervency that many pursue gold. Amen.*

THE MINISTRY OF THE MASTER—TUESDAY
A Spirit Lifter

"My wooden leg sure gave me a lot of pain last night," complained the old gent to his friends at the general store. "That's too bad. What seems to be wrong?" inquired a sympathetic listener.

"Oh, nothing is wrong with the leg and how it fits. It's just that last night my wife hit me over the head with it."

God's Promise

"...by which he has granted to us his precious and very great promises, that through these you may escape from the corruption that is in the world because of passion, and become partakers of the divine nature." (II Peter 1:4, RSV)

Practicing His Presence

Through what incident or person did you sense the presence of the Lord yesterday? Was the reality of this presence a conscious effort on your part?

God's Health Care Plan—Goodness

Goodness is eternal. It cannot be destroyed. It may not be appreciated and many may want to minimize it, but it is of God and shall last forever. It is the tangible expression of love which never ends.

Walt Whitman wrote,

"In my mind roaming in thought over the universe I saw the little that is good steadily hastening toward immortality; and the vast that is evil I saw hastening to merge itself and become lost and dead."

As Christians we believe that ultimately evil and wrongdoing will be destroyed. Evil cannot win. Its influence in God's universe and plan is not eternal.

I can conceive of goodness continuing into the eons of time. In fact, I cannot conceive of goodness ever being destroyed. It is the very nature of God.

There is much evil in the world today. There are many evil individuals. The temptation is for you to be overcome by evil instead of your overcoming evil by goodness. The Bible tells us to triumph through goodness and not to be defeated by evil.

PRAYER: *Lord Jesus, in the midst of all the evil of this day help me to be aware of your tender mercy and goodness. Amen.*

THE MINISTRY OF THE MASTER—WEDNESDAY
A Spirit Lifter

"When anything goes wrong around our house, I just get busy and fix it." said the proud husband. "I'll say he does. Since he fixed the clock, the cuckoo backs out and asks, 'What time is it?' " said the wife.

God's Promise

The following promise is a great one to remember!

"We know that God makes all things work together for the good of those who have been called according to his decree." (Romans 8:28, NAB)

Practicing His Presence

Perhaps you were aware of His presence in a baby's smile, in a gentle hug from a loved one, or in a view of the countryside. Continue to develop this awareness in your life.

God's Health Care Plan—Goodness

The Lord Jesus Christ put goodness up front when He said,

> *"...do good to them that hate you, and pray for them which despitefully use you, and persecute you." Matthew 5:44, KJV*

And what is the importance of this type of living? What significance does it have for you as a believer? Our Lord gave the answer. He said,

> *"That ye may be the children of your Father which is in heaven..." Matthew 5:45, KJV*

He goes on to point out the goodness of the Lord is not confined to the devout saints. His goodness is part of the everyday experiences of life.

> *"...for he maketh his sun to rise on the evil and on the good, and sendeth rain on the just and on the unjust." Matthew 5:45, KJV*

John Fountain has stated:

> *"Happy are men if they but understand there is no safety but in doing good."*

When you retaliate, individuals will retaliate toward you. The more good you do, the more it grows into an abundant life for you and for others. There are moments when you may question the value of the good you do, but the long view will keep you on the right path.

PRAYER: *Thank you, Father, for the sunshine and the rain. Thank you for all the things in life which sustain your children. Amen.*

THE MINISTRY OF THE MASTER—THURSDAY
A Spirit Lifter

The husband was becoming disgusted with the amount of time his wife was spending training the dog. "You will never succeed in making that dog obey you."

His wife calmly replied, "Yes, I will. It is only a matter of patience. I had a lot of trouble with you at first, also."

God's Promise

"The afflicted and the needy seek water in vain, their tongues are parched with thirst. I, the Lord, will answer them; I, the God of Israel, will not forsake them." (Isaiah 41:17, NAB)

Practicing His Presence

I pray that being aware of His presence each day has been meaningful for you. How did you sense His presence yesterday?

God's Health Care Plan—Goodness

Goodness as an aspect of God's health care plan and of Christian living is important because it keeps a person in tune with the Lord of the universe. God is a good God. He wants His children to live the life of goodness. He wants us to live this life unto Him and to His glory.

William Penn expressed his philosophy of life with,

"He that does good for goodness sake, seeks neither praise nor reward, though sure of both at last. And may the final praise be only from God."

Rudyard Kipling in his poem, "When Earth's Last Picture Is Painted," has some find words about our actions.

"And only the Master shall praise us,
And only the Master shall blame,
And no one shall work for money,
And no one shall work for fame."

I feel these words should be applied to the life of goodness. Our life should be devoted to doing good unto others.

The healthy person seeks what is good for himself or herself while, at the same time, doing nothing which would be harmful to others.

It is not a trite statement but a powerful truth, *"Be good for goodness sake."*

PRAYER: *Deliver me, O Lord, from even thinking; let alone doing evil to anyone. Amen.*

THE MINISTRY OF THE MASTER—FRIDAY
A Spirit Lifter

"Jack, dear," said the bride, "let us try to make the people believe we've been married a long time."

The newlywed replied, "All right, dear. You carry both suitcases."

God's Promise

When I have difficulty sleeping, the following verse helps me.

"When you lie down, you will not be afraid; when you lie down, your sleep will be sweet." (Proverbs 3:24, NIV)

Practicing His Presence

You perhaps had a busy day yesterday. I pray that, amidst your activity, you were able to pull apart and sense the Lord's presence.

God's Health Care Plan—Goodness

Often people are affected more by an act of goodness than they are by volumes of words. Years ago I had a friend whose relative was a missionary in Japan. He served as a medical missionary endeavoring to win the Japanese to Christ. His efforts were to no avail. The response was practically nil.

There was an epidemic which broke out in his area of labor. Many were ill and a large number died. People were afraid to care for the ill and to bury the dead because of the dread disease. The medical missionary did not hesitate to minister to the needy. He was a physician with the high calling of doing good in every possible way.

Several days after he had ministered to many who were ill and had carried dozens to their grave, he came down with the malady. He did not recover but died as a faithful servant unto the Lord.

Following his death several of the Japanese accepted the Lord Jesus Christ. This life of goodness had influenced them far more than any amount of words could do.

The whole life is more than one free from bodily disease. It is one of being obedient to the high calling of Christ Jesus. This doctor had a wholeness which many of us lack. His good deeds will last through eternity. He knew what was really important and he did it. This is victorious living at its best.

PRAYER: *Today, Lord, I want to control my thoughts and attitudes toward others. May I lift them into your light and love. Amen.*

THE MINISTRY OF THE MASTER—SATURDAY
A Spirit Lifter

The football team had great difficulty with college entrance exams. Finally it was decided to change the exams in order to help them get into the school. The first question on the exam was a puzzle to one of them. It was, "What did Old MacDonald have?" He leaned over and asked his friend, "What did Old MacDonald have?" "A farm." came the whispered reply. A few moments later the same person asked, "How do you spell farm?" "Dummy," his friend replied, "it's 'e-i-e-i-o'."

God's Promise

"Every man according as he purposeth in his heart, so let him give; not grudgingly, or of necessity: for God loveth a cheerful giver." (II Corinthians 9:7, KJV)

Practicing His Presence

I believe you will have a great day if you are anticipating being aware of the Lord's presence. How did you do this yesterday?

God's Health Care Plan—Goodness

If you do not feel goodness contributes to your wholeness, then may I suggest you carefully consider,

"For he that will love life, and see good days, let him refrain his tongue from evil, and his lips that they speak no guile; let him eschew evil, and DO GOOD; let him seek peace, and ensue it." I Peter 3:10,11, KJV

Peter knew that the healthy attitude included goodness. It was essential to the triumphant Christian of his day. It is essential to the triumphant Christian of our day.

Seneca was on the right track with his insight,

"What is beautiful is good and who is good will soon also be beautiful."

The good life is the beautiful life. If this is true, then should you not seek to do good and to forsake evil? The last witness of the man buried in Thewsbury, England is truth to be applied to your life and mine. This was inscribed upon his tombstone.

"For the Lord Jesus Christ's sake, do all the good you can, to all the people you can, in all the ways you can, as long as you ever can. Amen."

If you and I pursue this admonition, life will be more zestful, happier, and healthier.

PRAYER: *Deliver me from the temptations of this day, O Lord. Help me to resist all of them. Amen.*

205

THE MINISTRY OF THE MASTER—SUNDAY

A Spirit Lifter

The wife was ill and hubby was the chief cook and bottle washer. He was doing great but could not find the tea. He looked high and low, long and hard. Finally, he called to his wife, "I can't find the tea."

"I don't know why you can't," came the peevish reply. "It's right in front, on the cupboard shelf, in the cocoa tin marked matches."

God's Promise

Perhaps you or someone you know is ill at this time.

"The Lord will strengthen him upon the bed of languishing: thou wilt make all his bed in his sickness." (Psalm 41:3, KJV)

Practicing His Presence

Do you find that an awareness of His presence is determined to some degree by how you feel? Was there any time yesterday when you knew the spiritual life was the most important aspect of your being?

God's Health Care Plan—Goodness

When I practice God's health care plan, including goodness, I rise above my pride and permit goodness to issue forth.

Some individuals have done me injustices. You have had this happen to you, I am sure. Sometimes those who appear to be our best friends end up doing us the greatest evil. It influences us to respond in a very negative and sometimes even harmful way toward them.

Goodness of spirit triumphs when each of us continues to say, "Father, forgive them. They know not what they do." Even though they do know they are hurting you, they cannot possibly be aware of all the consequences.

A speaker was extolling the attractiveness of this age and the advances of technology. He pointed out that people had more and better things than ever before. After he had finished, the audience was sobered with the remark of an elderly gentleman,

"I don't know how you feel about it; but, as for me, I believe to be better off is not necessarily to be better."

He knew what Bishop Horn knew.

"In the heraldry of heaven goodness precedes greatness and so on earth is more powerful. The lowly and lovely may often do more good in their limited sphere than the gifted."

PRAYER: *Today I want to practice your presence, Lord Jesus. Thank you for your precious reality in my life. Amen.*

GOD'S HEALTH CARE PLAN—FAITHFULNESS

The Lord desires wholeness for you and for me. Yet, this wholeness can be impaired and sometimes completely destroyed by acts of unfaithfulness. These acts may be toward God or toward others.

It is certainly to my detriment when I turn my back upon the Lord and become unfaithful to Him and His promises. This creates great stress of spirit, mind, and body.

In like manner, when I am unfaithful to others in work, attitude, actions, or intent, stress is brought into my life. What is true for me is true for you.

I have counseled with many people who have been unfaithful to their employer, family members, spouse, neighbor or fellow church member. This unfaithfulness never produced the desired goal. The stark reality is that the sweet, wonderful fruit anticipated in most cases was ultimately bitter fruit and an unproductive harvest.

Faithfulness is a stirring word. Just to say it does something to me on the inside. It is a strong word. It almost shouts its message of devotion, firmness, loyalty, trust, trustworthiness, truth, and unwaivering style of life.

Faithfulness is a respected way of life in the world. It is the required way of life in the sight of God.

We are experiencing much unfaithfulness today. Promises are being broken and lives ruined by this spirit of unfaithfulness.

This is especially true in the area of marriage. It has become commonplace to have marriages of many years fall apart. One or both of the partners are left devastated. The problems which issue forth create all kinds of diseases, discomfort, and distress.

"Fear none of those things which thou shalt suffer: ...be thou faithful unto death, and I will give thee a crown of life."
Revelation 2:10, KJV

POINTS TO PONDER

1. What is the definition of faithfulness?
2. What example of faithfulness have you experienced?
3. Is there more or less faithfulness toward family, church, and friends today than in the past?

Daily Bible Study and Daily Prayer Concerns

GOD'S HEALTH CARE PLAN—FAITHFULNESS

1. A tale-bearer reveals secrets, but he that is of a _____ _____spirit conceals the matter. *Pro. 11:13*
2. A faithful_____will not lie: but a false witness will utter lies. *Pro. 14:5*
3. The one who is faithful is that which is_____ is faithful in that which is much. *Lu. 16:10*
4. It is required in stewards that a man be found_____ _____. *I Cor. 4:2*
5. The Lord thy God is the _____ God. *Deut. 7:9*
6. Thy faithfulness reaches unto the _____. *Ps. 36:5*
7. I will make known thy faithfulness unto all _____ _____. *Ps 89:1*
8. Commit your soul unto him in well doing, as unto a faithful _____ _____. *I Pet. 4:19*
9. The _____ is faithful who shall establish you, and keep you from evil. *II Th. 3:3*
10. If we believe not, yet he abideth _____: he cannot deny himself. *II Tim. 2:13*
11. Jesus Christ is the faithful _____. *Rev. 1:5*
12. The saying is faithful, that if we died with him, we shall also _____ _____ with him. *II Tim. 2:11*
13. He is faithful that_____. *Heb. 10:23*
14. Christ is our faithful high _____ in things pertaining to God. *Heb. 2:17*

DAILY SCRIPTURE

Mon.   Pro. 11:12-23
Tues.   Luke 16:10-13
Wed.   I Cor. 4:1-5
Thurs. Ps. 36:5-12
Fri.   I Pet. 4:12-19
Sat.   II Thess. 3:1-5
Sun.   Heb. 10:19-25

PRAYER CONCERNS

Your Family & Relatives
Government Leaders
Missionaries
For the Unbelievers
Churches & Denominations
Your Own Church
Prayer and Praise

NOTE: You will be spiritually strengthened by completing two questions each day, reading the suggested scripture, and ministering in prayer for the concerns of the day.

THE MINISTRY OF THE MASTER—MONDAY
A Spirit Lifter

The husband casually mentioned, "That couple across the street certainly is in love. Every morning I see him kiss his wife on the back steps of their house." The wife rather longingly said, "Why don't you ever do that?" His reply revealed where his thoughts were lodged. "How can I? I don't even know her?"

God's Promise

Consider this promise throughout your day.

"So, whether you eat or drink, or whatever you do, do all to the glory of God." (I Corinthians 10:31, RSV)

Practicing His Presence

I am amazed how often the Lord has felt near to me while I am involved in the ordinary experiences of life. The more I practice His presence, the more I behold Him in all things.

God's Health Care Plan—Faithfulness

Faithfulness to the Lord and those we love is more than doing certain things. It also involves not doing certain things. The snares of Satan are subtle, but even in their innocence they are deadly.

The faithfulness to which we are called is unto the Lord. However, this is tangibly expressed in relationship of daily actions and faithful living.

"Can a man take fire in his bosom, and his clothes not be burned? Can one go upon hot coals, and his feet not be burned? So he that goeth in to his neighbor's wife; whosoever toucheth her shall not be innocent." Proverbs 6:27-29, KJV

The writer is trying to point out that unfaithfulness will not reap the anticipated joys. The end result is bitterness, not blessings.

The call of God's word is to faithfulness. He states that if you are to be whole, strong, and wholesome, then faithfulness must be part of your total being.

The faithful person has accepted the facts that God has called him to purposeful and pure living and also that evil will lead to chaos and destruction.

PRAYER: *Help me to control my inner being, Lord Jesus. May I realize all the issues of life spring from the heart. Amen.*

THE MINISTRY OF THE MASTER—TUESDAY
A Spirit Lifter

"What is yours is mine and what is mine is mine," is a philosophy pursued by some people. However, this is about the furthermost I have ever seen this spirit carried by anyone.

Woman to the bank teller: "I want to make a withdrawal from my husband's half of our joint account."

God's Promise

"The God who made both earth and heaven, the seas and everything in them, He is the God who keeps every promise." (Psalm 146:6, TLB)

Practicing His Presence

Was there at least a little time during your busy schedule when you sensed His presence yesterday? How did this make you feel?

God's Health Care Plan—Faithfulness

Why are we inclined to yield to the temptation to be unfaithful to God, others, and to ourselves? Why are we willing to step from the light of openness and truth and walk into darkness and unfaithfulness?

Jesus points out some reasons which are presented in the eighth chapter of St. Luke's gospel. In the first place, He points out in verse 12 that Satan causes unfaithfulness. The moment a person hears of the better way of life, Satan snatches away this good word and the individual is left floundering.

Many individuals desire to lead faithful lives. They long and yearn for it. However, with many of them it is only a fleeting thought, even though a sincere one at the moment. This call to the highest is immediately ignored or suppressed, and Satan has another victory.

Some people are of the opinion that they can change their lives any time they choose and that they are not in the clutches of the evil One. How foolish! Even while speaking of being faithful, they continue a lifestyle of unfaithfulness.

They are like Mark Twain who said he could quit smoking any time he wanted to. He knew this to be true because he had quit a thousand times. It is obvious he was only fooling himself and satirically proclaiming a truth.

Satan does not desire the wholeness of faithfulness in your life. You must overcome him through the presence and power of the Lord.

PRAYER: *Father, may I depend upon your strength to help me live the disciplined life of self-control in all areas. Amen.*

THE MINISTRY OF THE MASTER—WEDNESDAY
A Spirit Lifter

A fisherman was hauled into court for catching ten more black bass than the law allows. "Guilty, or not guilty," boomed the judge. The quick reply, "Guilty." "That will be $57.00 plus cost." said the judge.

After cheerfully paying the fine, the defendant said, "Now, your honor, I'd like several copies of the court record to show my friends."

God's Promise

God's promise for belief is staggering.

"Let not your heart be troubled, ye believe in God, believe also in me." (John 14:1, KJV)

Practicing His Presence

You may have had a difficult day yesterday. I do hope, however, that you were able to put things into proper perspective and be aware of the Lord Jesus working in your life.

God's Health Care Plan—Faithfulness

The second reason Jesus gives for unfaithfulness is that often temptation cannot be resisted. Luke 8:13 describes the person who grasps the faithful life with enthusiasm.

This is fine until temptation again raises its head seductively. Its ugliness is obscured for the moment, and its appeal is such that the temptation is too strong to resist. Faithfulness is cast aside, and unfaithfulness issues forth.

I have seen many people begin a devout life. I have witnessed few who have pursued the journey through the years. The temptation to take the easy way and to choose short term benefits is too great. Often the temptations of the flesh are so strong that they succumb.

In the book, *"Daughter of Destiny,"* the life story of Kathryn Kuhlman, I was intrigued with those of her organization who could not remain faithful. Some of her co-workers succumbed to the temptation of sexual passions. Immorality caught up with them. In the presence of a person greatly used of God they could not maintain consistent and strong defense against temptation.

Even Kathryn's ministry was put in mothballs for nearly ten years and was affected to her death by her marriage to the man who left his family for her.

It is not easy to resist temptation, but it must be done if faithfulness is to be your lifestyle.

PRAYER: *Jesus, may my actions show forth goodness to all with whom I come in contact. Amen.*

THE MINISTRY OF THE MASTER—THURSDAY
A Spirit Lifter

The luckless fisherman went into the fish store on his way home. He ordered several fish. He refused to take them from the clerk but stepped back and said, "Toss them here to me," The amazed clerk said, "But why throw them to you?" The quick retort was, "So I can tell my family that I caught them. I may be a poor fisherman, but I am not a liar."

God's Promise

Here is a golden promise even in the midst of our leaden difficulties.

"If we suffer, we shall also reign with him; if we deny him, he also will deny us." (II Tim. 2:12, KJV)

Practicing His Presence

May you continually remain sensitive to the Spirit! How were you aware of His presence yesterday, and how did this make you feel?

God's Health Care Plan—Faithfulness

The reason for unfaithfulness is presented by Jesus in Luke 8:14. He was well aware of the fact that many are sidetracked by desire for material possessions. The concern for prestige, position, and prosperity has ruined many and produced unfaithfulness in the lives of a host of persons.

Life's attractions can be a snare to faithfulness unto yourself, others, and God. These attractions can produce an unhealthy attitude in you which will devour, instead of deliver, you. This attraction does not produce the fruit you need but produces bitter and harmful fruit.

Many a promising employee has been rising in his company, but he feels he is not moving fast enough. He begins to cheat and perhaps even to steal. His life ends up ruined. The desire for worldly things possesses him and unfaithfulness is the end result.

Many godly ministries have begun with the leader and participants really sincerely dedicated. In time, the lure of fame and fortune has changed that ministry to one of selfishness instead of one of sacrifice.

Jesus warns that the love of riches and glory is usually a creeping pilgrimage. It does not spring up over night but slowly one thing leads to another until es are off the true goal of life and on a lesser goal. This state of unhealthiness is sometimes ignored or not even detected until it is too late.

PRAYER: *Take control of my tongue, O Lord. May I speak only that which glorifies you and helps others. Amen.*

THE MINISTRY OF THE MASTER—FRIDAY
A Spirit Lifter

At breakfast the wife commented, "I'm sick and tired of being alone every weekend. If you think you're going out to golf today..."

The husband interrupted her, "Nonsense, dear, golf is the furthermost thing from my mind," as he picked up another piece of toast. "Please pass me the putter."

God's Promise

The promise of being known by the Lord is a comfort each day.

"My sheep hear my voice, and I know them, and they follow me." (John 10:27, KJV)

Practicing His Presence

Are you anticipating being aware of the Lord's presence throughout this day? If so, I am certain this will be a wonderful day for you.

God's Health Care Plan—Faithfulness

The spirit of unfaithfulness is not unique to our day. This has been a struggle through the centuries. The Apostle Paul certainly experienced unfaithfulness on the part of his friends and followers.

"For Demas hath forsaken me, having loved this present world..."
II Timothy 4:10, KJV)

Demas did what many have done and are doing today. He sought things instead of God. I have known many persons who have worked two, and sometimes three, jobs to secure possessions for their families only to discover they have lost their loved ones.

I have known people who have felt such a great need for more wealth that they have neglected worship. Adults and teenagers alike have put work ahead of worship. It seems to be a legitimate excuse in their hearts and minds to neglect the most important things in life. A teenager feels he must have a car; therefore, to secure it and pay the insurance he or she must work many hours each week. This means that fellowship with other believers is gone.

You need not look very hard to see many around you who are frantically trying to get more money so they can have more things which ultimately distract them from proper goals in life. In a crisis the things they sought will let them down. They will be of little, if any, value. They have sold their souls for a hot rod instead of a bowl of porridge, but the end result is the same. It cannot be regained, even though sought, with tears.

PRAYER: *My inner spirit yearns for you, O Lord. Help me to take time to be holy. Amen.*

THE MINISTRY OF THE MASTER—SATURDAY
A Spirit Lifter

Before her first plane ride a little old lady was told that chewing gum would keep her ears from popping. After landing she excitedly reported that it worked very well. However, her question to her traveling companion amazed him. "The chewing gum worked fine, but how do I get it out of my ears?"

God's Promise

The righteous life has its rewards.

"The righteous shall flourish like the palm tree: he shall grow like a cedar in Lebanon." (Psalm 92:12, KJV)

Practicing His Presence

Through what incident or person did you sense the presence of the Lord yesterday? How did this make you feel?

God's Health Care Plan—Faithfulness

I cannot stress enough this week that our faithfulness should be unto the Lord. We are called to worship Him and to put Him first. The benefits of this lifestyle are many and satisfying.

Moses was able to grasp this truth and to convey it to his people. They were not always willing to follow his advice, even though he gave them sound advice.

"Worship the Lord your God, and he will bless your bread and water. I will take away all sickness out of your midst. None shall miscarry or be barren in your land. I will grant you a full span of life." Ex. 23:25,26

God revealed to Moses that faithfulness began and ended with worship of Him as the only true God. The truth of the by-products of worship are presented.

These verses show to us that our daily needs of bread and water will be provided. In addition, sickness will be prevented. Our lot will not be as it is with those who do not worship.

The life which is centered on the Lord is a fuller and healthier life. In fact, Moses says that worship will grant you a full span of life. I believe that the span is more than quantity of years. I believe it is also quality of years.

Faithfulness is not something you and I do begrudgingly. It is not something which robs us of the pleasures of life. The call to faithfulness receives our willing response and adds pleasure, purpose, and power to our lives.

PRAYER: *Thank you, Lord Jesus, for your presence and the power you impart to me. Amen.*

THE MINISTRY OF THE MASTER—SUNDAY
A Spirit Lifter

When a Texan visited Canada, his host showed him the sights. The Texan's bragging spirit conveyed that nothing was so big and fine as that in Texas. Finally, the exasperated Canadian showed him Niagara Falls. "You don't have anything like this in Texas, do you?" he boasted.

"No, but we have a plumber down there who could fix that leak in no time flat," was his straight-faced response.

God's Promise

That evil deeds will not triumph is God's promise.

"For there is nothing covered, that shall not be revealed; neither hid, that shall not be known." (Luke 12:2, KJV)

Practicing His Presence

I pray you were very much aware of the Lord's presence in your life yesterday. Can you recall some specific incident or person which helped this awareness?

God's Health Care Plan—Faithfulness

The response to faithfulness is climaxed this week with the words by the writer of the book of Hebrews.

"But without faith it is impossible to please him: for he that cometh to God must believe that he is, and that he is a rewarder of them that diligently seek him." Heb. 11:6, KJV

Faithfulness unto the Lord is not merely believing that He exists. It includes believing Him. It includes believing that what He has revealed in the written Word is true. It includes believing that what He has revealed through the Living Word, Jesus Christ, is true.

Although unfaithfulness is not new, it is no more excusable today than it was in Paul's day, or in Christ's day, or in the days of Moses. The unfaithful person is held accountable for unfaithful acts, thoughts and motives.

"Loyal", trustworthy", "true blue", "devoted", and "faithful" are all strong, positive words. Do they describe your lifestyle in relationship to God and others? Are they descriptive of how you picture yourself?

I feel these are questions of prime importance in your life and in mine. Our calling is to faithfulness. Life cannot really be whole unless this be true.

The consequences of unfaithfulness are too great and the risk too immense for anyone. The Lord has been faithful. My desire is to be like him. I pray this is your desire as well.

PRAYER: *Lord Jesus, I give you my pride. Help me to walk humbly before you and to practice goodness and mercy. Amen.*

215

Theme for the Week
GOD'S HEALTH CARE PLAN—SELF CONTROL

I want to continue this week to emphasize that God desires wholeness for you. He gives us guidelines in His Holy Book to help achieve this wholeness. Among the suggestions are that they bring forth the fruit of the spirit. The fruit has the aspects of love, joy, peace, long-suffering, gentleness, goodness, faith, meekness, and self-control.

Self-control or temperance is something which God says should be a part of the life of every believer. It is needed by everyone. It is self-control which enables you to live a life of greater wholeness. It is lack of self-control which leads to deterioration of our devotion to God and to others. The neglect of self-control leads to dire consequences in emotions, body, mind, and spirit.

The lack of self-control may not affect you at the moment, but in the years ahead come back to haunt you. This was dramatically revealed in the life of a friend of mine.

While under the influence of drugs and in a moment of lack of self-control, he beat up the driver who did not make a left turn as fast as he felt he should. Years later he applied for a job and discovered that the personnel manager was the person he had dragged from the car and severely beaten. You can understand why he was not employed for the position he wanted in that company.

Self-control is your high calling in the area of your time, your desires, your passions, your ambitions, and your motives. All life must be under the control of the spirit or what is unleashed will ruin your spirit.

A self-controlled life is a more productive and purposeful life. This control is made possible because of the presence and power of the Lord.

The balanced life is a result of the controlled life. Self-control is laying aside that which hinders and clinging to that which enhances and brings wholeness.

POINTS TO PONDER

1. What is your definition of self-control?
2. In what areas of life do you find control to be most difficult?
3. How do you apply the spiritual power to your areas of self-control?

GOD'S HEALTH CARE PLAN—SELF-CONTROL

1. He that is slow to anger is better than the_____
_____. *Pro. 16:32*
2. As Paul reasoned of righteousness and self-control and the _____
_____to come, Felix was terrified. *Acts 24:25*
3. Let not sin reign your mortal _____.
Rom. 6:12
4. If any man offend not in _____ the same
is a perfect man. *James 3:2*
5. Add to your knowledge self-control; and in your self-control _____
_____. *II Pet. 1:6*
6. Keep thy _____ from evil. *Ps. 34:13*
7. Whoso keepeth his mouth and his tongue keepeth his soul from _____
_____. *Pro. 21:23*
8. He that will_____ life, and see good days, let
him refrain his tongue from evil. *I Pet. 3:10*
9. He that loveth his son _____ him. *Pro. 13:24*
10. Withhold not correction from the child, for if thou beatest him with the
rod, he shall not _____. *Pro. 23:13*
11. Train up a child in the way he should go; and when he is old, he will
not_____from it. *Pro. 22:6*
12. Thou shalt teach them diligently unto thy _____
_____. *Deut. 6:7*
13. What son is he whom the _____ chastenth not?
Heb. 12:7

DAILY SCRIPTURE

Mon.   Pro. 16:25-33
Tues. Acts 24:24-27
Wed.   Rom. 6:12-14
Thurs. I Pet. 3:8-12
Fri.   Deut. 6:4-9
Sat.   Ps. 94:8-15
Sun.   Heb. 12:3-11

PRAYER CONCERNS

Your Family & Relatives
Government Leaders
Missionaries
For the Unbelievers
Churches & Denominations
Your Own Church
Prayer and Praise

NOTE: You will be spiritually strengthened by completing two questions each day, reading the suggested scripture, and ministering in prayer for the concerns of the day.

THE MINISTRY OF THE MASTER—MONDAY
A Spirit Lifter

A woman, traveling by bus, told of her visit to San Jose, California. Her friend said, "You pronounced that wrong. In California all 'j's' are pronounced like 'h's'. When were you there?"

The lady looked puzzled for a moment and then without hesitation replied, "In Hune and Huly."

God's Promise

God promises good to the one willing to be reproved and corrected. *"A fool despiseth his father's instruction: but he that regardeth reproof is prudent."* (Proverbs 17:10, KJV)

Practicing His Presence

If you are like me, you sometimes experience things which seem to cloud the reality of His presence. What do you do when that happens to you?

God's Health Care Plan—Self-Control

The wholeness of self-control starts on the inside and issues forth on the outside. The victorious life is one which has put the important and pure issues at the core of your life. It is the better idea for each and every person.

There is a story of two Chinese individuals arguing. It became more intense all the time. An American standing in the group surrounding them started to yell at the one, *"Hit him, hit him. Let him have it."* One of the Chinese turned to all in the group and said,

"Neither one would ever hit the other, because the first one to strike a blow would be admitting he had run out of ideas."

Self-control is admitting that you have ideas on living and do not have to lash out at people, events, or circumstances.

Lack of control leads to overindulgence in many areas of life. It may be in the wasting of time, energy, and thought. It can lead to overweight, sexual immorality, dependence upon drugs, indifference to the feelings and needs of others, and an extremely selfish view of life.

Any or all of these things lead to defeat, remorse, frustration, depresson, and even to spiritual bankruptcy. The wholeness you desire will be more adequately achieved if you practice the self-control for which you yearn.

PRAYER: *Father, may I have an attitude of self-control at all times. May I live out this spirit at all times. Amen.*

218

THE MINISTRY OF THE MASTER—TUESDAY
A Spirit Lifter

"What are you looking for in a secretary?" asked the enterprising personnel director as he tried to discover the president's needs before interviewing applicants.

"Nothing much," he said. "Just find me one who looks like a girl, acts like a lady, and works like a dog."

God's Promise

May you be comforted with this glorious promise.

"Whosoever therefore shall confess me before men, him will I confess also before my Father which is in heaven." (Mt. 10:3, KJV)

Practicing His Presence

Constantly remain sensitive to the spirit. Sense His presence often during your day. Can you recall a specific incident yesterday in which His presence was very evident?

God's Health Care Plan—Self-Control

How well can you control your own actions and reactions? The kingdom to be controlled is the kingdom within you. It is the greatest kingdom in the world and the one over which the Lord should reign.

A King of old was strolling through his garden. He was startled by the sudden appearance of an old man who darted out from behind the bushes. The king immediately asked who he was and was about to shout for the guards. The old man replied, *"I am a king!"*

"A king! Of what kingdom?" retorted the king. Then looking him over ever more closely, he lost some of his initial fear and calmly said, *"Pray tell me over what kingdom do you rule?"*

The response is a jewel to be placed in the crown of your mind and to be kept polished throughout your life. *"I rule over the kingdom that is within me,"* said the old man without hesitation.

He had the right idea. He was indeed a king. He did have a kingdom over which to rule. Every person can say, *"I am a king, or a queen, because I rule over the kingdom within."*

It is impossible for you to control the actions of others. You may intimidate, but you cannot rule. The world is not going to do all things according to your desires. The kingdom you can control is within and this you should seek to do constantly.

PRAYER: *Jesus, help me to put my priorities right. May I ever practice self-control. Amen.*

219

THE MINISTRY OF THE MASTER—WEDNESDAY
A Spirit Lifter

A man went into the restaurant and ordered a cup of coffee without any cream. A few minutes later the waitress returned and said,
"Sir, we are all out of cream. Would you mind taking your coffee without milk?"

God's Promise

"If we confess our sins, he is faithful and just to forgive us our sins, and to cleanse us from all unrighteousness." (I John 1:9, KJV)

Practicing His Presence

May you seek to quiet yourself this day and hear "the still small voice" speak to you. How were you aware of His presence yesterday?

God's Health Care Plan—Self-Control

I find that one of the areas of control which I must maintain is in my private devotional life. If I neglect this, all life loses much of its meaning. I do not remain so calm, relaxed, dedicated to what I should be doing, or so confident in the Lord as I would otherwise.

My prayer pilgrimage, *"A Ministry of Prayer,"* has been pursued by many people. It is amazing to me how many of them find it almost impossible to devote thirty minutes a day for these spiritual exercises. They are too busy to have a devotional time.

Jesus never spent His time in long prayers in public. The prayers for healing were short and to the point. Even when He raised Lazarus from the dead, He had but a short prayer. His power issued forth from his disciplined private life with the Father. It was not an expression of public display. He displayed power, not piety, because of the self-control He practiced in the area of devotional life.

The highest victory you can achieve is to triumph in your own devotional life. I feel all of life is permeated by the spirit we bring to it each day through our conscious communion with the Father.

The day is brighter and more meaningful when my self-control rules. It loses its glow when I neglect to discipline the inner spirit.

PRAYER: *My desire is to have a disciplined devotional life, Jesus. Please grant my desire. Amen.*

220

THE MINISTRY OF THE MASTER—THURSDAY
A Spirit Lifter

"Doctor, you must help me. My husband thinks he is a dog."
"That sounds strange. What kind of a dog?"
"A dachshund."
"That is serious. How long has this been going on?"
The wife replied, "Ever since he was a puppy."

God's Promise

"...Let him that heareth say, come. And let him that is athirst come. And whosoever will, let him take the water of life freely."
(Revelation 22:17, KJV)

Practicing His Presence

Are you finding being aware of His presence exciting? I certainly am! Did you have an exciting day yesterday?

God's Health Care Plan—Self-Control

Paul tells us that the one who achieves must be willing to pay the price of discipline and self-control.

"And every man that striveth for the mastery is temperate in all things. Now they do it to obtain a corruptible crown; but we an incorruptible." I Corinthians 9:25, KJV

Not everyone in high school goes out for football but those who do are willing to discipline themselves to the expectations of the coach and the rules of the game. This is true of any sport.

It is interesting to me that so few members of the church are willing really to discipline themselves to practice His presence. An ancient Greek scholar wrote,

"The conqueror of pleasure is not the man who never uses pleasure. Rather he is the man who uses pleasure as a rider guides a horse or a steersman directs a ship. So he directs pleasures as he wishes."

The purpose of our spiritual discipline is to help us deal with the vicissitudes of life. Problems will soon overwhelm us if we are not willing to practice the self-control needed to overcome.

I realize it is much easier to present problems than to present solutions. Even though there is no easy three-step method to the victorious life, self-control will help each conquer in his own way. The Lord is willing to grant the grace. Are you willing to receive His grace and apply it moment by moment to your situation?

PRAYER: *Father, I believe you have a plan for my life. Help me to walk by faith in this conviction. Amen.*

221

THE MINISTRY OF THE MASTER—FRIDAY
A Spirit Lifter

A lady phoned and obviously got the wrong number. She had dialed the real estate broker, but she was seeking information about maternity clothes. While the man said he did not handle such clothes, he captured the moment by saying, "But can I interest you in a larger house?

God's Promise

"But the path of the just is as the shining light, that shineth more and more unto the perfect day." (Proverbs 4:18, KJV)

Practicing His Presence

I have sought to remind you each day to be aware of the presence of the Lord. How do you find this taking place in your own life?

God's Health Care Plan—Self-Control

Abraham Lincoln once said, *"A lot of people I know have a two foot boiler and a nine foot whistle. And every time they blow the whistle it takes so much steam the engine stops."*

There may be some who say it is good to blow your top at times. Perhaps, but my experience has been that I have seen more damage from such experiences than I have seen benefit.

The loss of self-control leaves problems, scars, and situations which are not healthy. If you must blow your top, may I suggest you do so unto the Lord and not others. He can certainly take it much better. He does not have trouble recovering from the onslaught of your verbiage.

It is not easy to practice self-control toward others. Sometimes they can be very exasperating. Yet, the self-control that you need is usually in the area of relationship to others.

My first grade friend was having great trouble liking his teacher. He could not control his anger. I showed him how to pour a bucket of love on her each morning before class got started. He was helped by controlling his thoughts and emotions through the discipline of thinking love. This self-control affected the emotions and attitude of even a small boy. It can do the same for you.

PRAYER: *I rebuke the evil and distracting thoughts, O Lord. Help me to keep my mind on you this day. Amen.*

THE MINISTRY OF THE MASTER—SATURDAY
A Spirit Lifter
"What does your father do?" inquired young Sally's teacher.
"My dad follows the medical profession."
"Oh, I didn't know he was a doctor," exclaimed the teacher.
"He isn't," said Sally. "He's an undertaker."

God's Promise
Do you ever wonder what God has to say about bearing burdens?
"Bear one another's burdens, and so fulfill the law of Christ." (Galatians 6:2, RSV)

Practicing His Presence
Continue to exercise your spiritual powers through consciously practicing His presence. How did you sense the presence of His Spirit yesterday?

God's Health Care Plan—Self-Control
Now we are coming to the end of this week and our consideration of self-control. The bottom line is keeping the mind and heart on the Lord Jesus Christ. All of life must be disciplined in this direction.

The Apostle Paul gave sage advice.

"Finally, brethren, whatsoever things are true, whatsover things are honest, just, pure, lovely, good report; if there be any virtue, and if there be any praise, think on these things." Philippians 4:8, KJV

This is self-control at its highest level. It involves the control of the mind. It is within the person that the lack of self-control originates. It may manifest itself in outward actions, but it starts with inward thoughts.

Many a person has told me he wastes too much time. I feel the same way. If my time were more disciplined, I could accomplish much more than what I do.

But even more important than the use of my time is the use of my mind. If I could keep my mind on the things which elevate and away from the negative and defeating, what a healthy, wholesome outlook I would possess!

It is my prayer to apply more than ever the insights of Paul to control my mind and to keep them on the things of the Lord and His purity and power.

PRAYER: *It is you, and you alone, that I worship, O Lord. May I never get my eyes on lesser gods. Amen.*

THE MINISTRY OF THE MASTER—SUNDAY
A Spirit Lifter

"Tell me why you lost your last job." asked the personnel director.
"It was because of sickness, sir," was the applicant's reply.
"What was the nature of your sickness?" he asked.
"Oh, it wasn't me that was sick. The problem was my boss got sick of me!"

God's Promise

Inner peace and world peace are essential. God's promise is:
"Blessed are the peacemakers; for they shall be called the children of God." (Matthew 5:9, KJV)

Practicing His Presence

I hope that these past several days of being aware of His presence have been helpful to you. May you continually remain sensitive to the Spirit! How did this sensitivity affect your day yesterday?

God's Health Care Plan—Self-Control

This week I do not want to neglect the self-control of the tongue. This is the instrument which causes much trouble. James says,

"And the tongue is a fire, a world of iniquity...full of deadly poison." James 3:6-8, KJV
"The boneless tongue, so small, so weak
Can crush and kill," declares the Greek.
"The tongue destroys a greater horde,"
The Turks assert, "than does the sword."
The Persian proverb wisely saith;
"A lengthy tongue, an early death,"
Or sometimes takes this form instead:
"The tongue can speak a word whose speed,"
Says the Chinese, "outstrips the steed."
While Arab sages this impart!
"The tongue's great storehouse is the heart."
From Hebrew writ this saying sprung:
"Tho' feet should slip, ne'er let the tongue."
The Sacred writers crown the whole:
"Who keeps his tongue doth keep his soul."

Here is a good summary of the benefits of self-control.

"He that is slow to anger is better than the mighty; and he that ruleth his spirit than he that taketh a city." Proverbs 16:32, KJV

PRAYER: *Lord, help me to properly control my tongue. Amen.*

INNER ILLNESS

This week I want to consider a very important area of concern. It is inner illness. I realize there are as many physical afflictions which plague individuals today as always. There is the high incidence of heart disease and the widespread malady of cancer. However, with all the ravages of cancer, heart disease, and many other physical afflictions I still believe that our greatest problem today is inner illness.

It is not the affliction of the body which has put many in the depths of depression. It is the result of their distressed inner being. You can triumph over a disease or injury; but if you do not triumph in spirit all life is in vain.

Mary and I saw a film, "Joni." This is a marvelous example of someone who conquered because of inner wholeness. It was her inner spirit which enabled her to triumph over all things. Many individuals with good health and sound limbs are living defeated lives. They have been defeated on the inside.

Inner illness is not easy to diagnose nor is it easy to cure. It is varied, complicated, and devastating. We do not always know what brings it, nor are we able to know what will take it away. We do know many manifestations of it, and we do know that the Lord Jesus can bring His healing to this area of life.

There are telltale signs which will help you detect the presence of inner illness. There are ways by which you can be healed from the ravages of inner illness. There is hope for you and wholeness does await you.

This week I want to consider several facets of inner illness. I believe a big step toward wholeness is to realize the problem. The disease must be pinpointed before the treatment can be properly given. It is my candid opinion that you will be helped as you consider inner illness and that it will help you move on to inner wholeness.

POINTS TO PONDER

1. How would you define and describe inner illness?
2. Do you feel inner illness is prevalent in our modern world?
3. What do you feel is the answer to inner illness?

INNER ILLNESS

1. _____ not: for God is come to prove you.
   Ex. 20:20
2. There is no want to them that _____ him.
   Ps. 34:9
3. Whoever is _____ with his brother without a
   cause shall be in danger of judgment. *Mt. 5:22*
4. Love your _____ and bless them that curse you.
   Mt. 5:44
5. Where your treasure is there will your _____
   be also. *Mt. 6:21*
6. Take no thought for your _____, what ye
   shall eat or drink. *Mt. 6:25*
7. Thou _____ first cast out the beam out
   of thine own eye. *Mt. 7:5*
8. He giveth his beloved _____. *Ps. 127:2*
9. Be careful for nothing, but let your _____
   be made known to God. *Ph. 4:6*
10. Cast all your _____ upon him. *I Pet. 5:7*
11. When I awake I am still with _____.
    Ps. 139:18
12. Cease from _____ and forsake wrath. *Ps. 37:8*
13. Anger resteth in the bosom of _____. *Eccl. 7:9*
14. Remember not the sins of my _____. *Ps. 25:7*

DAILY SCRIPTURE

Mon.   Ex. 20:18-20
Tues. Ps. 34:1-10
Wed.   Mt. 5:21-26
Thurs. Phil. 4:4-9
Fri.   Ps. 139:13-18
Sat.   Eccl. 7:9-14
Sun.   Mt. 7:1-5

PRAYER CONCERNS

Your Family & Relatives
Government Leaders
Missionaries
For the Unbelievers
Churches & Denominations
Your Own Church
Prayer and Praise

NOTE: You will be spiritually strengthened by completing two questions each day, reading the suggested scripture, and ministering in prayer for the concerns of the day.

THE MINISTRY OF THE MASTER—MONDAY
A Spirit Lifter

Three Methodists showed up at Heaven's gate and were denied admittance. There was no room, and there would be no room until a remodeling program was completed. They were sent to hell to await the preparation of their mansion which would take six months.

Some weeks later the head angel got a call from Satan in hell. He said, "Would you get these three Methodists out of here? They have put on rummage sales, bake sales, weekly suppers, as well as other money raising projects. At the rate they are going, within three weeks they will have enough money to air condition this place."

God's Promise

What a wonderful promise to remember throughout your day! *"Be still, and know that I am God, I am exalted among the nations, I am exalted in the earth!"* (Psalms 46:10, RSV)

Practicing His Presence

This day as you use *"The Ministry of The Master"* consciously practice His presence. May you seek to quiet your body, mind and spirit! He is with you.

Inner Illness

Inner illness manifests itself in many different ways. My sermonettes this week will deal with some of these manifestations. Aimlessness is one of the signs of an inner illness which needs attention and wholeness which the high calling in Christ Jesus can bring.

Millions have no great goal in life. They are wandering aimlessly. It is as if they have nothing as their target in life and shoot at it each day.

I could not begin to tell you how many people have said to me, *"Pastor, I just can't find any meaning in life. I want so desperately to do something for God, but I don't know what to do or how."* They are looking for a big ministry and spectacular results and, in the meantime, roam through life.

James was a writer who attacked problems head-on. He showed the futility of aimlessness.

"A double minded person is unstable in all his ways." James 1:8

He knew that you cannot continue to remain emotionally and spiritually strong if you are torn on the inside. A goal must be established and all of your energies directed to the achieving of that goal. The aimless life is one of anxiety and frustration.

PRAYER: *Father, may the goal of my life be to serve you faithfully until my last breath. Amen.*

THE MINISTRY OF THE MASTER—TUESDAY
A Spirit Lifter

A lady purchased a dozen oranges at her local grocery. Upon arriving home, she discovered there were only ten oranges in her sack. She fumed at the owner concerning this problem. He pleasantly assured her he had her interest at heart with these words,

"This is part of our personal and special service, madam. Two of the dozen were bad, so I threw them away for you."

God's Promise

"Thou dost keep him in perfect peace, whose mind is stayed on thee, because he trusts in thee." (Isaiah 26:3, RSV)

Practicing His Presence

I seek to remind you each day to be aware of the presence of the Lord. How do you find this taking place in your own life?

Inner Illness

There are many other characteristics of a person plagued with inner illness. One of them is the spirit of anger. Now, granted, everyone will have moments of anger. This is part of being human. It is temporary and soon passes.

The individual who has a continual inner boiling of anger is the one who has a severe case of inner illness. Some people literally live with anger within their hearts. The account of the woman who drove her car onto the sidewalk and killed several innocent people is an account of an anger boiling over. She had lived a life of anger against society and finally reached a breaking point which resulted in the tragedy.

Another aspect of inner illness is anxiety. Again, this is not the temporary deep concern for some situation. This is a state of constant uneasiness. Yet, you really do not know why you are troubled nor what is really troubling you. You cannot pinpoint the problem, but you know that you are anxious all the time. The words of Jesus mean very little to you when you are in this state. He said,

"...Sufficient unto the day is the evil thereof." Matthew 6:3

He knew that His confidence was in the Father and that He need not be anxious for all the details of life. Inner illness will not permit you to live this way.

PRAYER: *Dear Jesus, grant to me your gentle and forgiving spirit. Remove any anger I may have toward any person. Amen.*

THE MINISTRY OF THE MASTER—WEDNESDAY
A Spirit Lifter

One apparently successful businessman wanted to impress an important client. He got on the intercom and snapped to his secretary, "Miss Smith, call my broker immediately!"

Back came this reply, "Certainly, sir. But which one? Your stock or pawn?"

God's Promise

"The Lord will strengthen him upon the bed of languishing; thou wilt make all his bed in his sickness." (Psalm 41:3, KJV)

Practicing His Presence

Continue to exercise your spiritual powers through consciously practicing His presence. How did you sense the presence of His Spirit yesterday?

Inner Illness

I continue to mention some of the manifestations of inner illness. It is my prayer that my calling attention to them will help you understand yourself and others better. The understanding of the problem is a step toward wholeness.

The spirit of condemnation is a disease which cripples many people. This spirit is not an effort to correct others because of a wrong they have done, but usually because of a feeling that they have done us wrong or are a threat to us. It is easy to condemn another's actions when it seems he has neglected you. The response often heard is,

"I can't understand why she did this. After I had done so much for her."

The condemning spirit can also be present because of jealousy. Your friend has received special recognition or is particularly talented. You feel that you will be exalted if he can be put down. This spirit frequently pervades. This sign of inner illness needs the healing touch of the Lord.

Watch closely how often you speak in a condemning manner toward others. Perhaps today you can seek to be alert to the condemning spirit in your life and seek to rebuke it in the name of Jesus.

PRAYER: *Shut my mouth, O Lord, when I am inclined to condemn others. May I speak in love always. Amen.*

THE MINISTRY OF THE MASTER—THURSDAY

A Spirit Lifter

This Army cook knew how to impress others.

He had just prepared breakfast of bacon and eggs for several hundred men. He was wearied by his efforts and took a few moments to relax and to write his sweetheart. His letter really sounded great when it started out with, "Darling, for the past three hours shells have been bursting all around me."

God's Promise

"If we confess our sins, he is faithful and just, and will forgive our sins and cleanse us from all unrighteousness." (I John 1:9, RSV)

Practicing His Presence

Are you finding being aware of His presence exciting? Did you have an exciting day yesterday?

Inner Illness

It is impossible for me to list all the manifestations of inner illness and to discuss them at length. However, I shall continue to mention briefly several more.

The spirit of confusion is a dreaded disease. We live in an age of confusion. Many conflicting solutions are presented for practically every situation. There are many false religions and false lifestyles from whence to choose. I believe that each of us must sound the clarion call of Christ to help individuals with this problem. It is a major one.

Confusion leads to despair, another aspect of inner illness affecting many. This despair seems to issue forth from the general despondency which pervades many souls. I feel this is one of the reasons so many turn to drugs. Alcohol and many other drugs are used to deliver them from these afflictions. Instead of being a cure, they become a part of the problem.

It is easy to understand how, in the face of financial problems, work situations, and the constant threat of global destruction, individuals move to a life of despair. Somehow, the positive message of Paul has not been understood nor applied. He found meaning with the truth,

"All things work together for good to them who love God..."
Romans 8:28

PRAYER: *How I need your sure guidance and direction, Lord Jesus. Give me understanding of your Word and Ways. Amen.*

THE MINISTRY OF THE MASTER—FRIDAY
A Spirit Lifter

Have you ever had the feeling that you were made responsible for things which were really out of your control?

"For this job we need a responsible person."

The applicant replied, "Well, sir, I am just your man. In all my other jobs when anything went wrong, I was always held responsible."

God's Promise

"Put on the whole armor of God, that you may be able to stand against the wiles of the devil." (Ephesians 6:11, RSV)

Practicing His Presence

May you seek to quiet yourself this day and hear "the still small voice" speak to you. How were you aware of His presence yesterday?

Inner Illness

The catalog of characteristics of inner illness is large. Many things afflict the inner being and stifle the wholeness desired and needed.

A rebellious and disobedient spirit is the attitude of many people. Children rebel against their parents, teachers, and anyone else in a position of authority.

Adults rebel against established and long proven moral concepts and violate the most sacred commitments. Any institution and almost all facets of the establishment are looked upon with suspicion by many. This attitude leads to frustration and to defeat.

The inner turmoil is blamed on society instead of the person's own approach to life. This illness is difficult to treat and, with many, almost impossible to cure. The Great Physician is the only answer.

I want to say a word about the problem of doubt. Honest doubt is healthy, and we all live with an element of doubt. However, many live with an abnormal amount of doubt. They doubt the Word of God, they doubt any believer who tries to help them, they doubt the good intentions of loved ones, and they even doubt the existence and love of God. The far-reaching effects of this inner illness permeates all areas of their life. It clouds all their efforts to find meaning and fullness in life.

PRAYER: *There are times when I have my doubts about your love and care, Father. Forgive me for these moments and give me steadfast faith. Amen.*

THE MINISTRY OF THE MASTER—SATURDAY
A Spirit Lifter

"Why did the foreman fire you?" asked his friend.
"Because he thought I was doing his job." "What do you mean?" came the response.
"Well, the foreman is the man who stands around and watches others work. He got jealous of me because a lot of fellows thought that I was the foreman."

God's Promise

"But prove yourselves doers of the word, and not merely hearers who delude themselves." (James 1:22, NASB)

Practicing His Presence

Constantly remain sensitive to the Spirit. Sense His presence often during your day. Can you recall a specific incident yesterday in which His presence was very evident?

Inner Illness

I do not want to appear too negative nor morbid this week. Inner illness is certainly not a topic to lift a person. At the same time, I think it has to be discussed to lay the ground work for the receiving of the Lord's wholeness of this problem.

This leads me to say a word about illness resulting from fear. The abnormal fear of failure, disapproval, sickness, losing one's job, not having enough pension, or dying, brings illness to a person. It is literally true that fear can make the heart stop. One can find himself awakening at night in a cold sweat because of fear. One can seek to avoid a situation because of the fear one possesses concerning it.

I deal with many people who possess unwarranted fears. The message of wholeness brings hope and help to them. I recall a lady who came to our healing service with an intense fear of dogs. Her life was practically paralyzed because of this fear. The Lord brought to her mind His touch of wholeness. It was amazing how the rest of her life was helped when this fear was removed.

Fear is a crippling disease which should be treated daily by all the means of grace available to you.

PRAYER: *Thank you, Jesus, for removing fear from my heart. Your presence is all that I have to combat the dread disease of fear. Amen.*

THE MINISTRY OF THE MASTER—SUNDAY
A Spirit Lifter

The way others look at something may be entirely different from the real situation.

The farmer was astonished as the soldier landed in his field. "You are indeed brave to come down in a hundred-mile gale like this in a parachute."

The soldier replied, "Sir, I didn't come down like this in a chute. I went up in a tent."

God's Promise

"Let your mind dwell on whatever is true, noble, right, pure, lovely, admirable, excellent, praiseworthy." (Philippians 4:8, TLB)

Practicing His Presence

If you are like me, you sometimes experience things which seem to cloud the reality of His presence. What do you do when that happens to you?

Inner Illness

Another disease which afflicts many people is guilt. It takes its toll of your whole being by affecting your nerves, your body, and your mind. It makes it impossible to live the most victorious life. It is a damper as far as the burning glow of the Holy Spirit is concerned.

A person came into my office bent over from pain and the aftermath of years of arthritis. As I talked with him, it became evident this stooped condition was not the result of any physical problem. He was burdened with guilt which was literally binding him in body.

After a time of confession I endeavored to point to the forgiveness of the Lord. The prayer of absolution produced the healing desired. He left walking upright and triumphantly. The years have seen this person develop into a very fruitful Christian. Guilt was the culprit. All the pills in the world would not have cured this person. Inner illness was the cause of the malady, and healing of the inner being was the only answer.

I suggest that you search your heart today and bring your guilt to the Lord. Your life will be healthier and your total being more effective if you do.

PRAYER: *Enable me, Lord, to really believe that you remember my sins no more, that I can be free of guilt. Amen.*

INNER ILLNESS

On page 11 of Betty Tapscott's book, *"SET FREE through Inner Healing,"* she says,

"Inner healing is a daily walk, daily cleansing, a daily forgiving, and being forgiven. It is not a one-time experience. It is a process."

I believe that Betty is correct and commend her insights concerning inner healing to you for your consideration. Because we desire inner healing, I think we must devote some time to inner illness.

We live in an age in which the computer can be used to harm many people. Our newspaper had an article about two high school students who tapped into a telephone line with their computer and caused a large company's computer to malfunction. It required more than fifty thousand dollars worth of computer hours to restore the company's computer to its original effectiveness.

There was a malfunction of a nuclear warhead sometime ago because of the failure of a computer. I have read of individuals who bilked companies and individuals of millions of dollars with false insurance policies. They had done it with computers.

Now, if a computer can be made to malfunction and to be used for wrong purposes, how much more can the human computer, the brain, be used improperly. Much of our stress and sickness springs from inner turmoil. It is inner illness which is attacking our very being. Inner illness is the number one plague of our day.

This week I am considering other aspects of inner illness. It is my prayer that the daily sermonettes will help you appreciate the many ways inner illness can get a foothold on you.

The understanding of the effect of the mind and spirit over all your well-being will help you seek to remain inwardly whole. This is your high calling and is a goal attainable to all who believe.

POINTS TO PONDER

1. Do you feel your mind has much effect on your total outlook?
2. What are some inner illnesses which you see in those around you?
3. What do you feel is the cure needed for inner illness?

INNER ILLNESS

1. There is no fear in _____. *I John 4:18*
2. Fear not for I am with thee, and be not dismayed for I am your ____
   _____. *Isa. 41:10*
3. God is our_____and strength. *Ps. 46:1*
4. I will trust and not be _____. *Isa. 12:2*
5. Thou shalt not be _____. *Ps. 91:5*
6. I will not fear what_____shall do unto me.
   Heb. 13:6
7. Fear ye not, stand _____, and see the
   salvation of the Lord. *Ex. 14:13*
8. Whoso hearkeneth unto me shall be quiet from fear of _____
   _____. *Pro. 1:33*
9. The Lord will not fail your nor _____ _____ you.
   Deut. 31:8
10. His heart is fixed, trusting in the _____.
    Ps. 112:7
11. When thou passest through the _____
    I will be with thee. *Isa. 43:2*
12. The Lord shall preserve you from all _____.
    Ps. 121:7
13. Let not your heart be _____. *John 14:27*
14. The Lord is on my side; I will not_____.
    Ps. 118:6

DAILY SCRIPTURE

Mon.	I John 4:13-21
Tues.	Ps. 46:1-11
Wed.	Isa. 12:1-6
Thurs.	Heb. 13:1-6
Fri.	Deut. 31:1-8
Sat.	Isa. 43:1-7
Sun.	John 14:25-31

PRAYER CONCERNS

Your Family & Relatives
Government Leaders
Missionaries
For the Unbelievers
Churches & Denominations
Your Own Church
Prayer and Praise

NOTE: You will be spiritually strengthened by completing two questions each day, reading the suggested scripture, and ministering in prayer for the concerns of the day.

THE MINISTRY OF THE MASTER—MONDAY
A Spirit Lifter

"When I went to work for you, didn't you say something about my getting a raise?"

The employer replied, "Yes, I did say you would get a raise if you did well at your work."

"I knew there was a catch in there somewhere," was the employee's mournful reply.

God's Promise

Friends are wonderful gifts, are they not?

"A true friend is always loyal, in time of need." (Proverbs 17:17, TLB)

Practicing His Presence

I pray that you were very much aware of the Lord's presence in your life yesterday. Can you recall some specific incident or person which helped this awareness?

Inner Illness

This view of healing would not be complete without reference to the spirit of jealousy, a crippling disease. Many good laws have failed to get on the books because of jealousy. Many wonderful people have been ruined because of jealousy.

Jealousy usually looms its ugly head when you feel you are being overshadowed by another person. If a brilliant pianist comes from China, your neighbors will not be jealous; however, if your son is a brilliant pianist, some of the neighbors may be jealous. They may put your boy down and comment that they know facts about him that the public really ought to know. Whenever there is an apparent threat to your total being, jealousy can often creep into the picture.

Lack of vision, laziness, resentment, sadness, and suspicion are further examples of a form of inner illness. The horizon of some is so near that they cannot see beyond themselves. This lack of vision leaves them confined to the misery of their own feelings and the despair of their own interpretation of life.

Springing forth from this lack of vision are actions which make it difficult for the person, as well as those around them. Laziness and resentment can ruin a person. Check your own life as far as the spirit of suspicion is concerned. If we are not careful, we can become almost paranoid. You do not need this. Rather you need His wholeness.

PRAYER: *I really don't want to be jealous of anyone, O Lord. Thank you for removing this spirit from me. Amen.*

THE MINISTRY OF THE MASTER—TUESDAY
A Spirit Lifter

Some persons cannot do anything well but follow suggestions to the nth degree.

Here is a story about a rookie who took his sergeant's advice and put on a clean pair of socks every day. A week passed by and he showed up at drill in his stocking feet.

"Where are your shoes?" snapped the sergeant. The bewildered rookie replied, "I can't get them on over these seven pairs of socks."

God's Promise

"Take my yoke upon you, and learn from me; for I am gentle and lowly in heart, and you will find rest for your souls. For my yoke is easy, and my burden is light." (Matthew 11:29, 30, RSV)

Practicing His Presence

Through what incident or person did you sense the presence of the Lord yesterday? How did this make you feel?

Inner Illness

Today I call your attention to what I term the "un" syndrome. This covers such things as unbelief, unforgiving, unrealistic goals, unrelenting pressure, and unrighteousness.

This disease is characteristic of many and will not be cured by penicillin. There are no miracle drugs for these afflictions.

Unbelief is normal within limits; but when it goes to the very core of your being and disputes the graciousness and goodness of God, it ruins your life. Some people live with such a complete spirit of unbelief that they can in no way face life with a positive attitude.

The unforgiving spirit quickly attacks your body. I have known individuals who suffered pain in the neck, back, and elsewhere who could discover no relief. When they conquered the spirit of unforgiveness in their hearts, they realized to their surprise that the pain left their bodies.

Unrealistic goals cripple many people. The achievements desired by parents and friends may far surpass the ability of the person. The frustrated opera singer, baseball player, preacher, pianist, or actress is proverbial. They set a goal which could never be attained. Another example is the person whose goal is winning the lottery and who expects everything then will be all right.

PRAYER: *Father, give me the strength and faith to eliminate the "un" spirit from my life. Amen.*

A Spirit Lifter

The personnel director said, "Have you any references?"

"Oh, I sure do," replied the applicant. He produced the following brief letter.

"To whom it may concern. John Jones worked for us one week and we're satisfied."

God's Promise

I love the following verse. I hope you find it helpful also today.

"For we are fellow workmen for God." (I Corinthians 3:9)

Practicing His Presence

Are you anticipating being aware of the Lord's presence throughout this day? If so, I am certain this will be a wonderful day for you.

Inner Illness

I have not begun to list all the facets to inner illness. However, I have covered enough to help you realize the scope and seriousness of this malady.

But what brings this inner illness? How was I "infected" in spirit? These are good questions which I will seek to answer.

The wounds of the spirit are inflicted in many ways and by many people. One such way is your undue concern for some past action or statement. Sometimes things you have done or said in the past come back to haunt you. When they do, they bring an inner illness that is tremendously difficult to cure.

One of my most difficult counseling situations was with a society lady of the community. She was attractive, well off financially, and loved by all. However, she was frequently ill. At one time the illness had become emotional to the extent that she had to be confined to the hospital.

My visits with her revealed that she had lived a fast life during the Roaring Twenties. A pregnancy resulted in a willful abortion. Later, she met a fine man and married. They reared a wonderful family. Her act was hidden in the recesses of her mind, but came back to haunt her in her mid-fifties.

The healing did not come easy to her. The only thing which was able to help her was to realize that the Lord forgives and imparts His wholeness. Medicine could not do it.

PRAYER: *Jesus, may the soothing oil of your presence bring healing to my wounded spirit. Amen.*

THE MINISTRY OF THE MASTER—THURSDAY
A Spirit Lifter

A gentleman was to pick up a visiting pastor at the airport. He had never met him before and had to take his chances as to identifying the right person.

Several persons had come up the ramp, but the man could not tell which one was the pastor. He went to one likely prospect and asked whether he was a pastor. His reply,

"No, I am not." The man was a little embarrassed and stammered, "I'm sorry, but I thought you looked like a pastor." The reply "I am not, but I did have a little airsickness just before we landed."

God's Promise

This day, be sincerely thankful for your many blessings.

"Bless the Lord, O my soul, and forget not all his benefits." (Psalm 103:3, KJV)

Practicing His Presence

May you continually remain sensitive to the Spirit! How were you aware of His presence yesterday, and how did this make you feel?

Inner Illness

Many persons end up prisoners of the past and plagued by the past.

Sometimes an incident, unconsciously forgotten, still attacks emotionally your inner being. I counseled with a woman who desired to be a loving and gracious wife. However, the intimacies of her marriage were nightmare experiences for her. This frustrated her and her husband greatly. He felt bad because he thought that it might be his fault. She became depressed and despondent as she tried to assure him that it was not his fault and yet could not help herself.

One day, as we were talking, she recalled that, when a young girl, she had been molested by a close relative. This incident had been removed from her mind, but its trauma could never be erased. Even though the incident had been forgotten, the effects continued to be manifest in her life.

This inner illness needed the healing touch of the Great Physician. The darts of the devil will not penetrate your bones. They penetrate your inner being. The result is sickness of soul and hampering of the fullest life for you.

PRAYER: *I can't remember all of the incidents which have influenced my life, Father, but I give all of my being to you for your healing touch. Amen.*

THE MINISTRY OF THE MASTER—FRIDAY
A Spirit Lifter

You cannot always tell a person's intelligence by his appearance. Even his ability to communicate verbally is not the final test. The boss was interviewing a girl for a secretarial vacancy. He decided to test her spelling accuracy.

"How do you spell Mississippi?" was his initial question. Her unabashed reply spoke volumes.

"The river, or the state?"

God's Promise

"Then let us no more pass judgment on one another, but rather decide never to put a stumbling-block or hindrance in the way of a brother." (Romans 14:13, RSV)

Practicing His Presence

You may have had a difficult day yesterday. I do hope you were aware of the Lord Jesus working in your life.

Inner Illness

I am intrigued by the discoveries of the effect of the emotions upon a person prior to birth. It is obvious to me that certain drugs can affect the baby in the womb. It is more difficult for me to accept the psychological impact of emotions and statements prior to birth. However, I am convinced this is real and something to be considered if you are plagued with inner illness.

While speaking at a healing conference in a far western state, a man sought me out after the message and prayer concerning inner healing. He told me that on three different occasions he had been professionally treated for an emotional problem. Although he had been helped by the psychiatrist, he had never been able to rid himself of a negative inward spirit. He would slip back again into depression.

It was at this service that he realized that he was an unwanted child. It was from the time of his conception that his mother and father rebelled. He was an accident in their lives and not a blessing. He realized that he had heard her say this and that from the beginning he was not wanted. His parents' attitude caused inner illness which spread to every other area of his life.

The ministry of inner healing brought the healing he had been seeking. It changed him deep within as well as without.

PRAYER: *Deep within my soul, Father, impart the joy of your presence and the reality of your understanding and love. Amen.*

THE MINISTRY OF THE MASTER—SATURDAY
A Spirit Lifter

There are some people who are sincerely humble. They do not put on an air of superiority in knowledge, position, or heritage.

The sign on his desk said, "If you are looking for a little information, check with me. I have as little as anybody around here."

God's Promise

I certainly love this promise from the Lord Jesus himself.

"But seek first his kingdom and his righteousness, and all these things shall be yours as well." (Matthew 6:33, RSV)

Practicing His Presence

I am amazed how often the Lord has felt near to me while I am involved in the ordinary experiences of life. The more I practice His presence, the more I behold Him in all aspects. Is this true of your life?

Inner Illness

How can I deal with inner illness and not mention the illnesses caused by remarks of relatives, friends, and associates. What we say sometimes affects another person the rest of his life. This is one reason why we must be careful of our words and, as much as possible, live at peace with all.

I know of a gentleman who was a very dedicated worker. He was faithful in attendance, diligent in his work, and loyal to the company. He knew he was appreciated and looked forward to work each day.

His company was going through an adjustment period. One day he overheard some of the officers talking. Unaware of his presence, they stated that they would like to find a gracious way to dismiss this man. The realization that he was no longer wanted or needed devastated him.

The inner illness which resulted nearly killed him and brought great discomfort and inconvenience to his family. The outward graciousness of his superiors could not remove the inner knowledge that he was not wanted. Much prayer and counseling were needed to help him realize that his talents and experience would be valuable to others. This proved to be the case, but not until he had gone through much inner illness.

PRAYER: *Jesus, the unkind words of others have taken their toll on my inner being. May these negative feelings be turned to positive ones by You. Amen.*

THE MINISTRY OF THE MASTER—SUNDAY
A Spirit Lifter

Slips of the tongue have plagued individuals throughout the centuries.

A teacher asked her class of student stenographers, "What do you do when your employer buzzes to take dictation?

The one girl promptly answered, "When you are called; pick up your notebook and pencil and answer the buzzard immediately."

God's Promise

Do you enjoy this brief time of reflecting upon God's promises?

"Blessed are the pure in heart, for they shall see God." (Matthew 5:8, NASV)

Practicing His Presence

Do you find that an awareness of His presence is determined to some degree by how you feel? Was there any time yesterday when you knew the spiritual life was the most important aspect of your being?

Inner Illness

Have you ever watched the auto races which involve the parachute unfolding to slow down the car? They fascinate me. I have often thought that many of us have emotional parachutes which create a great drag for us.

These emotional parachutes are filled with inner hurts and problems of the past and present. Our lives become a drag because we cannot go forward to the victory desired and attainable.

Moments of dishonesty, immoral acts, and outright lies all come to plague us. Your inner being can take only so much of this. Your physical and emotional parachute opens and all of these things are swept into it. Somehow, you must get rid of this trash and receive the tender touch of the Lord.

Many years ago I counseled a man whose parachute was filled with filth. He confessed fathering a child with a neighbor woman. He said that he wanted to tell his wife. I telephoned her, and she came to the study. He revealed the sordid story to her. I will never forget her reaction.

After several minutes of silence she asked him whether it was really true. He said, *"Yes."* After another short period of silence she said, *"Well, we better get home and finish the painting."*

They had the happiest years of their life from that moment. He had emptied his parachute. He received what pills could not give. He experienced inner healing for his inner illness.

PRAYER: *Lord Jesus, I come to you and empty the filth of my life before you. Thank you for cleaning me up through your purity and presence. Amen.*

HOW TO REBUKE SATAN

Are you struggling within and defeated without? Who is trying to defeat you? Is it God? A resounding *"No"* must be forthcoming. The Lord is not out to keep you defeated. He wants His victory to be yours. He wants you to live triumphantly.

I have been speaking concerning inner illness. I believe it is the most prevalent disease of our age. There is but one cure for the epidemic of inner illness in the world. That cure is Jesus Christ.

The one who is bringing the onslaught of inner illness is Satan. He may be given great assistance by people's actions, but ultimately he is the source of discouragement, despair, defeat, and death.

Many persons walking around are dead in spirit. They do not realize that Satan is in the process of killing their spirit and their enthusiasm for life. He wants you defeated. He rejoices in ruination. He hates redemption and recovery.

The steps to wholeness must include understanding the source of illness. The complexities of creation and life are too great to understand completely. There are no complete and simple answers. However, life is faced most adequately when we walk in the light which has been revealed through His Word.

Jesus and His disciples acknowledged Satan as the source of illness. They credit him for the frustrations of soul, the diseases of body, and the disturbances of mind which possessed many unto whom they ministered. Jesus healed the woman with the infirmity which had afflicted her for eighteen years. His response to indignant Sabbath worshippers was,

"And ought not this woman, ...whom Satan hath bound, lo, these eighteen years, be loosed from this bond on the sabbath day?" Luke 13:16

There are two very important things to learn if inner wholeness is to be received and maintained.

First, you must learn how to rebuke Satan in all facets of your life.

Second, you must learn how to release the power and purpose of the Lord in your life.

It is my prayer the daily teachings of this book, the *"Ministry of The Master,"* will help you to be able to rebuke the evil one and to release the positive power of the Lord in your life.

POINTS TO PONDER

1. What is disease?
2. Is disease sent from God?
3. Do you feel Satan is a factor in inner illness? How and why?

HOW TO REBUKE SATAN

1. Now the _____ was more subtle than any beast of the field. *Gen. 3:1*
2. Jesus was led of the Spirit to be_____. *Mt. 4:1*
3. When anyone hears the word of the kingdom, then comes the_____ _____ one that takes it away. *Mt. 13:19*
4. You are of your father the _____. *John 8:44*
5. Satan is transformed into an_____of light. *II Cor. 11:14*
6. Giving heed to seducing spirits, and doctrines of_____ _____. *I Tim. 4:1*
7. The one that commits _____ is of the devil. *I John 3:8*
8. Might destroy him that had the power of death, that is, the_____ _____. *Heb. 2:14*
9. Do not give place to the _____. *Eph. 4:27*
10. Submit yourselves to God: resist the _____. *James 4:7*
11. Because your adversary the devil is a roaring _____ _____. *I Pet. 5:8*
12. We need not be ignorant of the devices of _____ _____. *II Cor. 2:11*
13. Put on the whole _____ of God. *Eph. 6:11*
14. The devil is a_____and the father of it. *John 8:44*

DAILY SCRIPTURE

Mon.	Gen. 3:1-7
Tues.	Mt. 4:1-11
Wed.	Mt. 13:18-23
Thurs.	I Tim. 4:1-5
Fri.	Heb. 2:14-18
Sat.	II Cor. 2:5-11
Sun.	Eph. 6:10-20

PRAYER CONCERNS

Your Family & Relatives
Government Leaders
Missionaries
For the Unbelievers
Churches & Denominations
Your Own Church
Prayer and Praise

NOTE: You will be spiritually strengthened by completing two questions each day, reading the suggested scripture, and ministering in prayer for the concerns of the day.

THE MINISTRY OF THE MASTER—MONDAY
A Spirit Lifter

It is difficult to separate facts from fancy, especially for children. The family was discussing the resurrection story. The little five-year-old had her own version. She said,

"Easter is when Jesus comes out of the grave. Then if He sees His shadow, He goes back in for six more weeks."

God's Promise

"Lay not up for yourselves treasures upon earth, where moth and rust doth corrupt, and where thieves break through the stall, but lay up for yourselves treasures in heaven." (Matthew 6:19, 10)

Practicing His Presence

I believe you will have a great day if you are anticipating being aware of the Lord's presence. How did you do this yesterday?

How To Rebuke Satan

One of the biggest steps to release from your inner illness is the realization of the source of your illness. I realize that life is complex. I know there must be proper diet, rest, chemical balance, and an overall wholesome approach to life. All these things I acknowledge and advocate. At the same time, there are areas of disease which are not the result of any of these. It is a spiritual warfare, and Satan is our adversary.

Satan needs to be rebuked and bound. He cannot be permitted to continue to control your life nor the life of a loved one.

When I read prayers from the prayer books used through the centuries, it is interesting to discover that some of them thank God for illness. It is as though the writers feel the one ill is favored of the Lord. The ill person in their minds seem to be signaled out by God for a blessing through illness.

Granted that the Lord may use the illness to help you spiritually and emotionally, but to believe it is a special act of kindness on His part to impart the illness to you is beyond my comprehension.

The Lord is in the healing business. He is not in the business of bringing illness. He desires your wholeness. He does not want you sick. He desires to deliver and not to destroy.

PRAYER: *Jesus, in your Name I rebuke the presence and power of Satan in my life. Amen.*

THE MINISTRY OF THE MASTER—TUESDAY
A Spirit Lifter

She was an only child and the 28-year-old single lady included the following in her prayer.

"Lord, I am not selfish and so really do not want anything for myself. But please give my mother a good son-in-law. Amen."

God's Promise

"Verily I say unto you, inasmuch as ye did it not to one of the least of these, ye did it not to me." (Matthew 24:45, KJV)

Practicing His Presence

I pray that amidst you. busy da. you will be able to pull apart and sense the Lord's presence. How did you do this yesterday?

How To Rebuke Satan

In His ministry of the wholeness of the Lord, Jesus always desired to help individuals. He brought them hope. He did not present them hell. '' . evidently felt individuals had had enough hell. What they needed was hope and help.

I feel this is vividly revealed in what He did not do, as well as through what He did do. We have no record whatsoever of Jesus' saying to a person,

"You aren't very religious; therefore, I am going to make you sick."

"You have missed synagogue attendance for eight weeks. I am going to give you a crippled hand."

"The rabbi reports you have not been paying your tithe. I am going to give you a lame leg."

"You haven't prayed as you should. I am going to make you blind."

These ridiculous remarks could go on and on. They are repulsive and cruel. What Jesus did was to heal the individuals with crippled arms, lame legs, blindness, deafness, or disturbed spirits. He was the healer. It was Satan who did the binding and who crippled.

Jesus wants you whole. It is Satan who desires to keep you sick of mind, body, and soul.

PRAYER: *Thank you, Lord Jesus, for bringing your wholeness to me and your desire that I maintain this wholeness of spirit, mind, and body. Amen.*

THE MINISTRY OF THE MASTER—WEDNESDAY
A Spirit Lifter

The little five-year-old awakened at 3:00 a.m. He insisted on getting into bed with his parents. Finally, he consented to return to his room if his light was kept on all night. His father tried to correct this situation with, "Imagine, a big boy like you being afraid of the dark."

The little boy replied, "Yes, it is all right for you, but you've got mommy to look after you."

God's Promise

"For God so loved the world, that he gave his only begotten Son, that whosoever believeth in him should not perish, but have everlasting life." (John 3:16, KJV)

Practicing His Presence

I pray that being aware of His presence each day has been meaningful for you. How did you sense His presence yesterday?

How To Rebuke Satan

Inner illness is not easily conquered. Many do not understand that the battle is against forces which are not measurable on scales or in test tubes.

"We wrestle not against flesh and blood, but against principalities, against powers, against the rulers of the darkness of this world, against spiritual wickedness in high places." Ephesians 6:12

You can be afflicted in body and still live a triumphant spiritual life. You can be apparently whole of body and live a life of defeat in spirit, morals, and attitude.

It would be much easier if your problems could be diagnosed and treated with pills or surgery. The sad commentary is that many illnesses are not of the kind which science can treat. They are of the spirit. They are of the evil one and must be seen in this light. This truth will help to set you free.

I have counseled with many people who could not conquer their inward illnesses. Many of them have been helped when I pointed out that Satan did not want them well and that he must be dealt with conclusively and convincingly. Their freedom came in rebuking him and permitting the Lord Jesus to bring His healing touch to every facet of their lives.

PRAYER: *Help me, Jesus, to realize who my enemy really is. Help me to face the onslaughts of Satan. Amen.*

THE MINISTRY OF THE MASTER—THURSDAY
A Spirit Lifter

She had noticed that near her home was a dry cleaning establishment. Also, she had observed that Sunday worship service usually lasted about an hour. She put this together for some pretty good theology.

One day, going by the "One Hour Cleaning" place, she said to her daddy, "Is our church a one hour cleaning place?"

God's Promise

"Whoever would love life and see good days must keep his tongue from evil and his lips from deceitful speech." (I Peter 3:10, NIV)

Practicing His Presence

Perhaps you were aware of His presence in a baby's smile, in a gentle hug from a loved one, or in a view of the countryside. Continue to develop this awareness in your life.

How To Rebuke Satan

One of Satan's tools is downgrading you. He wants to make you feel bad, act bad, and be defeated.

We real these words in the book of Revelation,

"And I heard a loud voice saying in heaven, Now is come salvation, and strength, and the kingdom of our God, and the power of his Christ: for the accuser of our brethren is cast down, which accused them before our God day and night." Revelation 12:10

One way to rebuke Satan is to realize he is the accuser. He brings accusations against you, such as that you are worthless, useless, or no good.

If he can bring you to the point where you feel you are without worth, then it is just a short step to feeling you have no reason to live. You may feel no one loves you and that you cannot even love others.

He accuses you of being so iniquitous that you cannot be saved by the Lord. He points out your useless life and wicked actions. All these add up to your defeat and his delight.

I have dealt with many people who have much to commend them, but they have been accused by Satan to the point they cannot accept any good about themselves. That is the spirit which needs to be rebuked in your life and mind.

PRAYER: *In your name, Lord Jesus, I command Satan to get off my back and out of my heart. I am redeemed and he knows it. Help me to always believe it. Amen.*

THE MINISTRY OF THE MASTER—FRIDAY
A Spirit Lifter

This conversation illustrates how priorities are set by what we have and not necessarily by what we need.

The doctor said to the patient, "If I find the operation necessary, will you have the money to pay for it?"

The patient promptly retorted, "If I find I don't have the money, will you find the operation necessary?"

God's Promise

"Come to me, all who labor and are heavy laden, and I will give you rest." (Matthew 11:18, RSV)

Practicing His Presence

Can you recall a specific incident or person which helped your awareness of the Lord's presence yesterday? Take a moment to reflect upon this.

How To Rebuke Satan

It is Satan who is out to bring disunity and disharmony to your life. He takes special delight in disrupting the individual as well as the group. This is one way by which he can apparently conquer.

This disunity is accomplished in cunning ways. The Word tells us,

"Lest Satan should get an advantage of us: for we are not ignorant of his devices." II Corinthians 2:11

One of the ways you can rebuke Satan is to learn to control your anger. I meet many who are angry at others, themselves, or at God. This creates a climate in which the powers of evil can thrive.

Some nurture their anger. They feed it with resentments and plans of revenge. The Apostle Paul spares no words in dealing with anger. He says,

"Be ye angry, and sin not: let not the sun go down upon your wrath. Neither give place to the devil." Ephesians 4:26,27

Deep inner problems create a vicious circle of discontent and defeat. Permitting attitudes and spirits to remain a part of your life makes the ground fertile for the Tempter. The Tempter leads you down dead-end streets bringing further discontent and defeat. This circle must be broken. The only One who can really break it is Jesus Christ. Seek the Lord's help to care for your spirit of anger or resentment and rebuke Satan. This is the path to victory.

PRAYER: *I pray, Father, for wisdom to know if I am a source of disunity among other believers. Help me to see myself as I really am. Amen.*

A Spirit Lifter

There is always a half-truth answer which can help a person side step just about any question.

She was being interviewed, and the personnel manager was reviewing her application form. He politely said,

"I see that your birthday is May 3, may I ask what year?"

Without hesitation, the woman replied, "Every year."

God's Promise

"And let us not grow weary in well-doing, for in due season we shall reap, if we do not lose heart." (Galatians 6:9, RSV)

Practicing His Presence

I do believe it is helpful to be reminded of the spiritual awareness which each of us should develop.

How To Rebuke Satan

The spirit of submission to the will of God is the spirit of victory. The rebuking of Satan is a two-pronged approach. It involves submitting to God and His righteousness and fleeing from Satan and his evil.

This clearly is revealed in the sacred Word.

"Submit yourselves therefore to God. Resist the devil, and he will flee from you." James 4:7

I love this verse. It assures me that I need not be defeated by Satan. He cannot conquer, but he has to flee. My calling is to humbly trust the Lord and to walk in His ways. He will take care of the devil for me if I remain under His protecting wings.

"Put on the whole armour of God, that ye may be able to stand against the wiles of the devil." Ephesians 6:11

We hear much about defense today. Some say we should spend billions of dollars to defend ourselves. Others point out the fallacy of trying to defend ourselves through arms.

The true defense comes from the Lord. The devil is the enemy we shoud be fearing. It is he who will ultimately destroy you. No nuclear bomb can destroy you. You are eternal.

PRAYER: *Thy will be done in my life, Father, is my earnest prayer. Amen.*

THE MINISTRY OF THE MASTER—SUNDAY
A Spirit Lifter

A restaurant customer had waited long and had tried several times to get the waiter's attention, but to no avail. Finally being unable to control his temper any longer, he shouted across the room,

"Your service is awful!"

The young waiter stopped, stared for a moment, and said, "How do you know? You haven't gotten any yet."

God's Promise

"Let brotherly love continue. Do not neglect to show hospitality to strangers, for thereby some have entertained angels unawares." (Hebrews 13:1,2, RSV)

Practicing His Presence

May you seek to quiet yourself today and hear "the still small voice" speak to you. How were you aware of His presence yesterday?

How To Rebuke Satan

The week has gone very fast. There is much which I feel should be said concerning Satan. He indeed is your adversary and the one you should constantly rebuke.

I Peter 5:7-9 tells us that our confidence should be in the Lord. It is upon Him that we should cast our cares. Satan is seeking to devour, and only as we cast ourselves upon the Lord will we be delivered.

Another way to rebuke Satan is to maintain a vital prayer life. Jesus said,

"Watch and pray, that ye enter not into temptation..." Matthew 26:41

Another important aspects of rebuking Satan is a spirit of praise. Do not let him get a foothold on you. In every situation seek to praise the Lord. He is there to sustain you, and you need not become disgruntled. The disgruntled spirit is an open invitation to Satan and all of his forces. You cannot stand fast if this spirit pervades your soul.

You can rebuke Satan by reminding him that your inheritance is peace, power, and purpose. These things are of the Lord.

I minister in prayer through rebuking Satan in my life and in the life of the one unto whom I minister.

PRAYER: *Praise to Thee, O Lord, praise to Thee. This is my prayer and heart's desire. Amen.*

Theme for the Week
INNER HEALING THROUGH GOD'S LOVE

Betty Tapscott in her book concerning inner healing presents a wonderful definition of inner healing.

> *"Inner healing is the healing of the inner person, the healing of the mind, the emotions, the painful memories, the dreams. It is the process through prayer whereby we are set free from feelings of depression, resentment, self-pity, guilt, fear, sorrow, inferiority, condemnation, or worthlessness."*

In the light of the above it is evident that all of us need healing at one time or another. In fact, most of us are in constant need of inner healing.

My experience has shown that many people are healed when they understand the love of God for them. It is relatively easy to concede that God loves the world but very difficult to conceive that He loves me. If I could believe with all my heart that God loves me all the time, I would be spared most of the problems which I endure.

God loves with no set limits. He loves you regardless of how unlovable you may be, regardless of your inner illness, or regardless of your outward wickedness. He does not want you to negate the realities of hell, but He does want you to be aware of the realities of His Kingdom. He does not choose to threaten with hell, but to deliver to heaven.

I have confidence that, if I could believe every moment of my life that God really loves me, then most of my problems would be solved. I would be spared many heartaches, much stress, and anxiety.

We must get back to the basics if we are going to come to the wholeness within that the Lord desires and has for us. He has called us unto Himself and bathed us in His love. Inner wholeness is yours when this fact is recognized and appropriated to life.

POINTS TO PONDER

1. How do you define the love of God?
2. What areas of the inner being do you feel need to be touched by God's love?
3. Do you feel God loves the unlovable? How and why?

INNER HEALING THROUGH GOD'S LOVE

1. Love one another even as I have _____you.
   John 15:12
2. You were taught of God to _____ one
   another. *I Thess. 4:9*
3. Let us love one another: for love is of _____.
   I John 4:7
4. If a man say, I love God, and hates his _____,
   he is a liar. *I John 4:20*
5. Have all knowledge, and great faith, without love I am_____
   _____. *I Cor. 13:2*
6. Thou shalt love thy neighbor as _____. *Mt. 22:39*
7. You shalt love your _____ as yourself.
   James 2:8
8. Love is the fulfulling of the _____. *Rom. 13:10*
9. That a man lay down his_____for
   his friends. *John 15:13*
10. Who shall _____ us from the love of God.
    Rom. 8:35
11. The Lord said, I have loved you with an _____
    love. *Jer. 31:3*
12. God loved the _____. *John 3:16*
13. The love of Christ passeth _____. *Eph. 3:19*
14. _____one another with a pure heart.
    I Peter 1:22

DAILY SCRIPTURE

Mon.	John 15:12-17
Tues.	I Thess. 4:9-12
Wed.	I John 4:7-12
Thurs.	James 2:8-13
Fri.	Jer. 31:1-6
Sat.	John 3:16-21
Sun.	I Peter 1:13-25

PRAYER CONCERNS

Your Family & Relatives
Government Leaders
Missionaries
For the Unbelievers
Churches & Denominations
Your Own Church
Prayer and Praise

NOTE: You will be spiritually strengthened by completing two questions each day, reading the suggested scripture, and ministering in prayer for the concerns of the day.

THE MINISTRY OF THE MASTER—MONDAY
A Spirit Lifter

Have you ever noticed that the person responsible is often unaware of being a problem?

The office manager was chiding his secretary with,

"If you can't work any faster, I'll have to get another girl."

The secretary, oblivious to her shortcomings, replied, "Thank you! I certainly can use some extra help."

God's Promise

A good promise from the Lord is his assurance. His presence is our only security.

"My presence shall go with thee, and I will give you rest." (Ex. 33:14)

Practicing His Presence

I am certain this will be an exciting day for you if you seek to quiet yourself and practice His presence. Have a golden day!

Inner Healing—Through God's Love

One of the best ways to convey God's love to another is to seek to identify with the person's problem or affliction. The disease may be terminal or minor, but it is still important to that person.

A rabbi displayed the art of a master in getting others to understand another's needs. This story is told of his visiting a wealthy man of his congregation. The rabbi was prompt for the appointment he had requested. They sat by the fireplace, sipped tea, and visited for some time. The man wondered when the rabbi was going to get down to business and state the purpose of the meeting. Finally, the rabbi said he must leave and asked for his coat, for it was a very cold winter night. As he was about to leave, he asked the man, *"Would you please step out on the porch with me? I have something I would like to discuss in private."*

It was very cold on the porch, and the rabbi took a while to get to the point. The man's teeth began to chatter, and he said, *"I thought you wanted to talk with me about something important! I'm freezing out here with no heat on this porch."*

The rabbi responded, *"I'm glad you brought that up. That's the reason I'm here. We have several families in our congregation who have no coal. They have no fires in their homes, and they are freezing. I thought you might want to make a donation."* He got help from this man. He helped him to identify with others who needed a tangible expression of God's love.

PRAYER: *Help me to be sensitive to the needs of those around me, Father. Amen.*

THE MINISTRY OF THE MASTER—TUESDAY
A Spirit Lifter

Do you find it difficult to correct people?

A professor was about to leave the campus. One of the students noticed his hat and said politely,

"Pardon me, Professor, but you've got your hat on backwards."

"Nonsense," he replied, "How do you know which direction I am going to walk?"

God's Promise

"For the Kingdom of God is not meat and drink; but righteousness, and peace, and joy in the Holy Ghost." (Rom. 14:17)

Practicing His Presence

Through what incident or person did you sense the Lord's presence yesterday? How did this make you feel?

Inner Healing—Through God's Love

"Pastor, the Lord has told me that I should talk with Jim and tell him that, if he really wanted to be well, he could be. His problem is himself, and he must snap out of it."

This was stated to me by one of our good church members. Jim had many emotional illnesses and had been ministered unto by many people of the church and medical field.

This friend wanted to heap more guilt and illness upon him. Often we do not minister the love of God but the frustration of our own ideas. There are individuals as helpless emotionally as some are helpless physically.

If you went to a friend's home and discovered she had fallen down the basement stairs and broken her back, you would not say, *"You better get up and get to a doctor."* When she replied, *"But I can't. It is impossible for me to move,"* you would not retort, *"If you really wanted to, you could."* This would be cruel.

Yet, some people are just as cruel in the area of the emotions. I explained to this well-intentioned member that Jim did not need further downgrading. He needed the love of God released in his life.

The most important goal in an individual's life is to be healed spiritually and to appreciate the love of God for them.

I am happy to report that throughout the years Jim has improved very much. Improvement came because some persons understood, took the time, and revealed the love and power of God to him.

PRAYER: *Jesus, give me insights into the difficulties so many face. Help me to understand them and not to belittle them. Amen.*

THE MINISTRY OF THE MASTER—WEDNESDAY
A Spirit Lifter

The age of innocence is not past. It exists in employees as well as with friends.

An employer, upset because the new stenographer was late every morning, tried to correct this habit. One morning, in exasperation, he said. "You should have been here at nine!"

She cooly replied, "Why? What happened?"

God's Promise

"I am a light into the world, that whosoever believeth in me should not abide in darkness." (John 12:46)

Practicing His Presence

I believe as you exercise your spiritual powers you will become more aware of the spiritual side of life. How did you sense the presence of His Sprit yesterday?

Inner Healing—Through God's Love

It is one thing to know God loves the world and another thing really to believe God loves you as a person. When the truth of His personal love for me became real, it changed my life.

I felt called to be a pastor when I was about ten years old. This call never left me. I strayed from devotion to God and His church through some of my teenage years, but I never had this sense of being called forsake me.

My early college years were very difficult for me emotionally and spiritually. I sought the advice of pastors and tried to explain my situation. It seemed to me that the first one I went to was a spiritual giant, but he could not handle my frustrations. He cut me off with, *"You'll be all right. Don't worry. Just hang in there."* I went to another, and the only thing he could say was, *"Just preach for awhile, and you will come out all right."*

Their remarks left me feeling worse than before I went to them. They were unwilling to identify with my problem and to bring the love of God to me.

I thank God that a lay person, Leonard Perkins of Elgin, Illinois, came along who took the time to listen and to reveal to me the healing God can bring. He took the time to show me God's love was all for me, even while it is all for others. I was healed spiritually. The inner healing I needed came because of his revelation to my inner being of God's love.

PRAYER: *Father, may I be willing to identify with the needs and deep yearnings of others. Amen.*

THE MINISTRY OF THE MASTER—THURSDAY
A Spirit Lifter

Sometimes we read into an innocent speech or remark far more than originally intended.

The family had gone to hear a speaker and had ordered their dinners. While they waited to be served, the speaker was introduced and her topic was announced as, "Tell Me What You Eat and I'll Tell You What You Are!"

Suddenly, the small son excitedly whispered to his parents, "Cancel my order for the shrimp salad."

God's Promise

"Trust in the Lord, and do good; so shalt thou dwell in the land, and verily thou shalt be fed." (Ps. 37:3)

Practicing His Presence

Can you recall a spiritual feast you had yesterday as you sensed the Lord's presence? Be aware of the Lord in your daily work and play today.

Inner Healing—Through God's Love

The love of God can be released in the innermost part of your being. Jesus can go where no one else can go. Jesus can reach into areas of your life where no pill, person, nor treatment can penetrate.

I like to illustrate this with the appearance after the resurrection of our Lord while the disciples were behind the locked door.

"And after eight days again his disciples were within, and Thomas with them: then came Jesus, the doors being shut, and stood in the midst, and said, Peace be unto you." John 20:26

He did not open the door but He was there. He could enter as no one else could enter.

He reveals God's love to each of us in the deep recesses of our life. There are the doors of unbelief, doubt, hurts, resentments, grief, despair, frustration, drugs, immorality, and a host of other doors. These doors cannot be opened by another person. However, Jesus can enter without opening the door and bring His peace. His inner healing is yours.

I urge you to believe by faith that the Lord has entered the most troubled area of your life. Accept His presence and peace. If you do, you will respond as Thomas did and say,

"My Lord and my God." John 20:28

PRAYER: *Lord Jesus, thank you for reaching deep into my being where no one else can ever enter. Amen.*

257

THE MINISTRY OF THE MASTER—FRIDAY
A Spirit Lifter

The waitress noticed a heavy frown on her supervisor's face. She said, "You sure look worried."

"Listen," he replied, "I have so many worries that if anything happens today to worry about, I won't have time to worry about it for another two weeks."

God's Promise

"Jesus said unto him, If thou canst believe, all things are possible to him that believeth." (Mk. 9:23)

Practicing His Presence

It takes conscious effort to be aware of the Lord in the small aspects of life. How did this consciousness affect your day yesterday?

Inner Healing—Through God's Love

The inner healing you desire is received to a greater degree if you realize that, regardless of how bad you may feel, the Lord does love you. He is with you, and His love is not conditional. It is ever being extended to you.

My years in the pastorate have revealed that the biggest problem I deal with is getting people to believe God loves them. Most believe they love God. They may do it in their own way, but they feel they believe in God and try to love Him. This love may be expressed in attendance at worship services, or being good, or even reading the Bible. They miss the most important factor that God loves them.

Love that goes one way is miserable love. This is true toward others as well as toward God. The most miserable individual is one who loves a person who does not return this love.

I see this all the time with married couples. One of them finds another lover. That one is not the miserable one, it is the one who has been forsaken. He or she continues to love a person who does not love him or her. It is a living hell.

In like manner, if a person cannot believe God loves him, he is spiritually miserable and often physically ill.

Accept His love and your life will be changed. He is reaching out to you in love. The telephone line to God is not dead. He is listening on the other end and responding.

PRAYER: *Thank you for your love, Father. It overwhelms me. May I ever believe that you do love me. Amen.*

THE MINISTRY OF THE MASTER—SATURDAY
A Spirit Lifter

The two men had sat beside each other on the plane for some time. The one said, "I just got out of prison yesterday, and it is going to be tough facing old friends."

His traveling companion replied, "I can sympathize with you. I'm just getting home from the state legislature."

God's Promise

"For his anger endureth but a moment; in his favour is life: weeping may endure for a night, but joy cometh in the morning." (Ps. 30:5)

Practicing His Presence

Continue to exercise your spiritual powers through consciously practicing His presence. How did you sense the presence of His Spirit yesterday?

Inner Healing—Through God's Love

I encourage you today to realize that God's love is the only love you can really trust. All other love is conditional. Regardless of how much another may say that he loves you, this love can be affected by how you act. There is a limit to human love. There is no limit to the love of God.

Although He does not desire that you live a life of sin and degradation, He does not cease loving you when you do. His love pursues you like the bloodhound pursues the fugitive.

Far too often and for far too long individuals try to discover inner wholeness through other people. Others are needed, but they are not the final answer. Only God's love can ultimately meet your innermost needs.

If you do not find wholeness through God, you will ultimately be bankrupt of love. Any other person would ultimately be bankrupt of love. People fall short of the glory and power of the Lord. Blending two bankruptcies does not create a stable bank. Regardless of how many bind together, they cannot be sound if they have no assets.

God is not bankrupt, and He never will be. His love is inexhaustable. He is ever willing to love and to heal.

If today you feel that you are desperately endeavoring to love God and still cannot find peace and victory, I suggest that you seek to believe that God loves you. Place your mind and heart upon this truth.

PRAYER: *I am open to your peace and victory, Lord Jesus. Thank you for these two precious things. Amen.*

THE MINISTRY OF THE MASTER—SUNDAY

A Spirit Lifter

The right place, the right way, and the right wording are important for a compliment really to be appreciated.

The lady tried on many hats. Finally, the sales person exclaimed, "That one makes you look ten years younger!"

"Oh really," said the lady. "Then I don't want it. I can't afford to put on ten years every time I take off my hat."

God's Promise

"He shall call upon me, and I will answer him: I will deliver him, and honor him." (Isa. 41:17)

Practicing His Presence

May you continually remain sensitive to the Spirit. How did this sensitivity affect your day yesterday?

Inner Healing—Through God's Love

The story is told of a person asking the famed theologian, Karl Barth, what he felt was the greatest truth he had gleaned from the Bible. His answer was simple, but powerful.

> *"After many years of studying the Bible, the greatest truth to me is 'Jesus loves me, this I know.' "*

Your heart and mine has a hunger which can never be satisfied except by the Lord. The appropriating of His love to your life will change your life. It will bring healing to you.

A gentleman came to counsel with me. Although he had been to many physicians and psychiatrists, he did not improve. After listening to his story, I responded with, *"I have some good news for you."*

It was then that I related the love of God for him. I pointed out that in spite of the fact that he had been trying to love God, the big problem was that he was not accepting God's love for himself. I am grateful that he perceived this truth. I could see him begin to change.

After a few minutes he said, *"Why didn't someone tell me this years ago?"* I pointed out that probably many had attempted to do so, but he had not perceived it. He has continued to improve and still rejoices in the Lord.

Your inner healing can come through God's love. Believe that He does love you. Herein is wholeness.

PRAYER: *Thank you, Jesus, for the sure knowledge you have given to me that you love me. Amen.*

STEPS TO INNER HEALING

It is one thing to talk about the inner healing you need and another to present guidelines to help you receive this inner healing. I am of little help to individuals if most of my time is spent in analysis. The great need of our day, as in the past, is for solutions to our problems and healing for our diseases.

We live in a marvelous technological age. I read recently of a new plane being designed which will carry hundreds of passengers at speeds in excess of 1,800 miles per hour. The plane is so designed that there will be no sonic boom when it breaks the sound barrier.

Yet, with all the marvels of our age no one has yet discovered a technological method of reaching deep within the heart and bringing the wholeness which is needed.

There are no instantaneous remarks or actions which can bring the inner wholeness many so desperately need. This pilgrimage begins with a step and continues as a walk with the Lord.

There is the inner gnawing that something is not right which affects practically everyone in the world. Ann Landers was asked, *"What do you find to be the most pressing problem in the lives of those who write to you?"*

Her reply was *"The most pressing problem seems to be that individuals keep asking, 'What's wrong with me? Why am I not like other people?'"*

The basic problem is couched in thoughts such as, why am I despairing, why am I discouraged, why am I impatient, why do I carry resentment, why am I not able to meet people and feel at ease with them, why am I so ugly, etc.

All of these things indicate an inner problem which must be solved if wholeness is to be experienced to its fullest.

This fog which has settled in upon the soul must be lifted. People do not know from whence has come the fog nor how to dispel it or to rise above it.

This week I want to present some steps which will help bring the inner healing you so need and desire.

You do not have to continue defeated and despairing. There is an answer and that answer is Jesus Christ. He is the way, the truth, and the life. He is the inner wholeness you are seeking.

POINTS TO PONDER

1. Do you feel inner problems are prevalent today? Why?
2. Do you agree with Ann Landers that the average person is asking the question, "What's wrong with me?"
3. Will the inner problems ever be solved by technology?

Daily Bible Study and Daily Prayer Concerns
STEPS TO INNER HEALING

1. My flesh and my heart fail, but God is my _____
   _____ forever. *Ps. 73:26*
2. The Lord will _____ us. *Hosea 6:1*
3. He has sent me to preach deliverance to the_____
   _____. *Lu. 4:18*
4. The words of the flesh are manifest, such as idolatry, and _____
   _____. *Gal. 5:19,20*
5. Ye shall know the truth and the truth shall set you_____
   _____. *John 8:32*
6. Where the spirit of the Lord is there is_____.
   II Cor. 3:17
7. You have been called unto_____. *Gal. 5:13*
8. If we confess our sins, he is faithful, and just to _____.
   I John 1:9
9. Saul said unto Samuel, I have_____.
   I Sam. 15:24
10. If you do not forgive men their trespasses, neither will the Father ____
    _____forgive your trespasses. *Mt. 6:15*
11. Jesus said, you shall forgive _____ times
    seven times. *Mt. 18:22*
12. Be ye kind and _____ even as Christ has
    forgiven you. *Eph. 4:32*
13. Forgive all of my_____. *Ps. 25:18*
14. The Lord will abundantly _____. *Isa. 55:7*

DAILY SCRIPTURE

Mon.   Ps. 73:21-28
Tues.   Hosea 6:1-3
Wed.   John 8:31-38
Thurs. II Cor. 3:12-18
Fri.   I John 1:5-10
Sat.   Mt. 18:15-22
Sun.   Isa. 55:1-9

PRAYER CONCERNS

Your Family & Relatives
Government Leaders
Missionaries
For the Unbelievers
Churches & Denominations
Your Own Church
Prayer and Praise

NOTE: You will be spiritually strengthened by completing two questions each day, reading the suggested scripture, and ministering in prayer for the concerns of the day.

THE MINISTRY OF THE MASTER—MONDAY
A Spirit Lifter

I feel this little incident conveyed the truth of how many of us handle our responsibilities in life.

Father called home to check on things. The little six-year-old answered the phone. His first comment was,

"Don't talk too loudly, Dad. The babysitter is asleep."

God's Promise

The promises of the Lord are for you and me. He has granted us great power.

"...whatever you bind on earth is bound in heaven, and whatever you free on earth will be freed in heaven." (Matthew 18:18, LB)

Practicing His Presence

Today seek to consciously be aware of the Lord Jesus. The practice of His presence is an art which you need to develop. It does not come with indifference. It comes with concentrated effort.

Steps To Inner Healing

The ancient writer, Plato, is reported to have said,

"All diseases of the body precede from the mind or the soul. Whatever disease the body may have it is accented unless..."

He perceived evidently what modern research has revealed that unless there is wholeness on the inside all the outward diseases are accented. In fact, many outward diseases can be prevented or cured if things are right on the inside.

The problems of the inside will engulf you more and more on the outside. I liken the inner problems to the characteristics of leather. You can bind a gun handle or other things with leather. You simply wet the leather thoroughly. Then you wrap the item you want to bind and let the leather dry. This pulls it tightly. Do you realize there are many lives in this condition? The inner disturbed emotions are pulling like leather around their hearts. The squeeze is becoming tighter and tighter.

Circumstances, remarks of people, events in your life, all serve as moisture in a sense which makes a situation from which you feel you can never recover. At times you feel you could just scream, but then you wonder if anyone would hear you if you did.

A big step in conquering inner illness is to realize it is a problem which is not confined to only you. It is universal and there is victory for you.

PRAYER: *Help me to renew my mind, O Lord, and to live to your glory and honor. Amen.*

THE MINISTRY OF THE MASTER—TUESDAY
A Spirit Lifter

What determines many of the decisions you make? Is it circumstances or a pre-determined plan? I guess most of us make decisions on the spur-of-the-moment like this mother.

"That settles it," exploded the distraught mother to her child who had just knocked over a very expensive vase. "You're going to be an only child!"

God's Promise

"When someone becomes a Christian he becomes a brand new person inside. He is not the same any more. A new life has begun." (II Corinthians 5:17, LB)

Practicing His Presence

Who irritated you the most yesterday? Did this serve to unnerve and to defeat you? Or did you seek to make it a time when you sense the presence of the Master?

Steps To Inner Healing

I cannot stress enough that the Lord is the only One who can really bring the inner wholeness you desire. There are many things which promise wholeness, but only One who can deliver.

We live in an age which provides many false cures. The false gods are on every hand The false gods take the form of drugs, the occult, and even the concept of self help. None of these can meet the need which you have deep within your soul.

It is amazing to me the number of people who have turned to the occult. There are even thousands who are turning to witches. This is supposed to be an enlightened age, but in some ways it is a dark age.

The seers carry influence far beyond their power to help and to direct in the lives of their followers. I read that of all the predictions made by the world's leading seers, less than one percent, came to pass. Now can you imagine a ball player being kept on the team with such an abysmal batting average?

During the presidential campaign I read of one prominent seer who predicted Carter's election because of the way the stars were in his life. Another predicted Reagan would be elected. Now, since there were only two running, someone had to be right.

A basic step to wholeness is to forsake that which can only bring more illness. Seek only the Lord and his wholeness.

PRAYER: *Lord Jesus, I know there is no One but You who can really bring the wholeness I need. Help me to always remember this. Amen.*

THE MINISTRY OF THE MASTER—WEDNESDAY
A Spirit Lifter

The exasperated mother said to her young son, "Every time you do something naughty I get another gray hair."

The little five-year-old applied his logic and said, "Gee, Mom, you must have been terrible when you were my age. Just look at Grandma!"

God's Promise

"The Lord said to Moses, Is there a limit to the power of the Lord? You will see this very day whether or not my words come true." (Numbers 11:23, NEB)

Practicing His Presence

I encourage you to take a few moments and picture youself completely at ease. As you do this let His presence pervade your whole being.

Steps To Inner Healing

Jesus Christ is the only One who can give to you the freedom, peace, and purpose you desire. This sounds so simple, but is absolutely true.

One of the big steps to inner healing is to realize this and to believe it with all of your heart. He gives an inner healing which will enable you to face all of the outward problems and diseases.

One of the ancient martyrs was being burned at the stake. A person was about to light the faggots at his back. He said,

"Please, please come around to the front and light them so I can see you do it. I am not afraid."

This man had inner wholeness. As the flames flickered around him and ultimately consumed his body he sang songs of victory. He knew the power of Romans 10:9.

"If thou shalt confess with thy mouth the Lord Jesus and believe in your heart that God has raised Him from the dead, you shall be saved."

Saved from what? Saved from your miserable self! When you are delivered from self and healed on the inside you are whole. You are free indeed!

PRAYER: *I give myself to Thee, O Lord, that I might be delivered from self. Amen.*

THE MINISTRY OF THE MASTER—THURSDAY
A Spirit Lifter

Our actions sometimes get us into complex situations. It takes much verbal gymnastics to get out of some of them.

The old lady was delighted by the gift and cheerfully said to the little boy and his friends,

"Tommy, tomorrow at church I'll thank your mother for this lovely pie."

"If you don't mind," Tommy nervously suggested, "would you thank her for two pies?"

God's Promise

The Lord promises benefits to those who fear Him.

"The fear of the Lord is the beginning of knowledge, but fools scorn wisdom and discipline." (Proverbs 1:7, NEB)

Practicing His Presence

Your spiritual powers are exercised as you practice His presence. It will make a difference how you approach today and tomorrow.

Steps To Inner Healing

Often individuals have told me that they felt much better after talking with me and unloading their souls. My being willing to hear their confession was a step to their being healed.

The secret to meaningful confession is to confess your own sins. I have known many who delight in confessing the sins of others. It may be more fun to confess someone else's sins, but it is not nearly as helpful.

Your spouse, neighbor, friend, relative, and fellow worker must do their own confessing. If you take care of your sins it will be amazing what happens to others. Your inner problem is crucial. The wholeness you desire is possible, but confession may be the step you need today.

I would suggest that you tell God of your disobedience. You may do this anywhere and at any time. There are times when you will be helped if you confess to another person. The Lord will use this means to help you. The Bible imparts truth through the statement,

"Therefore confess your sins to one another, and pray for one another, and then you will be healed." James 5:16, NEB

PRAYER: *"Give me, Father, a sharp eye for my own sins and blind me to the faults of others. Amen.*

THE MINISTRY OF THE MASTER—FRIDAY
A Spirit Lifter

Is it any wonder some people have trouble balancing the budget? A young woman had taken an examination for a job. The employer was concerned about her ability when he read the answer to the question,

"If you buy an article for twelve dollars and eighty cents, and you sell it for fourteen dollars and forty cents, do you gain or lose?"

Her answer, "I gain on the dollars. I lose on the cents."

God's Promise

Many fail to appreciate the real freedom they must have and can have.

"...God will break the chains that bind his people and the whip that scourges them..." (Isaiah 9:4, IB)

Practicing His Presence

Who is the biggest crook with whom you have had to deal? When you think of that person does it almost make you sick? It is in this situation you need to develop the ability to be aware of His presence.

Steps To Inner Heaing

Among the steps to inner healing must be listed the spirit of forgiveness. It is not an easy step to take, but it is an essential one. By the Grace of God we are called to forgive any and all.

I realize you have been hurt by others. The words they have said about you. The crooked deals they have pulled. The scandalous acts they have committed. Any one or all of these things have happened to every adult. Yet, they are not a license to continue to carry resentment.

The forgiveness needed must be an act of yours. The Lord has chosen to limit Himself to the point that He can't forgive you completely until you have forgiven others. Isn't it interesting that He would limit Himself in this area. He created a universe. He sustains this immense universe. Yet, Jesus tells us that unless we forgive others the heavenly Father cannot forgive us. It is the only part of the model prayer which He explains in detail.

"For if ye forgive men their trespasses, your heavenly Father will also forgive you."

This sounds all right, but notice the next verse and then you really receive the message of the necessity of forgiveness.

"If you forgive not men their trespasses, neither will your Father forgive your trespasses." Mt. 6:14,15

PRAYER: *I want your forgiveness so much, dear Lord, that I am willing to forgive others as completely as humanly possible. Amen.*

THE MINISTRY OF THE MASTER—SATURDAY
A Spirit Lifter

There are some people who expect us to accept the flimsy excuse. A dairyman was charged with selling watered down milk. The judge asked if he had anything to say about this dastardly deed. His response was, "Well, your Honor, the night before it rained awfully hard and the only thing I can figure is that the cows must have got wet clear through."

God's Promise

You can put your trust in the Lord because He is always the same.

"For I am the Lord, I change not; therefore ye sons of Jacob are not consumed." (Malachi 3:6, KJV)

Practicing His Presence

"The still small voice" is nestled in your heart. He is not perched on your shoulder. Permit the ears of the heart to be attuned to His voice.

Steps To Inner Healing

I want to continue in the area of forgiveness. This is so important as a step to your inner healing. I deal with many people and this is one of the most crucial areas of concern. Resentment, unforgiveness and the harboring of ill will are all forms of disease which will cripple you for life.

Someone has penned these thoughts,

> *"Saints are men who permit God's forgiveness to come into them so fully that not only are their sins washed out, but also their very selves. Their egos are the root of their self will. I forgive at the level that I have been forgiven and if that level is moderate, because I wanted to lose only my vices and not myself I can only forgive people who have offended moderately. And my forgiveness helps them only moderately."*

The point of this insight is that we must forgive completely. This is our high calling in Christ who forgave even those who killed Him.

One gentleman with whom I counseled had difficulty in practically every area of his life. He could not fulfill job responsibilities. He was at odds with every other member of his family. The general characteristic of his life was misery.

Through our talks together the Spirit revealed to him the seriousness of the grudges he held against members of his first family. When he truy forgave them he was truly healed.

PRAYER: *Though my actions are not perfect, Father, may my heart be stayed on Thee always. Amen.*

THE MINISTRY OF THE MASTER—SUNDAY
A Spirit Lifter

"So your name is Joshua. Is that right? Are you the man that made the sun shine for extra hours?"

"Oh no, sir. I am the Joshua that makes the moonshine."

God's Promise

You don't have to worry about the universe. The Lord made it, and He is going to care for it.

"All things were made by him; and without him was not anything made that was made." (John 1:3, KJV)

Practicing His Presence

"I am so sensitive" is often said by people. Our high calling is to be sensitive to His presence. So often we are sensitive to the hurts of others instead of the helps of Jesus.

Steps To Inner Healing

The steps to inner wholeness are not once in a lifetime ones. The inner wholeness you desire is a daily walk. These steps must be maintained. Inner wholeness is a pilgrimage. It is not a point of arrival.

The centuries have revealed some helpful ways for believers to keep whole in the Lord. Among them are such things as the study of His word, the meeting together faithfully with other believers, the developing of prayer as a life style, and the willingness to be disciplined by other believers.

You are not the only one in the world with inner illness. This is something which is common to human beings. You need not be defeated by this illness. The victory lies in your willingness to be healed and your willingness to continue to feed and nurture the things of the spirit.

You are more than flesh and blood. You are more than the sum total of all of your experiences. The real you is spiritual. This real you must be treated constantly. Now and in the future do not permit anything to bring inner illness to you.

The disciplines of the spirit-led life will enable you to reap many wonderful results.

PRAYER: *Help me, Lord Jesus, to walk moment by moment with you and to glorify you in my walk. Amen.*

A PRAYER FOR INNER HEALING

How can you receive the ministry of inner healing? What can be done to bring healing to the inward most part of your being? How can you best come to know that the Lord is reaching out to heal in every part of your past as well as the present?

I am convinced that individuals need help in the area of prayer for inner healing. I wish there were thousands of people trained and willing to minister to others in this way.

It has been my privilege to minister to many people through prayer. Each has had a different situation and yet each needed the same Master to touch and to heal.

I hope this week you will very carefully read the prayer. I have presented some aspect of the prayer each day. This is a week when you may want to read all of the sermonettes at one sitting and then day by day review the portion in the sermonette.

Every person has inner hurts. Every person has memories which are negative and destructive. Every person has emotional and spiritual scars which are as painful as physical adhesions.

The Lord Jesus has a message of hope for you. He said, *"I am come that you might have life and that you might have it more abundant." John 10:10*

He desires victory for you. He does not want you cast down and to be defeated. The problem with most of us is that the accumulation of the years has clogged our total being. There seems to be no way to escape. The message of inner healing proclaims there is an escape! You can be delivered.

As you read the sermonettes this week you will know your hurts. You will know where and how you desire the Lord to speak to you and to bring His healing. This is going to be a sacred pilgrimage for you. My prayers are with you.

POINTS TO PONDER

1. Do you feel everyone is in need of inner healing?
2. Is it possible for a person to pray the prayer of inner healing for himself?
3. What does it mean to receive inner healing?

A PRAYER FOR INNER HEALING

1. He shall call upon me, and I will _____ him. *Ps. 91:15*
2. Then shalt thou call, and the Lord shall _____. *Is. 58:9*
3. Ask, and it shall be given you; seek, and ye shall find; knock, and it shall be_____unto you. *Luke 11:9*
4. If ye shall ask anything in my_____, I will do it. *John 14:14*
5. And ye shall seek me, and find me, when ye shall _____ _____ for me with all your heart. *Jer. 29:13*
6. Therefore I say unto you, what things soever ye desire, when ye pray, _____that ye receive them. *Mark 11:24*
7. Give me now _____ and knowledge. *II Chr. 1:10*
8. If any of you lack wisdom, let him_____ of God. *James 1:5*
9. Is any among you afflicted? Let him_____. *James 5:13*
10. And they went out, and _____ that men should repent. *Mark 6:12*
11. But I have prayed for thee, and when thou art _____ _____, strengthen thy brethren. *Luke 22:32*
12. For this _____ I bow my knees unto the Father of our Lord Jesus Christ. *Eph. 3:14*
13. Therefore glorify God in your _____ and in your spirit, which are God's. *I Cor. 6:20*
14. Should live unto righteousness; by whose stripes ye were _____ _____. *I Peter 2:24*

DAILY SCRIPTURE   PRAYER CONCERNS

Mon.	Ps. 91:1-16	Your Family & Relatives
Tues.	Luke 11:1-13	Government Leaders
Wed.	Jer. 29:10-19	Missionaries
Thurs.	James 1:2-11	For the Unbelievers
Fri.	James 5:7-18	Churches & Denominations
Sat.	Eph. 3:14-21	Your Own Church
Sun.	I Peter 2:18-25	Prayer and Praise

NOTE: You will be spiritually strengthened by completing two questions each day, reading the suggested scripture, and ministering in prayer for the concerns of the day.

THE MINISTRY OF THE MASTER—MONDAY
A Spirit Lifter

The church had instructed the building committee to come back with a proposal concerning the new building and the future of the old building. Here is their proposal.

1. We shall build a church.
2. The new building is to be located on the site of the old one.
3. The material in the old building is to be used in the new one.
4. We shall continue to use the old building until the new one is completed.

God's Promise

"...It is not for you to know the time or times which the Father has put under his own authority." (Acts 1:7, Lamsa)

Practicing His Presence

There are many things which may cloud the sense of His presence. It might be an incident, some comments by others, the mood I am in for the day, etc.

A Prayer For Inner Healing

Lord Jesus, I pray that at this very moment I will realize you are receiving me just as I am. You know every thought of each second of my present and past life. You know every hurt I have experienced and every fear that I carry. You know every painful memory which haunts me. You are completely aware of the areas of guilt that leave me defeated.

MY FUTURE

Now, Lord Jesus, I want to give to you my future. A future which I often dread and fear because of the pressures and problems of the past. A future which is frightening because of the uncertainty of what lies ahead. I ask that you reach into my mind right now in such a way as to take away the fear of the future. Help me to walk into that future fully aware of your power, presence and love. Enable me to leave the future in your hands and with confidence. I now commit my life to you anew and at greater depth. I know that the peace you give this moment is the same peace I can have a year from now, or 10 years or a hundred years from now. It is your peace you have given to me and no one can take it from me. It is your peace and the world cannot give it. It cannot take it away. Yes, Lord, as never before I say and believe my future is in your hands.

PRAYER: *Thank you, Lord Jesus, that you love me just as I am. I come with all my faults and failures. Amen.*

THE MINISTRY OF THE MASTER—TUESDAY
A Spirit Lifter

There are many ways to evade the factual answer, but this gal was about the most clever I have read about.

Lawyer: "Don't forget you are under oath to tell the truth. Now, how old are you?"

Witness: "Twenty-nine and some months."

Lawyer: "How many months?"

Witness: "One hundred and thirty-three."

God's Promise

"But when the Holy Spirit comes upon you, you shall receive power and you shall be witnesses to me both in Jerusalem and in all Judea..." (Acts 1:8, Lamsa)

Practicing His Presence

"Lo, I am with you always..." are words of assurance. This assures you that the Lord desires to be your constant companion. He is always there.

A Prayer For Inner Healing

Today, think of your present situation and condition. May you keep in mind that the Lord is in every aspect of your living. He cannot be confined to the sanctuary. He cannot be put in one corner of your life. He is your all and all.

MY PRESENT

And now, Lord Jesus, I want you to take all that I am at this very moment and impart your wholeness. I believe you have much to give to me and I want, yes, I sincerely want, all that you have for me.

I invite you to come into the areas of my life which weigh heaviest on my heart. I want to have you enter those areas which are most disturbing to my mind. I want you to touch my body and to impart your wholeness.

Lord, I pray for your help with my anxiety for the problems I now face. In the midst of the problems help me to see that you stand there triumphant. I ask that you not only be with me, but also with all of my family and loved ones. May your love permeate every one of them.

I believe you are in the NOW of my life. You are helping me to face each moment and each situation. You are revealing to me the fact that you love me now, just as I am. Help me to believe this and heal me from devastating doubts. Amen.

PRAYER: *This very day is yours, Lord Jesus. I want to consciously give my all to you today. Amen.*

THE MINISTRY OF THE MASTER—WEDNESDAY
A Spirit Lifter

Communication is one of the great problems we all face.

The organist desired to impress the distinguished visiting preacher. Knowing that the one working the pumping mechanism had been a little slack lately, she had the pastor give him a note. The pastor misunderstood and thought the note was for the visiting preacher who opened it and read, "Keep blowing away until I give the signal to stop."

God's Promise

Pause to let this promise become a part of your innermost being.

"So do not fear, for I am with you; do not be dismayed, for I am your God. I will strengthen you and help you..." (Isaiah 41:10, NIV)

Practicing His Presence

Who touched your life yesterday and made you realize the power and presence of the Lord? Maybe it was someone who did a good deed for you. Maybe it was someone who did you wrong.

A Prayer For Inner Healing

Today, I want you to quiet yourself and permit the Lord Jesus to bring His healing touch to all facets of your past life. This is the beginning of the prayer for the healing of memories which can speak powerfully to any who are willing to have it do so. You may desire to read and reread this prayer and to permit it to become very much a part of your whole being.

MY PAST

And now, Lord Jesus, I invite you to heal my memories of the past. The immediate as well as the distant past I want to bring to you. I pray you will heal my yesterday. I pray you will heal in the areas where I suffer because of the past week, or past month, or of events of many years ago.

There are areas where I have failed and I ask you to forgive me. I cannot forgive myself and no one else has been able to help me accept forgiveness.

Lord, I ask that you take the troubled areas of my mind and heart and cleanse them. I give them all to you for your touch. They cling so tenaciously that I cannot rid myself of them. You alone can deliver me.

PRAYER: *Yesterday still clings to me, Jesus. Please remove any negative aspects of my yesterdays. Amen.*

THE MINISTRY OF THE MASTER—THURSDAY
A Spirit Lifter

Here is another one which reveals the complexities of communication. The newspaper advertisement was great, but the message in it could be interpreted in different ways.

Armageddon-The Earth's Last War-How and Where It Will Be Fought! At the First Baptist Church

God's Promise

"The Lord is gracious and compassionate, slow to anger and rich in love. The Lord is good to all; he has compassion on all he has made." (Psalm 145:8,9, NIV)

Practicing His Presence

Through what incident or person did you experience the presence of the Lord yesterday? If you are alert to His always being with you, then incidents and conversations will be seen in the light of His presence.

A Prayer For Inner Healing

This sermonette continues to take you through the past events of your life. This is not the ordinary sermonette. It is a prayer for inner healing. It is a sacred journey into your past with the desire for Jesus to touch and to heal. I join you in this prayer. Together we seek His wholeness.

MY PAST (continued)

Lord, please walk through my conscious memory of my working years. I want your healing for the many hurts, frustrations, and failures of people with whom I have worked. Also, I give you all the frustrations of the jobs I have attempted to do and to which I have given much of my life.

I want to open unto you the years when I left home to establish my own home. During this time I received wounds from parents, friends, and even my spouse. The scars remain from these wounds. Please take away even the scars. Where there have been resentments help me to be renewed with a spirit of forgiveness.

There have been many frustrations which defeated me often. I pray you would enter into this facet of my defeated life and bring your victory. Help me to realize that your presence and spirit can heal and help me to accept this healing. Amen.

PRAYER: *The many hurts at work sometimes overwhelm me, Father. Help me to forget and to forgive. Amen.*

THE MINISTRY OF THE MASTER—FRIDAY
A Spirit Lifter

Some things are hard on pastors. A pastor was informed that a man in his congregation with a very bad heart condition had inherited a million dollars. Everyone was afraid of what this shock might do to him and asked the pastor to break the news.

The pastor started off with, "Jim, what would you do if you inherited a million dollars?" Without hesitation Jim replied, "I would give half of it to the church." And the pastor had a heart attack.

God's Promise

The real challenge to you and me is to let that which endures be the prime goal of life. His promise helps us.

"But now abideth faith, hope, love, these three; and the greatest of these is love." (I Corinthians 13:13, RSV)

Practicing His Presence

Are you believing the Lord is going to be with you today? If so, it will make a difference in all that you say and do. You practice His presence not only in thought, but also in action.

A Prayer For Inner Healing

I want you to continue to permit the Lord Jesus to walk through your past. This is sometimes a traumatic experience, but it is worth the pain. The refreshing healing is worth the agony of the moment. Jesus is the tender One and ever so gently He imparts His touch.

MY PAST (continued)

Lord Jesus, at this time I want to bring my teenage years to you. It was a time when I rapidly moved through the trauma of many new emotions. They were not my happiest years. I feel guilty thinking they should have been, but they were not. Others thought I was happy, but so often I was miserable and this negativism I have had trouble removing from my life.

I developed a lot of new fears. This has left me with many painful memories. I especially want your forgiveness and healing in the areas of my teenage years in which the incidents left me humiliated and with feelings of guilt. I never realized the after-effects of my thoughts and actions would linger so long in my mind and heart. I beg you to remove the negative effects of them.

I truly give these years to you and thank you for your healing. My memories are now seen in the light of your glorious presence and for this I am grateful. Amen.

PRAYER: *Jesus, the hurts of my teenage years I give to you. I don't want them any more. Amen.*

THE MINISTRY OF THE MASTER—SATURDAY
A Spirit Lifter

There is more to life than formal education.

The mountain school teacher was presenting all the drawbacks to ignorance and the value of education to an absentee girl.

"Now look here teacher, Grandma didn't get no education and she got married. My maw didn't get no education and she got married. You got education and you haint married. So I just haint hankering for your education."

God's Promise

The Lord gives us a promise concerning truth.

"If any man will do his will, he shall know of the doctrine, whether it be of God..." (John 7:17, KJV)

Practicing His Presence

It is interesting to me that the more aware I am of the Presence of the Lord the more aware I am of the needs of others.

A Prayer For Inner Healing

Your approach and openness to this week's prayer pilgrimage will determine to a large extent the wholeness you will receive. The Lord is so willing. Your need is so great. This prayer brings together your needs and the One who can meet them.

MY PAST (continued)

Jesus, my junior high years come to my mind. I pray you would walk through them and heal. I want the scars of relationships and failures in other areas touched by you in this period of my life.

And, Lord, there are some childhood memories which are unpleasant. There were some people who affected me so negatively that I have not been able to cast off their destructive influence. Please help me bring them and the situations into your healing light.

I pray you would help me bring to your light the many things which I have suppressed through the years. Much of my childhood I have forgotten, but I know that I have not escaped the consequences of the events. I need your inner healing and sincerely trust you for it.

Lord Jesus, I even invite you to deal with my preschool years. I can't consciously remember much about them. Let your healing come even where my memory cannot go. May I be set free from those things in this period of my life which would hinder your fullness in me.

PRAYER: *Jesus, even the parts of my childhood which I can't remember I want you to touch and to heal. Amen.*

THE MINISTRY OF THE MASTER—SUNDAY
A Spirit Lifter

The famous preacher, Henry Ward Beecher, is reported to have received a letter with just one word written on it, "Fool." The next Sunday he referred to the letter from the pulpit by saying, "I have received many letters from people who have forgotten to sign their names, but this is the first time I've received a letter from someone who signed their name but forgot to write the letter."

God's Promise

Psalm 136 reminds us twenty-six times that the mercy of the Lord endures forever.

"O give thanks to the Lord, for he is good; for his mercy endures forever." (Psalm 136:1, Lamsa)

Practicing His Presence

The conscious awareness of the Lord will help you put the experiences of life into proper perspective. Satan is so desirous of feeding you lies. He wants to convince you that you have been forsaken by God. Do not believe him!

A Prayer For Inner Healing

It is my prayer that this week has been a meaningful devotional experience for you. My devotional guide is different, but I trust it is helpful. Please be open and honest as you continue to pray.

MY PAST (continued)

Jesus, I know you were present at the moment of my birth and during the moments of my breaking into this strange and terrifying world. May I feel and know your peace surrounding those moments. I ask that you even move through the months when I was carried in my mother's womb. May all of those moments be bathed in your love and tender care. I want you to be present in every emotion, even on the day I was conceived.

Now, Lord, I thank you for healing in every area of my life and every moment of my life. I desperately want to know your forgiveness. I desire your power. I want to be set free. Thank you that I do not ask in vain. Thank you that you hear and answer. Thank you for caring for my future, my present, and my past. Yes, Jesus, thank you for caring for my past fears, hurts, guilts, and failures. Thank you for caring for my future fears and worries. Thank you for being the same yesterday, today, and forever. Amen.

PRAYER: *Jesus, the sacredness of the moments and events surrounding my birth I lift unto you. Amen.*

OVERCOMING THE FEAR OF CRITICISM

Once a person has conquered in the area of inner healing there are many things which need continual attention. One of these areas is fear. There are so many fears which plague the average person. They must be dealt with extreme care and yet with a definite desire to defeat them.

One such fear is that of cricicism. Criticism can be used to your advantage. However, I feel in many cases it proves more of a defeating factor than it does a factor of deliverance.

Criticism means an inclination to find fault. It involves judging with severity. A criticial person is one who is over-occupied and skilled in negative criticism.

There are many so called good Christians who are experts at criticism. Practically everything in the world is viewed from their perspective and thus is seen as bad, done in poor taste, or not as it should be. It is absolutely impossible to please such a person.

Negative criticism cannot be escaped by any of us. You should not be permitted to escape it. It can be a positive influence in your life. However, this is true only when you receive it with a mature mind and proper attitude.

The critical spirit seeks to deprive others of their rightful possessions or personality uniqueness. It is that spirit which prevents success for churches, businesses, homes, neighborhoods, and other endeavors.

The lifestyle of our Lord Jesus Christ was one which lived above criticism. His was a high calling and He was going to fulfill it regardless of what others did. He knew all would not agree, but He knew His Father loved and cared.

He was dedicated to obedience and thus was not hampered by criticism. Your inner wholeness will be helped a great deal if you accept this fact and go on to the glory of God.

POINTS TO PONDER

1. Do you feel others ever speak in a critical way of you?
2. How could you check yourself on how negative you are toward others?
3. How do you feel you should handle your fear of criticism?

OVERCOMING THE FEAR OF CRITICISM

1. He maketh even his enemies to be at _____ with him. *Pro. 16:7*

2. Depart from _____, and do good; seek peace, and pursue it. *Ps. 34:14*

3. Fear _____; I will help thee. *Is. 41:13*

4. Be of good_____; it is I; be not afraid. *Mt. 14:27*

5. And Jesus came and _____ them, and said, Arise, and be not afraid. *Matt. 17:7*

6. For the Son of man is come to_____that which was lost. *Matt. 18:11*

7. _____the Lord in the beauty of holiness. *Ps. 29:2*

8. O magnify the_____ with me. *Ps. 34:3*

9. Blessed are the pure in _____. *Matt. 5:8*

10. Now the end of the Commandment is charity out of a pure_____ _____. *I Tim. 1:5*

11. Set your affection on things above, not on things on the _____ _____. *Col. 3:2*

12. For whatsoever a man_____, that shall he also reap. *Gal. 6:7*

13. But to be spiritually minded is life and_____. *Rom. 8:6*

14. But he that soweth to the Spirit shall of the Spirit reap life _____ _____. *Gal. 6:8*

DAILY SCRIPTURE

Mon.	Ps. 34:7-15
Tues.	Matt. 14:22-27
Wed.	Matt. 18:11-14
Thurs.	Ps. 34:1-6
Fri.	I Tim. 1:3-7
Sat.	Col. 3:1-11
Sun.	Gal. 6:1-10

PRAYER CONCERNS

Your Family & Relatives
Government Leaders
Missionaries
For the Unbelievers
Churches & Denominations
Your Own Church
Prayer and Praise

NOTE: You will be spiritually strengthened by completing two questions each day, reading the suggested scripture, and ministering in prayer for the concerns of the day.

THE MINISTRY OF THE MASTER—MONDAY
A Spirit Lifter

I wish I had this lady's quick comeback in all situations.

The mother was mailing a Bible to her son who was away at college. The postal clerk asked if the package contained anything breakable. She replied, "Yes, the Ten Commandments."

God's Promise

The good life does not go unrewarded.

"Surely the righteous shall give thanks to thy name; the upright shall dwell in thy presence." (Psalm 140:13, Lamsa)

Practicing His Presence

Life is too short not to use God's methods for victory in Jesus. One of these methods is to practice His presence. The quality of your life will be greatly enhanced as you do.

Overcoming The Fear Of Criticism

It is impossible to please everyone. Any concerted effort to do so can only lead to great frustration and needless inward worry and fear.

I like the story of the ancient Persian poet who had a donkey and a son. One day the three of them began a journey. The first village they entered some began to gossip about them. The comments were of their stupidity. They had a donkey and both were walking. How stupid that neither one of them rode the beast of burden.

After this they both decided to ride the beast. In the next town they were chastised for being so mean. How dare they load a small donkey with a man and a large boy! The poet said to his son, *"You ride and I will walk."*

In the next town they heard, *"Why that mean young man. He is riding the donkey and letting his father walk."*

It was then that the son decided to walk and let the father ride. Comments from the next village let them know that it was awful that a young boy would have to walk until exhausted while an indifferent father rode.

The poet concluded there was no way to please all the people. He learned that one way to overcome the fear of criticism was to face the fact that it would be received.

PRAYER: *Father, help me to put criticism in its proper perspective. May I learn from it, but not be defeated by it. Amen.*

THE MINISTRY OF THE MASTER—TUESDAY
A Spirit Lifter

Good Samaritans are hard to find. Especially the kind who can be compassionate as well as truly helpful.

The teacher had finished teaching concerning the Good Samaritan and going out of one's way to help another person. To clinch the truths she was seeking to impart she asked,

"What would you do if you saw a man bleeding beside the road?"

A student responded, "I'd throw up."

God's Promise

I like the promise the Lord gives that it is good to sing.

"Praise the Lord; for it is good to sing praises to our God' for it is pleasant, and praise is comely." (Psalm 146:10, Lamsa)

Practicing His Presence

There is no way you can really triumph in life without the Lord. If you believe this and practice His presence today you will be blessed. Try it with all your heart.

Overcoming The Fear Of Criticism

The fear of criticism can be overcome when you realize that in many situations the comments are made because of jealousy. Those nearest to you come in for the sharpest criticism. Those who are the most challenge to you are your targets of criticism. Those who are a threat to you are prime targets for your criticism.

I would encourage you to seek the comfort and help of the Lord during the moments of intense criticism. Your fighting back is not going to help a great deal. Vengeance belongs to the Lord and not to you.

Abraham Lincoln had been criticized again and again by a person. One of his friends told him he ought to lash back at him. Lincoln gave a classic reply.

"If I were to try to read much less to answer all the attacks made on me, this office might as well be closed for any other business. I do my very best that I know. The very best I can and I intend to keep doing so unto the end. If the end brings me out all right, what is said against me won't come out to anything. If the end brings me out wrong, ten angels swearing I was right would make no difference."

PRAYER: *Enable me, Father, to let the harsh words of others concerning me to go no deeper than the surface of hearing. Amen.*

THE MINISTRY OF THE MASTER—WEDNESDAY
A Spirit Lifter

I have heard of blowing your own horn, but this is ridiculous! The famous star had his show canceled on TV. An employee at the studio asked him, "Do you answer personally the hundreds of letters that have come in every day demanding that your program be renewed?"

"Heavens no!" he responded. "I hardly have time to write them."

God's Promise

"In the same way the Spirit comes to the aid of our weakness. We do not even know how we ought to pray, but through our inarticulate groans the spirit himself is pleading for us..." (Romans 8:26, NEB)

Practicing His Presence

The realization of His presence can make your life a heaven even in the midst of much hell. The neglect of His presence can make your life a hell in the midst of what many would feel should be a heaven.

Overcoming The Fear Of Criticism

There are many people who cannot react to criticism as did Abraham Lincoln. They end up defeated. They end up so self conscious that it is impossible for them to carry on the normal activities of life. Such individuals are afraid to launch new projects.

Years ago I recall an interesting incident at our home. There was a national mail order company having a campaign to name their new tires. My father came up with a name and suggested to my mother and family that it be submitted. The family members laughed at his suggestion and my mother seemed especially negative. My father couldn't handle this reaction and so he did not submit his idea.

Would believe that when the name was chosen it was what my father had suggested? There are still famous tires in our nation with this name.

This is probably one of the reasons my father remained poor. He could not handle the negative. I am as guilty when it comes to being defeated by negative cricitism. My guess is that you are the same way.

May I suggest that one of the ways to overcome this fear is to move as the spirit leads regardless of what others may say.

PRAYER: *Father, help me to go on to victory and faithfulness to my high calling regardless of thoughts and words of others. Amen.*

THE MINISTRY OF THE MASTER—THURSDAY
A Spirit Lifter

If the shoe fits, wear it.

The speaker was annoyed by people talking during his speech. Finally in exasperation he said, "We seem to have a number of fools here this evening. Wouldn't it be better to hear one at a time?"

A man retorted from the audience, "Right! Go on with your speech."

God's Promise

"He will tend his flock like a shepherd and gather them together with his arms; he will carry the lambs in his bosom and lead the ewes to water." (Isaiah 40:11, NEB)

Practicing His Presence

Can you think of anyone you desire to pattern yourself after? I suggest you use this same power of imagination to see Jesus with you right now. Practice His presence and have power.

Overcoming The Fear Of Criticism

There are other attitudes spawned by the fear of criticism. Included would be lack of initiative, blaming others for your failures and defeats, accepting what you call fate and failing to seek to achieve, and just quitting.

Frequently many of these are the prime result of your not being able to take criticism. You take your ball glove and go home if things do not go your way. If they don't like the rules you use or the way you bat, you quit.

The late Harry Truman once said, *"If you can't stand the heat, get out of the kitchen."* Many cannot stand the heat and seek to withdraw from the kitchen of life.

I would suggest you seek to overcome this fear of criticism by stepping out for God. Some years ago I had a person say to me,

"Bartow, you are always out on a limb."

My response I feel was from the Lord. *"This may be true, but that is where the fruit is."*

Yes, you do not pick cherries at the trunk. They are on the ends of the branches. The meaningful and powerful moments of life come when you reject criticism and do something great to the glory of God.

PRAYER: *Dear Lord, help me to gather the sweet and spiritually nourishing fruit of daily obedience. Amen.*

THE MINISTRY OF THE MASTER—FRIDAY
A Spirit Lifter

Abraham Lincoln was a wise man. Some of his responses have really been a blessing to me.

Lincoln was in a big debate with Douglas. In the heat of the aftermath of the speeches a person accused Lincoln of being two-faced. His was a classic answer.

"I leave it to my audience. If I had two faces, would I be wearing this one?"

God's Promise

There is a reward for your living at peace with others.

"How good it is and how pleasant for brothers to live together! It is fragrant as oil poured upon the head and falling over the beard." (Psalm 133:1,2, NEB)

Practicing His Presence

Frequently the degree of the awareness of the Lord is determined by how a person feels. This is natural, but somehow we must seek to sense His presence by faith. Feelings are too unreliable.

Overcoming The Fear Of Criticism

Jesus gave keen insight concerning the reactions of others. His penetrating words, *"Woe unto you when all shall speak well of you for so did they to the false prophets,"* *(Luke 6:26)* are worthy of your serious consideration.

Sometimes you hear the statement, *"Everybody loved her."* Or, *"Everybody really liked him."* You will notice that in most cases these statements are made after the person is dead. It is a statement which is made after the threat of competition is gone.

Jesus knew that anything worthwhile would engender negative comments. He knew that there would be opposition to anything be it ever so worthwhile. His own life is a beautiful example of this.

I am always amazed that even on the occasion of raising Lazarus from the dead, there were those who wanted to do away with Jesus. You would think this fantastic event would enthuse the most negative person. However, some immediately headed to the authorities to plot how to eliminate Jesus.

Your fear of criticism will be helped if you seek to realize that some are going to downgrade you. In the face of this the presence of the Lord will help you to be strong.

PRAYER: *Father, I know there are some who don't care for me. Help me not to be harsh toward them, but to love them. Amen.*

THE MINISTRY OF THE MASTER—SATURDAY
A Spirit Lifter

It is hard to separate your words from that which consumes you.
The wife was complaining to her husband. Finally she said, "You think so much of your golf you don't even remember when we were married." "Oh yes I do," he retorted. "It was the day I sank the 36 foot putt."

God's Promise

"The Lord is my shepherd; I shall want nothing. He makes me lie down in green pastures, and leads me beside the waters of peace." (Psalm 23:1,2, NEB)

Practicing His Presence

I believe you will have a great day if you begin by planning to practice His presence. You may be stuck with continued burdens at home. Seek to see Christ with you.

Overcoming The Fear Of Criticism

I cannot end the week of considering overcoming the fear of criticism without pointing out the fact that Jesus was criticized again and again. Some called Him a drunkard. Others called Him a devil. Others said He was in league with the devil.

There were those who said He did not worship properly. He and His disciples did not wash their hands properly. He healed on the Sabbath. He associated with sinners. He was disrespectful of the religious leaders.

All of these accusations He was willing to receive in order to remain faithful to God. He knew the Lord was on His side and ultimately He would win.

His admonition to His disciples is sound advice for you today.

"Fear not them which kill the body, but are not able to kill the soul; but rather fear him which is able to destroy both soul and body in hell." Mt. 10:28

He could overcome the fear of criticism because He knew whom to fear. The only one to really fear would be God and this delivered Him from petty fears which could only make His life miserable.

PRAYER: *Father, as your dear Son was faithful unto death in spite of severe criticism, please help me to be as faithful. Amen.*

THE MINISTRY OF THE MASTER—SUNDAY
A Spirit Lifter

Many people have such a simplistic answer to even major problems.

The wife was reading a magazine and was startled by some statistics. She said to her husband, "I read here that somewhere in the world there is a woman having a baby every four seconds! Why that's awful. Something should be done about this."

The husband replied, "I should think so. They ought to find that woman and stop her."

God's Promise

Are there depths of your being which ache for comfort? Jesus has a promise for you.

"I will pray the Father, and he shall give you another Comforter, that he may abide with you forever." (John 14:16, KJV)

Practicing His Presence

One of the mysteries of the Christian faith is that in the midst of a turbulent moment the inward calm can be present. A most busy day and a most frustrating experience cannot delete His presence. Remember this!

Overcoming The Fear Of Criticism

You can be unshackled from the fear of criticism. You can change your outlook on life and your method of handling criticism. This is what I hope has happened to you this week.

The story is told of a man who carried two burlap sacks. The one on the front was used to throw in all the bad and rotten things people did and said concerning him. The one on the back was used to throw all the kindnesses, good things, and kind words people did for him or said about him. He kept looking at the front bag all the time and reviewing all the bad things. One day a friend said,

"Why don't you put the front bag on the back and the back bag on the front?"

The old man's eyes lit up and he said, *"You know, I never thought of that."* He did this and it changed his life.

The lesson is plain. Do not spend your time fretting over the criticisms aimed at you. Seek to see the good and go on for God. In addition may you seek to encourage others with your words and actions.

A famous leader of men once said, *"I have yet to find the person however exalted his station who did not do better work and put forth greater effort under a spirit of approval than under a spirit of criticism."*

PRAYER: *Heavenly Father, help me to keep before my eyes the goodness of others and not their meanness. Amen.*

OVERCOMING THE FEAR OF DEATH

The fear of death has plagued individuals since the beginning of time. I have known many people who almost die because of this fear.

It is amazing to me how many teenagers feel this way. They have their life before them and yet suicide is one of the leading causes of death among teenagers. They do the very thing which they fear.

The Lord Jesus was born that He might bring to you and me a message of life. His was not a message of fear. He knew that He had come from heaven and that He would return to heaven.

The message at His birth was a message of life and hope.

"Be not afraid, for behold I bring you good news of a great joy which will come to all the people. For to you is born this day in the city of David a Saviour who is Christ the Lord." Luke 2:10,11

A Saviour is one who delivers. Christ delivered from death. He gave a message of hope which excelled any message ever given to human beings.

An over concern with death is an indication of unbelief. It is a sign that fear has conquered and that faith has failed. This fear can affect all of life. It can make you nervous, short-tempered, and at times almost paralyze you as far as making decisions are concerned.

The good news is that Christ can conquer this fear. He has come to give you life abundant as John tells us as he quotes Jesus (John 10:10).

God is not dead. He is very much alive. He does not want you to live in dread fear of being dead. He knows this fear can stifle all of a person's other efforts.

The end of your life is not at the point of the cessation of physical life. You live on with Jesus. This assurance is your hope now and always. You can rebuke the fear of death and begin to live with the thought of life. This will be more to God's glory and certainly more to your good.

POINTS TO PONDER

1. Do you feel many people fear death?
2. When do you most fear death?
3. How do you feel you overcome this fear and receive His inner healing?

OVERCOMING THE FEAR OF DEATH

1. All _____ is given by inspiration of God.
   II Tim. 3:16
2. Heaven and _____ shall pass away.
   Matt. 24:35
3. If ye abide in me and my_____abide
   in you. *John 15:7*
4. Thy word is a _____ unto my feet.
   Ps. 119:105
5. Who hath _____ our report? *Is. 53:1*
6. And he did not many mighty works there because of their _____
   _____. *Matt. 13:58*
7. He heard me, and delivered me from all my _____.
   Ps. 34:4
8. There is no fear in love; but perfect love casteth out _____
   _____. *I John 4:18*
9. I will_____no evil. *Ps. 23:4*
10. In God have I put my_____. *Ps. 56:11*
11. The Lord is thy _____. *Ps. 121:5*
12. Our help is in the name of the _____. *Ps. 124:8*
13. With my mouth will I make known thy_____
    to all generations. *Ps. 89:1*
14. Ye were called unto the fellowship of his Son Jesus Christ our _____
    _____. *I Cor. 1:9*

DAILY SCRIPTURE

Mon.	II Tim. 3:10-17
Tues.	John 15:7-17
Wed.	Isaiah 53:1-6
Thurs.	I John 4:8-21
Fri.	Psalm 56
Sat.	Psalm 121
Sun.	I Cor. 1:4-9

PRAYER CONCERNS

Your Family & Relatives
Government Leaders
Missionaries
For the Unbelievers
Churches & Denominations
Your Own Church
Prayer and Praise

NOTE: You will be spiritually strengthened by completing two questions each day, reading the suggested scripture, and ministering in prayer for the concerns of the day.

THE MINISTRY OF THE MASTER—MONDAY
A Spirit Lifter

And how was your vacation? I hope you had a wonderful time.
"Where are you going on your vacation?" asked his friend.
"Yellowstone National Park."
"Well, don't forget Old Faithful."
"I won't," was his reply, "she's going with me."

God's Promise

Are you desperate for a promise to cling to throughout this day?"

"The Lord is my light and my salvation; whom shall I fear? The Lord is the strength of my life; of whom shall I be afraid." (Psalm 27:1, KJV)

Practicing His Presence

Pause for a moment and think. When did I get that gentle touch of assurance of the Lord's presence yesterday? When did I know beyond a shadow of doubt that He was with me?

Overcoming The Fear Of Death

A jester had superbly entertained the king. He was so impressed that he gave him his scepter. He told the fool,

"Now you keep this and if ever you find a bigger fool than you, you give it to him."

The years rolled by and the jester appeared in the same court. The king who had given him the scepter was terminally ill. The jester was not aware of this. The king spoke to him in veiled language by saying,

"I am going to make a long journey."

The jester asked, *"Where are you going and when are you coming back?"* The king replied, *"I will not be back. You see, I will never return."*

"What preparations have you made for the journey?" asked the jester. *"None at all,"* was the king's answer. *"That is my problem. I have not made any at all."*

It was then that the fool took the scepter and said, *"Here it is, sir. You may have it. You are a bigger fool than I am."*

One of the best ways to overcome the fear of death is to prepare for death in and through Christ Jesus our Lord.

PRAYER: *Jesus, I want to be prepared to live and prepared to die. Thank you for your help in both areas. Amen*

THE MINISTRY OF THE MASTER—TUESDAY
A Spirit Lifter

There are some people who are always late. And when they go to a meeting or out for the evening it takes ages to get ready.

Husband, "I have tickets for the dinner theater."

"Wonderful, darling, I'll start dressing right away."

"That's a good idea," he said. "The tickets are for tomorrow night."

God's Promise

You may feel inadequate in speech. Do not let this hinder your realizing the power of the Lord.

"For the kingdom of God is not in word, but in power." (I Corinthians 4:20, KJV)

Practicing His Presence

I visited a new mother and child at the hospital. The little girl was just beautiful. I thought of this little life fresh from the hand of God and it made me aware of His presence.

Overcoming The Fear Of Death

It is reported that one of the ancient Russian rulers was so afraid of death that he made it a law that no one of his subjects could ever refer to death in his presence. If this were done the person would be banished for life.

While visiting a relative there was a sudden death in the home. He rushed from the house and never did enter it again. His wife became so angry at his strong reaction to this event that she criticized him for his actions. He became so angry at her that he put her out of his life. He never saw her again. It was a lifetime of separation because of her reference to death.

In his final stages of illness he offered his personal physician a million dollars if he could guarantee him ten more years of life. Of course he could not, nor can anyone today, guarantee a longer life.

All of his authority and all of his wealth did not remove the fear which tormented him to his dying day.

It helps me to see how important life is when I acknowledge life is short. There is no way to live forever in this world.

The fear of death can be overcome, but it cannot be overcome by trying to ignore the reality of it.

PRAYER: *Lord Jesus, I give thanks that because of You I do not have to fear death. Amen.*

A Spirit Lifter

The effort to transfer the result of one field of knowledge to another can bring interesting insights.

The wife related to the husband that she had read that men tend to become bald much more than women because of the intense activity of their brains.

The husband appropriately applied this logic to women and said, "I guess that is why women can't raise beards because of the intense activity of their chins."

God's Promise

Consider this promise and invitation from the Lord.

"Lo, everyone that thirsteth, come ye to the waters, and he that hath no money; come ye, buy, and eat;... (Isaiah 55:1, KJV)

Practicing His Presence

Sometimes it is not easy to recall a specific incident or person who made you aware of His presence. It does not come easy. The continued victory comes with continued practice of His presence. Don't give up!

Overcoming The Fear Of Death

One of my fellowship classmates in college was the son of a physician. His parents were wonderful, but his mother had an abnormal fear of dying. She was constantly concerned about the well-being of her husband and children. She bent over backwards to protect them and keep them from being exposed to unnecessary dangers.

The good doctor was to attend a convention out west. He wanted to fly, but the wife insisted it was too dangerous. He therefore took the train. It was on the return trip that another train rammed into the rear of the passenger train and killed several people. Among those who lost their lives was this good doctor.

All of the planning in the world could not deliver him from the clutches of death. One of the best ways to overcome the fear of death is to live a normal life. Your efforts to be overly cautious in some areas is to live a normal life. Your efforts to be overly cautious in some areas can only lead to problems in others.

You are not to tempt the Lord, but at the same time are not to be too protective. Life lived sensibly to the fullest is the best protection you can possibly have. Life lived in confidence in the Lord is your high calling.

PRAYER: *Help me, Jesus, to live life to the fullest and not to be stifled by the haunting fear of death. Amen.*

THE MINISTRY OF THE MASTER—THURSDAY
A Spirit Lifter

Happy anniversaries.

The farmer's wife announced, "Tomorrow is our 25th wedding anniversary and I think I'll kill the big red rooster and roast him."

"Now, now, honey, why punish the poor chicken for what happened 25 years ago," the husband replied.

God's Promise

"Come now, and let us reason together, said the Lord; though your sins be as scarlet...; though they be red like crimson, they shall be as wool." (Isaiah 1:18, KJV)

Practicing His Presence

This is going to be an exciting day for anyone willing to completely relinquish all unto the Lord. He will honor this spirit of commitment and let you know He is with you.

Overcoming The Fear Of Death

You are a terminal case. Every person is a terminal case. I know there are the apparent incurable situations which are referred to as terminal cases.

However, when you think about it every person is a terminal case. Each of us will some day end our earthy sojourn. Even if you lived to be 200 years old there comes a point when it will be all over.

I feel you will be helped in overcoming the fear of death if you accept the fact that you are mortal. You are going to die. This is not fancy. It is a fact. It is common to all.

The termination date for you may be a little further down the line than for some others but it is coming. Longfellow is reported to have written,

"The young may die, the old must die."

The Bible tells us,

"It is appointed unto men once to die, but after this the judgment." Heb. 9:27

There is no reason why any of us should live in mortal fear of something which is the lot of every person. The fear of death can be rebuked and reduced in your life.

PRAYER: *Some day, Lord Jesus, I will have to lay aside this earthly container, but thank you for the hope of the new body. Amen.*

THE MINISTRY OF THE MASTER—FRIDAY
A Spirit Lifter

I am amazed at the devotion of some to sports. The deeply distressed husband was lamenting to his friend. "Everything has gone wrong. I see no hope. My house burned down, my daughter eloped with a scoundrel, my wife left me, I am facing a major operation, the bank is foreclosing on my mortgage, and the Tigers lost three to two in the ninth. Imagine that! ...three to two in the ninth! And they were leading!"

God's Promise

"For the prophecy came not in old time by the will of man: but holy men of God spake as they were moved by the Holy Ghost." (II Peter 1:21, KJV)

Practicing His Presence

Try to meditate as to what incident or person helped you to sense His presence yesterday. It will strengthen you in spirit, body, and mind.

Overcoming The Fear of Death

Socrates knew that no person could escape death. It is reported that one of his friends told him of his death sentence. He said,

"Thirty tyrants have pronounced death for you. You will have to drink the hemlock."

His reaction is beautiful.

"They have pronounced death for me, but nature has pronounced death for them."

Socrates knew that it would be only a matter of time when all who have passed the death sentence upon him would be as dead. The big difference was that Socrates had no fear of death. He had faced life and in so doing could face death.

One of the best ways to overcome the fear of death is to live life to its fullest. The preparation for death is made as daily you live to the glory of God.

Caesar the great leader of Rome said,

"I have provided in the course of my life for everything except death. Now, at last, I am to die although I am entirely unprepared."

Ready or not, death is coming. Do not fear it, but revere and rejoice in life.

PRAYER: *Your words, "The one who believes will never die," mean so much to me, Jesus. Thank you for them. Amen.*

THE MINISTRY OF THE MASTER—SATURDAY
A Spirit Lifter

It is a common tendency to blame someone else for your own shortcomings. The marriage counselor was trying to get to the root problem. He asked, "When things go wrong, do you blame each other?" The couple responded, "Not always. Sometimes we blame the children. Sometimes we blame the church or the cops. Then sometimes we just slam doors."

God's Promise

The proper goals are promised if the proper methods are pursued. *"He that followeth after righteousness and mercy findeth life, righteousness, and honour."* (Proverbs 21:21, KJV)

Practicing His Presence

The exercise of the muscles of the body make them stronger. The exercising of your spiritual faculties will make them stronger. The practice of His presence will help you know of His presence.

Overcoming The Fear Of Death

Inner illness has fertile soil in the heart of the person who lives in the fear of death. This fear can grow to huge proportions when fed by thoughts of despair concerning the end of your life.

The Christian's death is an act which elevates. It does not eliminate. It is not a transition that annihilates, but a transition that leads to a greater life. It is to be faced by faith and not by fear.

You will overcome the fear of death as you link your spirit with the eternal spirit of the Lord. You are not to live in fear as a servant frantically working for God to earn the right to live forever. You are by faith to believe the Lord has given to you the gift of eternal life. You will never finish everything you want to finish. You will never understand everything you wonder about. You will never know everything which now puzzles you. Life does not grant these answers to you.

However, you can know that you are a child of God. You are a friend of the Lord Jesus Christ. You are always in His care and undergirded by Him. You are saved by His grace and not your goodness.

PRAYER: *Jesus, there are so many things I want to accomplish and never will. Thank you for understanding. Amen.*

THE MINISTRY OF THE MASTER—SUNDAY
A Spirit Lifter

The two women were discussing husbands during their coffee klatsch. Their insights are applicable to many of us.

"My Bill is as helpless as a baby. He can't do anything for himself."

"That's the way mine is," replied the other. "He comes home from work with a button off or a hole in his sock and he is so helpless I even have to thread the needle for him."

God's Promise

"And he that keepeth his commandments dwelleth in him, and he in him. And hereby we know that he abideth in us, by the Spirit which he hath given to us." (I John 3:24, KJV)

Practicing His Presence

Did you have a spiritual feast yesterday as you sought to be aware of His presence? There is not much nourishment in doubts and denials of His presence. The power comes through believing Him.

Overcoming The Fear Of Death

Inner healing covers many areas of life. I wish I had the time to deal with the many fears which hinder victory. Spending a week considering some of them will help you and others as well.

I was visiting one of our members who was nearly 95 years old. She was a most faithful church member and in attendance until hindered by infirmities.

She said, *"Pastor, I am so weak, I don't know why I have lived so long. I am ready to go any time. It can't be too much longer. I have no fear."*

She went on to say that when she was young she had some fear of death. It is now all gone. She had lived well. She was prepared to die well.

Christians need to be taught how to die as well as how to live. John Wesley knew this. He lived to a ripe age. Almost his last words were, *"The best of all is God with us. God with us. Farewell, farewell."* It was then he died.

David Livingston, the great missionary to Africa, was found by his friends kneeling by his bed. He closed out his life in communion with the Father. He didn't have a morbid fear of death. He had a marvelous faith in life. He, too, could say,

"Father, into thy hands I commend my spirit." Luke 23:46

PRAYER: *Jesus, thank you for your promise that I will be with You for all eternity. Amen.*

Theme for the Week
THE LAYING ON OF HANDS WITH PRAYER

I write *The Ministry of the Master* to enable me to visit with you each day with the message of wholeness. There are billions of dollars spent each year and millions of hours given to maintain wholeness or to regain it.

It is my sincere feeling that the teachings of the message of wholeness are needed in our day. The Bible abounds with guidance.

One important facet of the healing ministry is the laying on of hands with prayer. This is a ministry which is part and parcel of the teachings of the Bible. There are five occasions for the laying on of hands in the New Testament.

1. The Ordination of deacons is described in Acts 6. We are told that, *"...when they had prayed, they laid their hands on them." (Acts 6:6)*
2. The Holy Spirit was received with the laying on of hands. *"Then they laid their hands on them, and they received the Holy Ghost."(Acts 8:17*

3. The commissioning of missionaries was a time when the laying on of hands was done. *"And when they had fasted and prayed, and laid hands on them, they sent them away." (Acts 13:3)*

4. The imparting of spiritual gifts involved the laying on of hands. *"Neglect not the gift that is in thee, which was given thee by prophecy, with the laying on of the hands of the presbytery." (I Tim. 4:14)*

5. The ill received the ministry of the laying on of hands with prayer. *"...and they shall lay hands on the sick and they shall recover." (Mark 16:18)*

Traditionally the church has retained the ministry of the laying on of hands for ordination and commissioning of missionaries.

POINTS TO PONDER

1. What have you been taught concerning the laying on of hands?
2. Do you feel Jesus instructed His disciples to lay on hands for the sick?
3. Does a basic understanding of the faith involve an understanding of the laying on of hands with prayer?

THE LAYING ON OF HANDS WITH PRAYER

1. Then _____ they their hands on them. *Acts 8:17*
2. Of the doctrine of baptisms and of laying on of_____.
   Heb. 6:2.
3. ...The gift of God, which is in thee by the putting on of my _____
   _____. *II Tim. 1:6*
4. These things command and _____. *I Tim. 4:11.*
5. You are a chosen generation, a_____priesthood...
   I Pet. 2:9
6. And the _____ of my hands as the evening sacrifice.
   Ps. 141:2
7. ...I will _____ up my hands in thy name. *Ps. 63:4*
8. ...they anointed...many that were sick, and_____them.
   Mk. 6:13
9. ...put your_____in the Lord. *Ps. 4:5*
10. The elders of the congregation shall lay their _____
    upon the head of the bullock. *Lev. 4:15*
11. ...lay thy _____ upon him. *Num. 27:18*
12. *Then I will turn to the people a pure _____...Zeph. 3:9*
13. ...the good _____ of his God upon him. *Ezra 7:9*
14. And these_____shall follow them that believe...
    Mk. 16:17

DAILY SCRIPTURE

Mon.	Heb. 6:1-3
Tues.	I Tim. 4:6-16
Wed.	I Peter 2:4-10
Thurs.	Mark 6:7-13
Fri.	Psalm 4:1-8
Sat.	Num. 27:18-23
Sun.	Mark 16:14-18

PRAYER CONCERNS

Your Family & Relatives
Government Leaders
Missionaries
For the Unbelievers
Churches & Denominations
Your Own Church
Prayer and Praise

NOTE: You will be spiritually strengthened by completing two questions each day, reading the suggested scriptures, and ministering in prayer for the concerns of the day.

THE MINISTRY OF THE MASTER—MONDAY
A Spirit Lifter

"Why did you fire that secretary you had?"

"She couldn't spell — kept asking me how to spell every other word when she took dictation."

"And you couldn't stand the interruptions?"

"It wasn't that. I just didn't have time to look up all those words."

God's Promise

God desires that you and I guard our conversation. The following should be helpful.

"Whoever would love life and see good days must keep his tongue from evil and his lips from deceitful speech." (I Peter 3:10, NIV)

Practicing His Presence

Did you have a spiritual feast yesterday as you sought to be aware of His Presence? There is not much nourishment in doubts and denials of His Presence. The power comes through believing Him.

The Laying On Of Hands With Prayer

Please do not recoil negatively to my suggestion that the laying on of hands is a facet of the faith which should be studied and practiced by all believers.

I would encourage you to consider the Word and its emphasis upon this practice. The writer of the book of Hebrews knew the importance of this practice.

"Therefore leaving the principles of the doctrine of Christ, ...not laying again the foundation of repentance...baptisms, and of laying on of hands, ...resurrection...eternal judgment. And this we will do, if God permit." (Heb. 6:1-3)

You have heard Sunday morning messages concerning repentance, the resurrection, judgment, and baptism. Most people I ask tell me they have never heard a message on Sunday morning concerning the laying on of hands. Yet this is included among the very foundations of the faith. May I ask, why should it be neglected?

I firmly believe that New Testament practices produce New Testament results. Therefore, I believe the church should practice the laying on of hands and especially for the ill and troubled. This should be a part of the Christian expression of each believer and each congregation.

PRAYER: *Father, open my eyes to the truths concerning healing which are found in your word. Amen.*

THE MINISTRY OF THE MASTER—TUESDAY
A Spirit Lifter

Developing dinner manners is one continuous facet in rearing children. This mother was determined to instruct her offspring properly.

A lioness saw her young cub chasing a hunter around a bush. The lioness growled and said, "Junior, how often do I have to tell you not to play with your food?"

God's Promise

"When the Spirit of truth comes, he will lead you to the complete truth, since he will not be speaking as from himself but will say only what he has learned." (John 16:13, JB)

Practicing His Presence

I recently visited a new mother and child at the hospital. The little girl slept as we gazed through the glass. I thought of this little life fresh from the hand of God and it made me aware of His Presence.

The Laying On Of Hands With Prayer

I do not believe there is any magic in the laying on of hands. It is not something which is done simply to influence someone psychologically. It is a practice in keeping with the teachings and practice of our Lord Jesus.

For some reason which cannot be completely explained, God has chosen that the laying on of hands is a channel of healing and help to others. It is a channel he has chosen to use to bring a wholeness of body, mind and spirit.

I can see no reason why the church as a whole should confine the ministry of the laying on of hands to the ordination of officers or to the confirming of new members. There are appropriate occasions, but there is more to this ministry.

It has been my experience that a blessing is received by those unto whom this ministry is given. It helps as a tangible expression of love and concern. It reaches deep into the recesses of the troubled life to have another believer express concern with the touch of the hand as well as the prayers.

I wish it were possible for me to minister unto each person reading this with the laying on of hands. I know this is impossible because of time and distance. However, may you open your mind and heart to receive this ministry and perhaps the Lord will send someone your way to minister unto you in this fashion.

PRAYER: *Thank you, Father, for the tangible expression of your love through the laying on of hands and prayer of another believer. Amen.*

A Spirit Lifter

We've all noticed a change in prices through the years. This has led to some changes in the way we spend our money and how we evaluate channeling our earnings. This couple faced such a decision.

Husband to wife: "Honey, what do you say we take this money we have been saving toward a new car and blow it on a movie?"

God's Promise

"When someone becomes a Christian he becomes a brand new person inside. He is not the same anymore. A new life has begun." (II Corinthians 5:17, LB)

Practicing His Presence

Today seek to consciously be aware of the Lord Jesus. The practice of His presence is an art which you need to develop. It comes with concentrated effort.

The Laying On Of Hands With Prayer

An aspect of wholeness which is needed by many is an appreciation of the gifts which they possess. Paul instructs Timothy concerning his gift.

Timothy was very open to the message concerning spiritual matters. Paul discerned in him a young man whose dedication and talents could be greatly used to the glory of God and the good of the church.

There were weak moments for Timothy as far as his service for the Lord is concerned. He was young and evidently was faced with negative criticism of older Christians. Paul sought to encourage him to realize the Lord would use him even though he was young.

The Presbytery made their concern more tangible than a word of encouragement or a promise to pray for Timothy. The members of presbytery laid hands upon Timothy. They were channels for the imparting of spiritual gifts to him. The community of believers surrounded Timothy with love and devotion. He came to realize the church is not comprised of hermits. It is composed of believers with a common Lord and common purpose.

The laying on of hands helped to implant and to nurture this truth for Timothy. Fear and discouragement can often be overcome through the praying community which ministers in the name of Jesus and uses His methods.

PRAYER: *Lord Jesus, thank you for the many spiritual gifts you have given to me. May they be accented through the ministry of others unto me. Amen.*

A Spirit Lifter

This child's analysis seems perfectly logical.
Teacher: "What was the title for the former rulers of Russia?"
Student: "Czar."
Teacher: "And the title for his wife?"
Student: "The Czarina."
Teacher: "That's right, and for his children?"
The student thought a minute and replied, "Czardines."

God's Promise

"...Thus says the Lord to you, 'Fear not, and be not dismayed at this great multitude; for the battle is not yours but God's.' " (II Chronicles 20:15, RSV)

Practicing His Presence

"The still small voice" is nestled in your heart. He is not perched on your shoulder. Permit the ears of the heart to be attuned to His voice.

The Laying On Of Hands With Prayer

I write this week with the intent of opening to your mind and heart the essential truth of New Testament practices being pursued by Christians today. The example and commands of our Lord have not been transcended by something better. They are still the norm for each believer and should be pursued.

It is plain from scripture that Jesus sent His disciples to minister to the sick. He did not hesitate to have them reach out and touch. He knew the gratifying results for the one ministering, as well as for the one unto whom the person ministered.

"And they cast out many devils, and anointed with oil many that were sick, and healed them." (Mark 6:13) These were the disciples of Jesus. They were individuals who knew the power of the Lord and wanted to see His power manifest in their midst.

Jesus did not send disciples to do what he did not approve. He was the One who set the pace. He was the one who instructed. If my Master felt it was important to minister to the sick, I certainly want to do the same.

Your openness to the Lord's methods will reap wonderful benefits. You will better serve others as you serve them in the way Jesus taught. The Master teacher cannot be shunned. He is to be followed.

PRAYER: *Thank you, Father, that I can bear witness of my faith in you through receiving the ministry of your presence through others. Amen.*

THE MINISTRY OF THE MASTER—FRIDAY
A Spirit Lifter

Appliances are certainly more efficient and time saving. This confused traveler certainly didn't get her money's worth.

Helen: "My cabin on the ship was nice, but I didn't like the washing machine on the wall."

Mary: "Washing machine? That was a porthole!"

Helen: "No wonder I never got my clothes back!"

God's Promise

God gives us insights concerning our work.

"Commit your work to the Lord, and your plans will be established." (Proverbs 16:3)

Practicing His Presence

I pray that you were very much aware of the Lord's presence in your life yesterday. Can you recall some specific incident or person which helped this awareness?

The Laying On Of Hands With Prayer

What happens when a person receives the laying on of hands with prayer?

One of the things which happens is that the person ministering is saying that he believes in the healing power of the Lord. He is acknowledging that the Lord is the healer. He is saying that our trust should be in Him.

Another aspect is that the person unto whom the ministry is being rendered is acknowledging that the Lord can help them. It is important that the one receiving the prayer is willing to be ministered unto. It is not essential, but still in most cases a very important ingredient.

I cannot explain the power released or why it is released through the laying on of hands and not through other means. I cannot explain why the Lord sometimes laid His hands upon a person and pronounced him healed. He did not have to do this, but He chose to do this. For some reason this power continues to be released through willing channels.

Faith which is imparted through the believing community takes on new and greater dimensions with the laying on of hands with prayer. It is as if a source of power is harnessed which otherwise remains inert. It is as though the power of the Lord is released because of this simple act of obedience. The results cannot be scientifically analyzed as to why, but they are evident in the healings which occur.

PRAYER: *I am grateful, Father, that you choose to use me and others to bring wholeness to the ill of body, mind, and spirit. Amen.*

THE MINISTRY OF THE MASTER—SATURDAY
A Spirit Lifter

Have you had a chance to say a kind word to someone today? We too often overlook such opportunities.

Mother: "Did you thank Mrs. Jones for the lovely party she gave?"

Christy: "No, mommy. The girl leaving in front of me thanked her and Mrs. Jones said, 'Don't mention it,' so I didn't."

God's Promise

"Many are the afflictions of the righteous; but the Lord delivers him out of them all." (Psalm 34:19, RSV)

Practicing His Presence

It's hard to sometimes remember a specific incident in which you really felt His presence, but try to do so.

The Laying On Of Hands With Prayer

Now I move to some practical results as to what happens with the laying on of hands with prayer. I have been engaged in the ministry of healing since 1959. It has been my privilege to behold the power of the Lord released through the laying on of hands.

I was directing a Faith at Work conference in a Baptist church when I witnessed a marvelous release of the power of the Lord. A person was brought to me for ministry. I had never seen them before and spoke only briefly to them of the power and presence of the Lord.

Immediately after the brief prayer and I had removed my hands from her head she mentioned that things were so different. I later learned she had been involved in an auto accident several years before and had suffered untold misery ever since. She was healed physically, emotionally, and spiritually at this time. She also received her new prayer language at this time.

I often think, "What would have happened if I had not ministered in this way to this person?" Someone could say she would have been healed anyhow. Perhaps, but at least up to that point all the ministries of physicians and therapists and all the prayers of her church had not brought the healing. This incident alone would keep me following the Master's example.

PRAYER: *Heavenly Father, please help me to believe as never before that you want me to be whole. Amen.*

THE MINISTRY OF THE MASTER—SUNDAY
A Spirit Lifter

There's always more than one way to get a job done.

An old mountaineer and his son were sitting in front of the fire smoking their pipes, crossing and uncrossing their legs. After a long period of silence, the father said, "Son, step outside and see if it's raining."

Without looking up, the son said, "Aw, Pa, why don't we jest call in the dog and see if he's wet?"

God's Promise

The following is a promise in which we should take heed.

"For God did not give us a spirit of timidity but a spirit of power and love and self-control." (II Timothy 1:7)

Practicing His Presence

I believe as you exercise your spiritual powers you will become more aware of the spiritual side of life. How did you sense the presence of His spirit yesterday?

The Laying On Of Hands With Prayer

Mark 16:18 speaks specifically of laying on hands and praying for the sick. Many believe this is a later addition to the gospel of Mark. They feel it was not a part of the original book because it is not found in many of the older manuscripts.

This may be true. However, to me this does not take away from the validity of the laying on of hands and prayer for the sick. In fact, it makes this ministry more valid. It shows to us that the church was using this method of ministry for the sick. It had to be a part of the practice of the church for it to appear as the thing to do. Thus, it confirms the practice instead of casting doubt upon it.

God does desire your wholeness. He does want you to do everything possible to have this wholeness. Our churches must get back to the practice of the early Christians of ministering meaningfully unto the sick. This ministry should not only be private prayers for the ill, but also the tangible expression of concern through the laying on of hands.

I trust as you study the Word and seek to do His will that you will accept and practice what Christ has taught. I pray you will be willing to be ministered unto by others and to seek to minister unto others. The laying on of hands is one way you can do this.

PRAYER: *Enable me, blessed Jesus, to be obedient to your practice and teaching. May I walk by faith doing what you would have me to do. Amen.*

THE LAYING ON OF HANDS WITH PRAYER

It is my opinion that the ministry of the laying on of hands with prayer is so important that I want to devote another week to this subject. There are many Christians who have never really given much study to this facet of the foundation of our faith. (Heb. 6:1-3)

"Therefore leaving the principles of the doctrine of Christ, let us go on unto perfection; not laying again the foundation of repentance from dead works, and of faith toward God, of the doctrine of baptisms, and of laying on of hands, and of resurrection of the dead, and of eternal judgment. And this will we do, if God permit." (Hebrews 6:1-3)

Recent years have witnessed a new emphasis on the laying on of hands as a channel of God's power for healing. It thrills my soul to see this long neglected practice being revived.

God uses many concerned hands for our well-being. He uses the hands of the skilled surgeon, the dedicated nurse, the sympathetic family physician, the friend who embraces you, the parent who soothes your hurts and concerns, etc. The touch of these many and varied individuals means much to your wholeness. In light of the importance of touch in our lives why should the church neglect the ministry of laying on of hands?

One of the tragedies of our day is that too often the church has abandoned her power and spiritual resources. It so often leaves practically all of the ministry to the ill to the physical sciences.

You haven't done all you can for yourself and those for whom you are concerned until you have received the ministry of the laying on of hands. There will be no one reading this week's devotional thoughts but what will not have dozens and dozens of concerns and problems. You will not want to spend your time begging God, but will want to release all of the forces of the Lord in your life. I am thoroughly convinced that one way to do this is through the ministry of the laying on of hands.

POINTS TO PONDER

1. Do you believe New Testament practices produce New Testament results?
2. How often and when does a person need the ministry of laying on of hands?
3. Is the ministry of laying on of hands something needed in your church?

THE LAYING ON OF HANDS WITH PRAYER

1. Hear the voice of my supplications. .when I_____ up my hands toward thy holy oracle. *Ps. 28:2*
2. Cast all of your _____ upon Him...*I Pet. 5:7*
3. ...confess with thy mouth...and _____in thy heart...*Rom. 10:9*
4. We have this treasure in earthen_____. *II Cor. 4:7*
5. ...I am the way, the truth, and the _____. *John 14:6*
6. Thy word have I hid in mine _____. *Ps. 119:11*
7. _____ unto me, all ye that labour and are heavy laden. *Mt. 11:28*
8. _____ to show thyself approved unto God...*II Tim. 2:15*
9. For God hath not given you the spirit of_____. *II Tim. 1:7*
10. Whosoever therefore shall _____me before men...*Mt. 10:32*
11. ...he laid his_____on every one of them, and healed them. *Lu. 4:40.*
12. ...there went virtue out of him, and _____ them all. *Lu. 6:19*
13. ...I pray_____your whole spirit and soul and body be preserved blameless...*I Th. 5:23*
14. ...the just shall live by _____. *Habakkuk 2:4*

DAILY SCRIPTURE

Mon.	I Peter 5:6-11
Tues.	Rom. 10:6-12
Wed.	John 14:6-14
Thurs.	II Tim. 2:14-26
Fri.	Matt. 10:23-24
Sat.	Luke 4:38-44
Sun.	I Thess. 5:12-24

PRAYER CONCERNS

Your Family & Relatives
Government Leaders
Missionaries
For the Unbelievers
Churches & Denominations
Your Own Church
Prayer and Praise

NOTE: You will be spiritually strengthened by completing two questions each day, reading the suggested scripture, and ministering in prayer for the concerns of the day.

THE MINISTRY OF THE MASTER—MONDAY
A Spirit Lifter

Children begin to learn the rudiments of fighting very young.

The children were in a free-for-all when Dad entered the room. "Billy, who started this?" he asked the nearest boy. "Well," replied Billy, "It all started when Tommy hit me back!"

God's Promise

"When you pass through the water, I will be with you; in the rivers you shall not drown. When you walk through fire, you shall not be burned; the flames shall not consume you. (Isaiah 43:2, NAB)

Practicing His Presence

Are you consciously making the effort to be aware of the Lord in the small aspects of life? I know if you are, these have been exciting days for you.

The Laying On Of Hands With Prayer

It is rather interesting to me that many believe God is able to create a vast universe with millions of galaxies and millions upon millions of stars, but they cannot accept the fact that He is big enough to care for their problems.

I urge you to accept the fact that the Lord of creation is the Lord of every detail of your life and that He desires the best for you. You can bring to him what is uppermost in your mind and heaviest upon your heart. Your problem, or the problem of the one for whom you come in prayer, may not be a physical affliction. It may be a financial problem, an emotional disturbance, or such things as worry or fears. Whatever, you can bring your problems to the Lord for His healing touch.

I feel that one of the tangible ways to bring your concerns unto the Lord is through the ministry of the laying on of hands. This is one of the most practical aspects of the ministry of any church or body of believers.

It is not easy for each person to believe the Lord desires to heal in his or her life. It is almost like believing the Lord Jesus died for the sins of the whole world, but being unable to believe He died for your own sins. Yet, what He did for all includes you. Believe this today!

PRAYER: *Thank you, Father, for caring for me even though the universe is so vast. Amen.*

THE MINISTRY OF THE MASTER—TUESDAY
A Spirit Lifter

The sergeant was drilling raw recuits. It was a hectic job. Finally he noticed one man alone was out of step.

"Do you know, soldier," he said sarcastically, "they're all out of step except you?"

"Well," replied the rookie, "you're in charge — you tell 'em!"

God's Promise

"If my people, which are called by my name, shall humble themselves, and pray, and seek my face, and turn from their wicked ways; then will I hear from heaven, and will forgive their sins, and will heal their lands."
(II Chron. 7:16)

Practicing His Presence

Through what incident or person did you sense His presence yesterday? Was the reality of this presence a conscious effort on your part?

The Laying On Of Hands With Prayer

The ministry of laying on of hands with prayer is going to take on greater significance for you if you really believe that the Lord is the source of your help and healing. He may use many instruments, but He is ultimately the source of your wholeness.

Several years ago I was seriously ill. I went to a physician who diagnosed my situation and concluded that I would have to receive a bicillen shot every month for the rest of my life. I am grateful for this physician and how God used him to help me. At the same time I blended the prayers of my believing friends as well as my own prayers. I can bear witness to the fact that the Lord healed me and I have not received a bicillen shot since 1961.

The Lord will use your physician as an instrument, but no human is your final solution. Your apparently unsolvable problem, apparently incurable disease is solvable or curable in God's sight.

The same Lord who forgives sin whether they be large or small in the sight of man can also bring healing and help to the little or big problems or illnesses.

The Lord has power and resources we never dreamed existed. You see only a fraction of the totality of life. He sees and uses it all.

PRAYER: *Father, I give thanks for all your instruments of healing — the physicians, the nurses, administrators, housekeepers, etc. Amen.*

THE MINISTRY OF THE MASTER—WEDNESDAY
A Spirit Lifter

This naive consumer was bargaining for more than the merchant expected.

The butcher informed the customer: "I can't give you any more credit. Your bill is bigger than it should be."

"I know that," said the customer, "just make it out for what it should be, and I'll pay it."

God's Promise

You can be sure that God will keep His promises.

"For all the promises of God in him are yea, and in him, Amen, unto the glory of God by us." (II Corinthians 1:20, KJV)

Practicing His Presence

How are you doing, being aware of His presence each day? I pray this has been a meaningful experience for you. How did you sense His presence yesterday?

The Laying On Of Hands With Prayer

Familiar and helpful words are, *"But my God shall supply all your needs according to his riches in glory by Christ Jesus."* (Phil. 4:19)

It is obvious from this verse that the person laying on hands and ministering in prayer to you, the physician, your company, your school, your parents, your spouse, etc. is not your ultimate source. They may serve as a channel but they are not God and never can be. Your needs are supplied by the Lord and no one else.

One thing which bothered me a great deal when I first began the healing ministry was my own illness. I started believing the Lord wanted me to do this. Yet, I was inwardly disturbed because I was so sick myself. One day He spoke a great truth to me with the question, "Now really, is the ministry of healing dependent upon you or upon Me?"

It was obvious that He is the healer. It was not then, nor is it now, myself who does the healing. He is the One who makes possible a perfect plan of salvation. His Son is the Saviour. I am not. You are not. In like manner neither you nor me are the ones who bring wholeness. We are His channels. It was at this time that I was taught that I am called to be a proclaimer of His truth and not an explainer. I can't understand many things in life, but I can proclaim the One who is the Life.

PRAYER: *Father, may I keep my eyes off of my own imperfections and keep them on your perfection. In Jesus Name. Amen.*

THE MINISTRY OF THE MASTER—THURSDAY
A Spirit Lifter

Even underdeveloped countries are discovering some modern items are applicable to their life style.

Two cannibals met in a hut. One was tearing out pictures of men, women, and children from a magazine — stuffing them into his mouth and eating them. "Tell me," said the other, "Is that dehydrated stuff any good?'

God's Promise

I'm sure you'll appreciate this important truth today.

"For the righteous Lord loveth righteousness; his countenance doth behold the upright." (Psalm 11:7, KJV)

Practicing His Presence

"I am so sensitive" is often said by people. It is good to have a sensitive spirit, but our high calling is to be sensitive to His Presence. So often we are sensitive to the hurts of others instead of the helps of Jesus.

The Laying On Of Hands With Prayer

It is my prayer as you continue to think of the Lord being your helper that you will be lifted from your problems to the Problem Solver. It is my prayer that you will get your eyes off of your problems and unto the One who can solve your problems.

My task is not to call attention to your illnesses and problems so much as to challenge you to come to the One who can really help. Christ is the source of help and healing. It was when I realized this more fully that I was set free to proclaim the truth of the Lord and not let this proclamation be dependent upon my feelings for perfection.

In fact, the Lord placed this truth upon me so deeply that I said to him in the midst of my affliction, "Lord, I will conduct services of healing to my dying day even if I have to do it from a wheelchair."

I can bear witness to the fact that a funny thing happened on the way to the wheelchair. Instead of becoming more ill, I have been healed and today am better physically than I was back in 1959.

Your willingness to acknowledge your inability to help or to heal will release power for healing and help. The Lord desires the open and willing channel. Openness comes when we close to our own abilities and open to His abilities.

PRAYER: *Lord, I acknowledge I am unable to heal myself. I depend upon you for my wholeness. Amen.*

THE MINISTRY OF THE MASTER—FRIDAY
A Spirit Lifter

During preliminary inspection at a Boy Scout camp, the director found an umbrella in the bedroll of a tiny Scouter. Since the umbrella was obviously not one of the items of equipment listed, the director asked the lad to explain. The boy countered with the question; "Sir, did you ever have a mother?"

God's Promise

The real challenge to you and me is to let that which endures be the prime goal of life.

"But now abideth faith, hope, love, these three; and the greatest of these is love." (I Corinthians 13:13, RSV)

Practicing His Presence

Who touched your life yesterday and made you realize the power and presence of the Lord? Maybe it was someone who did a good deed for you.

Maybe it was someone who did you wrong. Either may have led you to Jesus.

The Laying On Of Hands With Prayer

Have you ever thought of the fact that your receiving the ministry of the laying on of hands is one of the greatest ways to acknowledge your belief in the True God? This enables you week after week to say to the worshipping community, "I believe God cares for every aspect of my life. I believe God answers prayer. I believe He is interested in every individual. I believe He wants me to confess Him before others and my dependence upon Him."

The ministry of laying on of hands is not given or received for show. It is a public expresson of an inward faith. It is one way among many ways you can say to the church, yea to the whole world, that you are not ashamed of the Master nor of His methods.

There are many people who say they are not ashamed of Jesus. Yet, at the same time they live as if they were ashamed of His methods. If Jesus felt the laying on of hands was important, why should we neglect this ministry? His practices followed bring his results.

Jesus was not afraid to touch the problem people of His day and neither should we be afraid to do so. He touched the leper and the dead. He healed and He restored to life. There was no one He rejected and none that He refused to minister unto. He continues to call you and me to this ministry fo wholeness in the midst of a sin sick and distressed world.

PRAYER: *Thank you, Jesus, that you accept anyone who comes to you and that you help any problem brought to you. Amen.*

THE MINISTRY OF THE MASTER—SATURDAY
A Spirit Lifter

Advertisements bombard us daily. They promise a wide variety of high expectations. This driver expected the station to honor its displayed service.

Attendant: "I'm sorry, sir, but all business at this service station is strictly cash."

Motorist: "But the sign says plainly, 'Batteries Charged.' "

God's Promise

God wants you to be happy, and He can provide this joy. I've found the following helpful.

"...God hath made me to laugh, so that all that hear will laugh with me..." (Genesis 21:6)

Practicing His Presence

Life is too short not to use God's methods for victory in Jesus. One of these methods is to practice His Presence. The quality of your life will be greatly enhanced as you do. Seek to see Him in your life.

The Laying On Of Hands With Prayer

There are always some who have a difficult time accepting the fact that Jesus practiced the ministry of laying on of hands for the ill. Today I want to present some instances in His earthly ministry which present this aspect of His ministry.

"...Come and lay thy hand upon her, and she shall live." (Mt. 9:18) are the words of the ruler to Jesus concerning his desperately ill daughter.

Did the ruler come up with this splendid idea for wholeness? Did he have a sudden inspiration as to how the Master should minister? No! The ruler was only asking Jesus to do what he knew was His practice. He was asking Jesus to use the method he knew Christ had used for many others.

It is obvious that Jesus by precept and practice set a pattern for ministry unto the ill. The disciples and the members of the early church followed His guidance. I feel you would be blessed by considering the following scripture. All of them will help undergird your understanding of the ministry of laying on of hands. (Mk. 1:29-31, 40-45, 5:21-23, 6:1-6, 7:32-37, 8:22-26, 9:14-29; 10:13-16, 16:18; Lu. 4:38-44, 5:12-15, 8:49-56, 13:11-17)

All of these references will show that in the ministry of the Lord Jesus Christ the touch of the hand played a very important part.

PRAYER: *Lord Jesus, help me to be obedient to your method of ministering through the laying on of hands. Amen.*

THE MINISTRY OF THE MASTER—SUNDAY
A Spirit Lifter

This young lad found the long road to knowledge a bit discouraging.

It was Nicky's first day in school and when he got home his mother asked, "Did you learn anything today?"

"No," he replied in disgust, "I have to go back tomorrow!"

God's Promise

If you are feeling bound by bad attitudes and wrong habits, this will help.

"...if ye continue in my word, then are ye my disciples indeed. And ye shall know the truth, and the truth shall set you free." (John 8:31-32, KJV)

Practicing His Presence

The realization of His Presence can make your life a heaven even in the midst of much hell. The neglect of His Presence can make your life a hell in the midst of what many would feel should be a heaven.

The Laying On Of Hands With Prayer

I cannot emphasize enough that the focal point of the laying on of hands with prayer is the Lord Jesus Christ. He is the Great Physician. He is the One who imparts wholeness. He is the One upon whom we must depend.

It is my prayer that after spending two weeks studying and thinking about the ministry of laying on of hands that you will realize you have not done all you can for yourself and others until you have received this ministry.

My wife and I have discovered that a weekly healing service and at least weekly receiving this ministry is of great help to us and for others. Your church may not have a service of healing, but perhaps there is one in your community where you may attend. Or perhaps in your Bible Study group or prayer group you will have opportunity to receive this ministry. It is not something to do as a fad, but something to do as an act of faith.

I realize some of you are thousands of miles from me, but at this moment may I suggest you seek to pause in your mind and heart and as you read just imagine your receiving the ministry of the laying on of hands. As you do, this is the prayer I offer.

"Father, into your light and love I lift this your child. May your wholeness be imparted in body, mind, and spirit. In the Name of the Great Physician Jesus Christ. Amen."

PRAYER: *Jesus, you are the one I look to for my wholeness. There is no one else to whom I can turn. Amen.*

THE ANOINTING WITH OIL

I am grateful for the renewed interest in anointing with oil within the church today and of the change that is taking place as to the significance of anointing.

There is indeed today a new awareness of the power and presence of the Holy Spirit. Many are displaying an eagerness to know more about the scriptures and to follow the practices of the early church. They are beginning to appreciate that following New Testament practices brings New Testament results.

There are many references to anointing in both the Old and New Testaments. Are you aware of the fact that the word *anoint* is used 30 times in the Old and 5 times in the New Testament? *Anointed* appears 80 times in the Old Testament and 12 times in the New Testament. *Anointest* is used 1 time in the Old Testament and none in the New Testament and *anointing* appears 25 times in the Old Testament and 3 times in the New Testament.

Not all of these references refer directly to anointing with oil. Some refer to the anointed of the Lord as being blessed or especially empowered.

However, the specific references to anointing with oil do appear. Ex. 28:41 — ". . . shalt anoint them and consecrate them and sanctify them that they may minister unto me in the Priest office," shows the use of the oil for the consecration of leaders. This is true when David is anointed as king. (I Sam. 16:12)

It is especially in the New Testament that we discover the oil being used as a ministry unto the sick. It is a specific and generally accepted practice. "Is any sick among you? Let him call for the elders of the church; and let them pray over him, anointing him with oil in the name of the Lord." (James 5:14) Also, "And they cast out many devils, and anointed with oil many that were sick, and healed them." (Mk. 6:13)

POINTS TO PONDER

1. Do you associate anointing with oil with life or with death?
2. How important is confession to healing?
3. What can you do to help inform others of the importance of anointing with oil?

THE ANOINTING WITH OIL

1. Then Moses took some of the anointing _____.
   Lev. 8:30
2. Then Samuel took a vial of _____ and
   poured it on his head. *I Sam. 10:1*
3. Then Samuel took the horn of _____ , and
   anointed him in the midst of his brothers. *I Sam. 16:13*
4. ...and anoint themselves with the finest _____.
   Amos 6:6
5. ...they are not pressed out, or bound up, or softened with _____
   _____. *Isa. 1:6*
6. And they cast out many demons, and _____
   with oil many who were sick. *Mk. 6:13.*
7. ...let them pray over him anointing him with oil in the name of the
   _____. *James 5:14.*
8. ...and salve to anoint your _____.
   Rev. 3:18
9. Thou _____ my head with oil. *Ps. 23:5*
10. He hath_____me to preach the gospel.
    Lu. 4:18
11. How God_____Jesus of Nazareth. *Acts 10:38*
12. Then took Mary a pound of ointment...and_____
    _____ the feet of Jesus. *John 12:3*
13. Touch not mine_____, and do my
    prophets no harm. *Ps. 105:15*
14. Now know I that the Lord saveth his _____.
    Ps. 20:6

DAILY SCRIPTURE

Mon.	I Sam. 10:1-8
Tues.	Amos 6:1-7
Wed.	Mark 6:7-13
Thurs.	James 5:13-18
Fri.	Luke 4:16-30
Sat.	Ps. 23:1-6
Sun.	Rev. 3:15-22

PRAYER CONCERNS

Your Family & Relatives
Government Leaders
Missionaries
For the Unbelievers
Churches & Denominations
Your Own Church
Prayer and Praise

NOTE: You will be spiritually strengthened by completing two questions each day, reading the suggested scripture, and ministering in prayer for the concerns of the day.

THE MINISTRY OF THE MASTER—MONDAY
A Spirit Lifter

Sharing family responsibilities is a pleasant way to accomplish the household chores. This loving spouse took his job literally.

Wife: "Didn't I tell you to notice when the soup boiled over?"

Husband: "I did. It was half past four."

God's Promise

Remember these important truths today.

"Many are the afflictions of the righteous: but the Lord delivereth him out of them all." (Psalm 30:5)

Practicing His Presence

Through what incident or individual did you sense His presence yesterday? What was your response to this reality?

The Anointing With Oil

Why bother to anoint with oil is a logical question as I begin to teach in this area this week. I cannot explain all the facets or reasons for its effectiveness, but I will start with an example of what happened following an anointing.

I was called to a home of a man who suffered from an apparently incurable disease. His body was afflicted from head to toe. He was confined to bed, weak, and in constant pain. His wife would change his briefs four or five times a day because of the oozing of this diseased skin.

We responded to the call and on Saturday afternoon anointed him. Early Sunday morning I received a call from his wife to stop on the way to church. Myself and the two men who were present for the anointing stopped and were utterly amazed at the healing. He was sitting in bed pulling off the diseased skin. He would throw away strips of skin about a half inch wide and a few inches long. His waste basket ended up filled with the old skin and his body was left with normal skin. He was in his mid-seventies and the last time I saw him was at the celebration of his 90th birthday. He died at the age of 93.

What part did the anointing play? I cannot fully explain it, but one thing I know is that he had not been recovering prior to the anointing. His son was a physician and he certainly had received all the ministries of the medical field.

PRAYER: *Jesus, even the impossible can be done by you. Help me to believe this as never before. Amen.*

THE MINISTRY OF THE MASTER—TUESDAY
A Spirit Lifter

Learning Bible stories is a prime goal of all Christians. The chapters relate truths that are applicable even as we live in the 20th century. These kids were applying their knowledge in their own way.

"Scott," called the mother, "tell your sister to come in the house out of the rain."

"I can't, Mom, we're playing Noah's Ark and she's the sinner."

God's Promise

"When thou passeth through the waters I will be with thee: and through the rivers, they shall not overflow thee: when thou walkest through the fire, thou shalt not be burned; neither shall the flame kindle upon thee." (Isaiah 43:2)

Practicing His Presence

Did you have a spiritual feast yesterday as you sought to be aware of His Presence? What incident led you to be conscious of His Presence?

The Anointing With Oil

I feel those who are ill and the friends and loved ones of the ill have not done all they can until the ministry of anointing has been received. There is no magic in the anointing, but there is great power in obedience. The prayer of faith as mentioned in James 5:15 cannot be uttered without obedience.

We know from church history that the post apostolic church declined spiritually and during this decline there was neglect of many of the principles and teachings of scripture and of the early church. Some things were completely ignored and some distorted to the extent that they lost their Christian significance. One aspect which was greatly distorted was the anointing with oil. It became associated with death rather than life. It became the final rites instead of a rite of new beginnings.

I feel it is tragic that to this day many Christians associate anointing with oil with eminent death. This is completely contrary to scripture and certainly contrary to the nature of the ministry of Jesus who commanded that the oil be used. (Mk. 6:13)

It is not my interest to lead individuals to practice something which will place importance upon the act instead of upon the Lord. It is my intent that we see the importance of the tangible expression of our inward faith and heartfelt desires.

PRAYER: *Father, help me to see the importance of the tangible expressions of your concern for each person. Amen.*

THE MINISTRY OF THE MASTER—WEDNESDAY
A Spirit Lifter

The Trinity is the fuel that allows us to generate energy for living a Christian life. Earthly supplies are not as reliable.

"I've just discovered oil on our property," a man told his wife.

"Marvelous! Now we can buy a new car!" exclaimed the new wife.

"No, we better get the old one repaired. That's where the oil is coming from."

God's Promise

The Lord promises divine care in sickness.

"The Lord will strengthen him upon the bed of languishing: thou wilt make all his bed in his sickness." (Psalm 50:15)

Practicing His Presence

I have sought to remind you each day to be aware of the presence of our Lord. How did you find this taking place and what is it doing for you?

The Anointing With Oil

The reference of Mark 6:13 clearly teaches that Jesus guided His disciples into the practice of anointing with oil. James 5:14 shows how this practice continued within the early church. We know Jesus' disciples would not have done it contrary to His will and we know the early church would not have chosen a method contrary to the teachings of the Master.

I must emphasize there is no magic whatsoever in the oil. It is the Lord who heals and it is His Name which should be glorified. As Christians we anoint within the context of our belief in the Lord Jesus Christ as personal Savior and Great Physician. Further, we seek to lead the individual we are anointing to the place of confessing Jesus as Lord.

There may be times when the individual being anointed is unconscious or so seriously ill no response is possible. In such cases we anoint because of our faith and because we trust what the Lord and the scriptures have taught. It is the least we can do to help the ill.

It is my feeling *The Ministry of The Master* should be pursued. It should not be neglected. It is my high calling to faithfully follow the methods of my Master and to believe He will honor my faithfulness. My experiences through the years have justified this willingness to believe that what Jesus taught and the way Jesus ministered are worthy of my serious consideration and faithful pursuit.

PRAYER: *I want to do your ministry, Lord. Enable me to be faithful in all of your ways. Amen.*

319

THE MINISTRY OF THE MASTER—THURSDAY
A Spirit Lifter

Wouldn't it be interesting if our pets could talk and comment on our behavior? Two dogs were watching a teenage dance when one looked over at the other and said, "You know, if we acted that way, they'd worm us!"

God's Promise

"Behold, I give unto you power to tread on serpents and scorpions, and over all the power of the enemy; and nothing shall by any means hurt you." (Luke 10:19)

Practicing His Presence

The exercise of the muscles of the body makes them stronger. The exercising of your spiritual faculties will make them stronger.

The Anointing With Oil

I am sure you realize, as do I, that the anointing with oil is not something which is mechanically done, and God immediately responds. The will of the Lord is not like some piece of machinery which has run dry of oil and is malfunctioning because of lack of oil. We cannot set His power in motion simply by an outward act.

Those who are anointing, and as much as possible, the one being anointed should seek to exercise the prayer of faith. It is not simply the application of the oil, but the prayer of faith which the Lord honors. It is a corporate act of faith. That is, there should usually be more than one person present to help with the anointing. This is not a hard fast rule, but it does say, "Let them call for the Elders." This is plural and implies that more than one will respond.

When more than one ministering person is present when the prayer of faith is offered it helps keep us humble. No one will ever know which one had his or her prayer honored. It doesn't matter, because we are pulling together as a community.

When I anointed the man mentioned in Monday's sermonette, there were two other men present as well as his wife. Whose prayer was honored? It really doesn't matter, but not one of us could claim to be the healer. The important thing is that his healing was received.

PRAYER: *I acknowledge, Father, that it is not my perfection which brings healing. It is because of your grace and goodness that it is imparted. Amen.*

THE MINISTRY OF THE MASTER—FRIDAY
A Spirit Lifter

This student found his answer "udderly" simple.
The teacher asked her class to name five things that contain milk.
Jason replied, "Butter, yogurt, cheese, and 2 cows!"

God's Promise

"Therefore, my beloved brethren, be ye steadfast, unmoveable, always abounding in the work of the Lord, forasmuch as ye know that your labour is not in vain in the Lord." (I Corinthians 15:58)

Practicing His Presence

Can you recall a specific incident or person which helped your awareness of the Lord's presence yesterday? Take a moment and reflect upon this.

The Anointing With Oil

I feel another important aspect of the anointing with oil is that of confession of sin. Confession of sin and the prayer of absolution are often neglected aspects of Christian life. It is imperative that we confess our sin unto the Lord and also that we hear "thou art forgiven."

The confession of faults is very important to complete healing. One of the things which creates much illness is guilt and I believe there can never be complete healing if guilt weighs heavily upon the heart and the mind.

There are Christians who faithfully practice the confessing of other people's sins. We all find this easier and more fun. However, it is not near as helpful. You and I must get to the place where we confess

"Against thee, O Lord, have I sinned." Ps. 51:4

The sin is not only toward a person but is toward the Lord as well. The impact and heinousness of sin is never realized until we come to appreciate the fact is it against God as well as against a person.

It is wise to practice the deep spiritual principles like confession if the acts of the Christian Church, like anointing with oil, are to be most effective. It can very well be said that confession is good for the soul, but in like manner it can be said that confession is good for the body and mind.

PRAYER: *I confess, Father, my constant need of you. Help me to believe you are constantly with me. Amen.*

THE MINISTRY OF THE MASTER—SATURDAY
A Spirit Lifter

An enthusiastic leader can rev up a group and turn on more supporters. Unfortunately, this husband didn't have that luck.

An avid baseball fan took his dubious wife to a game. One fellow hit the ball over the fence and she said, "I'm glad they got rid of it, now we can go home."

God's Promise

Consider this promise throughout your day.

"Jesus said unto him, if thou canst believe, all things are possible to him that believeth." (Mark 9:23)

Practicing His Presence

I pray that you were very much aware of the Lord's presence in your life yesterday. Can you recall some specific incident or person which helped this awareness?

The Anointing With Oil

A believer should request the anointing with oil. You have the responsibility to request leaders of your church to come and anoint you or any other sick member of your family. The Bible did not leave the leaders of the church responsible for being aware of all illnesses and rushing there with the anointing oil.

You have not done all that you can for your problem or illness until you have been anointed. Very few pastors or church officers will turn down a sincere request for anointing with oil. Even if your church at the present time is not practicing this New Testament ministry, your pastor or other leaders will probably react positively to a request for anointing.

The Lord's wholeness is so needed and the needs today so great that I feel we must teach about everything which has been used by the Lord to help His people. The anointing with oil is not a procedure I thought of last week or a year ago. It is part and parcel of the teaching of God's Holy Word. It is not new, but it is of God. We must do it and believe Him as we do.

There is no guarantee of physical recovery because you are anointed, but I can guarantee that you have been more obedient if you request and receive the ministry of anointing. And after all, it is to a life of obedience that you are called.

PRAYER: *Father, may I be willing to call for others to come pray and anoint when I am afflicted. Amen.*

322

THE MINISTRY OF THE MASTER—SUNDAY
A Spirit Lifter

Occasionally a challenging question can be difficult to answer.

Trying to rest after a hard day, the father was annoyed by the endless stream of questions from Jason. "What did you do all day at the office, Daddy?" "Nothing!" shouted the father.

After a thoughtful pause, Jason asked, "Dad, how do you know when you're through?"

God's Promise

"When the poor and needy seek water, and there is none, and their tongue faileth for thirst, I the Lord will hear them, I the God of Israel will not forsake them." (Isaiah 41:17).

Practicing His Presence

Has it been the big events through which you have sensed His presence or have they been the common experiences of life?

The Anointing With Oil

It is essential that church leadership teach concerning anointing if individuals are going to know about it and request it. A person will not think to ask for anointing with oil if they are not aware of this practice.

For many years I took the position if someone called for me to anoint, I would do so. However, I had not taught concerning this practice and I did not encourage my flock to request anointing in times of illness. I felt I had delivered my soul by being willing to go if invited, but not going until invited. I got no invitations because no one knew this practice was for today and that it was an important part of the Lord's ministry of wholeness.

One day I read:

> *"And they cast out many devils, and anointed with oil many that were sick, and healed them." (Mk. 6:13)*

This is the result of what Jesus did. He sent His disciples to do this as we read in verse 7,

> *"And he called unto him, the twelve, and began to send them forth by two and two . . ."*

It was then that I realized Jesus had instructed His disciples how to anoint and sent them forth to do so. They informed the people of this practice and did anoint many. I now had to begin to teach concerning anointing. If I did not teach the truth, the blood would be on my hands. If I teach the truth and people reject it, the blood is on their hands. I want clean hands as well as a clean heart.

Anointing with oil is valid today. Let's practice it!

PRAYER: *May I be willing, Jesus, to accept the anointing with oil as a ministry from you. Amen.*

PAUL'S THORN IN THE FLESH

This week I want to present some insights concerning a controversial verse. I realize my thoughts will not solve all the problems related to this complicated topic but will at least challenge your thinking and hopefully encourage your heart.

I will deal with Paul's thorn in the flesh as mentioned in II Cor. 12:7 *"...there was given to me a thorn in the flesh..."*

What is meant by this thorn? Does it absolutely refer to a physical illness? What should this experience mean to a Christian today?

It is true that many Christians have been led to believe that the thorn in the flesh must be specifically a physical illness. This is then used as an excuse for their own physical illness. Their reasoning is that if the great Apostle Paul had an illness which was never cured then why should they feel they have a right to expect their illness to be cured?

I suggest that we take a very careful look at this portion of scripture. Does "thorn in the flesh" have to mean a physical illness? Could it possibly mean some other significant factor in Paul's life?

I feel that it does not necessarily have to be a physical illness to which Paul refers. Throughout the week I will present my reasons for rejecting the concept of physical illness as the thorn in the flesh.

Friend and foe of the ministry of healing discover that this verse turns out to be either a stumbling block or a stepping stone according to their interpretation of the total message of the Bible. I believe that the Bible is its own best interpreter, and to understand any one portion you must look at the whole.

It is my prayer that a proper understanding of the total message of God's book will help you to take a giant step forward towards your wholeness of body, mind and spirit.

POINTS TO PONDER

1. What difference would it make in the mind and heart of the average Christian if Paul's "thorn in the flesh" was not a physical illness?
2. Is illness sent of God or is illness of Satan?
3. What are some of the most common hindrances to wholeness?

PAUL'S THORN IN THE FLESH

1. There shall be no more a pricking briar...nor any grieving _____
   _____. *Ezek. 28:24*
2. ...there was given to me a_____
   in the flesh. *II Cor. 12:7.*
3. I will even destroy thee that there shall be no _____
   _____. *Zeph. 2:5*
4. But if ye will not drive out the _____ ___
   of the land. *Num. 33:55*
5. ...when thy_____and thy body are consumed.
   Pro. 5:11
6. For when we were in the _____, ...the law
   did work to bring forth death. *Rom. 7:5*
7. ...righteousness...fulfilled in us, who walk...after the _____
   _____. *Rom. 8:4*
8. Create in me a clean_____, O God. *Ps. 51:10*
9. ...depart out of that house or city, shake off the_____
   _____ of your feet. *Mt. 10:14*
10. I take pleasure in infirmities, reproaches, necessities, in_____
    _____. *II Cor. 12:10*
11. In the day of our king the princes have made him sick with_____
    _____. *Hosea 7:5*
12. So went _____ forth from the presence
    of the Lord. *Job 2:7*
13. Whom_____hath bound, lo, these eighteen years.
    Luke 13:16
14. Hope deferred maketh the_____sick.
    Pro. 13:12

DAILY SCRIPTURE

Mon.   II Cor. 12:1-7
Tues.   Num. 33:50-56
Wed.   Rom.7:1-6
Thurs.   Rom 8:1-18
Fri.   Matt. 10:5-15
Sat.   Job 2:1-8
Sun.   Luke 13:11-17

PRAYER CONCERNS

Your Family & Relatives
Government Leaders
Missionaries
For the Unbelievers
Churches & Denominations
Your Own Church
Prayer and Praise

NOTE: You will be spiritually strengthened by completing two questions each day, reading the suggested scripture, and ministering in prayer for the concerns of the day.

THE MINISTRY OF THE MASTER—MONDAY
A Spirit Lifter

A child from the city was visiting a farm for the first time. Everything was new and wondrous. Toward evening of the first day he stood intently watching the farmer's wife plucking a chicken. After a bit, his curiosity grew too great and he asked gravely, "Do you take off their clothes every night, lady?"

God's Promise

The good life does not go unrewarded. It may appear that way at times, but we know time will prove the Lord to be faithful.

"Surely the righteous shall give thanks to thy name; the upright shall dwell in thy presence." (Psalm 140:13, Lamsa)

Practicing His Presence

Do you find that an awareness of His presence is determined to some degree by how you feel? Was there any time yesterday when you knew the spiritual life was the most important aspect of your being?

PAUL'S THORN IN THE FLESH

This Monday morning I want to take you into the Word to consider the "thorn in the flesh" controversy. We shall consider some of the other biblical references to the thorn.

There are three such references in the Old Testament. They are:

"But if ye will drive out the inhabitants of the land from before you, then it shall come to pass, that those which ye let remain of them shall be pricks in your eyes, and thorns in your sides, ..."(Num. 33:55)

"Know for a certainty that the Lord your God will no more drive out any of these nations from before you; but they shall be snares and traps unto you, and scourges in your sides, and thorns in your eyes, ... (Joshua 23:13)

"...I will not drive them out from before you; but they shall be as thorns in your sides, ..." (Judges 2:3)

Paul was a student of the Old Testament. His life was saturated with the truths of the Old Testament. He was a Jew among Jews and had a thorough understanding of the message of the Old Testament.

It is evident from all three of the above references that "thorns in the side" refer to individuals, i.e. to inhabitants of the land where the children of Israel were to dwell.

PRAYER: *Father, help me as I seek to live with individuals who create problems for me. Amen.*

THE MINISTRY OF THE MASTER—TUESDAY
A Spirit Lifter

Two friends met who hadn't seen each other for some time. One was on crutches. "What happened?" "I had a car accident six weeks ago." "And you still have to use crutches?" "Well, my doctor says I could get along without them, but my lawyer says I can't."

God's Promise

Perhaps you are facing some financial difficulty.

"And God is able to make all grace abound toward you; that ye, always having all sufficiency in all things, may abound to every good work." (II Corinthians 9:8)

Practicing His Presence

I am amazed how often the Lord has felt near to me while I am involved in the ordinary experiences of life. The more I practice His presence, the more I behold Him in all things. Is this true of your life?

Paul's Thorn In The Flesh

One of the reasons I want to give more detail concerning the thorn in the flesh references in the Old Testament is to help you realize there is another viewpoint to Paul's affliction.

The verse, Num. 33:55, specifically speaks of the individuals who will oppose Israel as they settle in their new land. They will be a menace to them because of their false beliefs and immoral practices. The Israelites are told to refuse to intermingle with them or to accept their gods. Thus, this reference is not a physical malady but to the personalities who are stumbling blocks to those whom God has called.

Your life and mine is often hindered more by others than by maladies. Individuals can dampen our devotion and hamper our witness.

You will notice that Joshua 23:13 also refers to individuals who are a problem and not to a physical affliction. In like manner Judges 2:3 certainly speaks of people who hinder and not of diseases which happen to the people.

It is very evident that all three references refer to the pagan and carnal inhabitants of the land. Paul certainly knew this when he spoke of his thorn in the flesh. He had many who opposed him and there was never a time when all opposition was ended. He was opposed by some until his dying moment.

PRAYER: *There are many things of the flesh which attract me, Father. May I resist them through your grace and strength. Amen.*

A Spirit Lifter

Mother made the mistake of leaving the baby in her husband's care while she was sunbathing in the backyard. Father buried himself in the newspaper and forgot the baby until he heard a series of thumps and a horrendous wail.

"Janet," called the father excitedly out the back door, "Come quick! Tracey just took her first 23 steps!"

God's Promise

It's not always easy to obey God, is it?

"For it is God which worketh in you both to will and to do of his good pleasure." (Phillippians 2:13

Practicing His Presence

I believe you will have a great day if you are anticipating being aware of the Lord's presence. How did you do this yesterday?

Paul's Thorn In The Flesh

The first two sermonettes this week have presented the possibility of the thorn in the flesh being opposition of individuals rather than a physical illness. Paul had those who followed him wherever he went and constantly stirred up trouble. Could it be that even though he prayed much about just opposition that the Lord told him they would never be completely removed? He was called to be obedient regardless of the actions of others.

I am not saying that my insights are 100% correct. I am saying that it is good to consider another side to the issue. My position is further supported by Paul's interpretation of the word, "flesh." The word used in II Cor. 12:7 is the same word for flesh used by Paul in many places.

The other references do not refer to the physical body. Paul means by flesh one's carnal nature. He means all that is contrary to the things of the spirit. The concept of the carnal is evident from these words of Paul.

"For when we were in the flesh, the motions of sin, which were by the law, did work in our members to bring forth fruit unto death."
(Rom. 7:5)

He is speaking of the part of the nature of everyone which is contrary to the nature and will of God. He is speaking to your heart and to mine. He is saying that the flesh cannot really understand the spirit of the Lord.

PRAYER: *Enable me, Lord Jesus, to be willing to concentrate on the things of the Spirit and to trust in you. Amen.*

THE MINISTRY OF THE MASTER—THURSDAY
A Spirit Lifter

Even experts don't always agree on an issue.
Teacher: "Timmy, how do you spell 'imbecile'?"
Timmy: "i-m-b-u-s-s-u-l."
Teacher: "The dictionary spells it 'i-m-b-e-c-i-l-e'."
Timmy: "Yeah, but you asked me how I spelled it."

God's Promise

Forbidden things often seem appealing, don't they?

"The Lord knoweth how to deliver the godly out of temptations, and to reserve the unjust unto the day of judgment to be punished." II Peter 2:9)

Practicing His Presence

Sometimes it is not easy to recall a specific incident or person who made you aware of His Presence. It does not come easy. The continued victory comes with continued practice of His Presence. Don't give up!

Paul's Thorn In The Flesh

I feel some other Scripture references are appropriate at this time.

"For I know that in me (that is, in my flesh) dwelleth not one good thing: for to will is present with me; but how to perform that which is good I find not." (Rom. 7:18)

Here again Paul is speaking about that part of you which is contrary to the things and ways of the Lord.

He makes his point even more telling with these words.

"There is therefore now no condemnation to them which are in Christ Jesus, who walk not after the flesh, but after the Spirit." (Rom. 8:1)

The verses which follow have several references to the flesh. Now the same word for flesh is the word used in II Cor. 12:7. It should be clear by now that flesh does not necessarily refer to your body. The real flesh is the carnal spirit and not the blood vessels, bones, hair, etc.

The things which keep you from God are the things of the spiritual flesh. They are not the things of your physical body. It is not what goes into the body which defiles, but what comes from the heart. Paul puts it succinctly with, "So then they that are in the flesh cannot please God." (Rom. 8:8)

PRAYER: *May each step I take today be in keeping with your will and in harmony with your Spirit, O Lord. Amen.*

THE MINISTRY OF THE MASTER—FRIDAY
A Spirit Lifter

A man was complaining that he had just bought a prefabricated home and it had cost $100,000.

"One hundred thousand!" exclaimed a friend. "Isn't that a lot to pay for a prefab?"

"Yes," said the home owner. "It wasn't so much to begin with, but I told them I wanted it right away and they sent it by air mail!"

God's Promise

Don't forget this promise as you consider your daily work.

"Yet now be strong...and work: for I am with you, saith the Lord of hosts." (Haggai 2:4, KJV)

Practicing His Presence

This is going to be an exciting day for anyone willing to completely relinquish all unto the Lord. He will honor this spirit of commitment and let you know He is with you.

Paul's Thorn In The Flesh

We are coming to the point of concluding that Paul's thorn in the flesh may very well have been the people who constantly plagued him with opposition. He was never able to have complete success in any city. He was never able to lead everyone to accept the Good News.

Paul had much opposition wherever he went. It seems that in every city where he had a revival he also experienced a riot. He never completely conquered for Jesus.

This must have been a burden and heartbreak for Paul. I can well imagine that often he would fervently pray to be delivered from this intense opposition. It is my opinion that Paul could endure physical suffering. He had much of this. He gloried in this as it demonstrated that it was the Lord who was bringing victory and not himself. It was the Lord's strength and not his own which made his ministry possible.

He says as much with the words,

"Therefore I take pleasure in infirmities, in reproaches, in necessities, in persecutions, in distresses for Christ's sake; for when I am weak, then I am strong." (II Cor. 12:10, 11)

It doesn't sound from this that he was begging God to deliver him from some physical malady. I believe it is difficult for anyone to definitely refer to physical illness as Paul's thorn in the flesh.

PRAYER: *Father, even though I cannot be shielded from all problems I pray for your power to deliver me from being defeated by any problem. Amen.*

THE MINISTRY OF THE MASTER—SATURDAY

A Spirit Lifter

Teacher: "Kyle, what happened in the year 1732?"
Kyle: "George Washington was born."
Teacher: "And what happened in 1776?"
Kyle: George Washington was 44 years old."

God's Promise

Do you ever feel depressed, desperate, like I do? Remember, there is light at the end of the tunnel. *"...I am come that they might have life, and that they might have it more abundantly."* (John 10:10)

Practicing His Presence

Try not to finish this devotional time without meditating as to what incident or person helped you to sense His Presence yesterday. It will strengthen you in spirit, body, and mind.

Paul's Thorn In The Flesh

Why is it so important that we have an understanding of Paul's thorn in the flesh? I believe it is important because so many Christians accept their illness as from the Lord. They feel it must be His will that they suffer. They conceive that the Apostle Paul had a continual physical affliction and so there must be something almost sacred about being afflicted in like manner.

Now I want to point out that anyone who seeks to defend an illness by the "thorn in the flesh" theory will have to be very careful. Paul's thorn was not sent by God, but was sent by the devil.

"...there was given to me a thorn in the flesh, the messenger of Satan to buffet me..." (II Cor. 12:7)

This verse refutes the thought that some illness is the cross we must carry because God wants us to do so. If Paul's thorn was illness it was not sent by God. It was Satan's messenger! I believe the total message of the Bible is that anything of Satan we have a right to rebuke and to seek to remove from our lives.

The thorn was not sent from God. It was sent from Satan. I believe a strong case can be made that the thorn refers to the opposition. Paul's message was accompanied with signs and wonders. Yet, constantly there were those who tried to quiet, yea, to kill Paul.

PRAYER: *Thank you, Father, for loving me more than I love myself. Thank you for caring for me. Amen.*

THE MINISTRY OF THE MASTER—SUNDAY
A Spirit Lifter

First Space Cadet: "Meet you on Jupiter tonight."
Second Space Cadet: "But how do I get there?"
First Space Cadet: "When you get to the moon, turn left, You can't miss it.

God's Promise

"Blessed are they that do his commandments, that they may have right to the tree of life, and may enter in through the gates into the city." (Rev. 22:14)

Practicing His Presence

The exercising of the muscles of the body make them stronger. The exercising of your spiritual faculties will make them stronger. The practice of His Presence will help you know of His Presence.

Paul's Thorn In The Flesh

There are individuals who try to persuade me that people are deepened in their faith because of illness. This I find very difficult to believe. Unless a person is deeply committed prior to a serious illness there is slim chance of his accepting the Lord at this time.

Years ago I read of a survey made of hospital patients who were seriously ill. It was discovered that unless the patient had some commitment prior to the illness the chances of religious ministry meaning much was practically nil. The illness made the sick think God was punishing instead of chastising to bring to repentance.

I feel we must get to the point where our faith is activated to the place of believing and acknowledging that illness is of the devil. No longer can the thorn in the flesh concept be reserved for an escape hatch for one's physical illness. Rather each of us must seek His love and healing through the prayers of others as well as our own. I am not saying the medical insights of our modern day should be neglected, but I am saying God is in the healing business. This we should not forget.

Paul had many who opposed his message of wholeness. You and I have many who oppose our message of wholeness. In fact, each Christian has many a "thorn in the flesh" and needs no physical illness to attest to this.

PRAYER: *Lord Jesus, help me defeat the enemy, Satan, who sows discord and disease in my life. Amen.*

SOME KEY POINTS OF A MINISTRY OF HEALING

I meet many who feel that the ministry of healing comes automatically to anyone who desires to participate in such a ministry. May I assure you this is not so.

An effective ministry of healing is a demanding ministry. It takes time, effort, energy and great devotion. There is no such thing as an easy life even when in service of our Lord. It is work. It is demanding.

It is my firm conviction that every believer is called to be part of a ministry of healing. This was, and is, the ministry of our Master and every one of us is called to follow His example.

A ministry of wholeness within a local congregation must have the support of the pastor. The pastor helps set the pace for power and purpose in this ministry. Your pastor cannot do it alone, but at the same time must be willing to exercise the leadership qualities which will inspire and inform members of the congregation.

The Lord has revealed many things to me throughout the years. He did not reveal all things at once. I have had to struggle in study and practice. There have been many obstacles to overcome. There have been mistakes made on my part. There have been moments of doubt and times of great frustration. It has not been a steady climb to effectiveness and victory.

I have discovered that anything worthwhile takes work, time, and dedication. These are key points to a consistent and effective ministry of wholeness.

You must be willing to pay the price. There will be people who won't understand what you are doing. They will speak disparagingly of your efforts. They will look at what they feel are your failures and ridicule you.

This week's pilgrimage will not be comforting to the quitter, but will be a great blessing to those willing to pay the price.

POINTS TO PONDER

1. Does a person naturally have a ministry of wholeness or does this ministry require effort and time to understand and fulfill?
2. What is the importance of the pastor's leadership in a ministry of healing?
3. What does one do to develop an effective ministry of healing?

SOME KEY POINTS OF A MINISTRY OF HEALING

1. Ye shall be my _____ in Jerusalem and in all Judea. *Acts 1:8*
2. Phillip went to Samaria and _____ to them. *Acts 8:5*
3. Though I am absent in the flesh, I am _____ in the spirit. *Col. 2:5*
4. Put on charity, which is the bond of _____. *Col. 3:14*
5. You should pray without _____. *I Thes. 5:17*
6. By the space of three years I ceased not to warn everyone night and day with _____. *Acts.20:31*
7. We labour and suffer _____, because we trust in the living God. *I Tim. 4:10*
8. Let us lay aside every weight and the _____ which besets us. *Heb. 12:1*
9. Be ye holy, for I am _____. *I Peter 1:16*
10. Be ye _____ as your Father in heaven is perfect. *Mt. 5:48*
11. Seek ye first the _____ of God. *Mt. 6:33*
12. Of the doctrine of baptisms, and of _____, and of resurrection of the dead. *Heb. 6:1*
13. Whosoever shall do the _____ of God, the same is my brother, and my sister, and mother. *Mk. 3:35*
14. Neither is there _____ in any other. *Acts 4:12*

DAILY SCRIPTURE

Mon.	Acts 1:6-9
Tues.	Col. 2:1-5
Wed.	Col. 3:12-17
Thurs.	Mt. 5:43-48
Fri.	Heb. 6:1-6
Sat.	Mk. 3:31-35
Sun.	Acts 4:9-12

PRAYER CONCERNS

Your Family & Relatives
Government Leaders
Missionaries
For the Unbelievers
Churches & Denominations
Your Own Church
Prayer and Praise

NOTE: You will be spiritually strengthened by completing two questions each day, reading the suggested scripture, and ministering in prayer for the concerns of the day.

THE MINISTRY OF THE MASTER—MONDAY
A Spirit Lifter

Two little fellows coming home from Sunday School were discussing the lesson.

"Say, do you believe all that about the devil?"

"No, don't let them kid you. That's just like Santa Claus — it's just your old man."

God's Promise

Are you in trouble for some reason? Trust God.

"The Lord saves righteous men and protects them in times of trouble. He helps them and rescues them." (Psalm 37:39,40)

Practicing His Presence

Can you recall a specific incident or person which helped your awareness of the Lord's presence yesterday? Take a moment and reflect upon this.

Some Key Points Of A Ministry Of Healing

It is my firm conviction that every believer is called to be ruled by our Lord Jesus Christ. He is the example to follow and His ministry is the one to be imitated. There are leaders in every congregation who act as if they ruled the church. They never seem to grasp the truth that Christ is the head of the Church. We are called unto Him to be ruled by Him.

What was His ministry? His ministry was one of bringing wholeness to people. He was desirous of bringing hope to the hopeless. He didn't bring a message of hell, but one of hope. I feel this is one of the key points of His earthly ministry and one of the key points He wants His followers to pursue.

One of the principles of communication is that the further removed from the source, the more distorted and diluted the message. By the time information or commands get down through the proper channels it is often much different than when it started. This is the reason it is important for every believer to keep close to the Lord. This is the reason you must personally search the Word and learn for yourself the ministry of wholeness of our Lord.

It is essential that you not take the easy road, but that you understand the point of Christ being the One who rules in your life and empowers you for your ministry. Your ministry will be His ministry and your fruitfulness will be to His glory when you permit His wholeness to be channeled through you.

PRAYER: *Lord Jesus, I truly believe your ministry was and is a ministry of wholeness to me and to all. Amen.*

THE MINISTRY OF THE MASTER—TUESDAY
A Spirit Lifter

Everyone is looking for a bargain.
Tourist: "How much to carry baggage?"
Porter: "One dollar for the first parcel and then fifty cents for each additional parcel."
Tourist: "I will carry the first parcel and you take the other."

God's Promise

The Lord will reach down and comfort you during your times of grief. Praise Jesus!

"You will increase my honor and comfort me once again." (Psalm 71:21, NIV)

Practicing His Presence

I have sought to remind you each day to be aware of the presence of our Lord. How did you find this taking place and what is it doing for you?

Some Key Points Of A Ministry Of Healing

Even as I stress the importance of each person putting forth effort to develop a ministry of wholeness, I must at the same time stress that our efforts for Christ are of a corporate nature. You do not go it alone. There are always others involved. It is true a leader makes a great difference, but there can be no great leader without many others cooperating.

Moses led the children of Israel out of Egypt. However, there were many others involved with this. His brother Aaron and other leaders of the people were informed of God's plan and of the efforts to free His people.

A key point of an effective ministry of healing is to be surrounded by others who are like-minded. In every congregation there will be at least a few who will be willing to devote themselves to this ministry. You need not be alone.

In addition, throughout the community there will be several who will be like-minded. These interested individuals will come from several congregations but together they will be one. I feel it is important that you avail yourself of the opportunity to meet with others who believe the message of wholeness. You will not be able to remain strong if you do not see that the ministry is a corporate pilgrimage. The Lord will lead and you will follow with others.

The healing community is far more important than the individual healer. The fellowship of the believers is essential in an effective ministry of healing.

PRAYER: *I thank you, Father, for my friends who believe and put their hope in you. They mean so much to me. Amen.*

THE MINISTRY OF THE MASTER—WEDNESDAY
A Spirit Lifter

As Christians we attempt to live with Biblical guidelines as our goal. Worldly values and principles can be dramatically opposed to these values.
Stranger: "I've come out here to make an honest living."
Native: "Well, there's not much competition."

God's Promise

Sometimes I feel so tired that it is hard to cope. I appreciate this promise very much.

"...We, too, are weak in our bodies, as He was, but now we live and are strong, as He is, and have all of God's power." (II Corinthians 13:4)

Practicing His Presence

Perhaps you were aware of His presence in a baby's smile, or in a view of the countryside. Whatever situation you sensed His presence was, I am sure, unique for you. Continue to develop this awareness in your life.

Some Key Points To A Ministry Of Healing

If you are going to be a person who develops a ministry of healing you must come to appreciate the place of your being an intercessor for others. This is a key point which cannot be overstressed.

If you are going to effectively intercede for others you must seek to identify with them. When people are hurting they want the person ministering unto them to realize they are hurting. This is one of the reasons that many effective servants of the Lord have suffered much. They know what it is to be ill and to be afflicted in other ways. They understand the importance of intercession and of helping others when they are so weak and discouraged that they cannot help themselves.

When the Lord led me to begin public healing services I was very ill. He did this at a time of great need in my life. He used my affliction to help me appreciate the afflictions others have. He showed me that I must with compassion intercede in behalf of others.

It is interesting to me that most believers feel they should care for the busy work of a congregation. Yet, one of the key points to keep in mind in the ministry of healing is that you are called to intercede for others. The greatest work is prayer and the greatest prayer is intercessory prayer. It is not how cleverly you work, but how committed you are to the Great Physician which makes you a real leader in the ministry of wholeness.

PRAYER: *I lift into your light and love those you have placed on my heart, O God. Send your healing to them. Amen.*

THE MINISTRY OF THE MASTER—THURSDAY
A Spirit Lifter

It is a good idea to make a list of your goals and then endeavor to follow through on them each day.

Student: "What is the date?"

Teacher: "Never mind the date. The exam is more important."

Student: "Well, sir, I wanted to have something right on my paper."

God's Promise

I think you will like this excellent promise from the Lord Jesus Himself.

"Is anyone among you suffering? Let him pray." (James 5:13)

Practicing His Presence

I pray that being aware of His presence each day has been meaningful for you. How did you sense His presence yesterday?

Some Key Points Of A Ministry Of Healing

The wholeness you desire for yourself, your church, and your community will not be achieved by indifference on your part and on the part of others. The ministry of healing is a ministry of discipline. Your thoughts, your actions, your emotions must be kept under the control of Christ. He is the One who sets the example of discipline to be followed by His people.

Are you bothered by the fact that I mention discipline as a part of an effective ministry of healing? I believe it is a key point. The church through the ages has been responsible for disciplining its members. I do not always know what should be done, and often even if I know I may not do it. I need a disciplined group of people to help me. I need others to assess my efforts and to evaluate my goals and methods.

I believe that many of the illnesses which people suffer are the result of an undisciplined life. The average American spends several hours every day watching television. How can a person have a strong victorious thought pattern after exposing his or her mind to the junk on most television programs? The average citizen of our nation comsumes much food which is not good for them and many people indulge in smoking, drinking, drug usage, and other things which destroy mind, body, and spirit.

The Lord is not in the business of zapping us when illness strikes and immediately making us well. He is in the business of imparting His wholeness to disciplined minds and bodies. Your health will be determined to a large degree by your lifestyle. Don's abuse your mind, body, or spirit.

PRAYER: *Jesus, help me to live the disciplined and the healthy life to your glory. Amen.*

THE MINISTRY OF THE MASTER—FRIDAY
A Spirit Lifter

This neighborhood went a little too far in an attempt to enrich the surroundings.

Man: "Madam, I'm the piano tuner."
Lady: "I didn't send for a piano tuner."
Man: "I know lady, the neighbors did."

God's Promise

Do you ever worry about your appearance? Isn't it interesting to note how God views you?

"He has made everything beautiful in its time." (Ecclesiastes 3:11, RSV)

Practicing His Presence

You perhaps had a busy day yesterday. I pray that, amidst your activity, you were able to pull apart and sense the Lord's presence.

Some Key Points Of A Ministry Of Healing

Another key point to a ministry of wholeness to yourself and unto others is that you maintain a life of high morals. The Old Testament often refers to evil being purged from the people. This emphasis was not to cruelly punish offenders, but it was done to keep the group strong.

It is amazing to me how many people have brought physical problems upon themselves because they have transgressed the moral laws. You cannot violate the moral standards of God's Word and expect to be whole of body, mind, and spirit.

It is strange to me that some want to be whole, but refuse to live a wholesome life. I believe one of the most extreme cases of desire for wholeness in the midst of an evil life is the following. A young man came seeking advice to overcome his occasional impotency. This happened at times when he was having an affair with the wife of a close friend of his. He wanted a healing for a problem so that he could continue to sin. How ridiculous!

A ministry of healing is one built upon the moral life. There would be far more healings if there were more truly repentant people. Also, the healings would continue if a righteous life were pursued. You cannot separate wholeness from holiness. The unrighteous life will reap the fruit of unrighteousness.

PRAYER: *By your grace, O Lord, I want to put aside all sin and live unto righteousness. Amen.*

THE MINISTRY OF THE MASTER—SATURDAY
A Spirit Lifter

Motivation can come from a variety of sources and styles.

The teacher was going to give an object lesson.

"Tommy," she began, "why does your father put up storm windows every fall?"

"Well," said Tommy, "Mother keeps at him until he finally gives in."

God's Promise

Do you ever feel full of anxiety?

"You will keep in perfect peace him whose mind is steadfast, because he trusts in you." (Isaiah 26:3, NIV)

Practicing His Presence

I believe you will have a great day if you are anticipating being aware of the Lord's presence. How did you do this yesterday?

Some Key Points Of A Ministry Of Healing

Another key point to an effective ministry is to realize it takes work to develop this ministry. You must give yourself to taking time to study the Word, to meet with other believers, to developing a life style of prayer, and to reaching out to others.

I know there are some who attract large crowds as they proclaim the message of healing. This is true, but remember they started by reaching out to a few. Their ministry has expanded because they have worked at serving others. They have given of themselves and the Lord has given unto them. They have seen the truth fulfilled that the one who has will receive more.

I would encourage you to take the time and to put forth the effort to learn about prayer, anointing, laying-on-of-hands, etc. so that you can minister more effectively to yourself and to others. The Lord has some people to whom you can minister more effectively than anyone else. Your unwillingness to put forth the necessary work to know what to do will affect these people. There is no one person who can minister to the entire world. You, as a believer, have your area of responsibility. May you not neglect it. Whatever the price, may you be willing to pay it. May you be a channel of wholeness.

PRAYER: *May I be willing to accept the fact that it takes time and effort to learn of you, O Lord. Amen.*

THE MINISTRY OF THE MASTER—SUNDAY
A Spirit Lifter

There is tremendous satisfaction when we touch another life in a positive way. "I'm not the happiest person in the world, but I'm next to the happiest," murmured the supreme egotist as he took the sweet young thing into his arms.

God's Promise

"Be patient, brothers, until the Lord's coming. Think of a farmer: how patiently he waits for the precious fruit of the ground until it has had the autumn rains and the spring rains. You, too, have to be patient; do not lose heart." (James 5:7, 8, JB)

Practicing His Presence

Do you find that an awareness of His presence is determined to some degree by how you feel? Was there any time yesterday when you knew the spiritual life was the most important aspect of your being?

Some Key Points Of A Ministry Of Healing

The last key point I want to mention is that you keep your eyes on Jesus. He is the One who has called you unto Himself. He is the One to whom you must give the glory. He is the One who is most willing to impart wholeness.

I have seen people disgruntled in the healing ministry because they have felt neglected or abused by other believers. I have witnessed indifference developing because a person does not care for some facet of the message, the method, or the person. How tragic to see this happen.

There are no perfect movements or persons. In the context of imperfection the Lord brings His wholeness. It is as if He shows us again and again that in our weakness His strength is made perfect. It is as if He is saying that He takes the foolishness of men and brings forth the miracles to glorify Himself.

A Ministry of healing cannot be continually fruitful if the Lord Jesus is put in second place. He must always be first. It is His calling to you. He is the Great Physician. He is the One who heals and keeps. He is the One who will comfort you in difficult times and inform you when you know not what to do or say. His ministry is your ministry and your ministry should be His ministry. If this be your goal, you will always be on the right track and no one can take your ministry from you.

PRAYER: *It is to you and you alone, Lord Jesus, that I look at this time. Amen.*

HEALING—A SHARED MINISTRY

The Lord Jesus Christ had a ministry of wholeness. Wherever He went it was with the message of wholeness. He sought to bring deliverance to all and in every area of life.

However, the Lord did not confine this ministry to Himself. He shared it with others. He wanted them to share it with others and thus to spread the message of healing to all the world.

Mt. 4:17-25 describes the beginning of Jesus' ministry and the calling of His disciples. They were called to be fishers of men, but notice v. 24 which describes the method of fishing which Jesus used. He healed the sick. He delivered the possessed. It was then that great multitudes followed Him.

Now, to show you how He desired this ministry of healing to be shared with His disciples and to have them share it with others we read Mt. 10:1.

"And when he had called unto him his twelve disciples, he gave them power against unclean spirits, to cast them out, and to heal all manner of sickness and all manner of disease."

He did not keep the ministry unto Himself. Neither did He do the ministry and then have a group of lay people elected to sit in judgment of this ministry or to supervise the ministry. They were the ministry and they were to minister. The ministry was not administration, but a ministry of hope and help.

It is my feeling that most Pastors and lay persons need to be reminded that the Lord didn't call a person, but he called a people. Within the institutional church today there is too much emphasis upon the pastor as the leader of the congregation. If the church is but an organization this may be true, but if the church is a ministering body then this is a false approach.

The Lord has called Himself a people and not a pastor. His people are to be proclaiming His message of wholeness.

POINTS TO PONDER

1. Can you think of some incidents which convey Christ's ministry as a ministry of healing?
2. Does every Christian have a ministry?
3. Can the healing ministry be a shared ministry? If so, how?

Daily Bible Study and Daily Prayer Concerns

HEALING—A SHARED MINISTRY

1. Jesus said, _____ me and I will make you fishers of men. *Mt. 4:19*
2. Jesus called the twelve and gave them power to _____. _____ all manner of sickness. *Mt. 10:1*
3. Take heed to the flock over which the _____ made you overseers. *Acts 20:28*
4. I will make of thee a great _____. *Gen. 12:2*
5. There were 144,000 who had his _____ name written in their foreheads. *Rev. 14:1*
6. After these things I heard the voice of _____ people. *Rev. 19:1*
7. Go and gather the _____ of Israel together. *Ex. 3:16*
8. And the Lord said unto _____, go and meet Moses. *Ex. 4:27*
9. Moses called for the _____ of Israel. *Ex. 12:21*
10. Come up unto the Lord and _____ a far off. *Ex. 24:1*
11. The Lord _____ other seventy. *Luke 10:1*
12. The seventy returned with _____. *Luke 10:17*
13. Greater _____ than these shall he do. *John 14:12*
14. He that dwelleth in the secret place shall abide under the shadow of the _____. *Ps. 91:1*

DAILY SCRIPTURE

Mon.	Mt. 4:18-11
Tues.	Mt. 10:1-4
Wed.	Gen. 12:1-4
Thurs.	Rev. 19:1-4
Fri.	Ex. 4:27-31
Sat.	John 14:12-17
Sun.	Ps. 91:1-6

PRAYER CONCERNS

Your Family & Relatives
Government Leaders
Missionaries
For the Unbelievers
Churches & Denominations
Your Own Church
Prayer and Praise

NOTE: You will be spiritually strengthened by completing two questions each day, reading the suggested scripture, and ministering in prayer for the concerns of the day.

THE MINISTRY OF THE MASTER—MONDAY
A Spirit Lifter

This is a rare case in which a politician felt he had too many supporting constituents.

Nurse: "Mr. Politician, you are the father of triplets."

Man: "What?"

Nurse: "You're the father of triplets. TRIPLETS!"

Man: "I'll demand a recount!"

God's Promise

The following promise is quite blunt about your identity.

"You are no longer foreigners and aliens, but fellow citizens with God's people and members of God's household." (Ephesians 2:19, NIV)

Practicing His Presence

As you use *"The Ministry of the Master"* it is wonderful to consciously practice His presence. May you seek to quiet your body, mind, and spirit!

Healing—A Shared Ministry

It is impossible to convey all that is in the Bible concerning the fact that every believer should have a ministry. Also, that if this ministry is to be patterned after our Lord Jesus it will be a ministry of wholeness. The Lord did not speak only to the "spiritual" side of a person, He brought wholeness of body, mind, and spirit. I feel our calling cannot be less than this.

I may not say it right and I may not write it clearly, but I shall attempt to convey to you that your blessed right as a believer is to be a minister of wholeness. It is impossible to cover everything about the task of a believer. This is as difficult as to try to absorb all the energy that the sun exudes. In one second the sun exudes more energy than human beings have used since man was created. The energy of the sun provides light for our world, warmth, growth, and many other things. We have not begun to channel this power to the fullest.

So it is with the followers of our Lord Jesus. He is imparting far more power than is being used. His power and purpose is on every side, but it is often ignored or neglected.

I pray that this week you will begin to see more clearly than ever your place as a proclaimer of the healing power of the Lord. This message cannot be left up to your pastor or a few select people. You will minister to someone that no one else can.

PRAYER: *Thank you for your power, O Lord, and may I appropriate this power to your glory. Amen.*

THE MINISTRY OF THE MASTER—TUESDAY
A Spirit Lifter

I love the honest, impulsive responses that children add to a conversation. Teacher: "Johnny, can you tell me what a waffle is?" Johnny: "Yes'm, it's a pancake with a non-skid tread."

God's Promise

"Just as you trusted Christ to save you, trust him, too, for each day's problems; live in vital union with him." (Colossians 2:6, TLB)

Practicing His Presence

It takes conscious effort to be aware of the Lord in the small aspects in life. How did this consciousness affect your day yesterday?

Healing—A Shared Ministry

Luke chapter 10 describes the seventy disciples being sent out to proclaim concerning the Kingdom of God and to heal the sick. It is interesting that 70 is the number mentioned.

There are several references in the life of Moses where there were 70 elders who were closely involved in a shared ministry with him. I don't know whether this number stands for a large number or if it precisely means 70 people. This is not really important. The important thing is that many people were involved in a ministry of fulfilling the will of God.

A shared ministry is the ministry God desires not because any one person is busy and can't do it all, but because every person is a unique minister of wholeness to another unique person. I find many who feel the church should be so organized as to involve all in some detail of activity.

Not so, says the Word of God. Each believer is to be sharing the Good News of wholeness in his or her own unique way. The ministry is not activity, but an active faith in the Lord.

It is obvious from the Word that I do not have exclusive rights to ministry. You do not have exclusive right to ministry. We are in ministry together. It is the Lord who has called us unto Himself and unto a ministry of hope to all. The Lord is your healer and you are His channel of healing to others.

PRAYER: *Help me to realize my responsibility as your child, Father. May I be a channel of healing to others. Amen.*

THE MINISTRY OF THE MASTER—WEDNESDAY
A Spirit Lifter

Worrying about the future can be a devastating lifestyle.
Friend: "What's the matter? You sure look worried."
Man: "Work-work-work! Nothing but work from morning to night!"
Friend: "How long have you been at it?"
Man: "Oh, I start tomorrow."

God's Promise

"He had made known to us in all wisdom and insight the mystery of his will, according to his purpose which he set forth in Christ." (Ephesians 1:9, RSV)

Practicing His Presence

Can you recall a spiritual feast you had yesterday as you sensed the Lord's presence? Be aware of the Lord in your everyday living.

Healing—A Shared Ministry

The healing ministry becomes valid and helpful when you realize you must have the presence of God in your life. You cannot bring the wholeness desired and needed apart from being in Him and He being in you.

Exodus 24:1 speaks of a group of people coming together to worship the Lord. They were to enter into His presence and to have this serve as a time to help them realize He has entered into their presence.

> *"And he said unto Moses, come up unto the Lord, thou, and Israel; and Aaron, and Nadab, and Abihu, and seventy of the elders of Israel; and worship ye afar off."*

Exodus 24:10 tells of the glories of the Lord which they all beheld.

> *"And they saw the God of Israel; and there was under his feet as it were a paved work of a sapphire stone, and as it were the body of heaven in his clearness."*

All of the worshipping community beheld the presence of the Lord. It was not confined to Moses. It was for all of them.

There is no place in the Bible where the revelation of the presence and power of the Lord is confined to a professional priesthood. The Lord has called each person unto Himself. You and I have the responsibility to respond. How foolish that some feel the only way they can really receive the ministry of wholeness is through a pastor. We bear a common burden and we have a common ministry. It is a shared one.

PRAYER: *Father, I am just a humble child of yours. Yet, your promises are so great and sure. Help me to believe them. Amen.*

THE MINISTRY OF THE MASTER—THURSDAY
A Spirit Lifter

Teacher: "Which is more important to us — the moon or the sun?
Pupil: "The moon."
Teacher: "Why?"
Pupil: "The moon gives us light at night when we need it. The sun gives us light in the daytime when we don't need it."

God's Promise

"Only test me! Open your mouth wide and see if I won't fill it. You will receive every blessing you can use!" (Psalm 81:10)

Practicing His Presence

Through what incident or person did you sense the Lord's presence yesterday? How did this make you feel?

Healing—A Shared Ministry

Another aspect of a shared ministry is for all to believe that only the Lord God can save. There is no other who can deliver. He alone is our salvation, our physician, our counselor, and our hope.

Exodus chapter 12 presents the Passover lamb being slain and the blood placed upon the door posts. This provided the deliverance needed for the children of Israel.

The instruction to Moses and Aaron are detailed in the first part of chapter 12. Then in verse 21 it says, *"Then Moses called for all the elders of Israel, and said unto them..."* He continued a shared ministry. We have no record that Moses went to every family and warned them of the dangers of not observing the Passover. This was done by many people as they were directed by Moses. They received protection because they believed those who proclaimed a way of deliverance.

Today we have the privilege of bringing a message of deliverance to those who are in bondage. This bondage may be one of sin, physical illness, financial stress, etc.; but the message is needed. Every person has a chance to impart the message that the Lord is the only One who can really save. It is to Him that we must point all people. There is no answer other than Him. I cannot reach all people with this message and neither can you. We are called to do it together.

PRAYER: *I thank you, Lord Jesus, for a shared ministry. I praise you for the many others seeking to do your will. Amen.*

THE MINISTRY OF THE MASTER— FRIDAY
A Spirit Lifter

A word of encouragement can change a discouraged attitude into a positive feeling.

Mr. Wise: "You sold me this car two weeks ago."

Used car salesman: "Yes, sir."

Mr. Wise: "Tell me again all you said about it then. I'm getting discouraged."

God's Promise

Perhaps you are having a difficult day. Reflect upon this wonderful promise.

"Commit everything you do to the Lord. Trust him to help you do it and he will." (Psalm 37:5, TLB)

Practicing His Presence

I am certain this will be an exciting day for you if you seek to quiet yourself and practice His presence. Have a good day!

Healing—A Shared Ministry

There are some things which will help you minister the good news of wholeness. One of the first things is to listen to the voice of the Holy Spirit. It is sometimes absolutely amazing what is revealed when you are in tune with the Holy Spirit.

I again call your attention to the efforts of Moses to deliver the people of Israel. Exodus 3:16-22 reveals that Moses is to go tell the Elders about God's deliverance plan. It is not that they will completely and always believe him, but at least he is to proclaim the message to them.

Exodus 4:27 says, *"And the Lord said to Aaron, Go into the wilderness to meet Moses. And he went, ..."* Before Moses had returned to tell what had happened to him at the burning bush Aaron has had the message from the spirit to go to meet him. Aaron listened to the spirit and went to meet his brother and it was then Moses told him of his calling.

The Holy Spirit spoke prior to the event and His servant responded. Each of us must tenderly and affectionately seek to listen to the voice of the Holy Spirit. When you do you will be able to take a message of hope to many people. The Spirit will not use you to direct other people's lives, but he will use you to bring them a message of hope and wholeness. Tune in to Him and be calm in your soul.

PRAYER: *Holy Spirit, speak to me. I seek to hear you and will seek to obey you. Amen.*

THE MINISTRY OF THE MASTER—SATURDAY
A Spirit Lifter

"I resent your remark," said the fifth grader, "and I'll give you five seconds to take it back!"

"Oh, yeah," snarled the seventh grader. "Suppose I don't take it back in five seconds?"

"Well," said the first, "How much time do you want?"

God's Promise

"The Lord your God is with you...He will take great delight in you, he will quiet you with his love, He will rejoice over you with singing." (Zephaniah 3:17)

Practicing His Presence

May you seek to quiet yourself today and hear "the still small voice" speak to you! How were you aware of His presence yesterday?

Healing—A Shared Ministry

The calling of Moses to deliver the children of Israel is recorded in Exodus chapter 3. He beholds the burning bush and hears the voice calling him to a task of deliverance. He was not only to bring spiritual strength to his people, but was to enter into the practical aspects of their life. He was to minister to the whole person.

However, his was to be a shared ministry. Sometimes I feel we get the idea Moses did it alone. Well, granted there were times when he had to go it alone, but this was not the plan of God. The Lord called a people to a ministry of deliverance.

The corporate ministry is really evident when we read Ex. 3:16. *"Go, and gather the elders of Israel together, ..."* and also in verse 18. *"And they shall hearken to thy voice: and thou shalt come, thou and the elders of Israel, unto the King of Egypt, and ye shall say..."*

The ministry to which the Lord had called Moses was a shared ministry with the other leaders of Israel. There is no one person who can and who does impart all the mercy and blessings of the Lord. Each person is called to do his or her small part. The most famous can but touch the surface of need and the most unknown can meet some need.

There is someone within your family or circle of friends who needs your ministry of faith and wholeness today. Share it with them. Do not let the task up to others.

PRAYER: *Father, I pray I may do my part to bring wholeness to others today. Amen.*

THE MINISTRY OF THE MASTER—SUNDAY
A Spirit Lifter

Mark Twain said, "It is better to keep your mouth shut and appear stupid than to open it and remove all doubt."

Girl: "Don't you know what an operetta is?"

Blind Date: "Don't be silly, of course I do! An operetta is a girl who works for the telephone company."

God's Promise

Please remember the following promise.

"The name of the Lord is a strong tower; the righteous run to it and are safe." (Proverbs 18:10)

Practicing His Presence

It is difficult to remember a specific incident in which you really felt His presence. Yet it is helpful to be reminded of the spiritual awareness which each of us should develop.

Healing—A Shared Ministry

The church today needs to study carefully the ministry of the Head of the Church, Jesus Christ. His focus is often not our focus. His main ministry is frequently not our main ministry. He chose individuals to share His ministry of wholeness. The assignment given His disciples was to preach the Kingdom is at hand, and to heal the sick. He blended the two together. He did not say to seek to save the soul and then give some thought to individuals concerning their needs in body and mind. He gave Himself to the whole person.

The Bible message concerns a ministry of a people. Abraham was called to a new land. Why? He was to become a great nation. His ministry was to be a corporate one and not simply an individual one.

"And I will make of thee a great nation..." (Gen. 12:3)

The leadership Jesus proclaimed was one of example and power. He did not call people to rule over others, but He called individuals to preach good news of wholeness to others. He asked that they be ruled by Him and by His rules. His rules involved the expressions of faith, trust, hope, and confidence in the Lord. His shared ministry called for believing and not simply setting machinery in motion. His spiritual laws must be followed in our day as they were in His. It is a shared ministry with Him and with our fellow believers.

PRAYER: *Father, as you call me to new things I pray for your grace and strength to pursue them with enthusiasm. Amen.*

WHAT ABOUT FAILURES?

What about failures? This is a question often asked of many who are fearful of emphasizing the healing power of the Lord, because all are not apparently healed.

There are several things which this question reveals concerning a person. First of all, it indicates that the individual is primarily concerned with physical healings. They place prime importance upon the physical and neglect to see the whole person and the needs in all areas of life.

Second, this question indicates that the person hasn't taken into account the complexities of this universe. There is no method which brings 100% wholeness in every situation. There are too many factors involved to say that the laying-on-of-hands, anointing, or any other thing will guarantee wholeness. The Lord will not, and does not, let us manipulate Him this way.

Third, this question implies the person doesn't really understand failure and success as far as Spiritual Healing is concerned. The absence of physical healing does not mean something did not happen to the person.

It is important for me to impart to you that Spiritual Healing is a ministry to the whole person. It is not dependent upon every person receiving an immediate and dramatic physical healing.

Why is this so important? It is of utmost importance because there are many who will never receive a physical healing for themselves or for their loved ones. There will be some who will react to this with, "God has failed me," or "Why doesn't God ever answer my prayers?" or "Where is the God that people tell me will heal the sick?"

Regardless of the ministry, you will discover many who participate who will not be healed physically. It is important that you understand this and realize that the total person involves more than physical healing.

POINTS TO PONDER

1. What is failure in God's sight?
2. Do you feel most people overemphasize the physical aspects of healing?
3. What part of you as a total person needs God's healing touch now?

WHAT ABOUT FAILURES

1. For the Lord is a God of judgment; blessed are all they that _____ _____ on him. *Isa. 30:18*
2. ...Blessed is he that shall eat bread in the _____ of God. *Lu. 14:15*
3. ...blessedness of the man unto whom God imputeth righteousness without _____. *Rom. 4:6*
4. ...who hath blessed us with all_____ blessings. *Eph. 1:3*
5. Blessed is the man whom thou _____, O Lord. *Ps. 94:12*
6. ...Blessed are all they that put their _____ in him. *Ps. 2:12*
7. Blessed is the man that maketh the_____ his trust. *Ps. 40:4*
8. ...Blessed is the man that feareth the Lord, that _____ _____ greatly in his commandments. *Ps. 112:1*
9. Blessed are they that...seek him with the _____heart. *Ps. 119:2*
10. Blessed is the man that walketh not in the _____ of the ungodly. *Ps. 1:1*
11. Blessed are ye that _____ now: for ye shall be filled. *Lu. 6:21*
12. Blessed are the_____which die in the Lord from henceforth. *Rev. 14:13*
13. Blessed is the man unto whom the Lord imputeth not _____ _____. *Ps. 32:2*
14. Blessed is the man whose _____ is in thee. *Ps. 84:5*

DAILY SCRIPTURE

Mon.   Isa. 30:15-18
Tues.   Luke 14:15-24
Wed.   Eph. 1:1-10
Thurs. Ps. 40:1-8
Fri.   Ps. 1:1-6
Sat.   Lu. 6:17-31
Sun.   Rom. 4:1-8

PRAYER CONCERNS

Your Family & Relatives
Government Leaders
Missionaries
For the Unbelievers
Churches & Denominations
Your Own Church
Prayer and Praise

NOTE: *You will be spiritually strengthened by completing two questions each day, reading the suggested scripture, and ministering in prayer for the concerns of the day.*

THE MINISTRY OF THE MASTER—MONDAY
A Spirit Lifter

The young first grader was having his physical examination. The Dr. asked him, "Have you ever had any trouble with your ears and nose?"

"Sure," answered the boy, "They always get in my way when I take off my T-shirt."

God's Promise

Rejoice in this promise.

"But when the Holy Spirit comes upon you, you shall receive power and you shall be witness to me both in Jerusalem and in all Judea..." (Acts 1:8, Lamsa)

Practicing His Presence

Pause for a moment and think. When did I get that gentle touch of assurance of the Lord's presence yesterday? When did I know beyond a shadow of doubt that He was with me?

What About Failures?

I am sure you agree with me that most of us put the primary focus upon physical healings. This is a most natural thing to do. I discover this very quickly when I am leading groups by asking if anyone has ever seen a miracle. Most of the people will say no, and the ones who say yes will tell of a physical healing they have experienced themselves or have seen in another person.

Why is there such emphasis upon the physical? Well, the reason I feel is that this is the area easiest to describe. It is dramatic to witness someone discard his crutches, but how can you behold the inner healing of a longstanding resentment?

A famous doctor was in a meeting where I presented the message of wholeness. He left the service and went on outside, and noticed that he had left his cane hanging on the back of the pew. Now, he had not been able to walk without a cane for years. He was startled, and hurried back to get it. It was obvious he had received a marvelous healing.

However, talking with him later he told of the fact that he had received Jesus Christ as His Saviour at the time of his healing. The most exciting thing to him and that which brought tears to his eyes was not the healing of his body. It was the healing of his spirit. Yet, how can you see or know of this except if he tells you. It is not spectacular, but so important.

PRAYER: *Lord Jesus, above all else I want to know you and to know I have been forgiven by you. Amen.*

THE MINISTRY OF THE MASTER—TUESDAY
A Spirit Lifter

Father: "Does your boyfriend have any money?"
Daughter, "You men are all alike! That's the same thing that he asked about you!"

God's Promise

You and I are called to serve. *"...It is not for you to know the time or times which the Father has put under his own authority."* (Acts 1:7, Lamsa)

Practicing His Presence

Yesterday was perhaps a busy and difficult day for you. Were there moments when you sensed He was really with you?

What About Failures?

When I want to visually picture the complexity of healing, I draw a circle. It represents the total person comprised of body, mind, and spirit. Within this circle I write numbers which represent the many facets of the individual.

$$1$$
$$2 \quad 3$$
$$5 \qquad 4$$
$$6 \quad 7$$
$$8$$

Thus 1 may represent the illness of terminal cancer. But that is not all the person has. He will possess fear (2), financial stress (3), pain (4), concern for loved ones (5), and many other problems. When he receives the ministry of healing, it is more than the physical problem of cancer which he is bringing to the Lord. He brings everything else of his life. It is *essential* that he does this and that he *realizes* the Lord is interested in all of his concerns.

Now, the person may not be healed of the cancer, but tremendously healed in the area of fear or pain. He may be healed of cancer, but often this healing does not take place. The important point is that he will always be helped one way or another when he turns to the Lord. God reaches out to some facet of his being, and blesses him.

PRAYER: *Thank you for the confidence I have that you are always there to help, O Lord. Amen.*

A Spirit Lifter

We often ask others to live up to higher standards than we are able to achieve ourselves.

A woman declared she was going to fire her maid for taking off with two of her towels.

"Which towels did she steal?" asked the concerned husband.

"The ones we got from that hotel in Kansas City."

God's Promise

You don't have to worry about the universe. The Lord made it, and He is going to care for it.

"All things were made by Him; and without Him was not anything made that was made." (John 1:3, KJV)

Practicing His Presence

This is going to be an exciting day for anyone willing to completely relinquish all unto the Lord. He will honor this spirit of commitment and let you know He is with you. His presence is yours.

What About Failures

There has never been anyone who accomplished more miracles than our Lord Jesus Christ. His miracles were expression of the power of the Lord in the body, mind, and spirit of many people. He even did many miracles in the realm of nature such as walking on water, feeding the 5,000, etc. Yet, in the midst of all of this, He stressed the spirit as the most important part of a person's life. He did not minimize the physical, but He did let His disciples know the importance of the spirit above everything else.

Of course, the people were astounded that from a few loaves and a few fish Jesus could feed 5,000. He plainly taught His disciples in the very face of this miracle, that they should rejoice the most with the fact that they can feast on the Bread of Life and the one who eats of Him shall never hunger.

It is my firm conviction that any Christian healing ministry must be based upon the Lord Jesus Christ. Our high calling is to lead individuals to Him and to have them healed in spirit. Anytime a person receives the ministry of healing in the Name of Jesus something happens to them. They receive additional strength. The spirit is made alive in Jesus. They are given the courage to face tomorrow.

There may be physical healing but even if there isn't, there *is* a facet of wholeness imparted. Something always happens when we look to Jesus. There are no failures.

PRAYER: *You never forsake nor abandon, O Lord. I give praise unto you for this truth. Amen.*

THE MINISTRY OF THE MASTER—THURSDAY
A Spirit Lifter

A woman called the fire department and said, "Come quick! My house is on fire!"

"How do we get there?" the dispatcher asked.

After a short pause she replied, "Don't you still have your little red truck?"

God's Promise

The Lord does not change nor fluctuate in His love or desires.

"For I am the Lord. I change not; therefore ye sons of Jacob are not consumed." (Malachi 3:6, KJV)

Practicing His Presence

Sometimes I have incidents which seem to cloud the reality of His presence. What do you do when this happens to you?

What About Failures

Matthew 9:1-8 is another important passage as we consider the aspect of failures. The man sick of palsy is brought to Jesus by his friends. They want him healed in body. The first thing Jesus did was to heal him of his sins.

Jesus had no more trouble with the miracle of forgiving sins than He did with the miracle of having the man rise and walk. He had no more problem with healing the physical than with forgiving sins. I feel it is important to see the part that the spiritual had to do with all of this. It is evident the crowd was touched by the man walking, but also the deep truth is the Lord's willingness to heal in all areas.

When I minister unto someone, I simply do not deal with the physical. The emotions are always involved. Past events and present pressures can be of greater importance than a physical affliction. Jesus can heal in these areas also.

Some years ago I was asked by one of our Elders to visit his terminally ill friend in the hospital. A few minutes after I had left the room, Jesus appeared to this man. He told me and his family that the Lord appeared and smiled at him. He knew, though all his life he had felt unworthy, that Jesus loved him and forgave him all his sins. He died three weeks later, but the ministry was no failure. He had received the greatest of healings.

PRAYER: *Thank you, Lord Jesus, for forgiving me of my sins. Amen.*

THE MINISTRY OF THE MASTER—FRIDAY
A Spirit Lifter

Oh, that we all could have as high of a self image as this gentleman. The dimwit's first day at work, the personnel manager told him: "It looks to me as if you've been fired from every job that you ever had." "Well, he bragged, "you have to admit that I'm no quitter!"

God's Promise

Many fail to appreciate the real freedom they must have and can have.

"...God will break the chains that bind his people and the whip that scourges them..." (Isaiah 9:4, LB)

Practicing His Presence

Frequently the degree of the awareness of the Lord is determined by how a person feels. This is natural, but somehow we must seek to sense His presence by faith. Feelings are too unreliable.

What About Failures

You are more than a physical being. I like the way this is taught in Genesis 1:27. *"So God created man in His own image, in the image of God created He him; male and female created He them."*

If we are created in the image of God we are more than flesh and bones. We are of the Lord. Genesis 2:7 — *"And the Lord God formed man of the dust of the ground, and breathed into his nostrils the breath of life; and man became a living soul."* The human race became more than an animal. The Spirit of the living God entered. The Spiritual is eternal. The Spirit is of God. In a sense, the body is the container of the Spirit. The Bible describes that the body is the temple of the Holy Spirit.

These well known truths help you and me to realize the wholeness we seek to minister is to the whole person. Our ministry of healing cannot be dependent upon the percentage of physical illness which is healed. We are not in the percentage business. We are in the obedience business. The Lord has called you and me to proclaim His truths. He applies them and blesses them according to His will.

Anytime you can get to the place where you seek Him and not what you feel He might have for you, the victory is yours. There are no failures with this faith and attitude. He is going to touch some areas of your life.

PRAYER: *It is you, O Lord, that I seek and not simply your gifts. Amen.*

THE MINISTRY OF THE MASTER—SATURDAY
A Spirit Lifter

Teacher: (patiently) "If one and one makes two, and two and two makes four, then how much does four and four make?"

Pupil: "That isn't fair, teacher! You answer the easy ones yourself and leave the hard ones for me!"

God's Promise

The Lord promises benefits to those who fear Him.

"The fear of the Lord is the beginning of knowledge, but fools scorn wisdom and discipline." (Proverbs 1:7, NEB)

Practicing His Presence

I believe you will have a great day if you are anticipating being aware of the Lord's presence. How did you do this yesterday?

What About Failures

I don't want to stress the spiritual to the extreme that you believe there are no physical healings. This is not true. There are many wonderful healings of the body. I have witnessed them. I have experienced them.

I will cite a recent example in my own life. Mary and I participated in the live broadcast over Channel 40 in the Pittsburgh, Pa. area. Rus Bixler and his wife, Norma, served as the host and hostess. We had returned from dinner and were walking into the studio. Rus said, "Don, what's wrong with your eye." I explained it was weak and would go shut in bright light. My left eyelid just automatically droops when I am in bright sunlight and it has been this way all my life.

He said we should ask Jesus to heal it. He stretched out his hand and gently touched my eye, and had about a 20 second prayer. It was immediately healed. I never realized how tired my right eye became of carrying the whole load. The left eye has remained normal and now the eye strain is gone.

This was a physical healing. There is no doubt about it. So, I am not saying it does not take place. I am trying to impart this week that something always takes place when you are ministered unto with prayer. There are no failures. He gives victory in some area of your life all the time.

PRAYER: *Thank you for the victory we have in you, O Lord. We praise you for your goodness. Amen.*

THE MINISTRY OF THE MASTER—SUNDAY
A Spirit Lifter

Two housewives chatted as they started lunch at the diner. "That neighbor of yours is quite a gossip."

"I don't like to say," said the other, "but when she came back from her vacation her tongue was awfully sunburned."

God's Promise

I need to be reminded often of the great power of the Lord.

"Is there a limit to the power of the Lord? You will see this very day whether or not my words come true." (Numbers 11:23, NEB)

Practicing His Presence

I don't know about you, but for myself, having to think each day about the reality of His presence is making His presence more of a reality.

What About Failures

Brian became a good friend of mine. This didn't happen until after he had witnessed in our church of a healing the Lord brought to him. He was a high school student and loved his studies and sports. He was good in both.

He began to notice he was not playing football as well as he thought he could. He began to stumble more and to lose the ball more. Time revealed he had leukemia and he was getting progressively worse. He was hospitalized. He was critically ill when his pastor witnessed to him concerning the Lord. He received Jesus as Saviour and Great Physician. He was immediately healed in many ways. The following Sunday his testimony in his church led to over 30 people turning to the Lord.

On one occasion, I heard his testimony and he mentioned that he felt he still had the leukemia, but it didn't really matter. He had Jesus. He had been healed in spirit. He knew the source of power and comfort.

He died several months after the last service where I had heard him. But to Brian, the Lord had not failed him. He had been healed. He had a wholeness few would ever achieve.

Jesus said, "I am come that they might have life." There are no failures in Jesus. Seek the Giver and not His gifts. Receive His healing in body, mind, and spirit.

PRAYER: *Thank you, Father, that our every action can be directed to leading others to you. Amen.*

THE FOCAL POINT OF PRAYER

It is my firm conviction that prayer is a life style. It is not a program to persuade God to perform for you. He is not about to be manipulated or influenced simply by your words or even your desires. It is not that He may not be pleased with your words.

I do not seek to beg God for particulars or for a particular way of meeting my problems. He has His ways and His timetable. He has His channels and His blessings to bestow.

It is my conviction that an individual or situation should be lifted into the light and love of the Lord. He is most willing to reach out and to help us. It is our privilege to permit his presence to flow through us and to serve as a channel of the release of the power of wholeness.

The fact is that we are more than channels. We are children of the Lord. The focal point of a child is relationship with the father.

I would encourage you this week to seek to develop the life style of lifting all things unto Him. It is not necessary that you relate every gruesome detail of the illness or situation. The Lord alone knows all the details of the individual unto whom you minister in prayer or the situation for which you are so concerned.

The wholeness which you desire and which you desire for others can only be imparted by the Lord. Therefore, I feel I cannot tell Him what to do nor tell Him when to do it. The focal point must always be my relationship to Him. This is the most important part of prayer.

If relationship with the Lord be kept as our focal point, then a great deal can be accomplished. Otherwise, we continue to offer vain repetition. The Lord is more than a help in a "pinch." He is your strength and your salvation at all times.

POINTS TO PONDER

1. Do you feel a particular disease or situation should be the focal point of your prayer life?
2. How do you really minister to another person or situation through prayer?
3. What is meant by the proper relationship with the heavenly Father?

THE FOCAL POINT OF PRAYER

1. That your _____ spirit, soul, and body be preserved. *I Thess. 5:23*
2. _____that you do not enter into temptation. *Mk. 14:38*
3. Pray for whatever you _____. *Mk. 11:24*
4. _____for those who despitefully use you. *Lu. 6:28*
5. Pray that labourers be sent into _____ harvest. *Lu. 10:2*
6. Pray to be _____ to stand before the Son of man. *Lu. 21:36*
7. Jesus said I have prayed for you that your _____ fail not. *Lu. 22:32*
8. Lord _____ his eyes that he may see. *II Kings 6:17*
9. Pray for the _____ of Jerusalem. *Ps. 122:6*
10. Pray that the_____of the Lord may have free course. *II Thess. 3:1*
11. Is any among you _____? Let him pray. *James 5:13*
12. Withal praying...that God would open unto us a door...to speak of the mystery of _____. *Col. 4:3*
13. If anyone lack wisdom let him ask of _____. *James 1:5*
14. Let the _____ be called and pray for the sick. *James 5:14*

DAILY SCRIPTURE

Mon.   Col. 4:26
Tues.   James 1:2-8
Wed.   Mk. 11:20-26
Thurs. Mk. 14:32-42
Fri.   Lu. 6:27-36
Sat.   II Kings 6:11-19
Sun.   Ps. 122:1-9

PRAYER CONCERNS

Your Family & Relatives
Government Leaders
Missionaries
For the Unbelievers
Churches & Denominations
Your Own Church
Prayer and Praise

NOTE: You will be spiritually strengthened by completing two questions each day, reading the suggested scripture, and ministering in prayer for the concerns of the day.

THE MINISTRY OF THE MASTER—MONDAY
A Spirit Lifter

Our appearance sometimes reflects which lifestyle we choose.
Wife: "You're on the wrong diet — you eat too much soldier food."
Husband: "What do you mean soldier food?"
Wife: "Everything you eat goes to the front."

God's Promise

I believe you will find comfort in the following promise today.
"The eternal God is your refuge." (Deuteronomy 33:27, TLB)

Practicing His Presence

Reflect on yesterday just a moment. Can you recall a specific incident which occurred which helped make His presence more real to you?

The Focal Point Of Prayer

If the focal point of your prayer life is relationship to the Father then your prayers are not limited to only the dramatic situations in life. Prayer will permeate every facet of your being and every detail of your life. It is this concept which brings a sacredness to all of life. It is then that you live and act with the sure knowledge that the Lord is concerned about every detail of your life.

I feel that the focal point of prayer must be correct or else prayer will be seen as a means of turning on the spiritual faucet of God's favor. This favor is sought by most people only in a dire emergency. (This approach takes out a great deal of the trust in the Lord's approach to life.) It leaves a life empty of devotion except during crisis.

The Lord Jesus tried to verbalize a life style when He said,

"Therefore I say unto you, what things soever ye desire, when you pray, believe that ye receive them, and ye shall have them." (Mark 11:24)

To believe was not an exercise to strengthen a particular part of a person's being. To believe was to commit all of your life unto the Lord. There are to be no reservations. He, and He alone, is the focal point of everything if prayer is to be as it ought to be.

PRAYER: *Father, I want to be in right relationship with you above all else. Amen.*

THE MINISTRY OF THE MASTER—TUESDAY
A Spirit Lifter

Developing a life style of prayer is a goal worth pursuing.

It was bedtime and little Marty had a question. "Look, Mom, why can't we pray once a week or once a month? Why do we have to ask every day for our daily bread?"

"Why," said his little brother, "so it'll be fresh."

God's Promise

What a wonderful promise! *"Open my eyes to see wonderful things in your Word."* (Psalms 119:18, TLB)

Practicing His Presence

I have sought to remind you each day to be aware of the presence of the Lord. Have you valued this experience?

The Focal Point Of Prayer

If I emphasize that the focal point of prayer is relationships, there are some who would feel this takes away the challenge of faith and trust. This is not true. I do not minimize faith. In fact, faith becomes an even greater part of your life. It becomes the very thing which determines all of your actions, hopes, and desires.

The words of our Lord are appropriate.

> *"...if you have faith as a grain of mustard seed, ye shall say unto this mountain, remove hence to yonder place; and it shall remove; and nothing shall be impossible unto you." (Mt. 17:20)*

I do not believe Jesus meant you could go out to an earthly mountain and speak the word and it would move into the sea. I believe He was pointing out the fact that if our focal point of prayer is correct, we will accomplish far more than we ever dreamed possible. We will be able to go forward to His glory and honor. We will be found faithfully seeking to serve and to glorify Him.

The real potential within each of us cannot be released without prayer. However, you don't have to beg God to have this happen. Neither do you have to pray "if it be thy will." It is His will that you fulfill your destiny.

PRAYER: *Father, may I realize the potential within my entire being. Help me to live to your glory. Amen.*

363

A Spirit Lifter

There are a large variety of jobs and activities to select and the following is a unique enterprise.

Hazel: "My brother's got a job. He's a midget window cleaner."

Edith: "What in the world is a midget window cleaner?"

Hazel: "He goes around cleaning people's eye glasses."

God's Promise

"For the oppression of the poor, for the sighing of the needy, now will I arise, saith the Lord; I will set him in safety from him that puffeth at him." (Psalm 12:5, KJV)

Practicing His Presence

Quiet yourself and listen to the Lord. Feel His presence engulfing your total being. Make this a wonderful day by walking in his light!

The Focal Point Of Prayer

There are specific things which the Lord mentions for which you can pray. I do not deny this. However, these things were said in the light of His constant and perfect relationship with His heavenly Father. He knew that His prime task was to keep close to the Father. There was no doubt about this. He put aside all other things that He might possess the relationship. He did not put his emphasis upon possessions, but upon keeping in tune with the Lord.

One of the specifics of prayer is for labourers.

"...The harvest truly is great, but the labourers are few: pray ye therefore the Lord of the Harvest, that he would send forth labourers into his harvest." (Luke 10:2)

Even though this is a specific, it is obvious that it teaches a heart cannot be touched except the spirit of the Lord move upon the person. All the logic in the world cannot convince a person to serve the Lord. It takes the touch of the Holy Spirit to bring this to fruition.

PRAYER: *Help me, Lord Jesus, to always keep in tune with your desire for my life. Amen.*

THE MINISTRY OF THE MASTER—THURSDAY
A Spirit Lifter

Doctor: "You've simply got to have more diversion and relaxation."
Patient: "But Doctor, I'm too busy!"
Doctor: " Nonsense! The ants are hard working creatures, but they take time to attend all the picnics!"

God's Promise

"And he said unto me, my grace is sufficient for thee: for my strength is made perfect in weakness. Most gladly therefore will I rather glory in my infirmities, that the power of Christ may rest upon me." (II Corinthians 12:9, KJV)

Practicing His Presence

It is amazing to me how often the Lord has felt near while I am involved in the ordinary experiences of life. The more I practice His presence, the more I behold Him in all things. Is this true of your life?

The Focal Point Of Prayer

If the focal point of your prayer life is the right relationship with God, then this takes a great burden off of you. It helps you to understand that every aspect of the universe is not dependent upon you. In fact, sometimes there are individuals who feel they must control everything which goes on around them. If they do not, then they become suspicious, sarcastic, and very negative. It is as if the world must move as they desire or not move at all.

I have known families where a member will feel it their bounden duty to protect every other member from many of the realities of life. The wife will never tell the husband of any difficulties with the children, finances, or neighbors. They say this would upset him too much. Or it might be the husband who feels he should not share problems at work or home with the wife. This effort to shield often leads to only more frustration.

The particulars in your life and in the lives of others will be cared for by the Lord. He isn't out to forsake you. He will not forsake you if you try to hide reality nor will he forsake you if you expose it. He is the Lord of all and desires that His children live triumphantly with Him.

PRAYER: *Father, thank you that you will never forsake me. I praise you for this promise. Amen.*

THE MINISTRY OF THE MASTER—FRIDAY
A Spirit Lifter

You have an unconditional guarantee of God's love.

Mr. Wise: "Didn't you guarantee when you sold me this car that you would replace anything that broke?"

Salesman: "Yes, sir. What is it?"

Mr. Wise: "Well, I want a new garage door."

God's Promise

Do you enjoy this brief time of reflecting upon God's promises?

"Trust in the Lord, and do good; so shalt thou dwell in the land, and verily thou shalt be fed." (Psalms 37:3, KJV)

Practicing His Presence

Continue to make your days exciting by consciously being aware of the spiritual aspect of life. I certainly enjoy this opportunity and hope you do too.

The Focal Point Of Prayer

I do not have to discern the Lord's will for many areas of life. It has already been revealed. There is the problem of discerning His will for me in the area of specific activity perhaps, but there is no doubt of His will in the general areas of life.

For instance, I don't feel I have to pray "Lord, help me to forgive John, if it be thy will" or "Lord, help me to accept your Son as my Lord and Savior, if it be thy will." How foolish to offer prayers like these. You and I both know He is always willing that we do these things.

Now, I feel the same thing is true in regard to any area of brokenness. It is His will that you restore the brokenness between you and Him and that you do this through His blessed Son. It is always His will that you restore brokenness between yourself and any other person. In like manner, I feel this way about any disease. The Lord's will is that you be whole.

I don't need to waste time or energy praying for His will to be done, but praying "according to His will." I put myself in the flow of His spirit. When ministering to a person or particular situation I seek to picture myself pouring buckets of love over them. I visualize the bucket being filled with the love of God and then I throw it all on the person or situation. I can see it covering and permeating. This helps me to put all things in proper perspective and to maintain the right relationship.

PRAYER: *Wherever I see disease help me, Father, to seek to bring your deliverance. Amen.*

THE MINISTRY OF THE MASTER—SATURDAY
A Spirit Lifter

You've no doubt heard the old adage "If you want it done right, do it yourself."

Absentminded Professor: "A collection agent at the door? Did you tell him I was out?"

Maid: "Yes sir, but he doesn't believe me."

Professor: "Well, then, I shall have to go and tell him myself."

God's Promise

"For whatever was written in earlier times was written for our instruction, that through perserverance and the encouragement of the Scriptures we might have hope." (Romans 15:14, NASV)

Practicing His Presence

Through what incident or person did you sense the Lord's presence yesterday? Did this awareness make your day more fulfilling?

The Focal Point of Prayer

The focal point of prayer is the right relationship with the Father. Once this is achieved and maintained the power released will be unbelievable. One of the things which would be accomplished is the evangelization of the world. Paul did not ask for more money, organization, or preaching skills to help him open doors for the message of the gospel. Paul asked for prayer. He asked for prayer from the believers who were encouraged to be right with God and others.

"Continue in prayer, and watch in the same with thanksgiving; withal praying also for us, that God would open unto us a door of utterance, to speak the mystery of Christ...(Col. 4:2, 3)

Each Thursday I suggest your ministry of prayer time be devoted to the unsaved individuals you know and to the many non-Christians throughout the world. I suggest you offer special prayer for the atheistic nations.

This ministry is needed because unless hearts are touched and changed by the Holy Spirit, they cannot comprehend the things of the Spirit. There is no greater work in the life of your Church than the work of intercession for others throughout the world.

PRAYER: *Father, help me to do the greatest work, which is prayer. Amen.*

THE MINISTRY OF THE MASTER—SUNDAY
A Spirit Lifter

"I don't see why you haggled so much with the tailor about the price — you'll never pay his bill any way," said the one vagabond to his friend.

"Yes, but you see, I'm conscientious. I don't want the poor fellow to lose more than is necessary."

God's Promise

"Let your mind dwell on whatever is true, noble, right, pure, lovely, admirable, excellent, praiseworthy." (Philippians 4:8, TLB)

Practicing His Presence

If you are like me, you sometimes experience incidents which seem to cloud the reality of His presence. What do you do when this happens?

The Focal Point Of Prayer

"Is anyone sick? He should call for the elders of the church and they should pray over him and pour a little oil upon him, calling on the Lord to heal him. And their prayer, if offered in faith, will heal him, for the Lord will make him well." (James 5:14, 15 TLB)

The focal point in the prayer ministry is the proper relationship with the Lord. Once having established this relationship, there are results forthcoming. One of the results is the healing of the sick.

Even in this portion from James, the relationship aspect is stressed. This is the step to wholeness which is needed. It is the step which restores relationships and sets in motion the spiritual laws which issue forth wholeness.

My encouraging you to believe the Lord for your wholeness and for the wholeness of loved ones is not an effort to replace physicians or any type of proper medical care. However, you have not done all you can do for yourself and others until you have received the ministry of prayer for your illness. It is into His light and love that we come and it is from Him that we receive all that is necessary.

PRAYER: *Father, may those who are ill seek the fullness of your ministry. Even the anointing with oil. Amen.*

GOD'S GRACE

You may be one who feels you do not deserve to be well. Your sins must be punished. I want this week to call to your attention that all healing is because of the grace of God. It is not because of your goodness nor mine. His wholeness is His gift. You are dependent on Him. The health you possess is from Him.

What is meant by grace?

First of all, it means God's unmerited love and favor. You do not deserve nor have you earned God's love and favor.

The family unit is a good example of God's love given so freely. Our children and grandchildren are born into the world. They are loved immediately. They have done nothing to merit this love. They cannot do us a kind deed. In fact, they are completely dependent upon us. Yet we love them so much we would literally die for them.

We love them, not because they worked for the love; but because they are ours and in a sense are born in our image. Thus the Lord God loves each of us.

Second, the word grace implies the divine influence acting upon your heart. You would never turn to the Lord if it were not for His grace working in and upon your heart. This tremendous truth is brought forth in the second verse of the song, "Amazing Grace."

"Twas grace that taught my heart to fear,
And grace my fears relieved;
How precious did that grace appear
The hour I first believed."

Third, grace implies that the Lord gives to you the desire to continue to live for Him. His grace enters every aspect of your life and makes it possible for you to live victoriously. It would be impossible to live the Christian life, if it were not for the grace of God.

I am grateful that His grace is always being imparted to me. He doesn't take time off nor become disgusted with me and withdraw His marvelous grace.

His desire for your wholeness does not change and by His grace He will grant it to you. Accept this promise from Him and rejoice in Him throughout this week. Remember,

"Every good gift and every perfect gift is from above, and cometh down from the Father of lights, with whom is no variableness, neither shadow of turning."
James 1:17.

POINTS TO PONDER

1. Is it possible to get something for nothing?
2. How do you feel most people expect to get to heaven?
3. What are some of the most prevalent things people do to be right in God's eyes?

GOD'S GRACE

1. The Grace of God has brought_____and has appeared unto _____. *Titus 2:11*
2. What did God do because of His love? _____ *John 3:16*
3. When did Christ die for us? _____ *Romans 5:8*
4. To whom does God give grace? _____ *I Peter 5:5*
5. How effective is the grace of God in difficult situations? _____
   _____ *II Corr. 12:9*
6. How are we saved?_____ *Acts 15:11*
7. How plentiful is the grace of our Lord? _____
   I Timothy 1:14
8. What would make Christ's death in vain?_____
   Gal. 2:21
9. What did Jesus taste for every person? _____
   Hebrews 2:9
10. If we are saved by grace it is impossible for us to be saved by? _____
    _____ *Romans 11:6*
11. Since we are justified by grace we become? _____
    Titus 3:7
12. What do we have through the riches of Christ's grace? _____
    _____ *Eph. 1:7*
13. What is it that cannot save us? _____ *Titus 3:5*
14. What does the love of God entitle us to be called? _____
    I John 3:1

DAILY SCRIPTURE

		PRAYER CONCERNS
Mon.	John 3:1-7	Your Family & Relatives
Tues.	Acts 15:1-11	Government Leaders
Wed.	Rom. 3:21-26	Missionaries
Thurs.	Rom. 5:15-17	For the Unbelievers
Fri.	Rom. 11:1-6	Churches & Denominations
Sat.	Titus 2:11-14	Your Own Church
Sun.	Phil 3:1-11	Prayer and Praise

NOTE: You will be spiritually strengthened by completing two questions each day, reading the suggested scripture, and ministering in prayer for the concerns of the day.

THE MINISTRY OF THE MASTER—MONDAY
A Spirit Lifter

On the first day of school, each kindergartner arrived home with a note from the teacher. It read, "Dear Parents: If you promise not to believe all your child says happens at school, I'll promise not to believe all he says happens at home."

God's Promise

Here is a wonderful promise from the Lord Jesus Himself.

"...lo, I am with you always, even unto the end of the world." (Mt. 28:20)

Practicing His Presence

I don't know about you, but for myself, having to think each day about the reality of His presence is making His presence more of a reality.

God's Grace

I am always intrigued at how difficult it is for us to accept the fact that we can never become pure enough, clean enough, smart enough, wealthy enough, etc. to merit God's love. It is by His grace we are made whole. Do you realize this is true of your body as well as your spirit?

My teaching this week stresses your relying upon the grace of God for all of your needs. Some feel they can't possibly ask the Lord for anything because they have not been living a good life. Or, they have not been going to church. The Good News of His wholeness is that you can call upon Him now, regardless of what you have been doing. His grace is extended to help you call upon him and to help you after you have called.

If any of us waited until we were perfect, we would never turn to Him. You and I are not able to clean up our act by ourselves. We need Him and we need Him desperately.

There is no way you can work to earn what He has so graciously given. If I could lift my little finger and thus assure my salvation, I could say I did something to merit God's favor. Since this is impossible, we can only rejoice in His goodness and mercy.

One day I spoke to a man who had been confined to bed for many months. He was so ill with cancer and suffering a great deal. He had lived a life which was anything but devout. He feared the Lord could never love him.

I brought the Good News of spiritual wholeness to him. The grace of God was manifest in his heart and he was wonderfully changed. God loves you as you are and His grace will help you to become what he wants you to be.

PRAYER: *Father, even though I am imperfect in so many ways may I realize you love me completely. In Jesus Name, Amen.*

THE MINISTRY OF THE MASTER—TUESDAY
A Spirit Lifter

It seems that several ghosts were scaring off any and all who sought to live in this old house. The community Pastor asked if he could spend the night in the house. The next day he came forth triumphant. When asked what he had done to get rid of the ghosts he replied:

"First I tried quoting scripture, but to no avail. Then prayer and still they stayed. Then I decided to pass the offering plate and they all disappeared."

God's Promise

Whatever your situation today this promise should pick you up.

"I am come that they might have life, and that they might have it more abundant." (John 10:10)

Practicing His Presence

It takes conscious effort to be aware of the Lord in the small things of life. How and where did you sense His presence yesterday?

God's Grace

Everyone at one time or another has a yearning for more meaning in life. Some may not think of this as a spiritual facet of life but I believe it is.

The grace of God abounds throughout the world and strives with all. How sad that many do not recognize the source nor the reality of this grace. You really cannot deny the spiritual part of your being. You may scoff at the idea, but this does not eliminate the reality. You are more than flesh and blood. God's grace has and will continue to tug at your heart and life.

A stranger approached a young lad and inquired as to what he was doing. The little boy said that he was flying a kite. The man rebuked him by saying he could see no kite. How could the kid say he was flying one, especially when it could not be seen?

The boy's answer is a classic. *"I know the kite is there because I can feel the tug."*

The trees on the hilltop may have prevented one from seeing the kite, but the evidence was positive that a kite was out there.

Thus in your life and mine it is evident that the tug of the Spirit is with us. The fullest meaning to life cannot be discovered unless we respond to that tug.

The unseen is really the most real. I feel that in your life today there are things tugging at the very core of your being. Why not acknowledge it is the wooing of the Holy Spirit and respond. You will never be really whole until you do.

PRAYER: *Lord, I turn to you for meaning in life which is beyond what I find in things and people. Thank you for giving me yourself. Amen.*

THE MINISTRY OF THE MASTER—WEDNESDAY
A Spirit Lifter

A little boy and his friend spent some days at grandma's. After they had gone home the one asked his friend why his grandma spent so many hours reading her Bible.

The grandson thinking that grandma was pretty old responded, "Well, you see, she is cramming for her finals."

God's Promise

Isn't this a great promise in the midst of your many needs and frustrations?

"But my God shall supply all your needs according to his riches in glory by Christ Jesus." (Phil. 4:19)

Practicing His Presence

An awareness of His presence will help you to maintain and/or regain wholeness.

How did you sense His presence in the events of yesterday?

God's Grace

Many are searching for the Lord frantically and fail to appreciate the fact that He is with them. It is as if they feel God is lost and they must find Him.

They evidently have not read the words of Jesus where he says, *"Repent, for the kingdom of heaven is at hand." (Mt. 4:17)* Also, *"...for behold, the kingdom of God is within you."*

The Lord is everywhere. He is with you today. He desires to help you see that you can be part of His kingdom.

Some act as if there are some places where the Lord is not and that in their condition He cannot meet the need. This is not true. He is in your joys. He is in your sorrows. He is in your victories. He is in your defeats. He is with you.

A man who prided himself in his ability to reason said to some youngsters, "I'll give you a dollar if you can tell me where God is." Most of them were puzzled as they tried to come up with an answer so they could get the dollar. Finally one little boy blurted out, "I'll give you two dollars Mr., if you can tell me where He isn't."

Now I ask you, which was the smarter of the two? I give my vote to the boy. He knew the Lord was everywhere and in every facet of life.

PRAYER: *Father, I need your Spirit to remind me constantly that you are with me constantly. I need you every hour. Amen.*

THE MINISTRY OF THE MASTER—THURSDAY
A Spirit Lifter

A fellow explained cynically why he refused to buy life insurance. "When I die I want it to be a sad day for everybody!"

God's Promise

"Blessed is the man that endureth temptaton: for when he is tried he shall receive the crown of life, which the Lord hath promised to them that love him." (James 1:12)

Practicing His Presence

Isn't the awareness of the things of the spirit important to you? How did you sense His presence yesterday? How did you realize the grace of God in your life?

God's Grace

This would be a most terrible world if it were not for the grace of God. I am grateful that He has not withdrawn His grace, but continues to extend it to His world. It is His grace which adds a positive flavor to all of creation and makes wholeness possible.

The class teacher had requested the students to write a definition of salt. She received all kinds of answers, but the most interesting stated:

"Salt is what spoils the soup when you leave it out."

I believe the presence of the Lord is what spoils your life when you leave Him out. We need to be reminded of this again and again.

His presence is not a once in a lifetime experience. He is with you always. The awareness on your part of His presence must be cultivated. Although He is everywhere at all times you will not be aware of this unless you consciously put forth effort to cultivate the reality of His presence.

You do not water a plant and believe it will live with no further watering. If you do this, it will be only a few days until it wilts and a few days later it is dead.

You do not eat a huge meal when you are twelve and conclude it to be sufficient until you are twenty. No, each day you partake of food. Each day you refuel your physical cells.

I believe that each day you must refuel the spiritual aspect of your being. You cannot adequately fulfill the Ministry of the Master without constant refueling.

This devotional book will help you to remain aware of the presence of the Lord. It is one way to help you cultivate the reality of His constant presence.

PRAYER: *Your presence is my hope and stay, Lord Jesus. Sometimes I feel you have deserted me and I pray these moments will not last long. Amen.*

THE MINISTRY OF THE MASTER—FRIDAY
A Spirit Lifter

Office Boy: "I think you're wanted on the phone."
Boss: "What do you mean you 'think'?"
Office Boy: "The voice said 'Is that you, you old fool?' "

God's Promise

I pray this promise speaks to your heart today:

"And let us not be weary in well doing for in due season we shall reap, if we faint not." (Galatians 6:9)

Practicing His Presence

Can you recall what you had for lunch yesterday? Can you recall a spiritual feast you had yesterday as you sensed His presence?

God's Grace

The wholeness you desire for yourself and others is from the Lord. Even His perfect healing which comes after the death of the believer is because of His grace.

The following story will perhaps illustrate better than anything I can write the fact that we are saved by the grace of God.

A man died and went to heaven. He eagerly knocked on heaven's door and was greeted by St. Peter. He felt he would be ushered into the glories of the blissful estate. He was astounded when Peter asked why he should be permitted to enter heaven. The man's answer was that he had been a very good man while on earth and therefore was worthy of a place in heaven.

Peter told him that good men had to accumulate 10,000 points before being admitted to heaven. The points were earned through good deeds. The gentleman confidently asked Peter to add up his total score.

A heavenly computer screen revealed the points needed, points earned, and the number still needed to reach the 10,000 mark. Peter asked him to start recounting some of his moral deeds and credit would be given for each. The man said, "I was always a good moral man." Peter's reply, "A quarter of a point." "I never cheated on my wife." A quarter of a point. "I was a boy scout leader for 25 years and a member of the Order of the Arrow." A quarter of a point. "I have a string of pins which almost reaches the floor of perfect Sunday School attendance." Quarter of a point.

The man named many more but had only gotten to about 4½ points. He was getting exceedingly nervous and frustrated. Finally in desperation he blurted out, "But by the grace of God no one would get into this place." Peter immediately replied, *"That's right, brother. Come on in."*

PRAYER: *It is your goodness in which I trust, Lord. All my righteousness appears soiled beyond redemption in your presence. Cleanse me. Amen.*

THE MINISTRY OF THE MASTER—SATURDAY
A Spirit Lifter

Lady at front door: "Will you donate something to the Old Ladies Home?"
Man answering the door: "With pleasure. Help yourself to my mother-in-law."

God's Promise

Please think of this promise throughout your day.

"And this is the promise that he hath promised us, even eternal life." (I John 2:25)

Practicing His Presence

Has it been the big events through which you have sensed His presence or have they been the common experiences of life?

God's Grace

I marvel at the moment by moment grace which the Lord extends to each of us. The grace we need is not dispensed months and years in advance. It is provided as needed and it exists in such abundance that there will always be plenty for everyone, and for all situations. There is an abundance for you today regardless of how you may feel.

A devout believer was asked if he had grace enough to be a martyr. I feel his reply was a classic. *"No! What do I want with a martyr's grace now? If I am ever called to be a martyr, then a martyr's grace will be given me. What I need now is grace for my present circumstances."*

Whatever trial you may be facing today, you will discover the Lord's grace to be sufficient. The afflictions of body, mind, and/or spirit cannot be so severe as to overcome you completely if you rely upon His grace.

The Lord is interested in the smallest details of your life. He made this very clear when he spoke of knowing the number of hairs on each head. He tells us that even the hairs of our head are numbered.

I would encourage you today to let the message of this sermonette become a channel for applying the grace of God to your every day experiences. This will help bring the wholeness you desire.

PRAYER: *It is a comfort to me, Lord Jesus, to know you care about every little thing which happens to me. Amen.*

THE MINISTRY OF THE MASTER—SUNDAY
A Spirit Lifter

May this little story bring some sparkle to your life. I guess the moral is that it is all in how you interpret a situation.

A lady phoned the dog pound and asked that they send someone to her home right away.

She reported there was a nasty old salesman sitting in a tree teasing her poor German Shepherd.

God's Promise

What an encouraging promise!

"And we know that all things work together for good to them that love God, to them who are the called according to his purpose." (Romans 8:28)

Practicing His Presence

As you use this devotional book consciously practice His presence. May you seek to quiet your mind, heart and body to hear "the still small voice" speak to you.

God's Grace

Many years ago after the death of a devout believer, the following words were found among her papers.

"O Lord, give me grace to feel the need of thy grace, give me grace to ask for thy grace, and when in thy grace, thou has given me grace, give me grace to use thy grace."

I feel this is one of the most lovely prayers I have ever read. It is a perfect one to close this week of my endeavors to present facets of God's grace.

It is my prayer that you will become more appreciative of the fact that all that you are or ever hope to be is of the Lord. There is no way that we can take credit for accomplishments. We give to Him the glory.

There are no self-made individuals. Every one of us has been and is dependent upon others as well as the good Lord. Every person has had his/her diapers changed by someone. We all came helpless into the world and were utterly dependent upon others. We all are still dependent upon the Lord and others.

The message of God's grace is thrilling when it burns deep into the heart and plunges to the very core of our being. An understanding of God's grace is a big step toward wholeness of body, mind, and spirit.

PRAYER: *Your grace burns deep within my soul, dear Lord, and for this I am grateful. Help me not to depend upon my own merits. Amen.*

GOD'S GIFT

Isn't St. Augustine's statement a beautiful one? *"God loves each one of us as if there were only one of us to love."*

I know you agree with me that God's love cannot be separated from His gift and neither can His gift be separated from His love. The two blend together perfectly and it would be impossible to remove either one and still have God be God.

He is a loving father who wants to give and give and give.

The gift I want to emphasize this week is that of eternal life. It is the gift the Lord Jesus made possible and has so graciously offered to all of us. This gift is not simply a promise of good things to come. It is the reality of good things now. The wholeness which our Lord proclaimed involves eternal life.

Eternal life implies more than quantity of time. Even more important is the quality that is involved in eternal life.

Eternity is no time because it is all time. It is all time because it is no time. It is always NOW. This is one of the reasons we can proclaim wholeness with confidence.

Jesus had capsuled time into the NOW. He can teach the reality of the Kingdom of God being here now. You are part of that Kingdom. You possess a quality of life which is God's gift to you.

I must stress that eternal life is more than *"pie-in-the-sky after you die."* This takes care of quantity of time in the future.

You need to hear that eternal life is also *"steak-on-the plate while you wait."* This graphically conveys the quality of time in the NOW of your life.

It is plain that eternal life does not begin at the point of your death. It has begun now in your life. Jesus tells us how wonderfully He is at work in each life now when He said,

"I am come that you might have life and that you might have it more abundant." John 10:10

This week may you meditate upon the gift of eternal life which is yours and which has worked the miracle of His presence and wholeness within you.

POINTS TO PONDER

1. Can a gift be given with no strings attached?
2. How do you convey to another person the concept of eternity?
3. How does a person express appreciation for a gift?

Daily Bible Study and Daily Prayer Concerns
GOD'S GIFT

1. What is God's gift? _____ *Rom. 6:23*
2. How is this gift received? _____ *Rom. 6:23*
3. How does Paul describe God's gift? _____
   II Cor. 9:15
4. What can a person receive except it be given from heaven? _____
   _____ *John 3:27*
5. How are you saved? _____ *Eph. 2:8*
6. What is the gift of God? _____ *Eph. 2:8*
7. What shall the Lord give to His people? _____
   Jer. 24:7
8. What shall the Lord put within His people? _____
   Ezek. 11:19
9. What shall the faithful be given? _____ *Rev. 2:10*
10. The Lord will freely give us _____. *Rom. 8:32*
11. God's gift of grace has come to us by _____.
    Rom. 5:15
12. What was the Lord willing to give the woman at the well? _____
    _____ *John 4:10*
13. What was God's greatest gift to the world? _____
    John 3:16
14. What did the Lord say He would give for the life of the world? _____
    _____ *John 6:51*

DAILY SCRIPTURE

Mon.   Rom. 6:15-23
Tues.   John 4:1-42
Wed.   II Cor. 9:10-15
Thurs. John 3:25-36
Fri.   Jer. 24:1-7
Sat.   Rev. 2:8-11
Sun.   Eph. 2:1-10

PRAYER CONCERNS

Your Family & Relatives
Government Leaders
Missionaries
For the Unbelievers
Churches & Denominations
Your Own Church
Prayer and Praise

NOTE: You will be spiritually strengthened by completing two questions each day, reading the suggested scripture, and ministering in prayer for the concerns of the day.

THE MINISTRY OF THE MASTER—MONDAY
A Spirit Lifter

The grocery clerk overheard two nuns debating as to which one should drive back to the convent. One said, "You drive, Sister Luke, and I'll pray." "What's the matter?" Sister Luke countered. "Don't you trust my praying?"

God's Promise

Please remember this today:

"And He said to me, My grace is sufficient for thee: for my strength is made perfect in weakness. Most gladly therefore will I rather glory in my infirmities that the power of Christ may rest upon me." (2 Corinthians 12:9)

Practicing His Presence

Believe as you practice His presence that He is with you every minute. It will make a difference in your day. Share with someone how you are seeking to practice His presence.

God's Gift

How long is eternity? How can it be measured? Is it possible to grasp the concept of living on and on and on?...

Believe me, it is difficult for my mind to grasp the fact that there is no end to time. Yet the truth is the ages will never end and the believer is forever with the Lord.

I find the following illustration to be of help to me when I try to contemplate eternity. It presumes that human beings can continue to make trips to the moon.

A crew goes to the moon and returns with a cubic inch of moon rock. A thousand years later another crew goes to the moon and returns with a cubic inch of moon rock. A thousand years later another expedition secures a cubic inch of the moon.

These voyages every thousand years continue until the entire moon has been carried to the earth. It has taken millions and millions of years and millions of trips. Even after the job has been completed eternity would have just begun.

The receiving of eternal life is important. It is this gift the Lord Jesus wants to give to you. In the light of the quality of life you desire now and the quantity of time you will receive later it is a gift worth receiving.

PRAYER: *I reach out by faith and receive and acknowledge your gift of eternal life, Lord Jesus. Thank you for it. Amen.*

THE MINISTRY OF THE MASTER—TUESDAY
A Spirit Lifter

"Mom," said the little boy, "I'm going to play elephant in the zoo, and I need your help."

"Okay," said the mother. "But what can I do?"

"You pretend you're the lady who comes to the cage and gives the elephant cookies and candy."

God's Promise

"Trust in the Lord, and do good; so shalt thou dwell in the land, and verily thou shalt be fed." (Psalm 37:3)

Practicing His Presence

May I ask: Are you seeking to consciously practice His presence? How did you do this yesterday?

God's Gift

I don't want to leave the impression that eternity is only a quality of life. There is quantity to it. There is the hope we have in Christ Jesus. There is the joy of the promised bliss.

Many years ago, a pastor announced a coming message concerning heaven. He received a letter from a dear soul which contained the following words:

Next Sunday you are to talk about heaven. I am interested in that land because I hold a title to a bit of property there. I've held it for over 55 years. I did not buy it — it was given to me without money and without price. The donor purchased it for me for the cost of a tremendous sacrifice.

It is not a vacant lot. For more than a half century I have been sending materials for which the greatest architect and builder of the universe has been building a home for me. This home will never need remodeled or repaired because this home will suit me perfectly. It will never grow old. Termites can never undermine its foundation because it rests upon the rock of ages. Fire cannot destroy it. Floods cannot wash it away.

I hope to hear your sermon, but I have no assurance that I shall be able to do so. My ticket to heaven has not been dated — I may not be here when you are talking next Sunday. I shall meet you there some day.

This person believed Jesus when He said, *"I go to prepare a place for you..."* This is all part of the gift of the eternal life. It is your gift from Jesus.

PRAYER: *Thank you for the touch of homesickness for heaven which you have placed in my soul. I am thankful for this hope. Amen.*

THE MINISTRY OF THE MASTER—WEDNESDAY

A Spirit Lifter

A pastor traveling for the first time on a jet seemed a little nervous. The stewardess asked if he cared for a drink.

"No thanks," he said. "We're too close to the head office."

God's Promise

"Therefore, I say unto you, what things so ever ye desire, when ye pray, believe that ye receive them, and ye shall have them." (Mark 11:24)

Practicing His Presence

You have been daily reminded to be aware of the presence of our Lord. How do you find this taking place and what is it doing to you?

God's Gift

The gift of eternal life is yours, not so much because you find the path leading to it, but because you enter the door. The door is not paneled by your personality, nor does it swing on the hinges of your good works.

The door to eternal life is a Person. The way to the abundant life is through relating to that Person and to His Father. This is our high calling and it is the invitation of that Person, Jesus.

On one of our journeys to the Holy Land, Mary and I and the group beheld hundreds of sheep and goats surrounding a watering trough. There were the women and men caring for these animals. It was as if we had been transported back several centuries to the Old Testament times.

My mind pictured many scenes as we watched the animals being watered. One of the scenes was the story I had read of the shepherd building a temporary fold for his sheep. They would be brought to this fold at night. The fold had no gate that could be opened or closed. The opening must be guarded. The shepherd himself lay down in front of the opening. He was the door. Sheep could not get out and preying animals could not get into the fold.

Is this not a beautiful picture of Jesus Christ? He is the door through whom we enter into eternal life. He not only gives the gift, but He is the gift. He is the door to your wholeness.

PRAYER: *Lord Jesus, I know you are the door to eternal life. I want to enter into your very being as you have entered into mine. Amen.*

THE MINISTRY OF THE MASTER—THURSDAY
A Spirit Lifter

Three-year-old Jennifer loves dogs. One day while she was playing in front of her home, she saw a huge boxer down the street and ran toward him, shouting, "Hi, doggie! Hi doggie!" The dog bounded to her, stopping just when they were nose to nose. She gazed up at him a moment with a puzzled expression, then breathed, "Hi, horsey!"

God's Promise

Why not keep this upon your heart throughout the day?

"For his anger endureth but a moment; in His favour is life: weeping may endure for a night, but joy cometh in the morning." (Psalm 34:19)

Practicing His Presence

Isn't it hard to sometimes remember a specific incident in which you really felt His presence? It is helpful to be reminded of the spiritual awareness you should develop. Were you aware of His presence yesterday?

God's Gift

The very nature of eternal life includes the concept of quality as well as quantity. The gift of eternal life is given to enrich you and not to curtail your joys.

There are more facets to the gift of eternal life than the promise that you are going to heaven when you die. It is also that you can have heaven in your soul while you are living here on earth.

There is the story of the depressed, dejected, cast down and wretched individual coming to Caesar to seek permission to commit suicide. He desired to kill himself and to end his misery. Caesar looked at that wrecked bit of humanity and said, *"Have you ever been alive?"*

This same question could be directed to many Christians. Have you ever realized there is an abundant life in Christ? If not, remember it is God's gift to you. Why not open the gift and rejoice today? Make today a better day than yesterday.

The Lord has given you a heart to know Him. He has also given to you all that is needed to enjoy Him. Claim your full rights in His Kingdom today.

PRAYER: *Thank you, Father, for your joy unspeakable. It lies deep in my heart and no one has been able to steal it. Amen.*

THE MINISTRY OF THE MASTER—FRIDAY
A Spirit Lifter

On the way home from church on Ash Wednesday, little Johnny queried his mother: "Is it true, Mommy, that we are made of dust?" "Yes, Darling." "And we go back to dust again when we die?" "Yes, dear." "Well, Mommy, when I said my prayer last night and looked under the bed, I found someone who is either coming or going."

God's Promise

Regardless of how depressed you may become at times, you are still very important in the eyes of God.

"Know ye not that ye are the temple of God, and that the Spirit of God dwelleth in you?" (I Corinthians 3:16)

Practicing His Presence

Practice makes perfect is what I was taught. If this be so, then you should be doing better with our awareness of the Lord. How were you made aware of His presence yesterday?

God's Gift

There is a greater quality to one's life, when seen in the light of eternity. It is when humanity is lowered to the realm of the animal that unhuman acts take place.

It is when individuals are seen as children of God, and that our actions toward others are weighed in the light of eternity, that the highest achievements are made.

On the triple doorway of the Cathedral of Milan, there are three inscriptions above the three splendid arches.

Carved over the one is a beautiful picture of roses and underneath the inscription,

"All that pleases is but for a moment."

Over the second arch is a sculptured cross and underneath the words,

"All that which troubles is but for a moment."

The great central entrance bears this inscription,

"That only is important which is eternal."

I feel this powerful message should be appropriated to your life. You have decisions to make today. Make them in the light of eternity. You will perform many acts today and it is my prayer that they be done in the light of eternity.

The gift of eternal life becomes very real when you consider it influences the quality and quantity of your life, and that it has a bearing on your wholeness of body, mind, and spirit.

PRAYER: *Father, help me to think and act today in the light of eternity. Thank you for so doing. Amen.*

THE MINISTRY OF THE MASTER—SATURDAY

A Spirit Lifter

When one of the vice presidents at a bank died, a young assistant went to his boss and inquired: "Do you think I could take his place?"

"It's okay with me," said the boss, "if you can arrange it with the undertakers."

God's Promise

Here is a wonderful promise from the Lord Jesus Himself.

"...if ye had faith as a grain of mustard seed, ye might say unto this sycamine tree, be thou plucked up by the root, and be thou planted in the sea; and it should obey you." (Luke 17:6)

Practicing His Presence

There are so many things to distract me from the life of the spirit. My guess is that you too have a hard time keeping in tune with the Spirit. How did you do yesterday as far as His presence and your awareness of this is concerned?

God's Gift

"Saturday Night is The Loneliest Night of the Week," is the title of a song which was very popular several years ago. This appraisal of Saturday does not have to be your Saturday. It can be another day lived victoriously for your Lord. It can be a time when you close the week with grateful heart and look forward to rejoicing with other believers tomorrow.

Every day is made exciting when you keep your heart and mind on the Lord. The possessions and cares of this world will not satisfy. He does and will satisfy as you permit Him to do so.

John Wesley was a wise man. He was visiting in a nobleman's home. It was beautiful and spacious. The estate was landscaped in breathtaking beauty. After he was there for awhile, he said to the nobleman,

"I, too, have a relish for these things, but there is another world."

This is the truth I have sought to impart this week. There is another world. This other world of the Spirit improves the quality of all your life and guarantees that you will never die. The gift of eternal life is yours — now and forever.

PRAYER: *Thank you, Father, for planting an understanding of the things of the Spirit in my heart. Amen.*

THE MINISTRY OF THE MASTER—SUNDAY
A Spirit Lifter

The junior executive arrived at the office after his vacation, tired and haggard. "What's the matter?" asked his secretary, "Vacation too much?"

"I guess so," was the reply.

"With the kids taking vitamins and me taking tranquilizers, it was a losing battle all the way."

God's Promise

Here is a wonderful promise.

"*...I am the bread of life: he that cometh to me shall never hunger; and he that believeth in me shall never thirst.*" (John 6:35)

Practicing His Presence

It is the quality of life which is important. You will increase the quality through conscious awareness of His presence. How did you do yesterday?

God's Gift

Are you ready to share the gift of life with others? You will cross paths with many people today, and in the days ahead. I pray that the quality of your life and the excitement of His presence will lead you to want to share His gift of eternal life. Perhaps you can provide someone with this daily devotional book to help them think upon the things which are eternal.

Whatever you do and however you do it, I do hope you will spread the message of the gift of eternal life. Isn't it great that we have the privilege to share with others what we have received for ourselves?

The legend tells of the man who had ascended the ladder from earth to heaven. He excitedly and expectantly knocked at the door. The voice within responded, *"Who is there?"* Proudly the man gave his name. *"Who is with you?"* asked the heavenly door keeper. *"No one,"* answered the man. *"I am all alone."* *"Sorry,"* replied the guardian angel of the door to heaven, *"but we are instructed never to open these gates for a single individual. Go, return and bring another soul with you and both of you will gain entrance to the city of eternal life."*

The wholeness you possess becomes even more precious when shared with another. A gift given is a gift received.

PRAYER: *Father, I pray for the wisdom, the courage, the knowledge, and the willingness to share the Good News of the gift of eternal life with others. Amen.*

GOD'S HEALTH CARE PLAN

God's grace and His gift of eternal life must be seen in the light of the fact that each of us has been created in the image of God. Every person is important. Every person is more than simply an animal. Each person is spirit as well as body. There may be theories about creation which omit the Lord and His spirit. However, as believers we know that we are more than cells. The spirit of life is kin to the One who is life, the Lord Himself.

Many years ago, I came across a poem which I feel teaches volumes about the sacredness of each person and concerning our being created in the image of God. I thought you would enjoy it.

Three monkeys once dining in a coconut tree
Were discussing some things they had heard true to be
What do you think, now listen you two
Here all you monkeys is something that cannot be true.
That humans descended from our pure race
Why it's simply shocking, a terrible disgrace.
Whoever heard of a monkey deserting his wife
Leave a baby starve and ruin its life.
And have you ever known of a mother monk
To leave her darling with a stranger to bunk.
Their babies are handed from one to another
And scarce ever know of the love of a mother.
And I've never known a monkey so selfish to be
As to build a big fence around the coconut tree.
So other monkeys can't get a wee taste
But would let all the coconuts here go to waste.
Starvation would force you to steal from me.
And here's another thing a monkey won't do
Seek a bootlegger's shanty and get in a stew.
Carouse and go on a whoopee, disgracing his life
Then reel madly home and beat up his wife.
They call this all pleasure, and make a big fuss.
They descended from something, but brother not from us.

Being created in His image involves understanding and truth. It calls us to seek that which is beautiful, creative, and right.

POINTS TO PONDER

1. What do you feel is meant when it is stated that man was created in the likeness of God?
2. Are most individuals able to grasp the fact that someday they will die?
3. How important, really, is an individual?

CREATED MAN

1. God created man in _____. *Gen. 1:27*
2. Man was created in the _____. *Gen. 5:1*
3. God breathed into man the _____ and he became a living _____. *Gen. 2:7*
4. God made man a little lower than _____. *Psalms 8:5*
5. Man was crowned with _____. *Psalms 8:5*
6. What is the candle of the Lord? _____ *Pro. 20:27*
7. What will every person see? _____ *Psalms 89:48*
8. The treasure of spiritual life is contained in _____ *II Cor. 4:7*
9. The one appointment all must keep is to _____. *Heb. 9:27*
10. Your days are as _____. *Psalms 103:15*
11. Through Christ, death is swallowed up in _____. *I Cor. 15:54*
12. A person's days are swifter than a _____ *Job. 7:6*
13. Individuals should fear him who can destroy both _____ _____. *Matt. 10:28*
14. Each person is worth more than the _____ *Matt. 16:26*

DAILY SCRIPTURE

Mon.	Gen. 1:26-31
Tues.	Psalms 8:1-9
Wed.	Psalms 89:46-52
Thurs.	II Cor. 4:7-18
Fri.	Heb. 9:23-28
Sat.	Matt. 10:26-33
Sun.	Matt. 16:24-28

PRAYER CONCERNS

Your Family & Relatives
Government Leaders
Missionaries
For the Unbelievers
Churches & Denominations
Your Own Church
Prayer and Praise

NOTE: *You will be spiritually strengthened by completing two questions each day, reading the suggested scripture, and ministering in prayer for the concerns of the day.*

THE MINISTRY OF THE MASTER—MONDAY
A Spirit Lifter

Mother (to small son): "Now Johnnie, you can't have the hammer to play with. You'll hit your fingers."

Johnnie: "No I won't, Mummie. Doris is going to hold the nails."

God's Promise

"And God shall wipe away all tears from their eyes; and there shall be no more death, neither sorrow, nor crying, neither shall there be any more pain: for the former things are passed away." (Revelation 21:4)

Practicing His Presence

Busy, busy, busy. Yet, in the midst of the ocean of activity is a quiet island. It is shaded by the presence of the Lord. Did you find any of this shade yesterday?

Created Man

Plato is reported to have defined man as *"a two-legged animal without feathers."*

A wag, in response to Plato, plucked the feathers from a rooster and holding him up for all to see cried out, *"Behold, Plato's man."*

There are those who see individuals as only creatures. They do not see them as created in the image of God.

The Bible, from the very beginning, teaches us that a person is more than a body. There is the spirit, which is more real and which is eternal.

Humans are lifted above the animals. Jesus reveals this through His temptations in the wilderness. He acknowledged that we do not live by bread alone. There is more to life than filling the stomach.

This week, I pray you will seek to see yourself as a child of God. Also, that you will seek to look at others in the light of the truth that they, too, are created in the image of God. You cannot treat others as if they were things. You must act toward them as sacred revelations from God.

PRAYER: *Father, you have created me in Your image. Grant me the willingness to accept and believe this truth always. Amen.*

THE MINISTRY OF THE MASTER—TUESDAY
A Spirit Lifter

An elderly lady who was visiting the Capitol Building for the first time went in to hear a debate which she listened to with puzzled interest.

"You know," she observed, "I'm sure if the nation's politicians were laid end to end, they would point in all directions!"

God's Promise

Why not claim this promise today?

"And we know that all things work together for good to them that love God, to them who are called according to His purpose." (Romans 8:28)

Practicing His Presence

Through what incident or individual did you sense the presence of the Lord yesterday? How did this affect you?

Created Man

You are amazing! Has anyone ever told you that? If they have, they are correct. If no one has, someone should and this person would be 100% correct.

Every person is a wonder of the all wise and all powerful God. I like what Carlisle said, "We are the miracle of miracles. The great inscrutable mystery of God." Isn't that exciting? And you have felt at times you weren't worth anything. This is not true. In fact, Jesus said each person is worth more than the whole world. You are valuable.

The valuable things in life are protected, cared for, appreciated and treated with respect. Isn't it about time that we began to look at ourselves and others in the light of the value the Lord places upon us?

Consider the fact that scientists would have to build a computer the size of three football fields in dimension and ten stories high to duplicate your brain, and even then the computer would not be as efficient as your few ounces of brains.

You are indeed smarter than you look and act at times. You are the amazing created child of God.

PRAYER: *May my amazing mind be renewed each day with the thoughts of your goodness and mercy toward me, O Lord. Amen.*

A Spirit Lifter

One editor of a small town paper, who became irritated with the number of complaints following his editorials, decided to run the Ten Commandments in place of his next editorial. A few days later a letter arrived reading: Cancel my subscription. You're getting too personal!

God's Promise

Why not consider these words throughout your day?

"For all the promises of God are in Him, Amen, unto the glory of God by us." (II Corinthians 1:20)

Practicing His Presence

I find the pilgrimage of being aware of His presence exciting. I trust you are finding it this way? May you keep sensitive to the Spirit.

Created Man

The scholarly Baillie has said, *"Each person should think of himself/herself as an act of God. The mind, a thought; and the life, a breath of God."*

This concept would change your attitude and mind, toward all of life. Too often, the negative is too prone to reign in the heart. It is then that some think people can be trampled underfoot and manipulated like animals. This practice is not of the Lord.

The child of God should know that faith is not an added dimension which can or cannot be present. Faith is the very essence of life. Since we are created in the image of God, it is our very nature to be concerned about the things of the spirit. We may abuse this nature. We may neglect to exercise faith. We may at times act like animals. However, this does not change the reality of the situation.

The Lord has created you for the things of the spirit. He wants you to constantly think of yourself as His child and to live accordingly.

PRAYER: *Father, as you have put the breath of life in me may I seek to live life abundantly through your Son the Lord Jesus Christ. Amen.*

THE MINISTRY OF THE MASTER—THURSDAY
A Spirit Lifter

Bill and Charlie were in a store when a hoodlum dashed in and announced, "This is a hold-up!"

While he was searching the patrons for valuables, Charlie nudged his friend and whispered, "Take this."

"Take what?" asked Bill.

"The $25.00 I owe you."

God's Promise

Remember these important truths today:

"Many are the afflictions of the righteous; but the Lord delivereth them out of them all. (Psalm 30:5)

Practicing His Presence

Yesterday was no doubt a busy and difficult day for you. Were there any times when you sensed He was really with you?

Created Man

I wish I could convey to many of my friends that they are missing out on life because they are neglecting the One who is the Life.

The physical sciences cannot provide all of the answers. Individuals must get back to their maker if they are to be tuned to the Spirit and equipped to meet the challenges of the day. No one else can do for them what their Maker can do.

It is reported that Alexander, the crown prince of Russia, purchased a very exquisite and complicated watch on one of his visits to England. He had a lot of money and he could purchase a watch which was one of a kind.

The watch was intricate. It was so mechanically different that when it broke down, there was not a person in Russia who could repair it. It had to be returned to its maker for service.

You are a great deal more complicated than a watch. There is only One who can bring the repairs you need. He made you. He can remake you. He can repair the broken heart. He can restore the diminished soul. He can renew the wounded spirit. He can bring the wholeness you desire and need.

PRAYER: *Father, help me to look unto you for the deep meaning to life instead of the many things of man's accomplishments. Amen.*

THE MINISTRY OF THE MASTER—FRIDAY
A Spirit Lifter

While riding on a bus, a little old lady noticed three children and told their mother: "I'd give 10 years of my life to have such fine and nice looking children." "That," the mother responded, "is just what it cost me."

God's Promise

The Lord promises divine care in sickness.

"The Lord will strengthen him upon the bed of languishing: thou wilt make all his bed in his sickness." (Psalm 50:15)

Practicing His Presence

Do you find that an awareness of His presence is determined to some degree by how you feel? Was there any time yesterday when you knew the spiritual life was the most important aspect of your being?

Created Man

Even though we are created in the image of God, we do not live in this life forever. The years pass very rapidly. Even if you live to be 150 years old, it is but a short time in the light of eternity.

The significance of each person is not dependent upon the length of your days. The years pass so rapidly. The older you become, the faster the time flies. I feel one of the reasons for this is that we have so many signs and events to consider as we get older.

For instance, I have traveled over 700 miles per hour in a jet airplane. However, it seemed as if I could get out and walk faster than we were traveling. The reason for this apparent slow pace was that we were 37,000 feet above the earth. There were no points of reference.

I have traveled 85 miles an hour in a car. The telephone poles, other cars, etc., were all points of reference which made it appear that we were really going fast.

Thus, as we get older, we have many points of reference. Children, friends, events are all points of reference for us. Birthdays, anniversaries, deaths, promotions, graduations, etc., are all points of reference. A second is still a second. A minute is still a minute. Yet, seen and experienced in the light of all that has happened in our lives, these seconds and minutes appear to pass more rapidly.

Your life is like the weaver's shuttle. It passes very fast. It is imperative that it be seen in the light of your being created in His image and to His glory.

PRAYER: *Thank you, Father, that you care for me until my mission is completed here on earth and that you have given to me the hope and assurance of eternal life. Amen.*

THE MINISTRY OF THE MASTER—SATURDAY

A Spirit Lifter

When the teacher asked the little boy if he were animal, vegetable or mineral, he answered proudly, "Vegetable. I'm a human bean."

God's Promise

"When thou passest through the waters I will be with thee; and through the rivers they shall not overflow thee; when thou walkest through the fire thou shalt not be burned; neither shall the flame kindle upon thee." (Isaiah 43:2)

Practicing His Presence

Are you anticipating being aware of His presence throughout this day? If so, I believe it will be a great day for you.

Created Man

I don't want to emphasize your being created in the image of God to the point that I fail to point out the reality of your humanity. This treasure of the spirit is contained in an earthen vessel.

Historians give us some insights concerning Roman generals which are very revealing. It is recorded that in the triumphant marches of the returning victorious general would be mingled reminders of his frailties.

The crowds would respond with shouts and applause of admiration as the general rode by in his chariot and with a crown on his head. However, they would also cry out in the midst of their praises these words of stark reality. *"Look behind you and remember you will die."*

Further, at the end of the procession would be the rejoicing soldiers who had fought under his command. They sang the general's praises, but they also shouted insults to keep the general humble. They did not want him to develop too much pride.

The frailty of life demands the life of faith. The power and purpose is not in you, but in the God who created you.

PRAYER: *May I seek to be humble before you, Lord, and to acknowledge my frailties and shortcomings. Amen.*

THE MINISTRY OF THE MASTER—SUNDAY
A Spirit Lifter

After crawling into Grandfather's lap, little Freddie asked, "Were you in the ark, Grandpa?" The grandfather replied, "Why, no son." The youngster persisted, "Then why weren't you drowned?"

God's Promise

"Behold, I give unto you power to tread on serpents and scorpions, and over all the power of the enemy; and nothing shall by any means hurt you." (Luke 10:19)

Practicing His Presence

Sometimes I have incidents which seem to cloud the reality of His presence. What do you do when this happens to you?

Created Man

Who are you? What are you? These and other questions arise in the heart and mind of many persons. I believe the Bible has the best answers to these questions. You are created in the image of God. Your life is important because He is all and all.

Richard Cole wrote,

"Man is like a book. His birth is the title page, his baptism the preface, his youth the table of contents, his life the body of the volume, his blunders the errors, his repentance the correction of them. Men, like books, are large and small, folios and tiny volumes. Some are better bound than others and some that lack in show make up in durability of binding and in the value of their contents. Some are pious, some are profane. Some are full of wisdom and some full of folly. But each must have a final page with the closing word 'final'."

Created man does not face death. Jesus said you should choose death that you might have life. He was speaking of dying spiritually that you might live to the wholeness of a quality of life reserved only for the devout believer.

PRAYER: *Father, I want to understand your Book. I want to study and to know your written Word as well as to know Christ the Living Word. Amen.*

Theme for the Week
FALLEN HUMANITY

The wholeness which once existed ended. The world which opened to Adam and Eve was shattered by the Fall. The sin which plagues us today entered and will be a part of life until Christ reigns supreme and puts all manner of evil under his feet.

However, at the same time we are called to a wholeness few experience to the fullest. The Fall left an impact which is inescapable. However, it did not completely defeat. The Lord God provided a way of deliverance.

I feel it is important for us to acknowledge the sinfulness of man if we are going to fully appreciate the sacredness of God.

This week, I want to present some thoughts concerning the fact that each of us has sinned and fallen short of the glory of God. It will help put things in perspective for us and to better appropriate the healing power and presence of the Lord.

Andrew Jackson in his inaugural address of 1829 said,

"I believe man can be elevated, man can become more endowed with dignity and as he does he becomes more God-like in his character and capable of governing himself."

What Jackson said in 1829 we know in 1981 to be absolutely false. Man cannot lift himself to the point where he can govern himself better. His sinful nature prevents the perfect achievement of dreams.

We live in an age of terrorism. It is an age of the rampant rush to the occult. Superstition abounds on every side in spite of the many who are supposedly highly educated.

I believe the Bible presents the proper insight when it says we have turned away from God. The natural person cannot discern nor appreciate the things of the spirit.

The wholeness which we proclaim is not that an individual will live for a thousand years. Fallen man has been condemned to die.

It is that in the midst of this sin there can be victories which make life worthwhile. Sin can be conquered in and through Christ.

The Good News is that you can triumph. It is not that you are an exception and will never die. It is that you are a chosen vessel and will and can live facing your fallen humanity, by receiving His blessed Spirit.

I pray that as you practice the Ministry of the Master this week, you will bring into sharp focus the fact that you have and do sin as well as the fact that the Lord has and does forgive.

POINTS TO PONDER

1. What do you feel was the forbidden fruit in the Garden of Eden?
2. Is the heart of each person really basically wicked?
3. Do you feel life is very brief?

FALLEN MAN

1. What was forbidden to Adam and Eve in the Garden? _____
_____ _____. *Gen. 2:17*
2. What is the purpose of knowing the measure of your days? _____
_____ *Psalms 39:4*
3. The thoughts of man are _____ *Psalms 94:11*
4. What would be the result of eating of the forbidden tree? _____
_____ *Gen. 2:17*
5. What are the conditions of a person's heart? _____
_____ *Jer. 17:9*
6. What assurance does fallen man have about tomorrow? _____
_____ *James 4:14*
7. The_____man receives not the things of the Spirit but they
are _____ to him because they are _____ ____
discerned _____. *I Cor. 2:14*
8. How many righteous are there?_____ *Rom 3:10*
9. What has every person done? _____ *Rom 3:23*
10. Our righteousness in the sight of God are as _____
_____. *Is. 64:6*
11. Out of the _____ proceed evil thoughts, etc. _____
_____. *Mark 7:21*
12. The world _____ but the one who does the will
of God _____. *I John 2:17*
13. Man's days are as _____. *Psalms 103:15*
14. There is_____that doeth good. *Psalms 14:3*

DAILY SCRIPTURE

Mon.   Gen. 3:1-24
Tues. James 4:13-17
Wed.   Ps. 103:1-22
Thurs. I John 2:7-17
Fri.   Mark 7:14-23
Sat.   Rom. 3:21-31
Sun.   I Cor. 2:6-16

PRAYER CONCERNS

Your Family & Relatives
Government Leaders
Missionaries
For the Unbelievers
Churches & Denominations
Your Own Church
Prayer and Praise

NOTE: You will be spiritually strengthened by completing two questions each day, reading the suggested scripture, and ministering in prayer for the concerns of the day.

THE MINISTRY OF THE MASTER—MONDAY
A Spirit Lifter

When the first grade student came home, the mother asked, "What did you learn in school today?" The lad replied, "I learned that 4 and 4 make 9." "But that's wrong," the mother protested.

"Well, in that case," said the son, "I didn't learn anything."

God's Promise

"Therefore, my beloved brethren, be ye steadfast, unmoveable, always abounding in the work of the Lord, forasmuch as ye know that your labour is not in vain in the Lord." (I Corinthians 15:58)

Practicing His Presence

Through what incident or individual did you sense His presence yesterday? How did you react to this reality?

Fallen Humanity

The little hand shot up and the face lighted with the joy of a new insight. I responded by giving the little girl a chance to ask her question. Little did I realize it was such a profound one.

"Pastor Bartow, why did God put that apple there in the first place?"

The girl was a fifth grader. I was a Seminary student teaching in Bible School. The question was profound and in a sense unanswerable. However, I have struggled with it through the years.

Why? Why? Why? This has haunted individuals through the ages. Why all the sin and distress in the world? Why all the illness and sorrow? Why all the suffering and uncertainty?

I have never come up with a better answer than the fact that man fell. He disobeyed the laws of the spirit and suffered the consequences. He failed to appreciate the fact that the Lord meant what He said.

The conclusion I have reached which has been of help to me is that it is not so much how I got into this mess; but how can I get out. I can do nothing about the beginning, but I can do something about the end.

I can acknowledge my own sinfulness and turn to the One who was sinless. My wholeness depends upon my realizing I am sick. This big step I take by admitting my need of the Lord in all areas of my life.

PRAYER: *Lord, I do not understand why all the evil in this world exists, but I do understand the reality of your forgiveness and the power for righteousness You impart. Amen.*

THE MINISTRY OF THE MASTER—TUESDAY
A Spirit Lifter

Returning to his stadium seat, popcorn in hand, a rather obese baseball fan leaned over and asked a woman seated on the aisle, "Did I step on your feet when I went out?" "Well," smiled the woman, ready to accept his apology, "as a matter of fact, you did." "Good," exclaimed the portly one, squeezing past her. "This is the right row, then."

God's Promise

Consider this promise throughout your day:

"Jesus said unto him, if thou canst believe, all things are possible to him that believeth." (Mark 9:23)

Practicing His Presence

The old song says, "...and He tells me I am His own..." Does the reality of His presence being this type of assurance to you?

Fallen Humanity

Humanity has fallen. Death has been passed upon each and every person. Yet, you don't have to stand by and let death defeat you. Jesus invites us to Himself for His ultimate wholeness of the gift of life.

He realizes our sin and failures. He imparts His righteousness and fullness. Don't just stand there, do something. That something is to really believe the Lord desires wholeness for you in your fallen condition. His is life.

I have read that in Ireland there is a bird called the Cock of the Wood. They travel in flocks. They never seem to be able to flee from danger. If you shoot one of them, the others simply stand and look at the dead one. You can shoot another and the rest look on. They stand still looking at the one recently shot until one by one the marksman can kill every bird in the flock.

This is not your lot. You are called not to look at the dead, but at the life. You are called not to be a target for death, but to aim toward the mark of your high calling in Christ Jesus. He is more desirous of redeeming your nature than you are of being redeemed. I hope you will sincerely believe this today.

PRAYER: *Father, I thank you for the redeeming power of your presence and love. May your gift of faith become more precious to me always. Amen.*

THE MINISTRY OF THE MASTER—WEDNESDAY

A Spirit Lifter

It's no wonder people pay so much for antiques. How often do you find something that outlasts the original guarantee?

God's Promise

Consider this truth throughout your whole day today:

"When the poor and needy seek water, and there is none, and their tongues faileth for thirst, I the Lord will hear them, I the God of Israel will not forsake them." (Isaiah 41:17)

Practicing His Presence

It has been amazing to me how often the Lord has felt so near while I am involved in the ordinary experiences of life. The more I practice His presence, the more I behold Him in all things. Is this true of your life?

Fallen Humanity

Socrates was sentenced to death for supposedly corrupting the minds of the youth of Athens. He had proclaimed truth and it was interpreted as false. He had faced reality and ended up accused of fantasy.

One of his friends told him that thirty tyrants had sentenced him to death. He calmy replied,

"Never mind. Nature has sentenced the thirty tyrants to death."

He know they, too, would die. Death is a matter of when and not of whom. All die. The Fall made this a certainty.

When I was younger, I thought I would live to be at least 100 years old. Also, by that time there would be a pill discovered which would enable me to live to be perhaps 200. Now, I know better.

In fact, there are times when I am not too concerned about living to be 100. I can face the fact that life is short and that the sinful nature of humanity is a part of me as well as everyone else.

Nature has ruled that you die. Christ has ruled that you can conquer this death. It is done through Him. He imparts this hope of glory and this wholeness of your being.

PRAYER: *Thank you, Lord Jesus, for the hope which I have in you. The hope and certainty of eternal life. Amen.*

THE MINISTRY OF THE MASTER—THURSDAY

A Spirit Lifter

Read in the will of a miserly millionaire: "...And to you my dear brother Arnold, whom I promised to mention in my will, Hi there, Arnold!"

God's Promise

Isn't this a wonderful promise? *"I love them that love me; and those that seek me early shall find me." (Proverbs 8:17)*

Practicing His Presence

The cultivating of the sense of His presence is an art. It does not come automatically. Do you feel it adds to your life experiences to be reminded He is with you?

Fallen Humanity

"As for man, his days are as grass: as a flower of the field, so he flourisheth." Psalms 103:15

This verse was certainly graphically illustrated in our time with the death of Pope John Paul I. I was a visiting professor at Walsh College, a Catholic school in our community, at the time of his election and death. I recall mentioning to the class a few days after the Pope's election that I did not feel he would live too long. I was astonished when he died after only 34 days in office. Even a Pope does not have a guarantee of long life.

However, there have been times in history when a Pope has had even a shorter reign. Pope Steven II died 3 days after his election. Marcellas II and Irvin VII each died 13 days after assuming the office. Bonaface VI reigned 15 days, Leo XI only 17 days and Theodore II was Pope for 20 days.

They may have been considered the head of the church. However, they could not reign over death. They were a part of fallen humanity.

This brevity of life should lead each of us to a greater appreciation of the sacredness of life. I feel it will help you and me to realize more than ever that only in the Lord can we have the life we desire.

PRAYER: *I know my life on earth is brief, Father, but there is your peace within my heart because I know I will spend eternity in your presence. Amen.*

THE MINISTRY OF THE MASTER—FRIDAY
A Spirit Lifter

Following a lot of dull, long-winded speakers at a sports dinner, a well-known athelete, noticing some guests who had dozed off, started his speech, "Friends and nodding acquaintances."

God's Promise

"God so loved the world that he gave his only Son that whosoever believes in Him should not perish but have everlasting life." (John 3:16)

Practicing His Presence

Through what incident or person did you sense His presence yesterday? Was the reality of this presence a conscious effort on your part?

Fallen Humanity

Several years ago, Mary and I attended our first Rose Bowl Parade. There were thousands present. The excitement was contagious and all seemed lost in the revelry of this spectacular event.

The floats were beautiful beyond description. The individuals riding in the floats were exuberant and gorgeous. They were dressed for the occasion both inside and out. Our places were reserved right on the blue line and thus we had an excellent view of all the floats as well as the bands, horses, etc.

The next day we went to the park where they take the floats following the parade. It was an exceedingly windy day. Would you believe, those floats looked like death warmed over? Yes, the flowers were still beautiful, but something was missing. There were no individuals on the floats to bring life to them. It was as if the spirit had departed from them. They had fallen from their original glory.

Fallen humanity needs the Spirit of the Living God to bring the beauty which is possible. We are called to be beautiful in Him and He in us.

PRAYER: *Spirit of the Living God fall afresh on me. Melt me and mold me after your will, O Lord, and enable me to rejoice in it. Amen.*

THE MINISTRY OF THE MASTER—SATURDAY
A Spirit Lifter

One of the most discreet, and yet explicit letters of reference ever read was made to a company asking for a reference on a former employee: "We have known Mr. X for a long time, and when you come to know him as well as we do, you will think the same of him as we do."

God's Promise

Isn't it wonderful to know that the Lord is at work in your life? I like the following:

"For it is God which worketh in you both to will and to do of his good pleasure." (Phillippians 2:13)

Practicing His Presence

Did you find the quiet island yesterday? Was there at least some time during the day when you sensed His presence?

Fallen Humanity

"I can't swallow that idea of original sin," was the sharp statement of a person to his friend. I liked the reply, "You don't have to swallow it. It is already in you."

It is true that in each of us is an imperfection which cannot be erased by any amount of positive thinking or disciplined training. You may call it Adamic sin, original sin, human frailty, natural tendency to do wrong, or any other term which fits your viewpoint of humanity. However, the bottom line is that every person is imperfect.

There seems to be a natural inclination toward that which seeks the lesser instead of the greater in life.

It is comforting news to hear that Christ made possible our triumph over sin. He met the problem head-on and destroyed what we could not destroy. It is this hope which sustains us in the midst of our defeats and keeps challenging us to greater things. He is our victory, because in and of ourselves, we will always be a failure. In Him is our victory.

PRAYER: *Lord Jesus, I give thanks to you for the strength you impart which helps me to be victorious over sin. Amen.*

THE MINISTRY OF THE MASTER—SUNDAY
A Spirit Lifter

"Hadn't you better go and tell your father?" asked the motorist of the farmer's boy who stood looking at the load of hay upset after the collision.
"He knows," said the boy.
"Knows — how can he know?"
"He's under it."

God's Promise

Patience is a good trait and this is the day to wait for God's promises to be fulfilled.

"Wait on the Lord, be of good courage, and he shall strengthen thine heart: wait, I say, on the Lord."
(Psalm 27:14)

Practicing His Presence

Through what incident or individual did you sense His presence yesterday? What was your response to this reality?

Fallen Humanity

The pastor had enthusiastically expounded upon the sinfulness and imperfection of every person in the world. Near the close of his message he asked the rhetorical question, *"Has anyone here ever known a perfect person?"* He realized there would be a negative response on the part of all.

However, to his surprise, a timid little man in the back of the church held up his hand. The pastor looked at him in surprise with the startled statement, *"You know a perfect person!"* *"Yes,"* he replied timidly, *"It was my wife's first husband."*

There are times when some would lead us to believe they are perfect or they have known someone who is. Each of us knows better. Even the constant reference to perfection cannot produce it.

Christ is our perfection. Our wholeness and perfection is in Him. This is the message which makes it possible to rejoice even in our sinfulness. We do not live in despair because of our imperfection, but live in His deliverance and joy.

PRAYER: *Thank you, Jesus, that you are my perfection. It is in thee that I put my trust and to you that I look for forgiveness. Amen.*

SIN—BARRIER TO WHOLENESS

The aspect of a barrier to wholeness which seems to escape many individuals is that of their own sinfulness. I believe each of us should take a hard look at sin and how it affects life. We are spiritually and sometimes physically ill because of sin. Spiritual wholeness cannot be sought, if we are unaware of the power of sin in life's experiences.

I believe we must consider the fact of being dead in our trespasses and sins before we can come to fully appreciate being alive unto righteousness and life in Jesus Christ.

What is meant by sin? How is sin a part of your life and mine? What wholeness is available in spite of the presence and power of sin?

There are many definitions of sin. The dictionary defines it as transgression from a rule or set of laws. It can be either overtly committed or committed by omission. It can be in thought or in deed. It is any lack of holiness. It is any defect of moral purity and truth, whether in heart or in life's actions. It can be either commission or omission.

The scriptures speak of sin as a state. It is a defect built into each of us. There are no perfect human beings.

"All have sinned and come short of the glory of God" (Rom. 3:23) is the way the Apostle Paul speaks concerning this eternal truth.

Every one of us lacks something which prevents us from reaching perfection and from being perfect.

I hope that this week you will be led to acknowledge as never before that you are not perfect. There is no amount of learning, wealth, fame, or length of years that can make you perfect.

Wherein do you find perfection and where do you go for the wholeness you desire and need?

I pray that both you and myself will cease to rely upon our own righteousness this week and turn afresh unto Him who is our great Physician.

POINTS TO PONDER

1. What really is sin in God's sight?
2. Are most individuals fooled as to the true values of life?
3. Do you really feel every person is a sinner?

Daily Bible Study and Daily Prayer Concerns
SIN—BARRIER TO WHOLENESS

1. Sin is_____to do good and_____
doing it. *James 4:17*
2. Whatever is not of_____is sin. *Rom. 14:23*
3. Sin is the_____of the law. *Rom 4:15*
4. Our own righteousness is as _____. *Is. 64:6*
5. The soul that sins shall_____. *Ezek. 18:4*
6. Lust brings forth_____and sin when it is
finished brings _____. *James 1:15*
7. Jesus said that _____ comes evil thoughts
and actions. *Mark 7:21*
8. There is a way which seems _____ unto man,
but the end is_____. *Pro. 14:12*
9. The face of the Lord is against them that do _____.
Ps. 34:16
10. My sin is not_____from God. *Ps. 69:5*
11. How many have sinned? _____ *Rom. 3:23*
12. The_____of sin is_____
Rom. 6:23
13. This _____ takes away the _____
of the world. *John 1:29*
14. If we _____ our sins the Lord will forgive.
I John 1:9

DAILY SCRIPTURE

Mon.	Ps. 34:11-22
Tues.	Is. 64:1-7
Wed.	Mark 7:14-23
Thurs.	James 1:12-18
Fri.	John 1:19-34
Sat.	James 4:13-17
Sun.	Ezek. 18:1-9

PRAYER CONCERNS

Your Family & Relatives
Government Leaders
Missionaries
For the Unbelievers
Churches & Denominations
Your Own Church
Prayer and Praise

NOTE: You will be spiritually strengthened by completing two questions each day, reading the suggested scripture, and ministering in prayer for the concerns of the day.

THE MINISTRY OF THE MASTER—MONDAY
A Spirit Lifter

There is this prayer inscribed on a wall of the Cathedral in Chester, England.
"Give me a sense of humor, Lord.
Give me the grace to see a joke.
To get some happiness from life,
And pass it on to other folk."
Whoever wrote the above is my kind of person. Right on!

God's Promise

"For thou hast made him a little lower than the angels, and hast crowned him with glory and honour." (Psalm 8:5)

Practicing His Presence

May you seek to quiet your mind, heart and body to hear "the still small voice" speak to you. He is with you.

Sin—Barrier To Wholeness

The concept of sin is not always easy to convey to myself and I am sure you struggle with it also. However, it is easy for me to grasp the fact that I never quite achieve the goals for which I strive. Somehow I always miss the mark. I fall short, overshoot, or veer to the left or the right. To be on target is my goal, but to hit that bullseye is impossible.

An artist was commissioned to paint a picture which would depict the thought of sin. It was a beautiful picture. It showed an expert archer shooting at a miniature bull's eye. Each of the arrows was off target. He always missed.

The picture graphically portrayed that in life we miss the mark. Our wholeness is impaired by the shortcomings within mind and actions.

I am sure that you realize how difficult it is to really do what you desire to do. It is so hard for you to 100% accomplish what you dreamed you would like to accomplish.

The Apostle Paul realized the struggle of seeking to hit that mark and always missing it.

"For I do not understand my own actions — I am baffled, bewildered, I do not practice or accomplish what I wish, but I do the very thing that I loathe (which my moral instinct condemns)." Rom. 7:15 Amplified.

PRAYER: *My failure to achieve my goals disturbs me, O Lord. Help me to realize the central goal of your presence is the most important one in my life. Amen.*

THE MINISTRY OF THE MASTER—TUESDAY
A Spirit Lifter

The rooster was strolling about the barnyard and stumbled upon an ostrich egg. He looked it over and hurried back to the hen house. He quickly rounded up all the hens and took them out to see the egg. His words of inspiration flowed as he said,

"Now ladies, I do not want to embarrass you, but I just want to show you what some have done."

God's Promise

Isn't this a neat promise to ponder upon this day? It sure helps me.

"The steps of a good man are ordered by the Lord; and he delighteth in his way." (Psalms 37:23)

Practicing His Presence

It takes conscious effort to be aware of the Lord in the small things of life. How and where did you sense His presence yesterday?

Sin—Barrier To Wholeness

What are the truly great sins in life? How do you appraise a life of holiness and devotion unto the Lord?

Many individuals feel that the worst sins in life can be covered by such specifics as smoking, drinking, dancing, going to movies, and perhaps even watching television.

Now any one of the above may be abused and thus be sin to an individual. However, to make specific acts the ultimate sin seems to really miss the mark as far as the Word of the Lord is concerned.

Sin is more than a specific action which may be disapproved by you or me. It is an attitude of rebellion against the Lord and against all that is right for you and others.

I don't feel the Lord is honored by my trying to be pure through staying away from some things and/or some people. There was a day, and shamefully some still feel this way, when Catholics felt Protestants were all lost and Protestants felt all Catholics were spiritually blind. It was easier to be against another religion than to really live one's own faith. This neither honors God nor does it help others.

Sin is deeper than a specific action. It is your reaction to actions. I pray today you will search your heart as to what is harbored there as well as looking at your outward actions.

PRAYER: *Create in me a clean heart, O God. Renew a right spirit within me. Help me to do right, but even more important help me to think right. Amen.*

408

THE MINISTRY OF THE MASTER—WEDNESDAY
A Spirit Lifter

A man went into the bank to cash his check. The only money the teller had to give him was badly soiled. The teller said that he hoped he had no fear of microbes as there were probably some on the money. The reply was, "Don't worry, a microbe couldn't live on my salary."

God's Promise

Life is sometimes very confusing, isn't it? I'd suggest you consider this truth along with me today:

"If any of you lack wisdom, let him ask of God, that giveth to all men liberally, and upbraideth not; and it shall be given him." (James 1:5)

Practicing His Presence

Can you recall what you had for lunch yesterday? We all need food for our bodies, don't we? Just as important, we need spiritual food for our spiritual bodies. Can you recall a spiritual feast you had yesterday as you sensed His presence?

Sin—Barrier To Wholeness

There is a basic defect in every person. Saying this does not mean a putdown. Rather it is simply reality.

Remember the story of the person who mentioned to his friend about not being able to swallow the idea of original sin. The friend had wisely replied, "You don't have to swallow it. It is already in you."

The wholeness Jesus desires for you involves facing the reality of your sin. It is acknowledging that you have sinned. It is admitting that you are in need of the Lord's forgiveness. It is saying that life is bigger than you and that you need someone bigger than life to help you.

Jesus never hesitated to be identified with sinful individuals. He was called a sinful person because He associated with the so-called sinful people. However, He lashed out at the apparently religious individuals and said they had cleaned the outside, but that inwardly they were filthy. They were like graves which were whitewashed, but they still had dead people in them. There is no amount of veneer which can cover to the point of eradicating your imperfection.

Spiritual wholeness is your worthy goal and Christ is the only One who can enable you to achieve it.

PRAYER: *I realize you look beyond my pretense and see the real me, Father. Thank you for your mercy when you do and for your forgiveness. Amen.*

THE MINISTRY OF THE MASTER—THURSDAY
A Spirit Lifter

The hobo approached the back door and his knock was answered by the lady of the house. She said to him, "And do you want employment?" His reply was a classic.

"Lady, I know you mean well, but you can't make work sound any more inviting by using words of three syllables."

God's Promise

Remember, there is light at the end of the tunnel:

"...*I am come that they might have life, and that they might have it more abundantly.*" (John 10:10)

Practicing His Presence

I believe as you exercise your spiritual powers you will become more aware of the spiritual side of life. How did you sense the presence of His spirit yesterday?

Sin—Barrier To Wholeness

I like this story. I think it is neat and really sums up how we often look at ourselves.

There was a man in the community who was not the greatest brain-wise, but was brilliant when it came to overlooking his own shortcomings. He always wore a multi-colored coat with large patches of brightly colored cloth sewn together. Those who met him would inquire concerning the coat and comment about its beauty. He would point out what each piece represented. Each piece stood for a particular sin of the people of the small town.

He would take great delight in mentioning the sins and telling about them and talking about the people who were supposedly committing them. On the back of his coat was a little patch. One day he was asked what it represented.

His reply, "*Well. that's my sin and I can't even see it.*" Isn't this often the way you act and the way I respond. The sins of others are obvious, but mine are not observed by myself or explained away as mere shortcomings of life.

It is like the person who said he had no faults. This he knew because he could easily see the faults in others and therefore if he had any he knew he would be aware of them.

PRAYER: *Father, help me to see and face my own shortcomings. Help me to be understanding of the shortcomings of others and to see them as your children. Amen.*

THE MINISTRY OF THE MASTER—FRIDAY
A Spirit Lifter

"I had an awful scare this morning about two o'clock," said Mrs. Rapp. "What in the world happened?" her friend inquired. "Well, I heard a noise downstairs, and I got up and turned on the light, and I saw a man's legs sticking out from under the bed." "The burglar was under your bed!" exclaimed her friend. "No, my husband's legs," replied Mrs. Rapp, "he heard the noise before it woke me."

God's Promise

Don't forget this promise as you consider your daily work.
"Yet now be strong...and work: for I am with you, saith the Lord of hosts." (Haggai 2:4)

Practicing His Presence

May you seek to quiet your mind, heart and body to hear "the still small voice" speak to you today. He is with you. How did you sense His presence yesterday?

Sin—Barrier To Wholeness

Spiritual wholeness is often neglected because we do not deal with sin as we should. It is seen as an innocent aspect of life when really it is deadly. Selfishness, an irritable spirit, unloving attitude, lack of faith, etc. can get a toe-hold in your life and before you know it the attitude influences a great deal of your life.

Sin is like the camel who appealed to its master's mercy. He asked the master to permit him to simply put his nose in the tent because it was cold. O.K. was the reply. A while later the camel said, *"My neck is also cold. May I just get it in a little ways."* It wasn't long until he had his shoulders in the tent. The climax came when he mentioned how cold his hump was.

Getting the hump under the protecton of the tent meant that the entire camel had ended up in the tent. The master chastised the camel and ordered it to leave. The response to this admonition was, *"If anybody gets out of this tent it will be you, not me. I'm in to stay."*

And pray tell me, who is going to fight with a camel. There are many camels which nuzzle their way into the tent of your life and mine. Once ..e have opened ourselves to sin the consequences are deadly. Spiritual surgery is needed for us to recover. Jesus is the surgeon and to Him we look for the wholeness He can impart.

PRAYER: *Lord, by your grace may I keep the little sins from my door. Give me the strength to resist the little temptations that I might be victorious over all. Amen.*

411

THE MINISTRY OF THE MASTER—SATURDAY
A Spirit Lifter

How gracious are you to friends who have gone on, and how diplomatic can you be about someone's eternal destination?

A new acquaintance, unaware that the person was a widow inquired, "Where is your husband?" "Poor Charles," she replied, "I hope he's gone where I suspects he ain't."

God's Promise

Perhaps you are feeling bound by bad attitudes and wrong habits today.

"If ye continue in my word, then are ye my disciples indeed. And ye shall know the truth, and the truth shall set you free." (John 8:31-32)

Practicing His Presence

I pray that you were very much aware of the Lord's presence in your life yesterday. Can you recall some specific incident or person which helped this awareness?

Sin—Barrier To Wholeness

The legend is told of the young fox out walking with his aged grandfather. The gray hair revealed his old age and the marks on his body gave evidence of the times he had escaped the teeth of the hounds.

The young fox inquired how he had managed to escape these many years, how he had been able to remain alive in the face of all the dangers. The reply is most fitting. *"All my experience forces me to the conclusion that the best thing to do is to go out of the way so as not to meet the dogs."*

I feel this is tremendous insight concerning sin. We should go out of our way to keep away from sin. There is really no way that a person can ultimately defeat sin. It conquers all sooner or later. Self-help cannot bring cleansing.

Sin is defeated only through the presence and power of the Lord. We are called to seek to not only resist sin, but to flee from it. This does not mean we are to forsake the world, but does mean we are not to permit the world to inundate our soul.

It is when we turn from sin and look unto the Lamb of God that taketh away the sin of the world that we are triumphant.

PRAYER: *O Lamb of God, thank you for taking away my sins. Thank you for revealing your love to me and letting me know that I am part of the world you have forgiven. Amen.*

THE MINISTRY OF THE MASTER—SUNDAY
A Spirit Lifter

How easy it is to interpret things in keeping with our own needs and situation and to miss the real intent of a statement.

The teacher was again disciplining verbally the most active child in the class. She retorted, "Johnny, I should think you'd be ashamed to have the class hear me scold you." "I am," retorted the little second grader, "but you won't keep still."

God's Promise

Remember, when you are feeling alone, God understands. I rejoice in this truth:

"God setteth the solitary in families: he bringeth out those which are bound with chains: but the rebellious dwell in a dry land." (Psalm 68:6)

Practicing His Presence

It's hard to sometimes remember a specific incident in which you really felt His presence, isn't it? Yet, I do believe it is helpful to be reminded of the spiritual awareness which each of us should develop. Were you aware of His presence yesterday?

Sin—Barrier To Wholeness

You and I must realize that sin cannot be completely destroyed in this world, but it can be defeated. There is no way we can make this a perfect world.

I am encouraged with the knowledge that the Lord understands my frailties and understands my sins. Ps. 103:14 is precious to me.

"He knoweth our frame; he remembereth that we are dust."

I take this to mean that He really understands that I am a human being. He knows that temptation will sometimes get the best of me. Sin does lie at my door. Sometimes I open the door and it comes in and exerts its dastardly power. This is not an effort to excuse myself and to find an easy out for my own sins. However, it does face the fact that the Lord is with me and understands even when I do sin. Ps. 103:13 has a great message for us.

"Like as a father pitieth his children, so the Lord pitieth them that fear him."

I feel a grand climax to this sermonette would be Ps. 103:12.

"As far as the east is from the west, so far hath he removed our transgressions from us."

What more can we ask? Amen!

PRAYER: *My heart rejoices, O Lord, when I think of my sins being forgiven. My heart rejoices when I know you are the One who has forgiven me. Amen.*

GOD IS HOLY

God is holy! This truth must permeate our very being. It is an eternal truth which I feel is often neglected.

When the Bible speaks of the Lord as holy it is emphasizing the fact that He is the only one that can be holy. There is none other who is holy.

You may question His love. You may doubt His personal concern for you. You cannot doubt His holiness. You must acknowledge there is a Lord God Almighty.

If God is God He must be different from his creation. Attributing holiness to any creature or aspect of creation is idolatry.

I believe it is well to consider some of the scripture in the Old and New Testaments which call attention to the holy God. Consider:

"There is none holy as the Lord: for there is none beside thee: neither is there any rock like our God." I Sam. 2:2

"Speak unto all the congregation of the children of Israel, and say unto them, Ye shall be holy: for I the Lord your God am holy." Lev. 19:2

"Exalt the Lord our God, and worship at his holy hill; for the Lord our God is holy."

Because it is written, Be ye holy, for I am holy." I Peter 1:16

The holiness of God refers to the mystery of God. It speaks of the otherness of God. It calls to our attention the sovereignty of God. He is completely separated from His universe, even as He is completely identified with His universe. He sustains the universe, but is not the universe.

The root meaning of the word holy is to be different. God is different. He is not His creation and never can be. He is an all perfect and all powerful person.

POINTS TO PONDER

1. What do you feel is meant by the word holy?
2. How is God different from you and from all humanity?
3. If God is so holy, how can you possibly believe you can relate to Him?

GOD IS HOLY

1. The seraphim cried,_____*Is. 6:3*
2. There is_____ holy as the Lord.
   I Sam. 2:2
3. You shall be holy because _____
   Lev. 19:2
4. The one who has called us is _____
   I Peter 1:15
5. The Lord is_____ in holiness.
   Ex. 15:11
6. The Lord is of _____ than to behold evil,
   and He cannot _____ on iniquity. *Heb. 1:13.*
7. The four beasts constantly are saying_____
   _____ *Rev. 4:8*
8. The Lord our God is _____ *Ps. 99:9*
9. Who alone is holy? _____ *Rev. 15:4*
10. The one who inhabitest the praises of Israel is_____
    _____ *Ps. 22:3*
11. _____ is the name of the Lord. *Ps. 111:9*
12. The Lord is the _____ of Israel.
    Ezek. 39:7
13. _____is the holy one of Israel. *Is. 12:6*
14. The temple of God is _____ *I Cor. 3:17*

DAILY SCRIPTURE

Mon.   Is. 6:1-8
Tues. I Sam. 2:1-10
Wed.   I Peter 1: 13-25
Thurs. Rev. 4:1-11
Fri.   Ps. 22:1-11
Sat.   Ps. 99:1-9
Sun.   Is. 12:1-6

PRAYER CONCERNS

Your Family & Relatives
Government Leaders
Missionaries
For the Unbelievers
Churches & Denominations
Your Own Church
Prayer and Praise

NOTE: You will be spiritually strengthened by completing two questions each day, reading the suggested scripture, and ministering in prayer for the concerns of the day.

THE MINISTRY OF THE MASTER—MONDAY
A Spirit Lifter

How gently we can sometimes be reproved, and how sharply we can sometimes react.

"You must have annoyed that customer a great deal to have him sulk out of the shop like that."

"I didn't really do anything to make him mad," said the new sales clerk. "He asked me what sort of hat I felt would suit his head and I simply said, 'A soft one,' and he left in a huff."

God's Promise

"When thou passest through the waters, I will be with thee; and through the rivers, they shall not overflow thee: when thou walkest through the fire, thou shall not be burned; neither shall the flame kindle upon thee." (Isaiah 43:2)

Practicing His Presence

You have been daily reminded to be aware of the presence of our Lord. How do you find this taking place and what is it doing to you?

God Is Holy

I hope this week's theme, *"God Is Holy,"* will help you appreciate His majesty. He is the only holy One.

The word holy is used in relationship to many things. We can talk of a holy day meaning usually Sunday or the sabbath, Saturday. We can speak of a holy people.

The Bible describes the holy of holies of the temple. There are holy orders, holy water, holy week, holy scripture, holy Catholic church, a holy life, a holy place, a holy person.

However, in all of the above references the point is that the place, day, person is different. It is not that any are perfect or completely removed from the frailities of life.

The reference to things or persons being holy implies there are some places and things and persons who are unholy. They are considered to be secular or profane.

The difference between holy and common lies in the nature of the person's concept. However, with the Lord He is holy by His very nature. He is set apart not by designation but by His very nature.

PRAYER: *Father, help me to see the sacredness in all of life. May I be lead to rejoice that all that I am and have is yours and can be to your glory and honor. Amen.*

THE MINISTRY OF THE MASTER—TUESDAY
A Spirit Lifter

An old time resident was escorting an excursion party and relating to them the wonders of the area. He referred to one area of the terrain as Lover's Leap bluff. "I sorter forgit jest why, but 'pears the story goes than an old maid proposed to a feller right here on this spot. He gave out a blood curdling yell and jumped off."

God's Promise

Feeling troubled today! God will help you, as he does me:

"These things I have spoken unto you, that in me ye might have good cheer; I have overcome the world." (John 16:33)

Practicing His Presence

How were you made aware of His presence yesterday? I pray this awareness has been helpful to you. In the days ahead, I believe this will become more and more meaningful to you.

God Is Holy

The light of God's holiness certainly shows up our imperfections. You and I are basically unholy. This imperfection is an integral part of you and me. There may be some people disturbed by the Bible's message that all fall short of the glory and purity of God. The most minute pollution renders something impure. It is my feeling that we should search to discover what lack of holiness means and seek to cast ourselves upon the One who is holy.

Some years ago Mary and I visited a pottery in Chester, West Virginia. It was fascinating to behold the common clay at one end of the shop and beautiful dishes and vases, etc. at the other end. However, between the one end of recently mined clay and finished product were many processes performed.

One of the most intriguing steps to me was the removing of impurities. The clay was mixed with water to the point that it was a free flowing liquid. It passed through a machine which removed all the impurities humanly possible. It was pointed out that minute particles of iron were in the clay and if permitted to remain would show up in the finished product.

We were told that they removed approximately one pound of iron from every forty to fifty tons of clay. I thought, what a small amount to produce visible imperfections in the finished products.

PRAYER: *It is unto you, O Lord, that I look for the impurities of my life to be faced and their guilt removed from me. I put my trust in You. Amen.*

A Spirit Lifter

The judge was dissatisfied. He announced, "I discharge this jury." A tall, lean member of the twelve unfolded himself and with all seriousness said, "Say, judge, you can't discharge me." "Can't discharge you? Why not?" thundered the irate judge. "Why," replied the juryman, pointing to counsel for defense, "I was hired by that guy over there."

God's Promise

"Now our Lord Jesus Christ himself, and God, even our Father, which hath loved us, and hath given us everlasting consolation and good hope through grace, comfort your hearts, and establish you in every good word and work." (II Thessalonians 2:16, 17)

Practicing His Presence

I believe as you exercise your spiritual powers you will become more aware of the spiritual side of life. How did you sense the presence of His spirit yesterday?

God Is Holy

Yesterday I spoke of the minute particles which can corrupt so completely. This corruption was within the clay. Contrasted to God's holiness we are indeed corrupt.

I feel it is good to realize that not only from within, but also from without we are unable to stand in the presence of God's holiness. He is the great Other and as created beings we cannot stand in His presence.

Paul Diuk of our church invited Mary and and myself to visit the steel rolling mill where he works. I was fascinated by the huge machinery, the vastness of the plant, and the magnitude of the noise. The marvels of modern technology were on every hand.

However, the thing which has lingered the most graphically in my mind is the imprint of a mosquito upon the steel. Can you believe that an object as tiny as a mosquito can make an imprint in a sheet of steel? It is literally true. I saw it with my own eyes. The shape of the mosquito was as evident as could be.

If perchance there would be a number of mosquitoes caught in some section of the steel they would have to scrap it. There are many frailties in your life and mine. We need to constantly seek His wholeness.

PRAYER: *I know, Lord Jesus, that in and of myself I am impure and imperfect. I rejoice in Your perfection. Amen.*

THE MINISTRY OF THE MASTER—THURSDAY
A Spirit Lifter

Did you ever try to impress the boss or someone else and discover you ended up in a worse situation?

The young enthusiastic new secretary eagerly sought to do what her boss asked her to do. He had dictated a number of letters and she was about to transcribe them. Wanting to do it right she went to him and asked, "Do you want the carbon copies single-spaced or double-spaced?"

God's Promise

"Who is the image of the invisible God, the firstborn of every creature: all things were created by him, and for him: And he is before all things, and by him all things consist." (Colossians 1:15-17)

Practicing His Presence

Are you consciously making the effort to be aware of the Lord in the small aspects of life? I know if you are, these have been exciting days for you.

God Is Holy

Have you ever felt you would like to see God? Have you felt that if only He would literally reveal Himself you would never doubt again?

My guess is that these questions have crossed your mind. They certainly have come to me. You and I are not alone if we sometimes long to really see the Lord. Moses had this problem. After a wonderful chat with the Lord he went further by saying,

"...I beseech thee, shew me thy glory." Ex. 33:18

The Lord's reply is fitting for us to ponder. He said that He would reveal some of His attributes. That is, His goodness, mercy, graciousness, etc. However, He said,

"...Thou canst not see my face: for there shall no man see me and live."

It is impossible to really look upon the Holy One. This is one of the reasons the Lord sent His Son. Jesus revealed the nature of the Father because it is impossible for us to really behold the actual presence.

If you want to behold the Lord then see Him in others and see Him as He is revealing Himself constantly. He is holy. Behold His holiness.

PRAYER: *I behold your glory, Father, in so many things and in so many ways. Thank you that through nature, others, and your precious Word you reveal yourself. Amen.*

THE MINISTRY OF THE MASTER—FRIDAY
A Spirit Lifter

What's in a name? How do we look at ourselves and others? The new preacher was invited to join one of the civic groups in his community. In introducing him, the speaker facetiously said they were electing him to be the "chief hogcaller" for the club. In responding, the preacher showed tremendous ability at quick thinking. "Gentlemen, I certainly appreciate the very great honor you have conferred upon me. When I came to this community, I had expected to be shepherd of a flock; but of course, you know your crowd better than I do."

God's Promise

"..If thou wilt diligently hearken to the voice of the Lord thy God, and wilt do that which is right in his sight, and wilt give ear to his commandments, and keep all his statutes, I will put none of these diseases upon thee..." (Exodus 15:26)

Practicing His Presence

Through what incident or person did you sense His presence yesterday? Was the reality of this presence a conscious effort on your part?

God Is Holy

I have been speaking of the otherness of God. I have stressed His holiness and the fact that He cannot be seen, but experienced.

Even as I do this I do not want to leave the impression that He has forsaken His universe. He's not a clock maker who makes such a fantastic clock that it never again needs attention.

We have all seen the eight day clocks, which need winding only occasionally. Some individuals act and believe as if God's universal clock was started in the beginning and God went off into the wild blue yonder. This is not true. His holiness pervades the entire universe. Even though He is holy He has not forsaken you and me.

"...Holy, Holy, Holy, is the Lord of hosts: the whole earth is full of His glory." Isaiah 6:3

The holiness of God is on every hand, if we look for it and accept its presence. Not accepting it does not remove it, but it does affect your life. The realization of His presence is what makes all things sacred. It is our high calling to see the spiritual aspect of creation.

PRAYER: *It is you, Father, who makes my days and ways holy. I know I cannot do it myself. My hope is in you and my confidence is in you. Amen.*

THE MINISTRY OF THE MASTER—SATURDAY
A Spirit Lifter

The preacher had come to sermon time and announced that this message would deal with gossip. He then asked the song leader to sing a hymn before the message. A ripple of smiles and subdued laughter resulted when the congregation turned to the announced page and discovered they would be singing, "I Love to Tell the Story."

God's Promise

"But let it be the hidden man of the heart, in that which is not corruptible, even the ornament of a meek and quiet spirit, which is in the sight of God of great price." (1 Peter 3:4)

Practicing His Presence

How are you doing, being aware of His presence each day? I pray this has been a meaningful experience for you. How did you sense His presence yesterday?

God Is Holy

If God is holy what should this do to you and me? How should it affect our thinking and our actions? Peter admonishes believers to forsake a life of sin and pursue a life of holiness.

"...But as he which hath called you is holy, so be ye holy in all manner of conversation." I Peter 1:15

The word, "conversation," is better translated "life." All of life is sacred and should be lived as holy unto the Lord.

The Pharisees and the Sadducees seemed to feel that minute keeping of the law would indicate a holy life. Our travels in the Holy Land have given us opportunity to see the members of the present day sect of Judaism who feel they must keep minute details of the law. They would feel better killing a person who would desecrate their section of Jerusalem on the Sabbath, than to violate their concept of Sabbath observance.

Monks through the centuries have felt the holy life to be the life which flees the cares and corruption of the world.

It is my firm conviction that Jesus called us to a holy life within the world. His disciples were not told that the Kingdom would soon be ushered in and perfection accomplished. What they were told at the time of Christ's ascension was that they would receive power to live in the midst of a troubled world. This is true holiness.

PRAYER: *Father, may the words of my mouth edify you and others. Help me to say and to do the positive. Help me to believe you are with me always and to bear witness of this truth. Amen.*

421

THE MINISTRY OF THE MASTER—SUNDAY
A Spirit Lifter

My father-in-law, the Reverend J. Leslie Bell, many years ago was preaching in Plain Grove, Pa. He became ill during the service and was taken to a side room. A doctor was present and attended to him. After several minutes one of the Elders reported to the congregation that the Pastor was ill and would not be able to continue with the service. You can imagine the smiles on the faces of some as they stood and began to sing, "Praise God from who all blessings flow..." to close the service.

God's Promise

"Peace I leave with you, my Peace I give unto you: not as the world giveth, give I unto you. Let not your heart be troubled, neither let it be afraid." (John 14:27)

Practicing His Presence

Perhaps you had a very busy day yesterday. Hopefully, though, there were times when you sensed He was really with you.

God Is Holy

I want to close this week of presenting the theme God is holy by calling attention to Psalm 22:1

"My God, my God, why hast thou forsaken me?" These same words were uttered by Jesus as he hung dying on the cross (Mt. 27:46). I agree with the biblical scholars who feel that the reference in the Psalms was fulfilled in Jesus Christ. I also agree that the feeling of being forsaken by the Father was because of the fact God is holy.

When Christ died on the cross, He bore your sins and mine. He assumed the sins of the entire world. God, who is holy, cannot look upon sin. In a sense, His Son was all alone at that point. Sin breaks the communion between the Lord and you. It is sin which you have committed. Sin does separate from God.

In the case of the Lord Jesus it was not sin which He had committed, but rather sin which He had assumed. It was your sin and mine.

The holiness of God meant that Jesus would have to be alone. I thank God that He was willing to go through this agony to make it possible for me to be delivered from it.

The crucifixion marvelously revealed the reality and importance of the holiness of God and at the same time revealed the sinfulness of humanity. I would that you would close the week by really trusting the One who took your place. He indeed bore your sins and the God who is holy can and does accept you because of this.

PRAYER: *There are those times, Father, when I feel forsaken by even You. Help me to see that even during those times you sustained me with your everlasting arms. Amen.*

GOD IS JUST

Wholeness is the goal of life which can be faithfully and directly pursued by each of us. The Lord desires that we be whole and that in body, mind, and spirit we live out this wholeness.

The totality of life's experiences involves more than seeking the Lord's wholeness when you are extremely ill or in an impossible situation.

The wholeness you and I need and desire must be seen in the light of all facets of the Lord. One area which is often neglected is the justice of God.

Most of my acquaintances will acknowledge that God exists. They then feel that logically He is a God who does not expect very much of anyone. From their viewpoint, He is the One who is kind and benevolent to all. In a sense this is true. However, they fail to appreciate His attribute of being a just God.

I believe we are taking a warped view of life when we neglect to consider that God is just. He has laws, expectations, and goals for each of us which cannot be broken or neglected without dire consequences resulting.

There are two main aspects of the thought of being just as far as scripture is concerned. First, just is synonymous with the statutes of God. His testimonies and His laws are just.

Second, there is the concept of His being just as far as nations and individuals are concerned. God is just when it comes to actions which are done individually or corporately. The practical implications of God as a just God are always in the now as well as always in the future. You are ever being seen in the light of God being just. You shall also be judged in this light.

POINTS TO PONDER

1. Is there really justice in this life?
2. Has there ever been a person who could look at an issue completely objectively and justly?
3. Is it fair that the person who has more is expected to be more responsible?

GOD IS JUST

1. The Lord is _____ in all His ways and _____
   _____ in all His works. *Ps. 145:17*
2. To whom much is given much is _____. *Luke 12:48*
3. The Father has committed all judgment to the_____
   _____. *John 5:22*
4. Christ said that his judgment is _____. *John 5:30*
5. The Lord shall _____ the living and the dead
   at His appearing. *II Tim. 4:1*
6. The day is coming when God will judge the_____
   _____ of man. *Rom. 2:16*
7. God is the judge of _____. *Heb. 12:23*
8. When the book of life is opened each person will be judged according
   to his/her _____. *Rev. 20:12,13*
9. Everyone will stand before_____. *Rom. 14:10*
10. What happened to those not found in the book of life? _____
    _____ *Rev. 20:15*
11. We must_____ appear before the judgment
    seat of Christ. *II Cor. 5:10*
12. The heavenly Father judgeth with _____.
    I Peter 1:17
13. The Lord is coming _____. *Rev. 22:12*
14. The Lord come to_____the earth.
    PS. 96:13

DAILY SCRIPTURE

Mon.   John 5:19-24
Tues.   Ps. 145:14-21
Wed.   II Tim. 4:1-8
Thurs.   Rev. 22:10
Fri.   Rom. 2:12-16
Sat.   Heb. 12:18-29
Sun.   II Cor. 5:1-10

PRAYER CONCERNS

Your Family & Relatives
Government Leaders
Missionaries
For the Unbelievers
Churches & Denominations
Your Own Church
Prayer and Praise

NOTE: You will be spiritually strengthened by completing two questions each day, reading the suggested scripture, and ministering in prayer for the concerns of the day.

THE MINISTRY OF THE MASTER—MONDAY
A Spirit Lifter

The pastor had presented a stirring message on the evils of alcohol. All alcoholic beverages were to be shunned by all. He closed with a fervent plea that all the alcohol of the community be taken immediately and dumped in the nearby river. Nearly exhausted from his 45 minutes of exhortation he closed the message and requested that a hymn be sung to close the service. The song leaders announced page 159 and the congregation began to sing, "Shall We Gather At The River."

God's Promise

"And not only so, but we glory in tribulations also; knowing that tribulation worketh patience; and patience, experience; and experience, hope." (Romans 5:3,4)

Practicing His Presence

Are you anticipating being aware of His presence throughout this day? If so, I believe it will be a great day for you.

God Is Just

As we begin a new week together I feel it is important to realize that our just God has conveyed the fact that justice is not something which is to wait until eternity to be revealed.

Each of us constantly lives under the judgment of God. If it were not for His mercy, we could not last at all.

Jesus beautifully pointed out the fact that judgment is not completely futuristic. He spoke the truth when he said,

"He that believeth in Him is not condemned: but he that believeth not is condemned already." John 3:18

When does the judgment begin? It is not only in the future, but now, isn't it? I am not trying to say there is not a time when we will be judged, but trying to point out that we should constantly be aware that the God of love is also a God who is just.

You are called to a life of holiness because the Lord is just. You are not called to live in abject fear because He is just, but to live constantly realizing that on your own you are indeed unworthy. This entire week I will endeavor to present aspects of our relationship to our God which will strengthen our devotion to Him.

PRAYER: *Lord Jesus, thank you for setting me free. Judgment is my lot, but your grace is my portion forever. Thank you. Amen.*

THE MINISTRY OF THE MASTER—TUESDAY
A Spirit Lifter

May I give you another one about hymns and singing in the church. A friend of mine was at a church where they had an annual singspiration service. This was fine, but the one year which will be remembered by most was when the promotional announcement read, "Sunday Nov. 10th will be our Annual Sinspiration Sunday." The "g" had been omitted. I hear there was more enthusiasm shown for sin than for singing. What do you think?

God's Promise

It's not always easy to obey God, is it? I struggle with this, and find the following verse helpful.

"For it is God which worketh in you both to will and to do of his good pleasure." (Philippians 2:13)

Practicing His Presence

Perhaps yesterday was a difficult day. I do hope, however, that you are taking the time to be aware of His presence each day. How was this done yesterday?

God Is Just

How do you seek to comprehend the justice of God? It is hard for me to do because I am just to a degree, but cannot really look at and judge all things at all times in a just manner.

I personally get a better concept of God's perfect justice when I think of it in comparison with time. Time is one thing which never varies. It is always the same. There is no way you can speed it up or slow it down. Time hurries for no one and it does not hesitate even for kings. You cannot really turn the clock of time up nor can you turn it back. Time simply marches on irrespective of anyone or anything.

Thus it is with the justice of God. He looks at everyone and every situation perfectly. He judges in the light of perfectly considering every aspect and facet of the event, thought, or action.

There is no way that you and I can change the justice of God any more than there is any way we can influence the rapidity of time. We may think we are, but we are not. We may at times feel time flies or drags, but in reality a second is a second regardless of how pleasant or how unpleasant it may be to you.

It is my prayer that I may live my life in the light of the Lord's perfect and unrelenting justice.

PRAYER: *Father, help me to know you love and care for me every moment of every day. May I not depend on my feelings, but help me to rest in your promises. Amen.*

THE MINISTRY OF THE MASTER—WEDNESDAY
A Spirit Lifter

Some people really interpret the Bible literally. They can find a scripture verse to fit every situation regardless of what it might be.

There was one church which is reported to have put I Corinthians 15:51 over the entrance to the Nursery. They are the profound words of the beloved apostle Paul, but really were given a modern application. As you entered where the babies were during the service you read,

"We shall not all sleep, but we shall all be changed."

God's Promise

Perhaps you are facing some difficulty. If so, the following verse, I'm sure, you'll find helpful:

"And God is able to make all grace abound toward you; that ye, always having all sufficiency in all things, may abound to every good work."
(II Corinthians 9:8)

Practicing His Presence

Do you find that an awareness of His presence is determined to some degree by how you feel? Was there any time yesterday when you knew the spiritual life was the most important aspect of your being?

God Is Just

The justice the Lord wants you and me to live out must be directed unto others. In a sense, we cannot render justice unto Him. He is perfect. He has not needs which we can help Him meet. However, His people have many needs which we can help meet.

Jesus beautifully speaks of our bringing justice to others when he tells the parable of doing things unto the least of individuals. He speaks of the last judgment and the separating of the devout from those who have misused their life. He doesn't separate people by how they have used their liturgy books, but how they have responded to others.

He cast from Him those who did not respond to the needs of others and bring justice into their life situation. The scripture speaks powerfully in this area.

"Depart from me, ye cursed, into everlasting fire, prepared for the devil and his angels: For I was hungry, and ye gave me no meat: I was thirsty, and ye gave me no drink: I was a stranger, and ye took me not in: naked, and ye clothed me not: sick, and in prison, and ye visited me not." Mt. 25:41-43

This is the day the Lord has made to reach out in justice to another person.

PRAYER: *Lord Jesus, make me sensitive to the truth that as I minister unto others I am ministering unto you. Thank you. Amen.*

THE MINISTRY OF THE MASTER—THURSDAY

A Spirit Lifter

Taking the words of scripture literally and applying them to our understanding can result in interesting comments.

"Mummy, when are you going to lay another baby?" asked the little child. "Now dear, you know babies are not laid, because Mummy is not a bird." "Yes they are," said the little boy, "because at Sunday School this morning the teacher said that Mary laid Jesus in a manger."

God's Promise

"The Lord knoweth how to deliver the godly out of temptations, and to reserve the unjust unto the day of judgment to be punished." (II Peter 2:9)

Practicing His Presence

Sometimes incidents happen to me which seem to cloud the reality of His presence. Does this ever happen to you? If so, what do you do to realize His presence?

God Is Just

There are so many needs in life and so many injustices. It is impossible for you and me to meet them all, but we can help alleviate some of them.

There are so many stories about St. Francis of Assissi and I especially love this one.

It is reported that St. Francis saw a leprous man and got down from his carriage and went over and put his arms around this hideous looking man. The dreaded disease did not keep St. Francis from bestowing his love.

St. Francis reports a miracle as he put his arms around the leper and looked into his eyes. Behold, the leper's face became the face of Jesus Christ.

It is in the little things of trying to do justly and to bring justice to all that we see Jesus. He is all around us, but we frequently miss Him because we are looking in the wrong places.

St. Francis was a very wealthy young man, because of his father's inheritance. However, all that wealth could not do for him what one occasion of sincere embracing of another child of God could bring. He gave away much, but he received much more.

PRAYER: *Lord, may I give myself to the poor, the needy, the despairing, the defeated. As I do, thank you for your strength and wisdom imparted to me according to your promises. Amen.*

THE MINISTRY OF THE MASTER—FRIDAY
A Spirit Lifter

This one is a dandy. It's not so much what you hear, but what you think you hear.

A church school teacher had carefully instructed the children concerning the story of Lot. She was especially dramatic when it came to the part where God told Lot to take his wife and flee out of the city. She excitedly told how the wife looked back and was turned into a pillar of salt. There was reverent silence for a few seconds and then a little boy's hand shot up. "Yes Jimmy." His question, "What happened to the flea?"

God's Promise

Do you ever have difficulty sleeping because of worry?

"When thou liest down, thou shall not be afraid; yea, thou shalt lie down, and thy sleep shall be sweet." (Proverbs 3:24)

Practicing His Presence

Through what incident or individual did you sense His presence yesterday? How did you react to this reality?

God Is Just

May I continue to stress the importance of you and me endeavoring to impart the justice as well as the mercy of God.

The story is told of a very devout Roman soldier. One day in his travels he saw a man shivering in the cold. This beggar had no way to possibly warm himself. The soldier had one old army coat with him. It was tattered and torn, but at least it kept him warm.

There were many beggars in his day. He could have said I can't help one or all will think I can help them. But he decided to do his small bit to bring some justice into the life of this poor soul. He took his coat and tore it in two parts and gave half to the beggar.

That night the soldier had a dream and saw that Jesus had his old tattered piece of coat on himself. The angels were asking the Master where he got the coat. The reply was, *"From one of my children."*

It is literally true *"inasmuch as you have done it unto the least of these you have done it unto me."* The God who is just desires that you and I seek to be just and helpful to others.

PRAYER: *Father, somewhere, sometime today may I see you in someone who crosses my path. Help me to minister with love and tenderness. Amen.*

THE MINISTRY OF THE MASTER—SATURDAY
A Spirit Lifter

Children can often adjust to their situation quite well. A little girl was sitting in church with her father and became suddenly ill. "I have to throw up," she whispered. Her father, not wanting to get up and disturb the service, told her to hurry to the restroom alone. In no time she was back. He asked how she had gotten down the hall and to the restroom so quickly. Her reply, "Oh, I didn't have to go all that way. Just outside the door there was a box which said, 'For the Sick'."

God's Promise

Perhaps you sometimes get confused as to what to believe. Consider the following:

"For the law was given by Moses, but grace and truth came by Jesus Christ." (John 1:17)

Practicing His Presence

It's amazing to me how often the Lord has felt so near while I am involved in the ordinary experiences of life. The more I practice His presence, the more I behold Him in all things. Is this true of your life?

God Is Just

Some years ago I shared leadership at a healing conference with a Catholic priest. He told of an incident in his life which really spoke to my heart. I will never forget it.

One day he was fervently praying in the chapel and pleading for Jesus to show Himself to him. He really wanted to see Jesus and to faithfully serve Him. It was during this sacred time that the doorbell of the rectory rang and he had to answer it.

There stood a beggar in the snowy cold asking for some help. The beggar asked for food and lodging. The priest prepared him a baloney sandwich as he inquired about his church and activity in church.

The beggar said he was a Catholic, but hadn't really been going to church. He gave him a lecture about neglecting his church and thought he had done his duty. He also gave him two dollars to provide for bus fare downtown and money for a room at a dingy hotel.

Then he dashed back to the chapel to finish his devotional time and to plead for Jesus to appear to him. As he voiced his desire for Jesus to come to him he got this clear answer, *"I was just here."* He dashed out to call back the beggar, but he was nowhere to be found even though there had not been enough time elapsed for him to have caught the bus.

PRAYER: *Lord Jesus, may I see you in each person you bring across my path each day. May I have the love you have for the person and seek to be a blessing. Amen.*

THE MINISTRY OF THE MASTER—SUNDAY
A Spirit Lifter

Some things just simply happen and who can we blame. A class of fourth graders sure knew how to put this point across as they presented a nativity play which they wrote themselves. The scene is at the inn.

Innkeeper: "Can't you see the NO VACANCY sign?"
Joseph: "Yes, but can't you see that my wife is expecting a baby any minute?"
Innkeeper: "Well, that's not my fault!"
Joseph: "Well, it's not mine, either!"

God's Promise

I think you'll benefit from this promise:

"Who satisfieth thy mouth with good things; so that thy youth is renewed like the eagle's. (Psalm 104:5)

Practicing His Presence

Was there at least a little time during your busy schedule when you sensed His presence yesterday? How did this make you feel?

God Is Just

Charles G. Finney, the famous evangelist, was about to finish his law training. He reports that one day the Holy Spirit seemed to say to him, *"What are you going to do when you finish your course?"*

Finney replied, *"I am going to put out a shingle and practice law."* Then what? *"I am going to get rich."* Then what? *"I am going to retire."* Then what? *"I am going to die."* Then what? He says these words come trembling to him, *"...and after that the judgment." Heb. 9:27*

He tells how he ran out into the woods about a half a mile away from his office. He fell on his knees and spent hours with God until he was so transformed that he felt compelled to give his time to proclaiming the Good News of the Gospel.

Time and time again you and I must ask the question, *"What then?"* The wheels of the justice of God may grind slowly, but they grind consistently, impartially, and continuously. St. Paul realized this when he wrote:

"For we must all appear before the judgment seat of Christ; that everyone may receive the things done in his body, according to that he hath done, whether it be good or bad." II Cor. 5:10

PRAYER: *Father, may I make the choice today to live to your glory and honor. You have told me what should be my chief aim. Help me to pursue it faithfully and seek you only. Amen.*

JESUS CHRIST—WHO IS HE?

"There lives a man, a singular character, whose name is Jesus Christ. He lives in Judea. The barbarians esteem Him as a prophet, but His own followers adore Him as the immediate offspring of the immortal God. He is endowed with such unparalleled virtue as to call the dead from their graves. And to heal every kind of disease with a word or a touch.

"This person is tall and eloquently shaped. His aspect is amiable and reverent. His hair flows into those beautiful shades which no united color can match. Falling into graceful curves below His ears, agreeably couching upon His shoulders, and parting on His head like the head of a Nazarite.

"His forehead is smooth and large. His cheeks without either spot, save that of a lovely red. His nose is smooth and formed with exquisite symmetry. His beard is thin and of a color suitable to the hair of his head, reaching a little below the chin and parted in the middle like a forge.

"He rebukes with majesty, commands with mildness, and invites with the most tender and persuasive language. His whole address in deed or word being eloquently graceful is characteristic of so exalted a being. No man has ever seen him laugh. But many have seen Him weep. And so persuasive are His tears, that the multitude cannot withhold theirs when joining in sympathy with Him. He is very temperate, modest, and wise. And in short, whatever this phenomenon may turn out in the end, He seems a heavenly presence from His excellent bearing and divine perfection, and in every way surpassing the greatest of men."

Isn't the above a beautiful presentation of our Lord?

POINTS TO PONDER

1. Do most people really understand who Jesus Christ is?
2. What difference does Christ make in the life of an individual?
3. How can Christ make you righteous and whole?

Daily Bible Study and Daily Prayer Concerns
JESUS CHRIST—WHO IS HE?

1. Christ was to be called _____
   Luke 1:35
2. Christ the Lord is a _____
   Luke 2:11
3. Christ is the_____which takes
   away the sin of the world. *John 1:29*
4. Christ is a faithful _____
   Heb. 2:17
5. Christ is the _____ of the new
   testament or covenant. *Heb. 9:15*
6. Christ is the end of the_____for
   righteousness for all who believe. *Rom. 10:4*
7. Christ is the good _____
   John 10:11
8. Christ is the _____
   John 1:1
9. Christ is the Lord of _____
   Acts 10:36
10. Christ is _____
    Rev. 19:16
11. Christ is _____
    Rev. 22:13
12. Christ is _____
    John 6:35
13. Christ is the _____
    John 11:25
14. Christ is the _____
    John 15:1

DAILY SCRIPTURE

Mon.	Luke 1:26-38
Tues.	John 1:29-34
Wed.	Heb. 2:14-18
Thurs.	Acts 10:34-43
Fri.	Rev. 19:11-21
Sat.	John 11:17-27
Sun.	John 15:1-11

PRAYER CONCERNS

Your Family & Relatives
Government Leaders
Missionaries
For the Unbelievers
Churches & Denominations
Your Own Church
Prayer and Praise

NOTE: You will be spiritually strengthened by completing two questions each day, reading the suggested scripture, and ministering in prayer for the concerns of the day.

433

THE MINISTRY OF THE MASTER—MONDAY
A Spirit Lifter

Have you ever had children, grandchildren, guests who just about did you in? Sometimes you feel you could put up with about anything but children. If so, this is your kind of story.

There was a terrible earthquake and many of the inhabitants of the area fled for fear of more of the same. One couple sent their four children to stay with an aunt and uncle in another area. A week later the parents received this telegram:

"Am returning your children. Send earthquake."

God's Promise

I'd appreciate your reflecting upon the following:

"There is that speaketh like the piercing of a sword: but the tongue of the wise is health." (Proverbs 12:18)

Practicing His Presence

May you continually remain sensitive to the Spirit. How were you aware of His presence yesterday, and how did this make you feel?

Jesus Christ—Who Is He?

It seems to me as we begin this week to consider our Lord Jesus Christ that it will be good to list the personal references stressing who he is. There are several occasions where Jesus said, *"I am..."* Consider them carefully, and perhaps you will want to turn to the scripture passages and read further concerning each instance.

The woman Christ met at the well refers to the Messiah. Jesus said to her, *"I am he,"* that is, I am the Messiah.

I am the bread of life - John 6:35
I am from above - John 8:23
I am the eternal One - John 8:58
I am the light of the world - John 9:5
I am the door - John 10:7
I am the resurrection and the life - John 11:35
I am the Lord and Master - John 13:13
I am the Way, the Truth, and the Life - John 14:6
I am the true vine - John 15:1
I am Alpha and Omega - Revelation 1:8
I am the first and the last - Revelation 1:17

PRAYER: *Lord Jesus, may I feast on you today, may I drink from your living fountain, and may I walk through the door to victory through you. Amen.*

THE MINISTRY OF THE MASTER—TUESDAY
A Spirit Lifter

Several of us served churches while attending Seminary. The one young man reported about his Sunday School teacher who was expounding on the first chapter of Mark verse 34 where it says, "...he healed many people of divers diseases."

The teacher tried to bring this teaching down to modern times and said that if we were putting it in our language we would say he healed people of "swimming cramps." And the really humorous part is that he was dead serious when he gave his profound insight.

God's Promise

God wants you to be happy and He can provide this joy.

"...God hath made me to laugh, so that all that hear will laugh with me..." (Genesis 21:6)

Practicing His Presence

I find the pilgrimage of being aware of His presence exciting. Are you also finding it this way? May your days ahead continue to be exciting.

Jesus Christ—Who Is He?

Jesus Christ is not only revealed by the statements of whom He is, but also by what He says He is willing to do. A person's character is certainly revealed more by action than by words. Today I would encourage you to mediate upon the "I will" aspect of our Lord Jesus. They will present to you His desire for your life in a very vivid and profound manner.

To His heavenly Father, *"not as I will"*—Mt. 26:39
To the leper, *"I will, be thou clean"*—Luke 5:13
To the believer, *"I will raise him unto life eternal"*—John 6:40
To the sinful world, *"I will draw all unto me"*—John 12:32
To impart hope to believers, *"I will come again"*—John 14:3
To what is expected of each person, *"If I will that he tarry"*—John 21:22

The above are strong and wonderful statements. You and I can bank our lives on them. They remain our source of strength and help.

It is my prayer and hope that you and I can say unto the Lord, *"I will"* instead of *"I won't."* He desires an obedient and faithful response from each of us.

PRAYER: *Jesus, I will be your faithful follower. I will believe you. I will seek to lift you up so others can behold your glories. Amen.*

A Spirit Lifter

What did your marriage do for you? What do you think it does for others? Well, the following is the way I got thanked by a young couple many years ago for officiating at their wedding.

In the letter she stated, "I want to thank you, Pastor Bartow, for *maring* Jim and me."

Well, I thought then and have since, I wonder how many are *marred*, instead of *married*.

God's Promise

"Now our Lord Jesus Christ himself, and God, even our Father, which hath loved us, and hath given us everlasting consolation and good hope through grace, comfort your hearts, and establish you in every good word and work." (II Thessalonians 2:16,17)

Practicing His Presence

Are you anticipating being aware of His presence throughout this day? If so, I am sure this will be a wonderful day for you.

Jesus Christ—Who Is He?

I can't help but get all excited when I seek to write about Jesus. He is the bright and glorious light of my life and I am sure you feel the same.

Others have so eloquently written of Him, and so I quote some comments which I feel are really great.

*"There was a knight of Bethlehem
Whose wealth was tears and sorrows.
His men at arms were little lambs,
His sentinels were sparrows."*

*"His castle was a wooden cross,
Where on he hung so high.
His helmet was a crown of thorns,
Whose crest did touch the sky."*

Jesus will be with you today. You must seek to be spiritually alert so as to be aware of His presence. There are precious truths on every hand and most of them are overlooked by most of us. The One who is the Truth is near at hand, and if you are not careful you will miss him.

PRAYER: *Enable me, Lord Jesus, to cease seeking the ultimate truth in science or modern technology. May I see that truth is a person and that person is You. Amen.*

THE MINISTRY OF THE MASTER—THURSDAY
A Spirit Lifter

The religious education teacher was having a terrible time with her weekly class. There was one little eight year old who was impossible. In exasperation she said, "Johnny, you are an incorrigible." He raised himself to full height and proudly replied, "I am not, I am a Presbyterian."

There may be a difference, right?

God's Promise

"If my people, which are called by my name, shall humble themselves, and pray, and seek my face, and turn from their wicked ways; then will I hear from heaven, and will forgive their sins, and will heal their lands." (II Chronicles 7:14)

Practicing His Presence

Are you finding it difficult to recall a specific incident in which you really felt His presence yesterday? I really believe, however, it is helpful to reflect on this each day so that you may develop a greater spiritual awareness.

Jesus Christ—Who Is He?

Someone asked the renowned Tennyson what he thought of Jesus. He replied in his own poetic fashion,

"What the sun is to that flower, so Jesus is to me."

The flower would soon be dead without light. The reason many are dead in their heart and soul today, even though they seem alive physically, is because they have not permitted the light of the world to enter into their innermost being.

Jesus did not have a long public ministry, but His truths are for all ages and all peoples. Socrates taught for approximately forty years. Plato was a famous teacher for fifty years. Aristotle taught for about forty years. Yet, their influence is very little compared to the impact of the teachings of Jesus Christ.

We cannot talk about whom He is without acknowledging Him as the greatest teacher that ever lived. Jesus painted no pictures, for instance. Yet He has inspired literally thousands and thousands of pictures.

Can you name any picture which is the result of inspiration of the artist by Socrates, Plato, etc.? Of course not. Jesus is the One who has captured the imagination of thousands in all areas of art.

PRAYER: *You are the light of my life, Lord Jesus, and it is to you that I turn for energy to live and to grow in my faith. Thank you for your help. Amen.*

437

THE MINISTRY OF THE MASTER—FRIDAY
A Spirit Lifter

The patient had just returned from an operation and remarked to others in the ward that he was glad it was all over.

One man said, "Don't be so sure. Mine was all over too, but they had to take me back and open me up again because they had left a sponge in me."

And behold another said, "Yes, and I had to be opened again because an instrument was left in me."

It was just at that time the surgeon came in and inquired, "Has anybody around here seen my hat?" You guessed it. The new patient shouted, "Oh no!" and fainted.

God's Promise

I'm sure you'll appreciate this important truth today:

"For the righteous Lord loveth righteousness; his countenance doth behold the upright." (Psalm 11:7)

Practicing His Presence

I pray that you were very much aware of the Lord's presence in your life yesterday. Can you recall some specific incident or person which helped this awareness?

Jesus Christ—Who Is He?

Someone has written concerning Jesus.

His birth was contrary to the laws of nature — He was born of the virgin Mary.

His life was lived contrary to others — He always sought to serve and desired not to have others minister unto Him.

His death was contrary to the laws of the nation — for it was a false trial.

He had no corn fields or fisheries, but yet he could feed over five thousand at one time and from a few loaves of bread and a few fish.

He walked on no beautiful carpets or velvet rugs — yet he walked on the Sea of Galilee.

He knew no sin — yet, he became sin for all.

He ended up being killed — yet, He brought life to all.

Every effort on my part to encourage you to really permit Jesus Christ to be Lord of your life is energy well expended.

One of the earliest and most simple of the creeds of the church stated,

"Christ is the Lord."

This He is, and your believing and yielding to this truth will lead to the abundant life for you and yours. He is your wholeness.

PRAYER: *Father, your Son is the One I love and in Whom I trust. Help me in every area of life to declare "Christ Is Lord."*

THE MINISTRY OF THE MASTER—SATURDAY

A Spirit Lifter

If the fruit of our actions are bad for some I guess they aren't much good for others, either. At least this seemed true of the doughnuts.

A country housewife had good intentions, but little knowledge concerning the making of doughnuts. Hers came out very heavy. She couldn't get anybody in the family to take more than one bite of them. In disgust she threw them out to the ducks. An hour later two of the neighborhood urchins tapped at her door and said,

"Say, lady, your ducks have sunk."

God's Promise

Do you need God's direction in your life?

"The meek will he guide in judgment: and the meek will he teach his way." (Psalm 25:9)

Practicing His Presence

If you're like me, you sometimes have incidents which seem tc cloud the reality of His presence. What do you do when this happens to you?

Jesus Christ—Who Is He?

Many will gather tomorrow to worship and to lift praise unto the Lord Jesus. I would encourage you to let this sermonette help prepare your life for a wonderful worship experience. You are opening yourself unto the One who knows you perfectly. Jesus Christ is aware of your thoughts, motives, desires, and actions. He is Lord of all.

Who is Jesus? He is the One who can put music in your life. He is the One who has inspired the great music you will hear in church worship tomorrow. He never wrote a word of music and yet Hayden, Handel, Beethoven, Bach, Mendelson, and many other famous composers were inspired by Jesus.

He is the One who must be born in your heart. He is the One to whom you must give an account of your decision for Him and for your actions.

"Even though Christ is Bethlehem
A thousand times be born.
If he is not born within your heart,
Thou are most forlorn."

There is no substitute for Jesus Christ within your own life. He alone is the one who takes away the sins of the world. — John 1:29.

PRAYER: *Come into my heart today, Lord Jesus. Come in to dwell and to stay. Come to cleanse and to empower. Come to bring assurance and to bring a challenge. Amen.*

THE MINISTRY OF THE MASTER—SUNDAY
A Spirit Lifter

Life is confusing. And this is sometimes especially apparent to the dear husband.

A man returned from vacation and said to his friends, "I will never figure out a woman. Last year we went on a vacation up in the mountains. She couldn't decide what to put on. This year we went to the beach and she couldn't decide what to take off."

God's Promise

You can be sure that God will keep His promises. I think this is a wonderful promise from the Lord Jesus Himself:

"For all the promises of God with him are yea, and in him, amen, unto the glory of God in us." (I Corinthians 1:20)

Practicing His Presence

Hopefully, these past few days, being aware of His presence has been exciting for you. May you continually remain sensitive to the Spirit. How did this sensitivity affect your day yesterday?

Jesus Christ—Who Is He?

The Bible tells us who Jesus is with the use of fitting names. It is said that He is the beloved Son of God. At the time of his baptism the voice from heaven designated Him as such.

"And there came a voice from heaven, saying, Thou art my beloved Son, in whom I am well pleased." Mark 1:1

Jesus is often referred to as the Son of God. Many of the people of His day spoke of Him as the Son of God.

"Then they that were in the ship came and worshipped him, saying, Of a truth thou art the Son of God." Mt. 14:33

The title which seems most appropriate as I close this week of devotional thoughts about Jesus is King of Kings. He is the One who is going to reign forever and ever.

"Which in his times he shall show, who is the blessed and only Potentate, the King of Kings, and Lord of Lords." I Timothy 6:15

You and I must some day face the One who is the King. It is our responsibility as well as privilege to make Him King of our life now. He desires and must sit on the throne of your heart.

PRAYER: *My heart is your throne, O Lord. I want you to reign there at all times. When I seek to displace you, may your spirit grant me wisdom to cease this foolish attempt. Amen.*